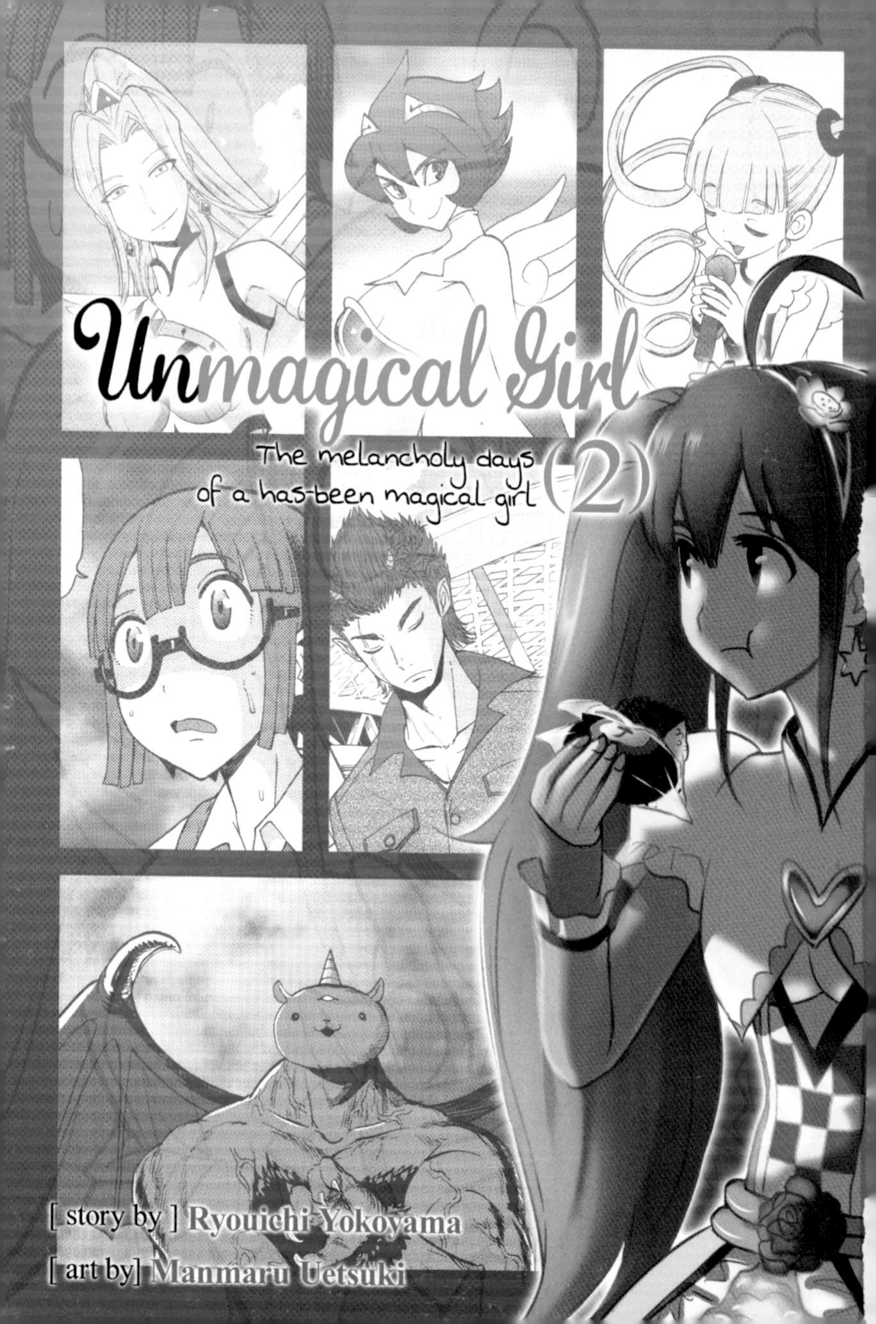
Unmagical Girl
The melancholy days of a has-been magical girl (2)
[story by] Ryouichi Yokoyama
[art by] Manmaru Uetsuki

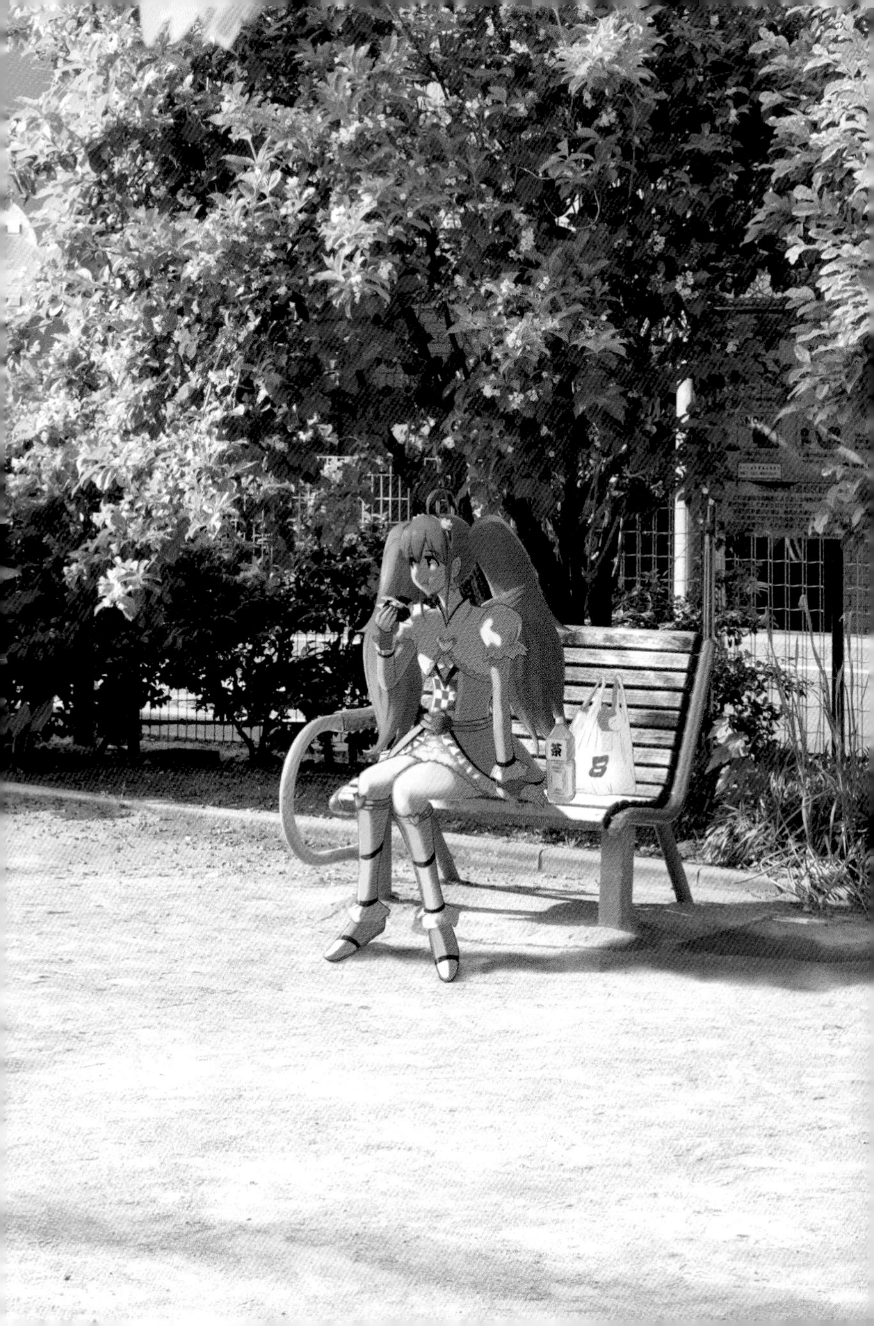
茶

Chapter 11: I Can Dream, Can't I?

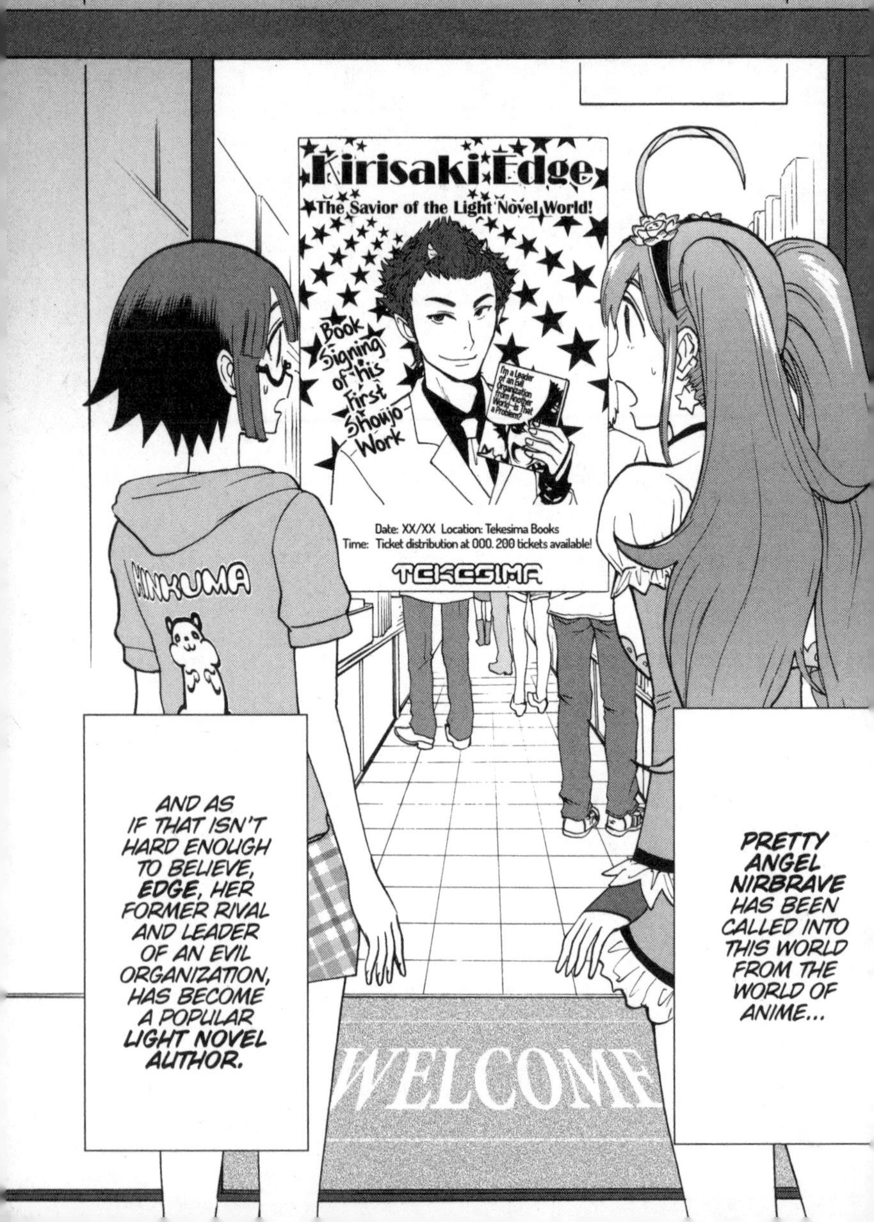
Kirisaki Edge
The Savior of the Light Novel World!
Book Signing of his First Shoujo Work
I'm a Leader of an Evil Organization from Another World—Is That a Problem?
Date: XX/XX Location: Tekesima Books
Time: Ticket distribution at 000. 200 tickets available!
TEKESIMA
HINKUMA
WELCOME
PRETTY ANGEL NIRBRAVE HAS BEEN CALLED INTO THIS WORLD FROM THE WORLD OF ANIME...
AND AS IF THAT ISN'T HARD ENOUGH TO BELIEVE, EDGE, HER FORMER RIVAL AND LEADER OF AN EVIL ORGANIZATION, HAS BECOME A POPULAR LIGHT NOVEL AUTHOR.

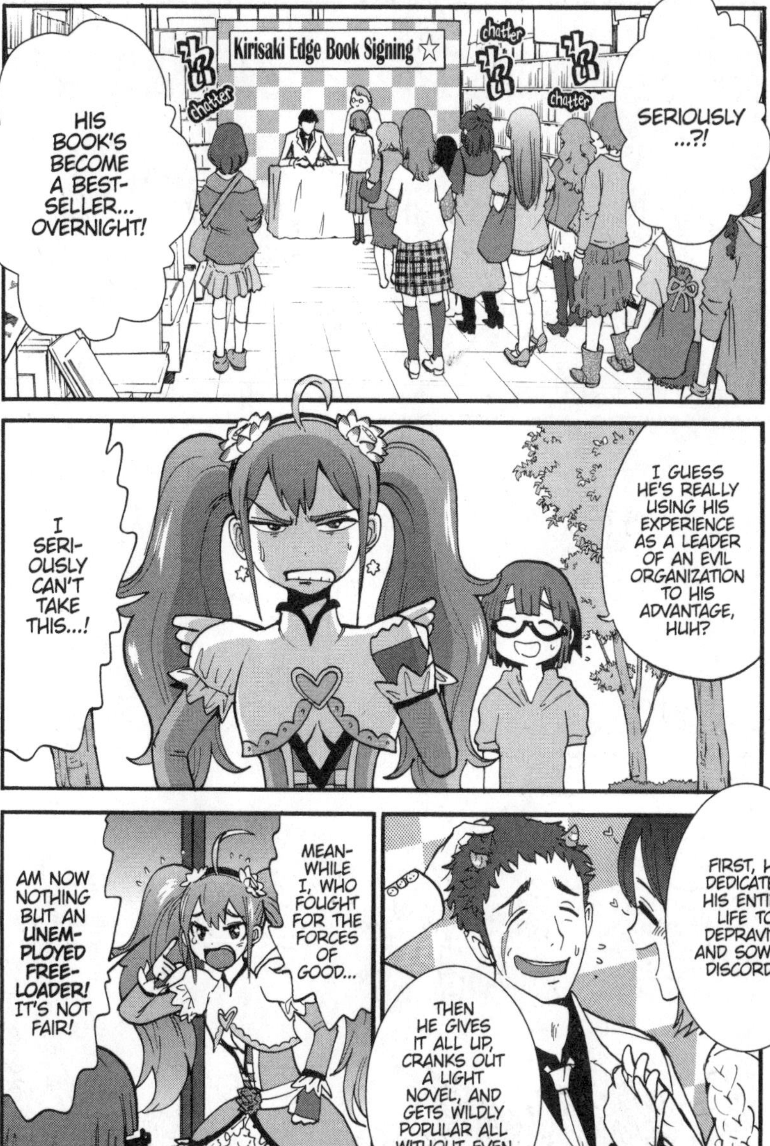
chatter
chatter
SERIOUSLY ...?!
Kirisaki Edge Book Signing ☆
chatter
HIS BOOK'S BECOME A BEST-SELLER... OVERNIGHT!
I GUESS HE'S REALLY USING HIS EXPERIENCE AS A LEADER OF AN EVIL ORGANIZATION TO HIS ADVANTAGE, HUH?
I SERIOUSLY CAN'T TAKE THIS...!
FIRST, HE DEDICATES HIS ENTIRE LIFE TO DEPRAVITY AND SOWING DISCORD...
THEN HE GIVES IT ALL UP, CRANKS OUT A LIGHT NOVEL, AND GETS WILDLY POPULAR ALL WITHOUT EVEN REALLY TRYING.
MEANWHILE I, WHO FOUGHT FOR THE FORCES OF GOOD...
AM NOW NOTHING BUT AN UNEMPLOYED FREELOADER! IT'S NOT FAIR!

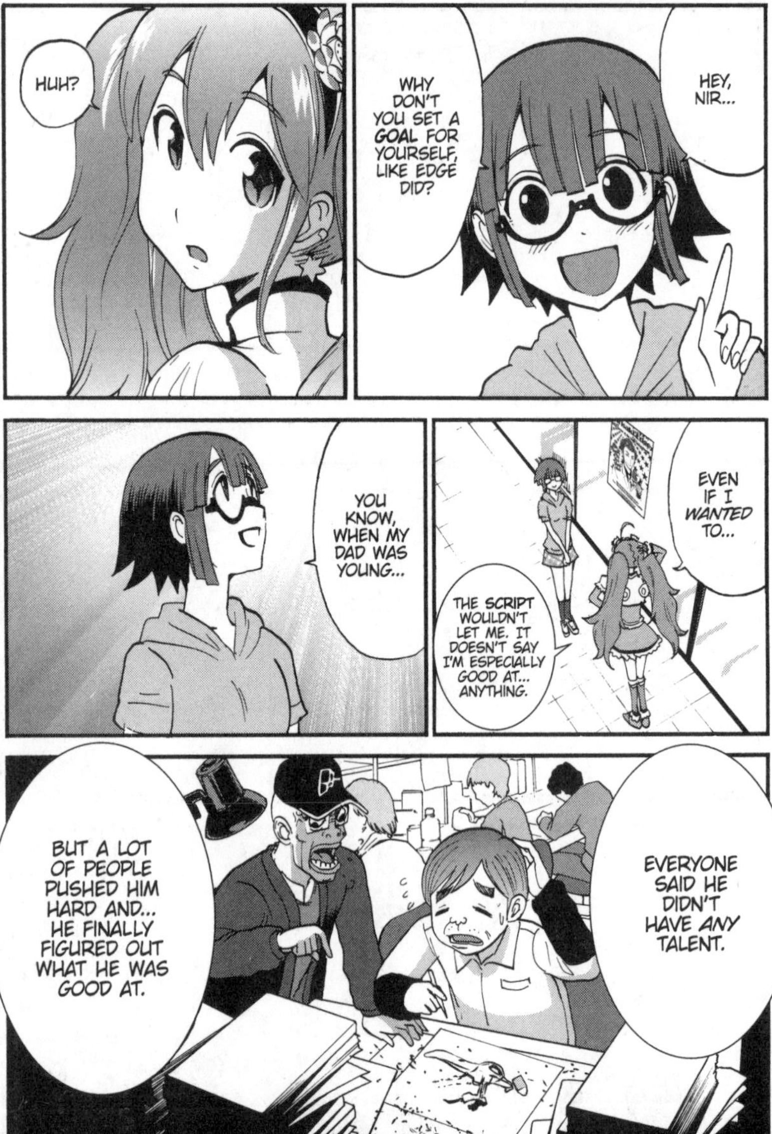
HEY, NIR...
WHY DON'T YOU SET A **GOAL** FOR YOURSELF, LIKE EDGE DID?
HUH?
EVEN IF I *WANTED* TO...
THE **SCRIPT** WOULDN'T LET ME. IT DOESN'T SAY I'M ESPECIALLY GOOD AT... ANYTHING.
YOU KNOW, WHEN MY DAD WAS YOUNG...
EVERYONE SAID HE DIDN'T HAVE *ANY* TALENT.
BUT A LOT OF PEOPLE PUSHED HIM HARD AND... HE FINALLY FIGURED OUT WHAT HE WAS GOOD AT.

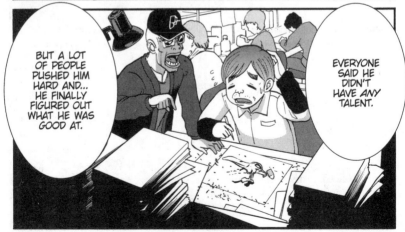

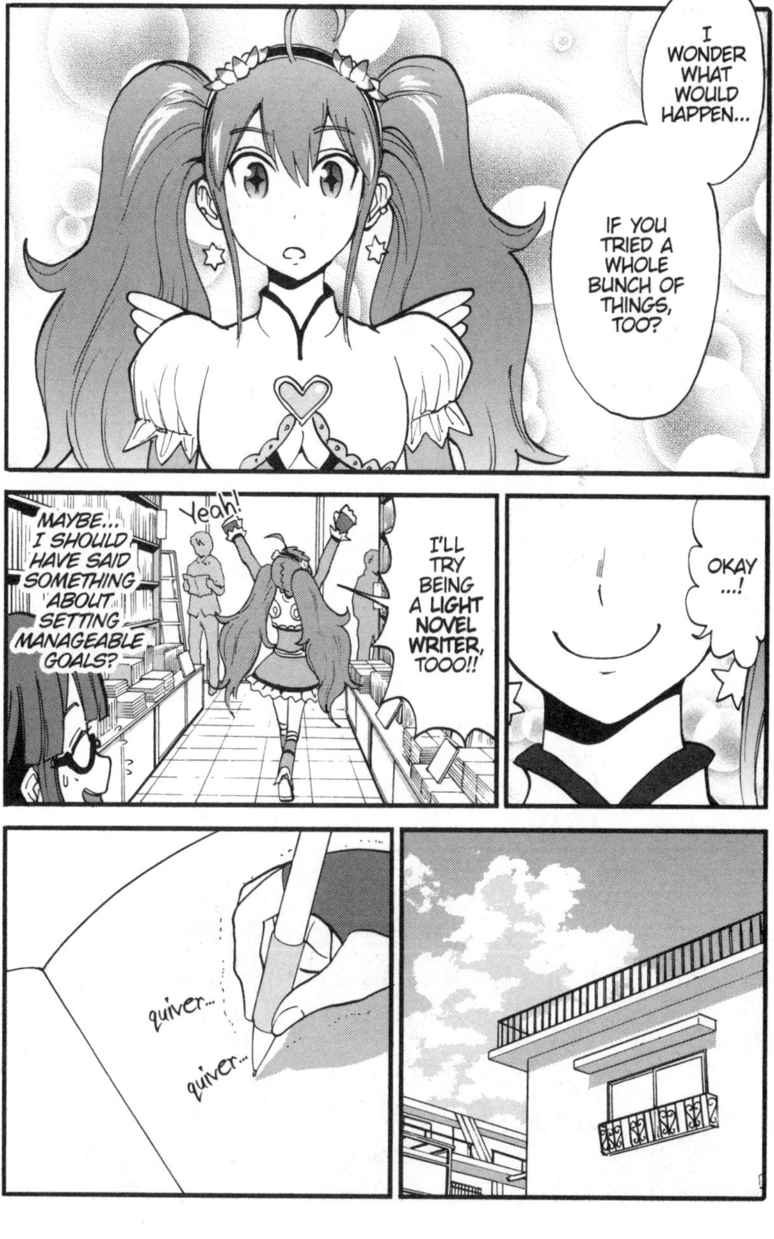
I WONDER WHAT WOULD HAPPEN...
IF YOU TRIED A WHOLE BUNCH OF THINGS, TOO?
OKAY ...!
Yeah!
I'LL TRY BEING A LIGHT NOVEL WRITER, TOOO!!
MAYBE... I SHOULD HAVE SAID SOMETHING ABOUT SETTING MANAGEABLE GOALS?
quiver...
quiver...

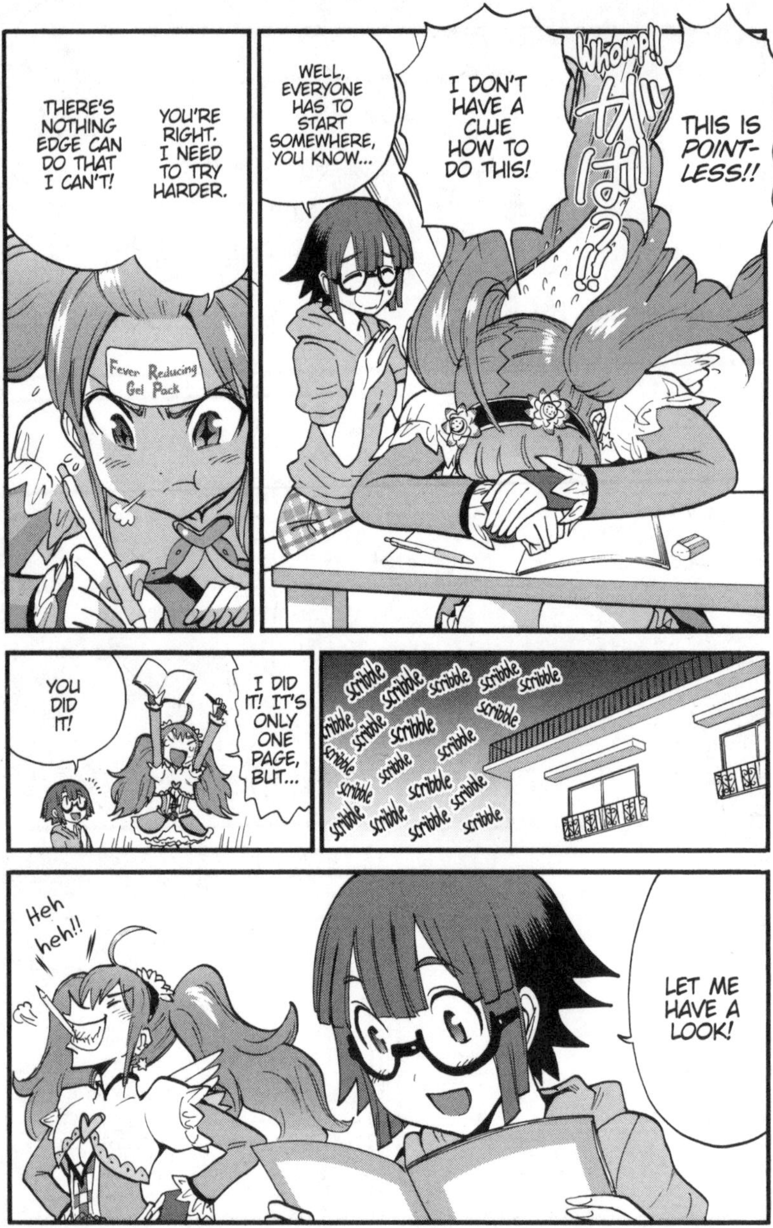
THIS IS POINT-LESS!!
Whomp!!
がばっ?!!
I DON'T HAVE A CLUE HOW TO DO THIS!
WELL, EVERYONE HAS TO START SOMEWHERE, YOU KNOW...
YOU'RE RIGHT. I NEED TO TRY HARDER.
THERE'S NOTHING EDGE CAN DO THAT I CAN'T!
Fever Reducing Gel Pack
scribble scribble scribble scribble scribble scribble scribble scribble scribble scribble scribble scribble scribble scribble scribble scribble scribble scribble scribble scribble
I DID IT! IT'S ONLY ONE PAGE, BUT...
YOU DID IT!
LET ME HAVE A LOOK!
Heh heh!!

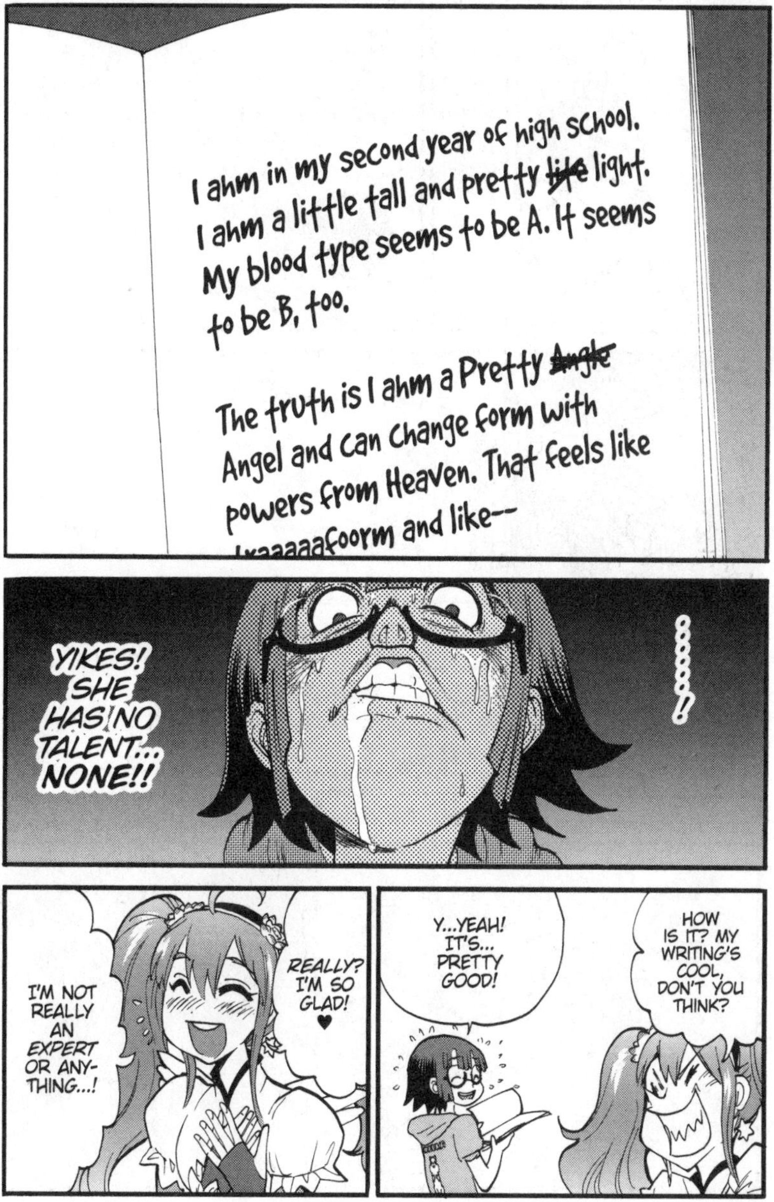
I ahm in my second year of high school.
I ahm a little tall and pretty lite light.
My blood type seems to be A. It seems to be B, too.
The truth is I ahm a Pretty Angle
The truth is I ahm a Pretty Angel and can change form with powers from Heaven. That feels like kaaaaaafoorm and like--
......!
YIKES! SHE HAS NO TALENT... NONE!!
HOW IS IT? MY WRITING'S COOL, DON'T YOU THINK?
Y...YEAH! IT'S... PRETTY GOOD!
REALLY? I'M SO GLAD! ♥
I'M NOT REALLY AN EXPERT OR ANYTHING...!

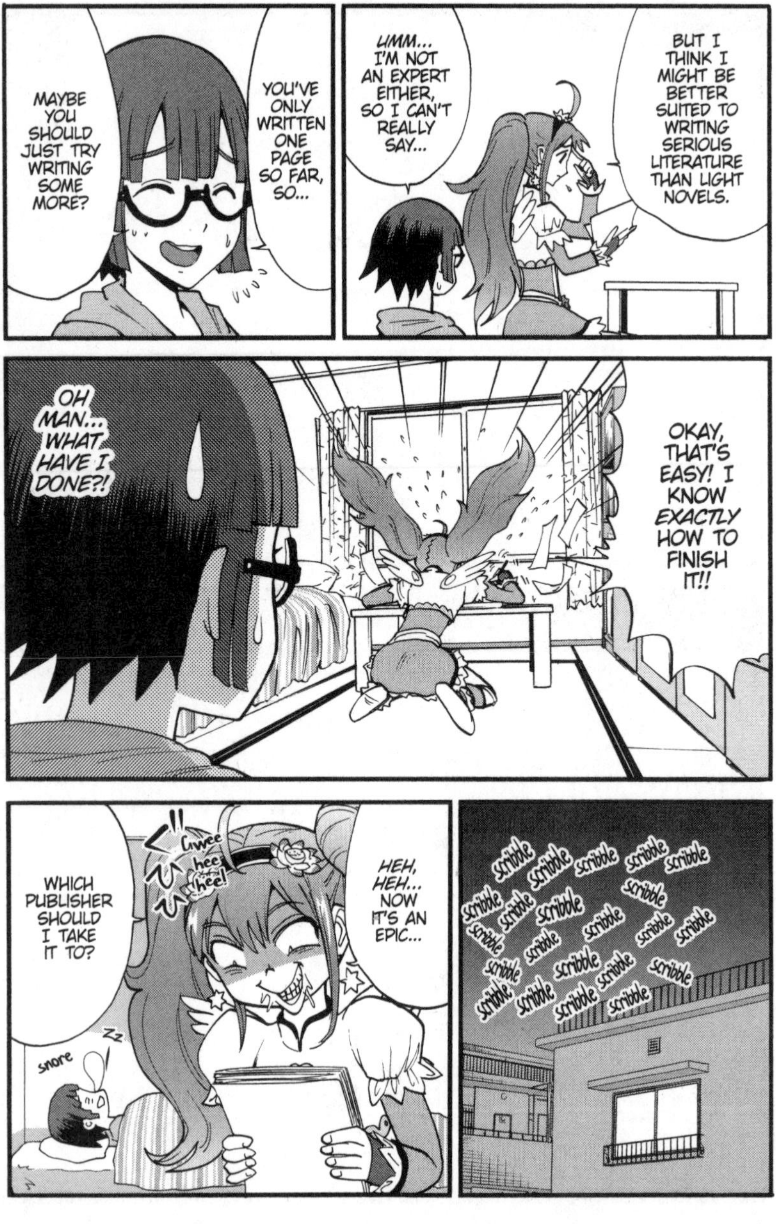
BUT I THINK I MIGHT BE BETTER SUITED TO WRITING SERIOUS LITERATURE THAN LIGHT NOVELS.
UMM... I'M NOT AN EXPERT EITHER, SO I CAN'T REALLY SAY...
YOU'VE ONLY WRITTEN ONE PAGE SO FAR, SO...
MAYBE YOU SHOULD JUST TRY WRITING SOME MORE?
OKAY, THAT'S EASY! I KNOW EXACTLY HOW TO FINISH IT!!
OH MAN... WHAT HAVE I DONE?!
scribble scribble
HEH, HEH... NOW IT'S AN EPIC...
Gwee hee hee!
WHICH PUBLISHER SHOULD I TAKE IT TO?
Zz
snore

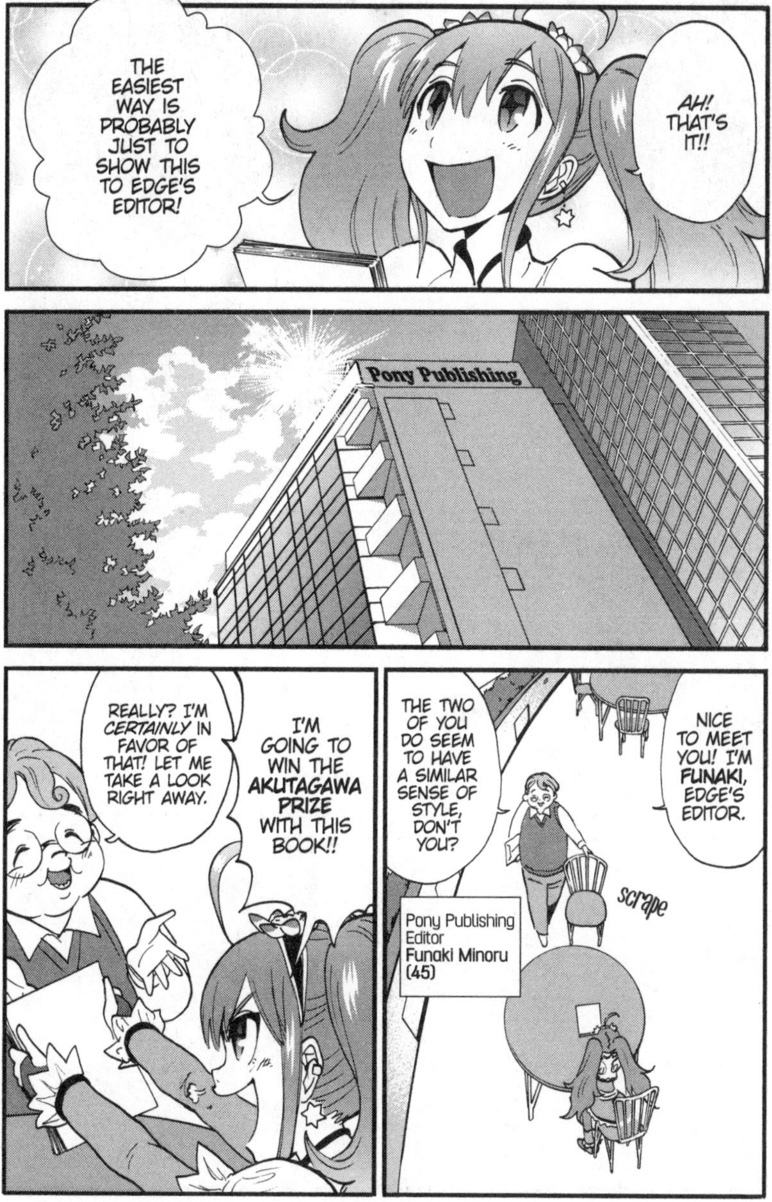
AH! THAT'S IT!!
THE EASIEST WAY IS PROBABLY JUST TO SHOW THIS TO EDGE'S EDITOR!
Pony Publishing
NICE TO MEET YOU! I'M **FUNAKI**, EDGE'S EDITOR.
THE TWO OF YOU DO SEEM TO HAVE A SIMILAR SENSE OF STYLE, DON'T YOU?
scrape
Pony Publishing Editor
Funaki Minoru (45)
I'M GOING TO WIN THE **AKUTAGAWA PRIZE** WITH THIS BOOK!!
REALLY? I'M *CERTAINLY* IN FAVOR OF THAT! LET ME TAKE A LOOK RIGHT AWAY.

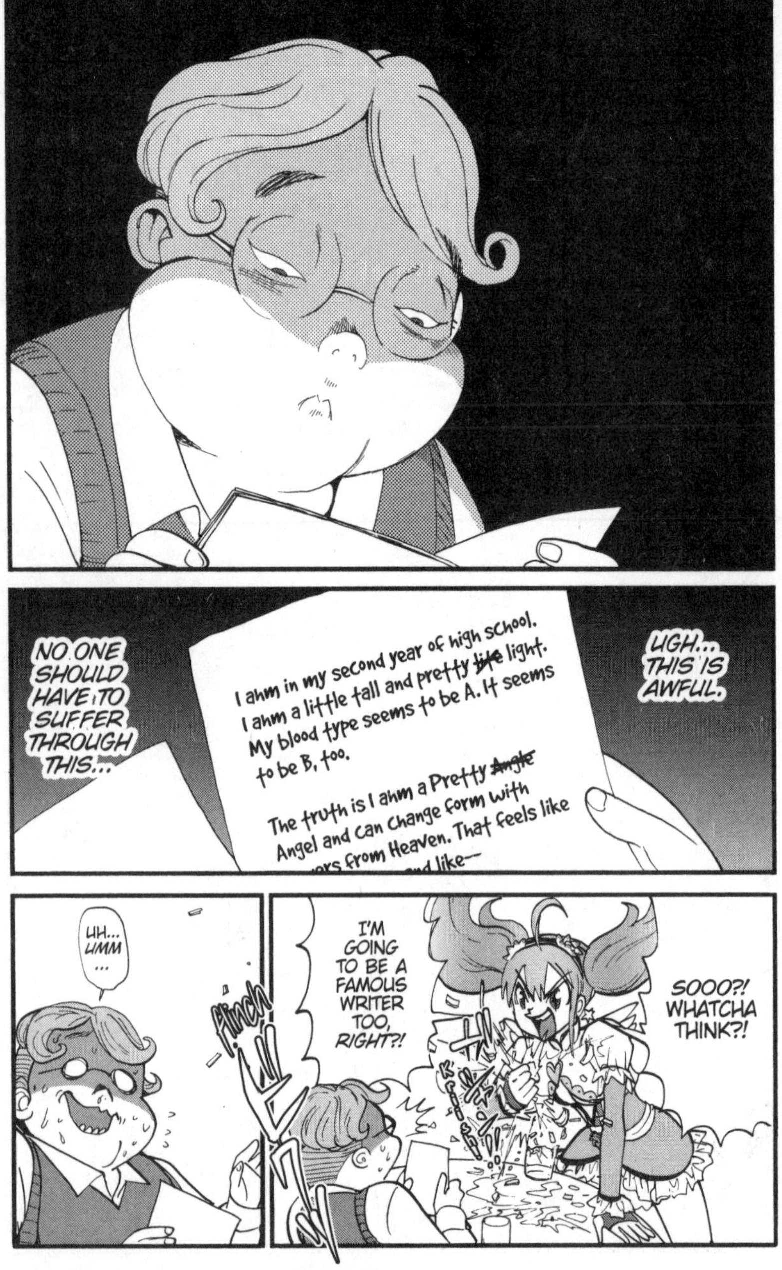
UGH... THIS IS AWFUL.
I ahm in my second year of high school. I ahm a little tall and pretty ~~life~~ light. My blood type seems to be A. It seems to be B, too.
The truth is I ahm a Pretty ~~Angle~~ Angel and Can Change form with
That feels like
NO ONE SHOULD HAVE TO SUFFER THROUGH THIS...
SOOO?! WHATCHA THINK?!
I'M GOING TO BE A FAMOUS WRITER TOO, RIGHT?!
Flinch
UH... UMM ...

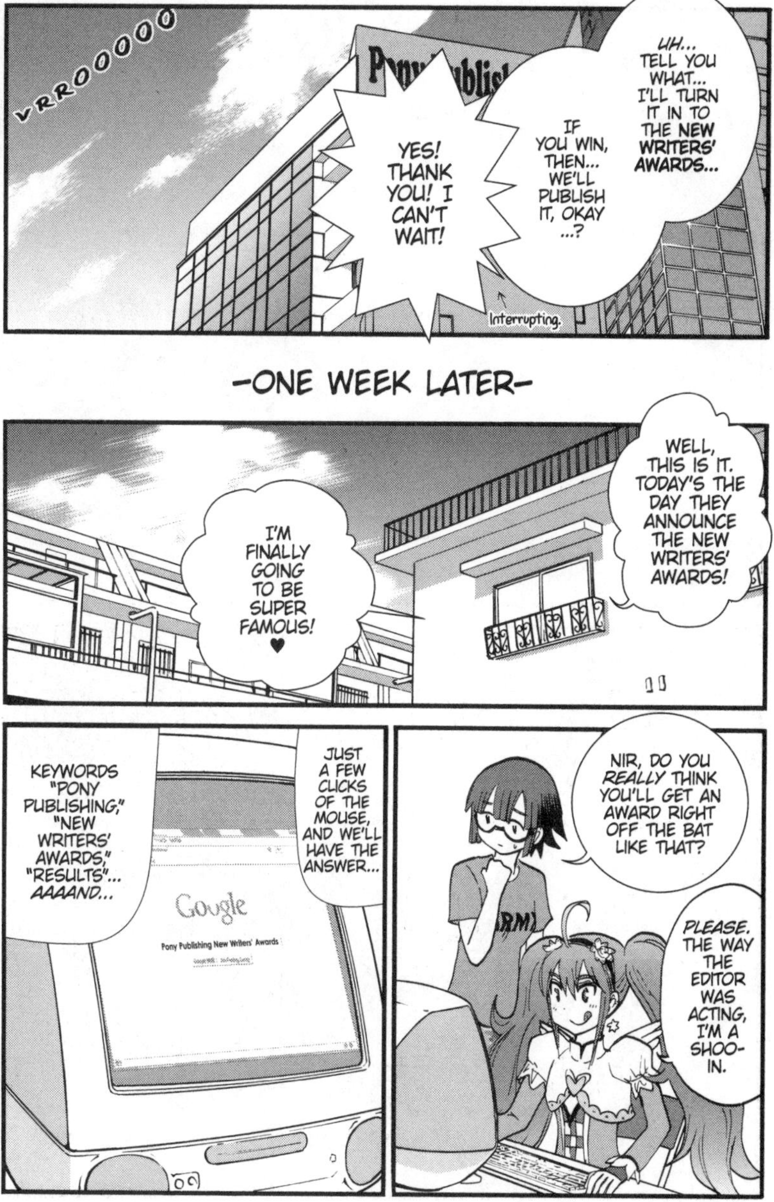
UH... TELL YOU WHAT... I'LL TURN IT IN TO THE NEW WRITERS' AWARDS...
IF YOU WIN, THEN... WE'LL PUBLISH IT, OKAY ...?
YES! THANK YOU! I CAN'T WAIT!
Interrupting.
VRROOOOOO
-ONE WEEK LATER-
WELL, THIS IS IT. TODAY'S THE DAY THEY ANNOUNCE THE NEW WRITERS' AWARDS!
I'M FINALLY GOING TO BE SUPER FAMOUS! ♥
NIR, DO YOU *REALLY* THINK YOU'LL GET AN AWARD RIGHT OFF THE BAT LIKE THAT?
PLEASE. THE WAY THE EDITOR WAS ACTING, I'M A SHOO-IN.
JUST A FEW CLICKS OF THE MOUSE, AND WE'LL HAVE THE ANSWER...
KEYWORDS "PONY PUBLISHING," "NEW WRITERS' AWARDS," "RESULTS"... *AAAAND...*
Gougle
Pony Publishing New Writers' Awards

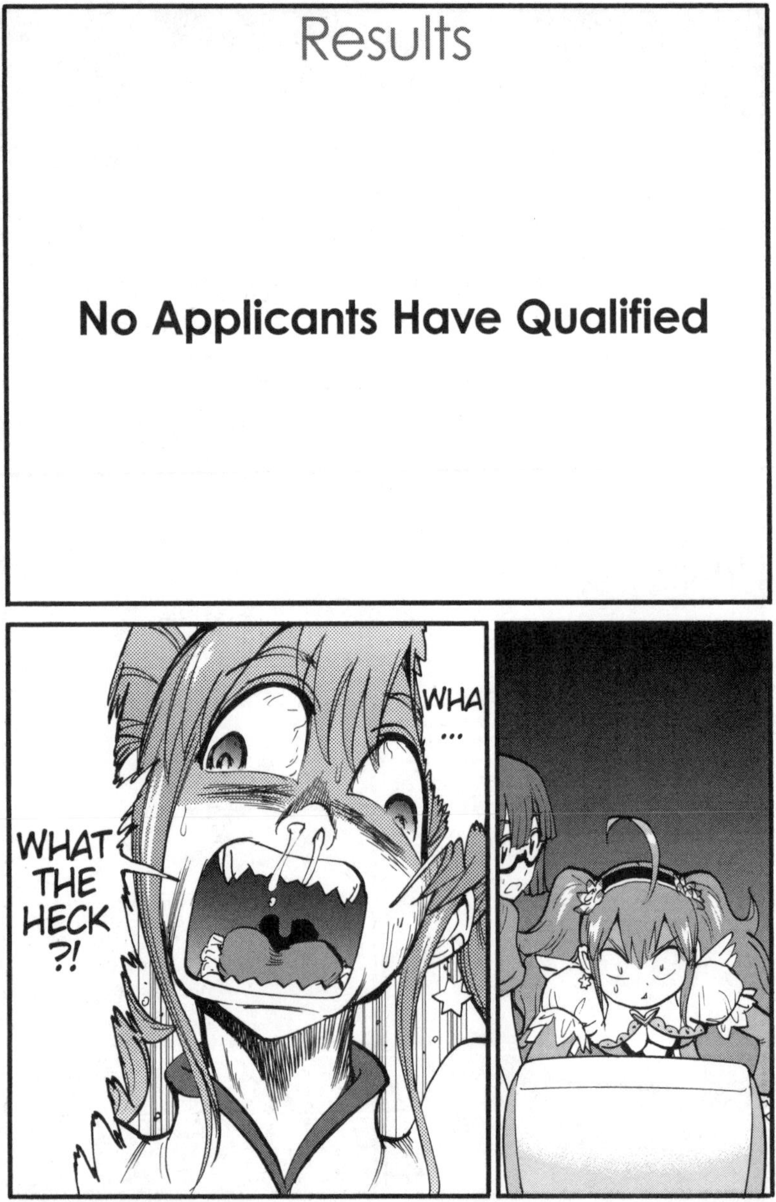
Results
No Applicants Have Qualified
WHA...
WHAT THE HECK?!

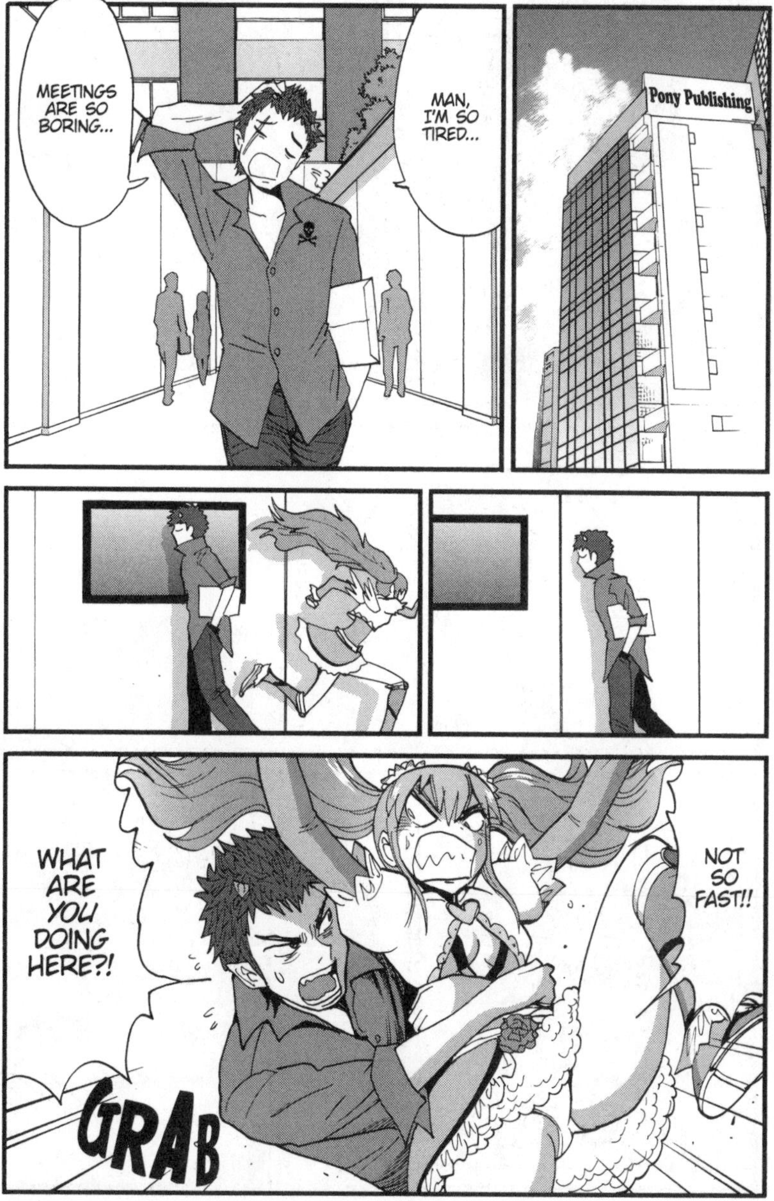
Pony Publishing
MAN, I'M SO TIRED...
MEETINGS ARE SO BORING...
NOT SO FAST!!
WHAT ARE YOU DOING HERE?!
GRAB

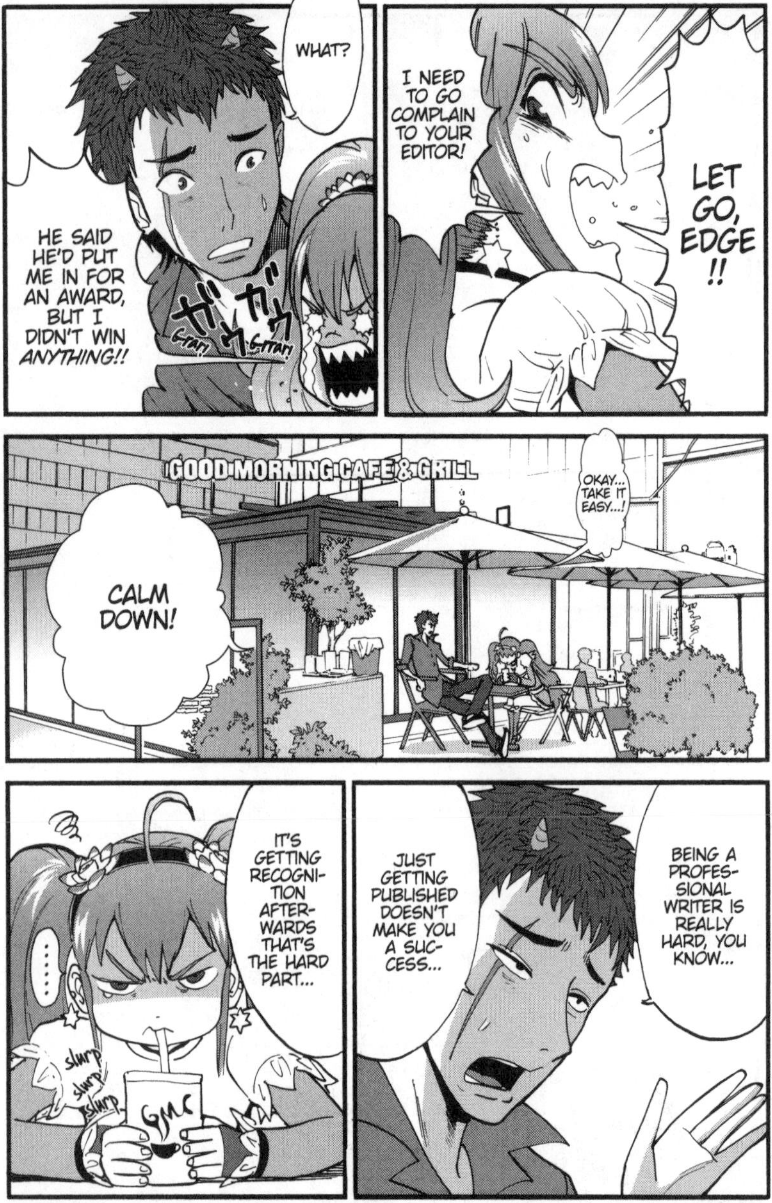
LET GO, EDGE!!
I NEED TO GO COMPLAIN TO YOUR EDITOR!
WHAT?
HE SAID HE'D PUT ME IN FOR AN AWARD, BUT I DIDN'T WIN *ANYTHING!!*
ガウガウ
Grrar! Grrar!
GOOD MORNING CAFE & GRILL
OKAY... TAKE IT EASY...!
CALM DOWN!
BEING A PROFESSIONAL WRITER IS REALLY HARD, YOU KNOW...
JUST GETTING PUBLISHED DOESN'T MAKE YOU A SUCCESS...
IT'S GETTING RECOGNITION AFTERWARDS THAT'S THE HARD PART...
......
slurp slurp slurp
GMC

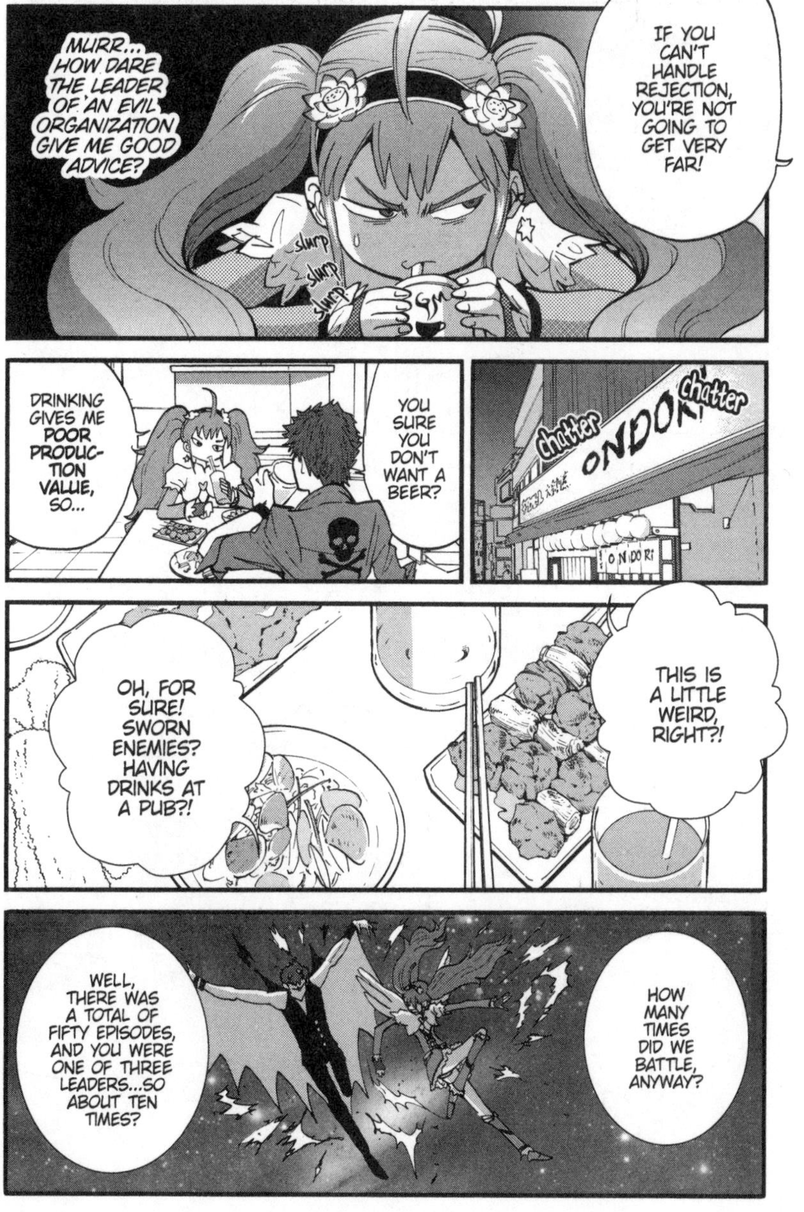
IF YOU CAN'T HANDLE REJECTION, YOU'RE NOT GOING TO GET VERY FAR!
MURR... HOW DARE THE LEADER OF AN EVIL ORGANIZATION GIVE ME GOOD ADVICE?
slurp slurp slurp
chatter
chatter
ONDORI
ONDORI
YOU SURE YOU DON'T WANT A BEER?
DRINKING GIVES ME POOR PRODUCTION VALUE, SO...
THIS IS A LITTLE WEIRD, RIGHT?!
OH, FOR SURE! SWORN ENEMIES? HAVING DRINKS AT A PUB?!
HOW MANY TIMES DID WE BATTLE, ANYWAY?
WELL, THERE WAS A TOTAL OF FIFTY EPISODES, AND YOU WERE ONE OF THREE LEADERS...SO ABOUT TEN TIMES?

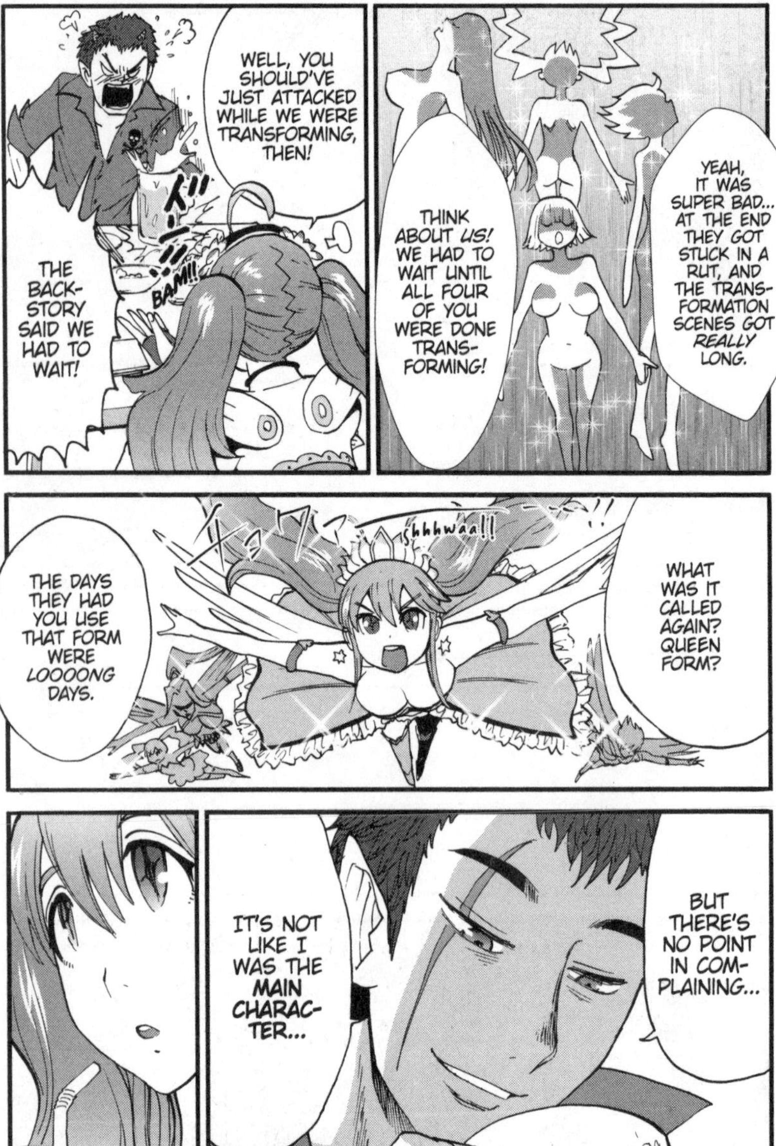
YEAH, IT WAS SUPER BAD... AT THE END THEY GOT STUCK IN A RUT, AND THE TRANSFORMATION SCENES GOT *REALLY* LONG.
THINK ABOUT *US!* WE HAD TO WAIT UNTIL ALL FOUR OF YOU WERE DONE TRANSFORMING!
WELL, YOU SHOULD'VE JUST ATTACKED WHILE WE WERE TRANSFORMING, THEN!
BAM!!
THE BACKSTORY SAID WE HAD TO WAIT!
shhhwaa!!
WHAT WAS IT CALLED AGAIN? QUEEN FORM?
THE DAYS THEY HAD YOU USE THAT FORM WERE *LOOOONG* DAYS.
BUT THERE'S NO POINT IN COMPLAINING...
IT'S NOT LIKE I WAS THE **MAIN CHARACTER**...

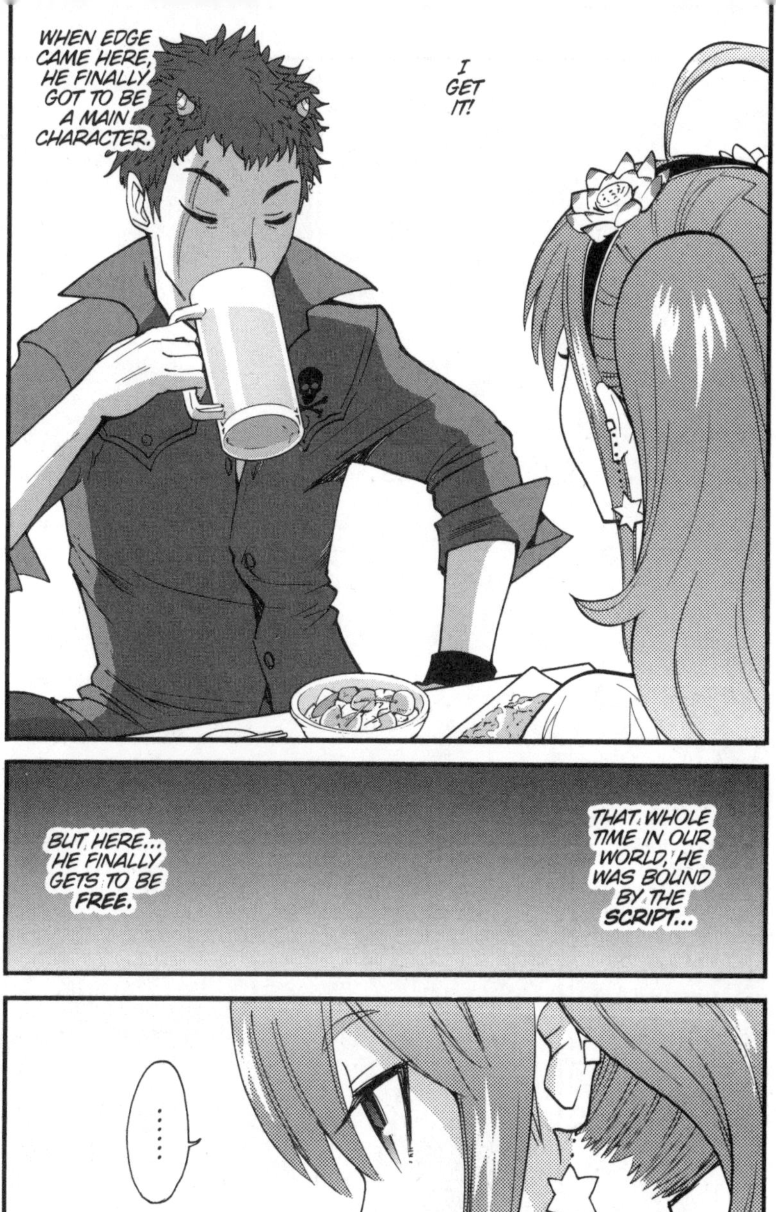
I GET IT!
WHEN EDGE CAME HERE, HE FINALLY GOT TO BE A MAIN CHARACTER.
THAT WHOLE TIME IN OUR WORLD, HE WAS BOUND BY THE SCRIPT...
BUT HERE... HE FINALLY GETS TO BE FREE.
......

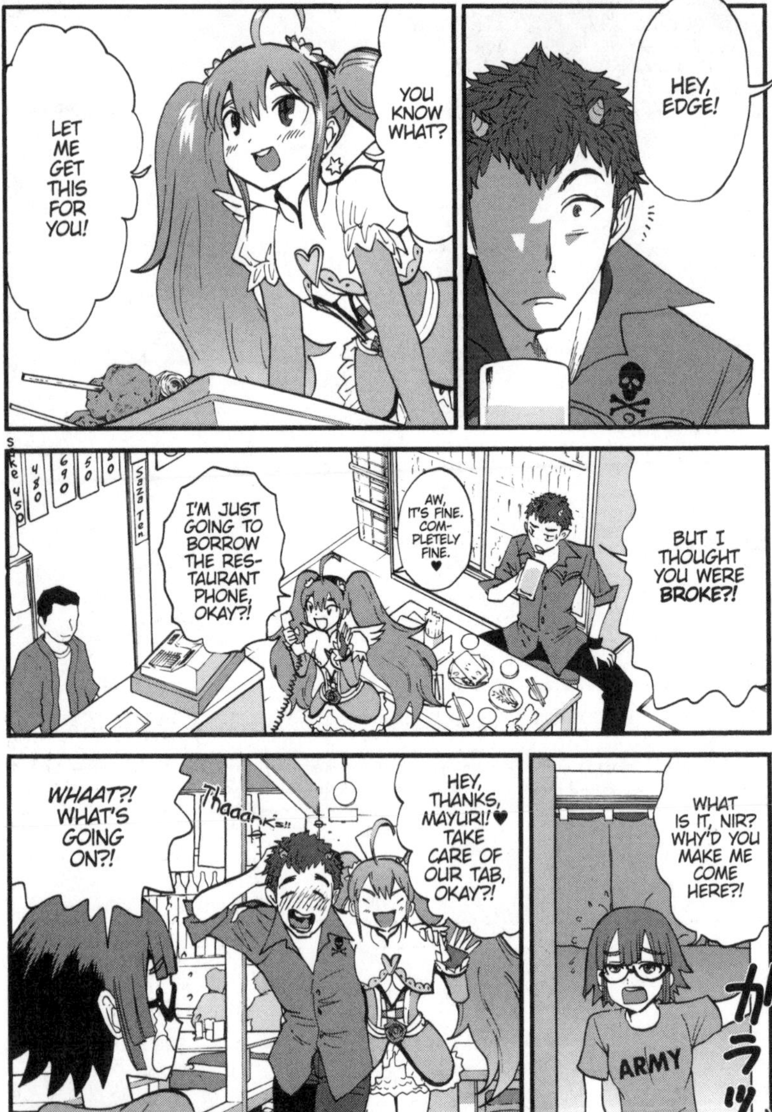
HEY, EDGE!
YOU KNOW WHAT?
LET ME GET THIS FOR YOU!
BUT I THOUGHT YOU WERE BROKE?!
AW, IT'S FINE. COMPLETELY FINE. ♥
I'M JUST GOING TO BORROW THE RESTAURANT PHONE, OKAY?!
WHAT IS IT, NIR? WHY'D YOU MAKE ME COME HERE?!
ガラッ
rattle
HEY, THANKS, MAYURI! ♥ TAKE CARE OF OUR TAB, OKAY?!
Thaaanks!!
WHAAT?! WHAT'S GOING ON?!

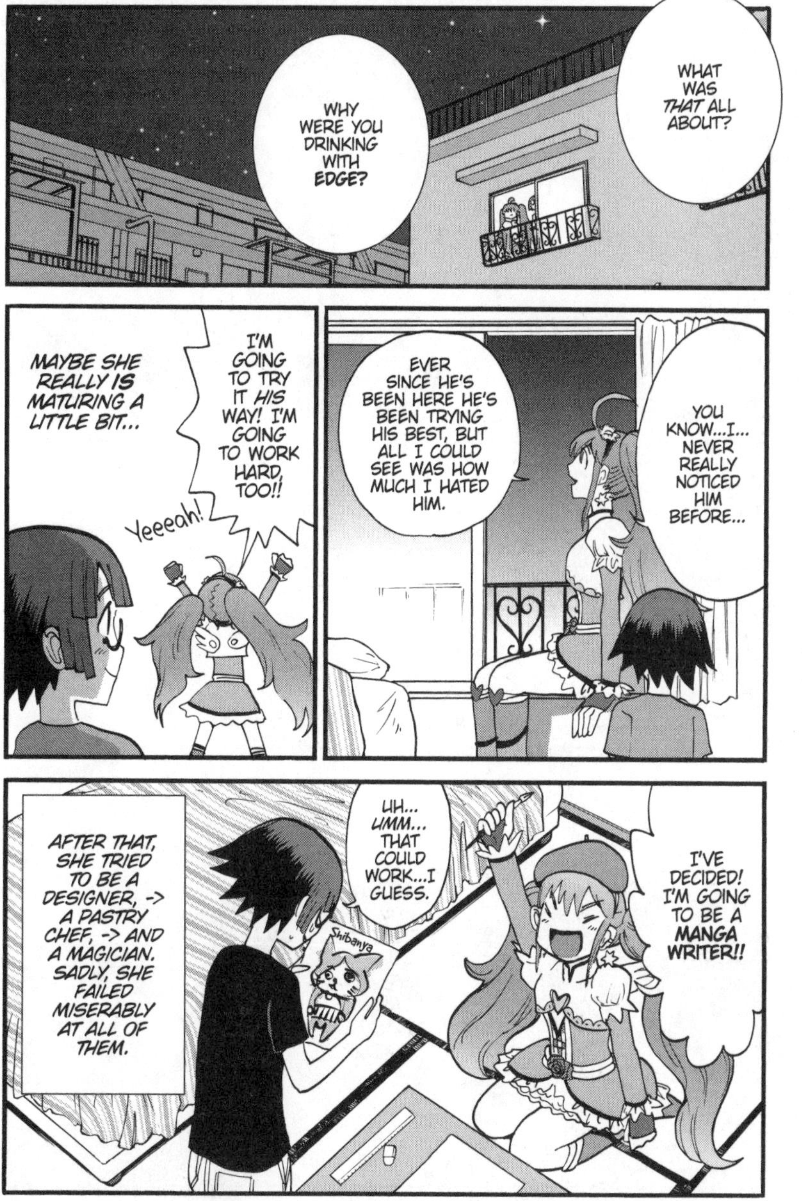
WHAT WAS *THAT* ALL ABOUT?
WHY WERE YOU DRINKING WITH **EDGE?**
YOU KNOW...I... NEVER REALLY NOTICED HIM BEFORE...
EVER SINCE HE'S BEEN HERE HE'S BEEN TRYING HIS BEST, BUT ALL I COULD SEE WAS HOW MUCH I HATED HIM.
I'M GOING TO TRY IT *HIS* WAY! I'M GOING TO WORK HARD, TOO!!
Yeeeah!
MAYBE SHE REALLY ***IS*** *MATURING A LITTLE BIT...*
I'VE DECIDED! I'M GOING TO BE A **MANGA WRITER!!**
UH... UMM... THAT COULD WORK...I GUESS.
Shibanya
AFTER THAT, SHE TRIED TO BE A DESIGNER, -> A PASTRY CHEF, -> AND A MAGICIAN. SADLY, SHE FAILED MISERABLY AT ALL OF THEM.

Chapter 12: I Went to a *Pretty Angel* Show!

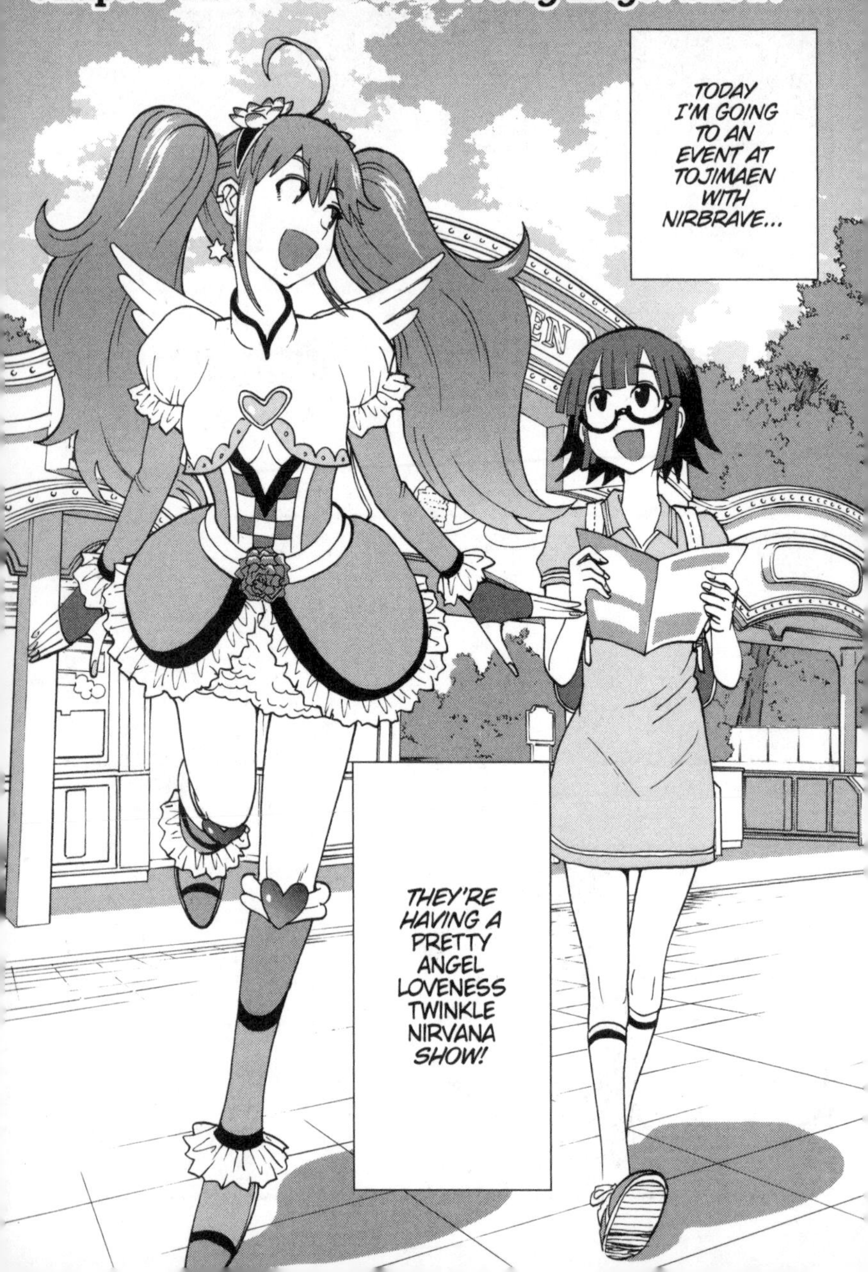
TODAY I'M GOING TO AN EVENT AT TOJIMAEN WITH NIRBRAVE...
THEY'RE HAVING A PRETTY ANGEL LOVENESS TWINKLE NIRVANA SHOW!

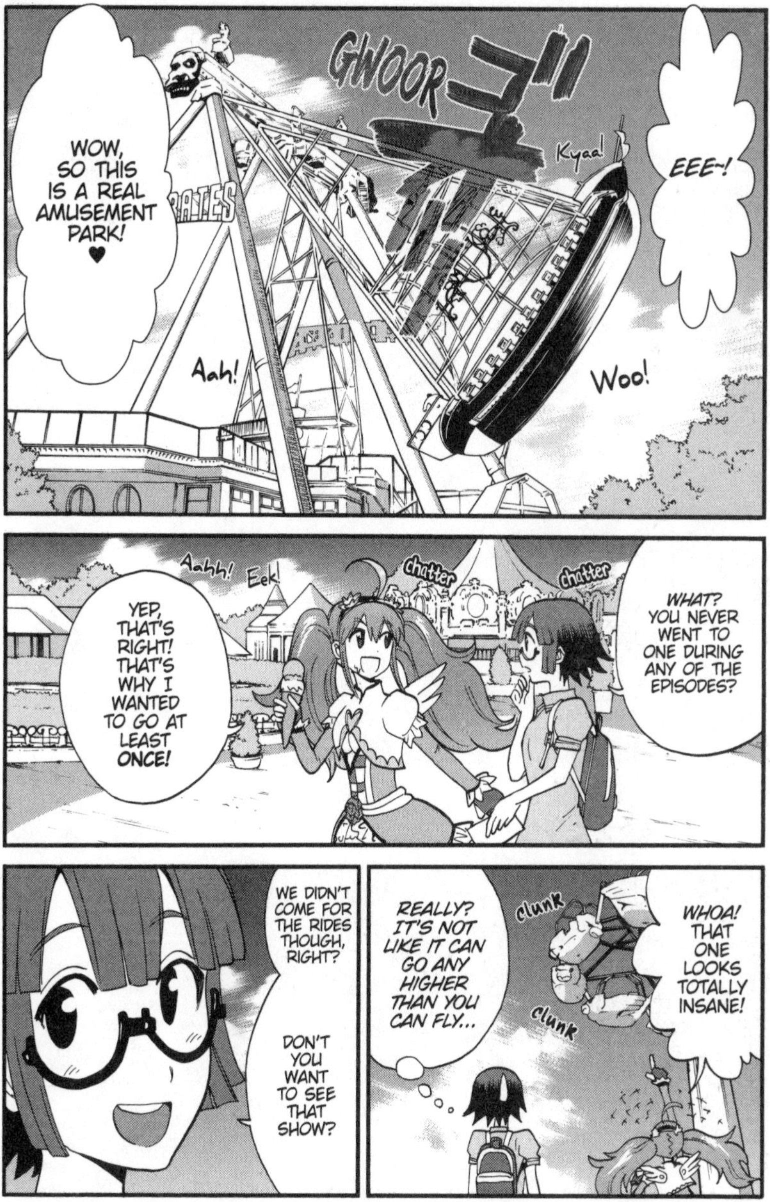
EEE~!
Kyaa!
GWOOR
WOW, SO THIS IS A REAL AMUSEMENT PARK! ♥
Woo!
Aah!
WHAT? YOU NEVER WENT TO ONE DURING ANY OF THE EPISODES?
chatter
chatter
Eek!
Aahh!
YEP, THAT'S RIGHT! THAT'S WHY I WANTED TO GO AT LEAST ONCE!
WHOA! THAT ONE LOOKS TOTALLY INSANE!
clunk
clunk
REALLY? IT'S NOT LIKE IT CAN GO ANY HIGHER THAN YOU CAN FLY...
WE DIDN'T COME FOR THE RIDES THOUGH, RIGHT?
DON'T YOU WANT TO SEE THAT SHOW?

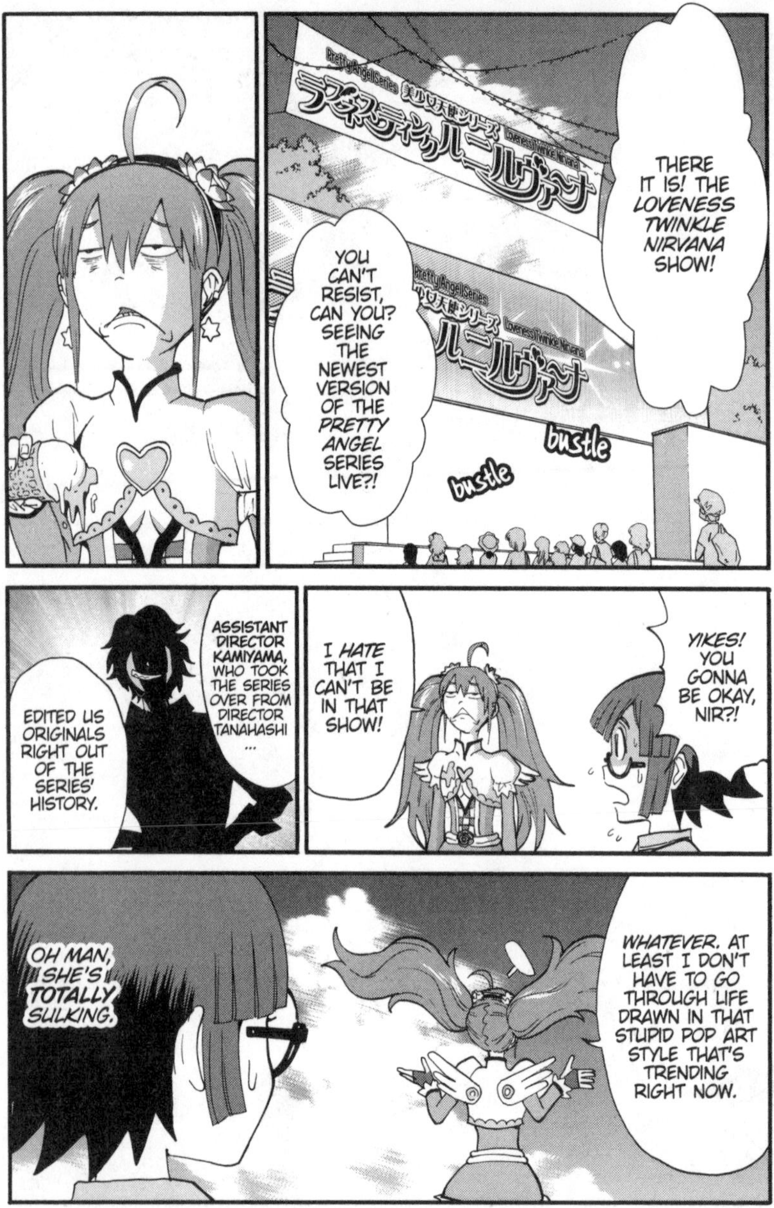
Pretty Angel Series
美少女天使シリーズ
ラブネスティンクルニルヴァ〜ナ
Loveness Twinkle Nirvana
THERE IT IS! THE *LOVENESS TWINKLE NIRVANA* SHOW!
YOU CAN'T RESIST, CAN YOU? SEEING THE NEWEST VERSION OF THE *PRETTY ANGEL SERIES* LIVE?!
bustle
bustle
YIKES! YOU GONNA BE OKAY, NIR?!
I *HATE* THAT I CAN'T BE IN THAT SHOW!
ASSISTANT DIRECTOR KAMIYAMA, WHO TOOK THE SERIES OVER FROM DIRECTOR TANAHASHI...
EDITED US ORIGINALS RIGHT OUT OF THE SERIES' HISTORY.
WHATEVER. AT LEAST I DON'T HAVE TO GO THROUGH LIFE DRAWN IN THAT STUPID POP ART STYLE THAT'S TRENDING RIGHT NOW.
*OH MAN, SHE'S **TOTALLY** SULKING.*

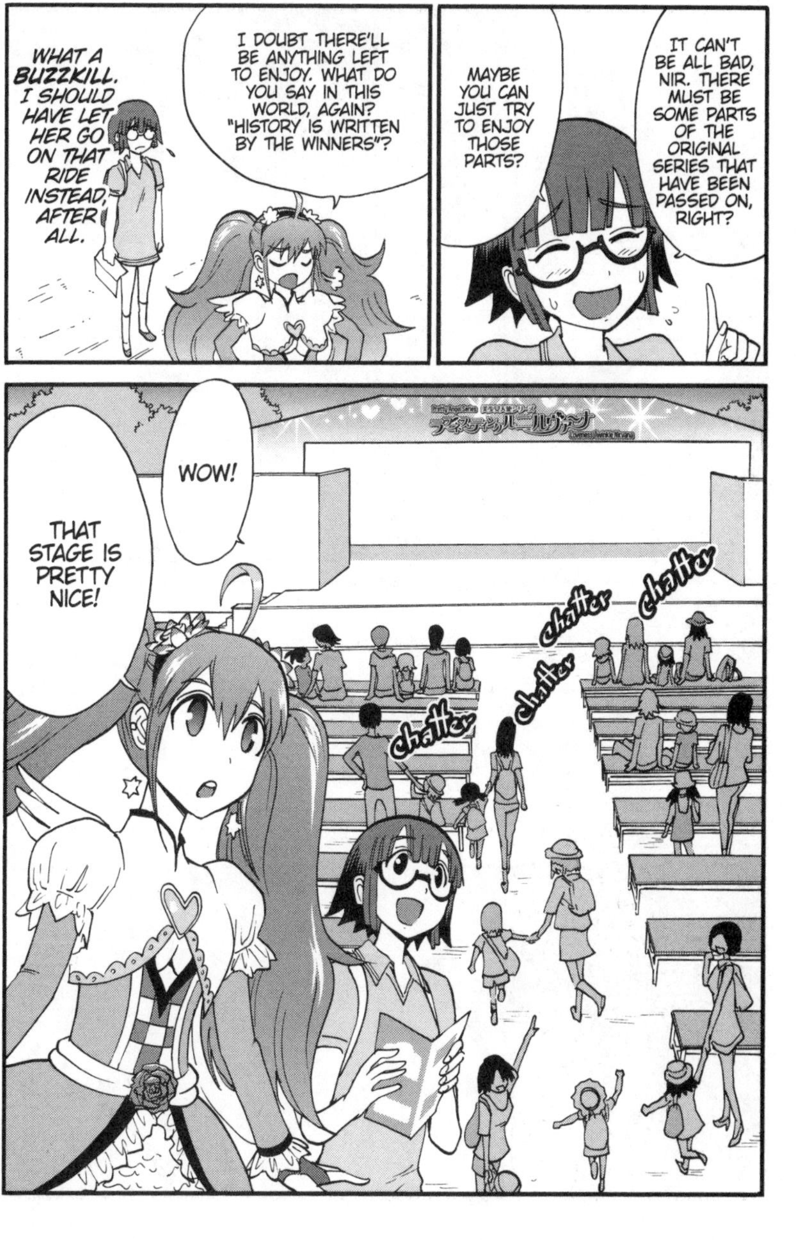
IT CAN'T BE ALL BAD, NIR. THERE MUST BE SOME PARTS OF THE ORIGINAL SERIES THAT HAVE BEEN PASSED ON, RIGHT?
MAYBE YOU CAN JUST TRY TO ENJOY THOSE PARTS?
I DOUBT THERE'LL BE ANYTHING LEFT TO ENJOY. WHAT DO YOU SAY IN THIS WORLD, AGAIN? "HISTORY IS WRITTEN BY THE WINNERS"?
WHAT A BUZZKILL. I SHOULD HAVE LET HER GO ON THAT RIDE INSTEAD, AFTER ALL.
WOW!
THAT STAGE IS PRETTY NICE!
chatter
chatter
chatter
chatter

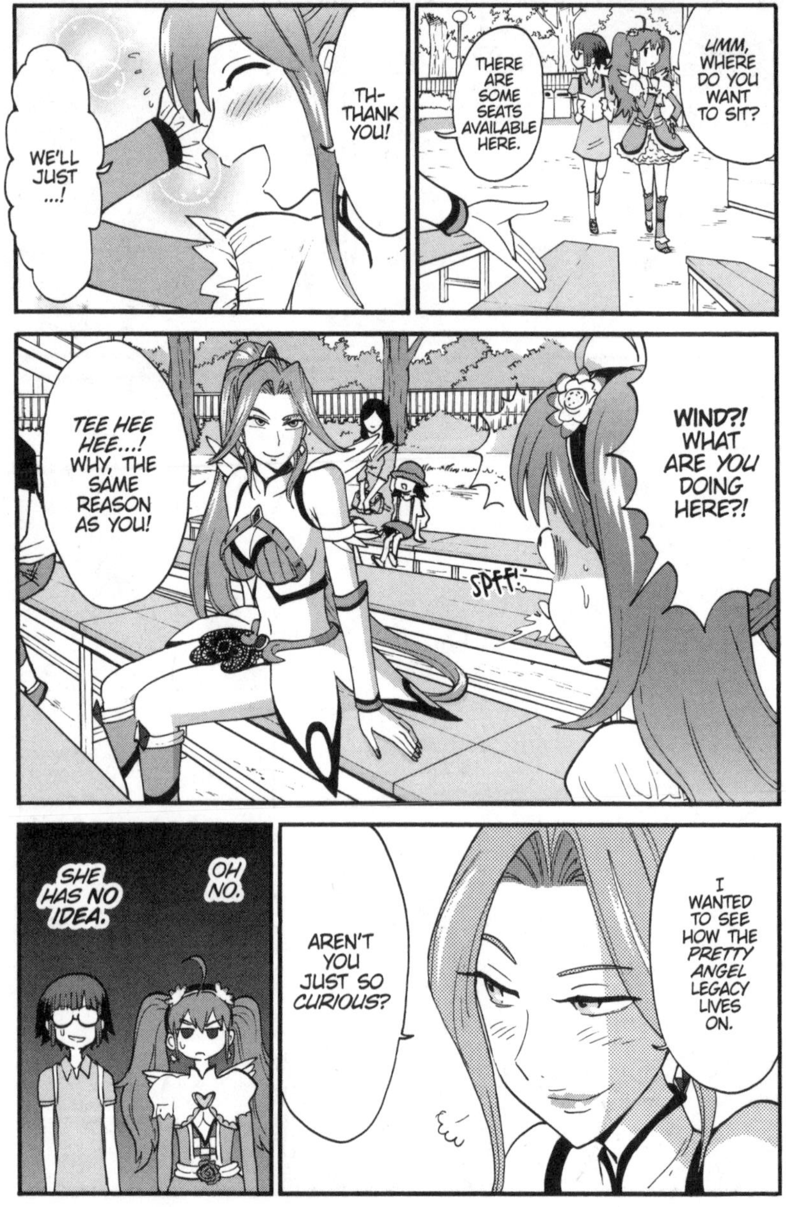
UMM, WHERE DO YOU WANT TO SIT?
THERE ARE SOME SEATS AVAILABLE HERE.
TH-THANK YOU!
WE'LL JUST ...!
WIND?! WHAT ARE YOU DOING HERE?!
SPFF!
TEE HEE HEE...! WHY, THE SAME REASON AS YOU!
I WANTED TO SEE HOW THE PRETTY ANGEL LEGACY LIVES ON.
AREN'T YOU JUST SO CURIOUS?
OH NO.
SHE HAS NO IDEA.

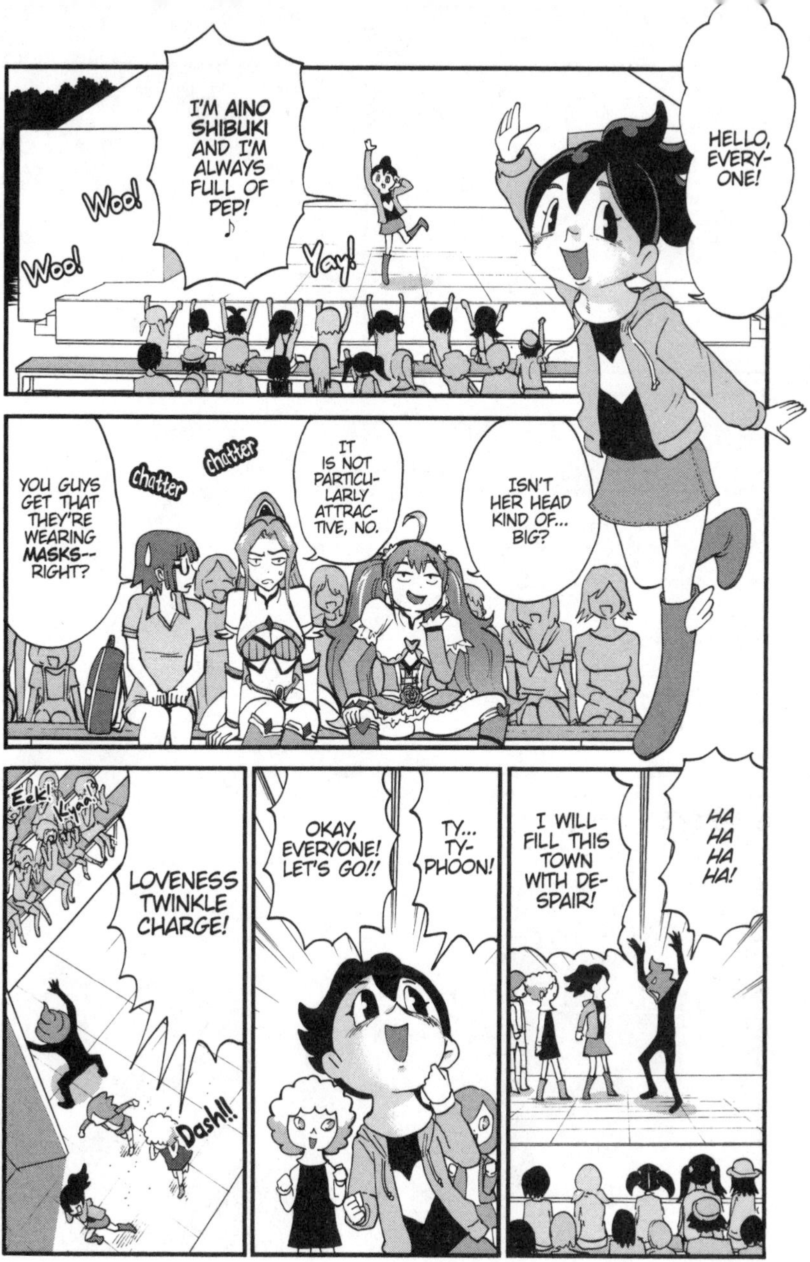
HELLO, EVERY-ONE!
I'M AINO **SHIBUKI** AND I'M ALWAYS FULL OF PEP! ♪
Yay!
Woo!
Woo!
ISN'T HER HEAD KIND OF... BIG?
IT IS NOT PARTICU-LARLY ATTRAC-TIVE, NO.
chatter
chatter
YOU GUYS GET THAT THEY'RE WEARING **MASKS**-- RIGHT?
HA HA HA HA!
I WILL FILL THIS TOWN WITH DE-SPAIR!
TY... TY-PHOON!
OKAY, EVERYONE! LET'S GO!!
LOVENESS TWINKLE CHARGE!
Eek!
Kyaa!
Dash!!

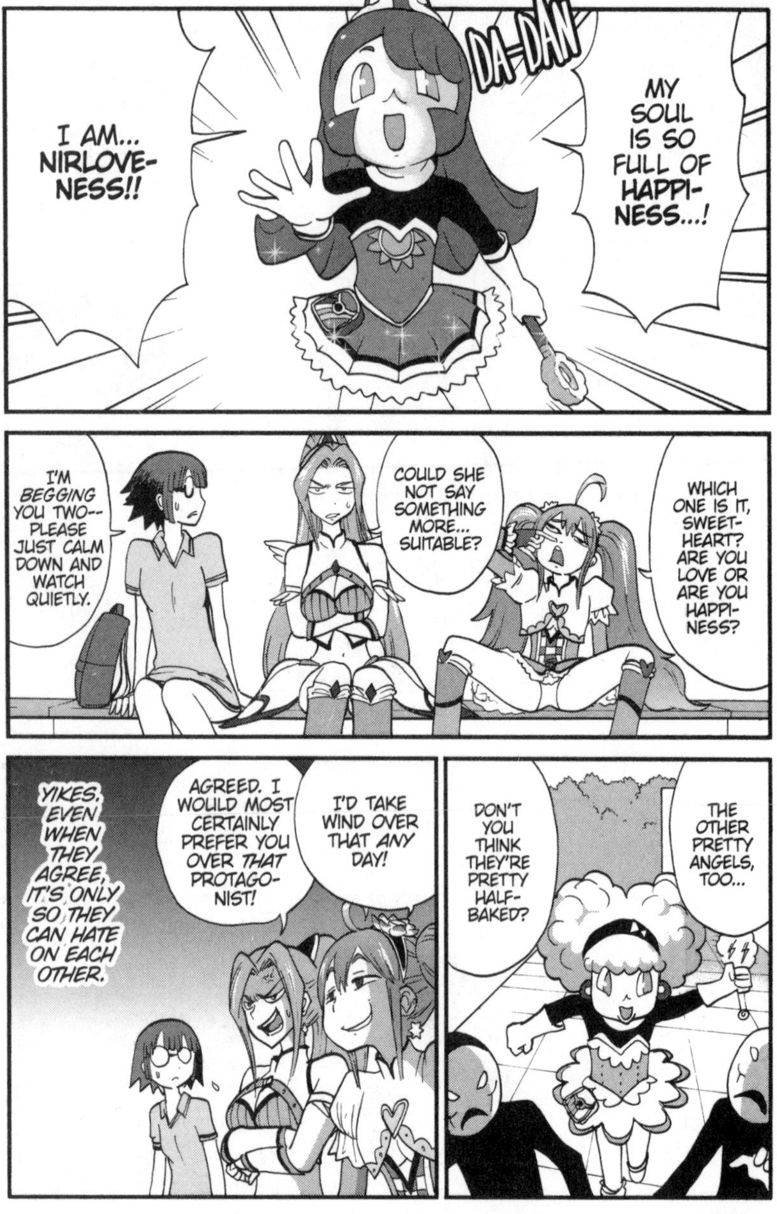
DA-DAN
MY SOUL IS SO FULL OF HAPPINESS...!
I AM... NIRLOVENESS!!
WHICH ONE IS IT, SWEETHEART? ARE YOU LOVE OR ARE YOU HAPPINESS?
COULD SHE NOT SAY SOMETHING MORE... SUITABLE?
I'M *BEGGING* YOU TWO-- PLEASE JUST CALM DOWN AND WATCH QUIETLY.
THE OTHER PRETTY ANGELS, TOO...
DON'T YOU THINK THEY'RE PRETTY HALF-BAKED?
I'D TAKE WIND OVER THAT *ANY* DAY!
AGREED. I WOULD MOST CERTAINLY PREFER YOU OVER *THAT* PROTAGONIST!
YIKES. EVEN WHEN THEY AGREE, IT'S ONLY SO THEY CAN HATE ON EACH OTHER.

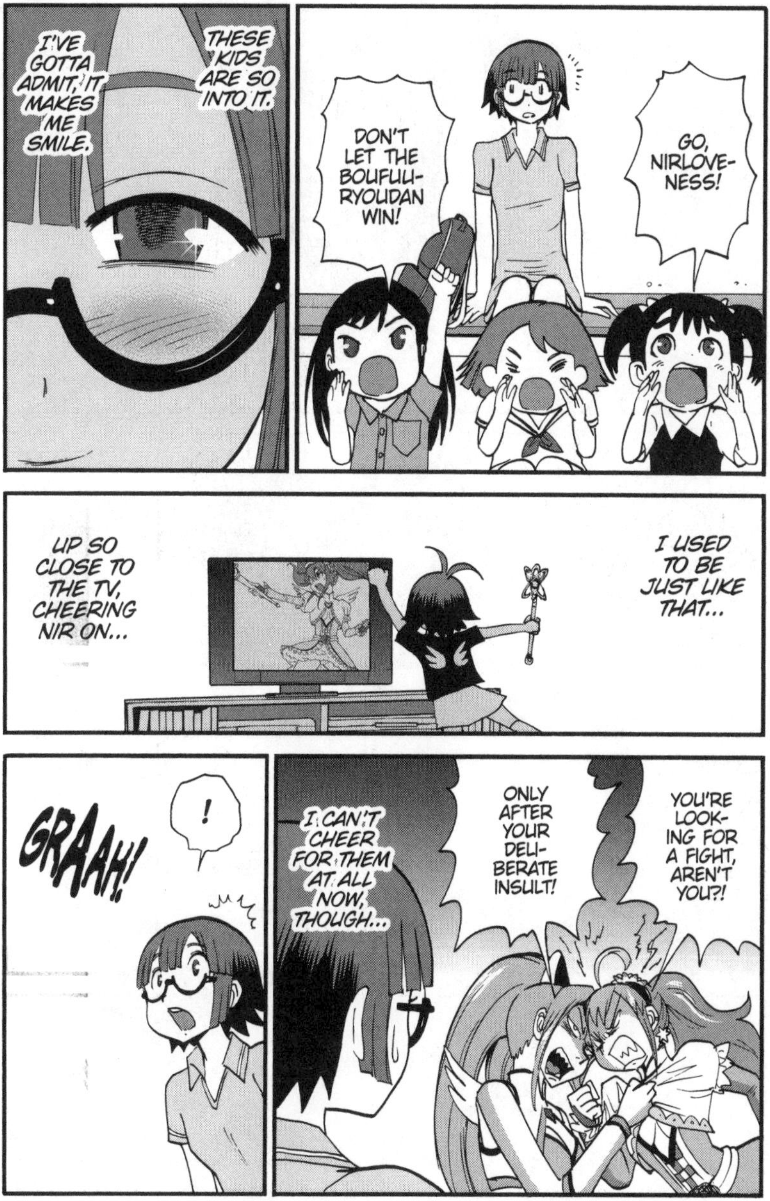
GO, NIRLOVE-NESS!
DON'T LET THE BOUFULI-RYOUDAN WIN!
THESE KIDS ARE SO INTO IT.
I'VE GOTTA ADMIT, IT MAKES ME SMILE.
I USED TO BE JUST LIKE THAT...
UP SO CLOSE TO THE TV, CHEERING NIR ON...
YOU'RE LOOKING FOR A FIGHT, AREN'T YOU?!
ONLY AFTER YOUR DELI-BERATE INSULT!
I CAN'T CHEER FOR THEM AT ALL NOW, THOUGH...
!
GRAAH!

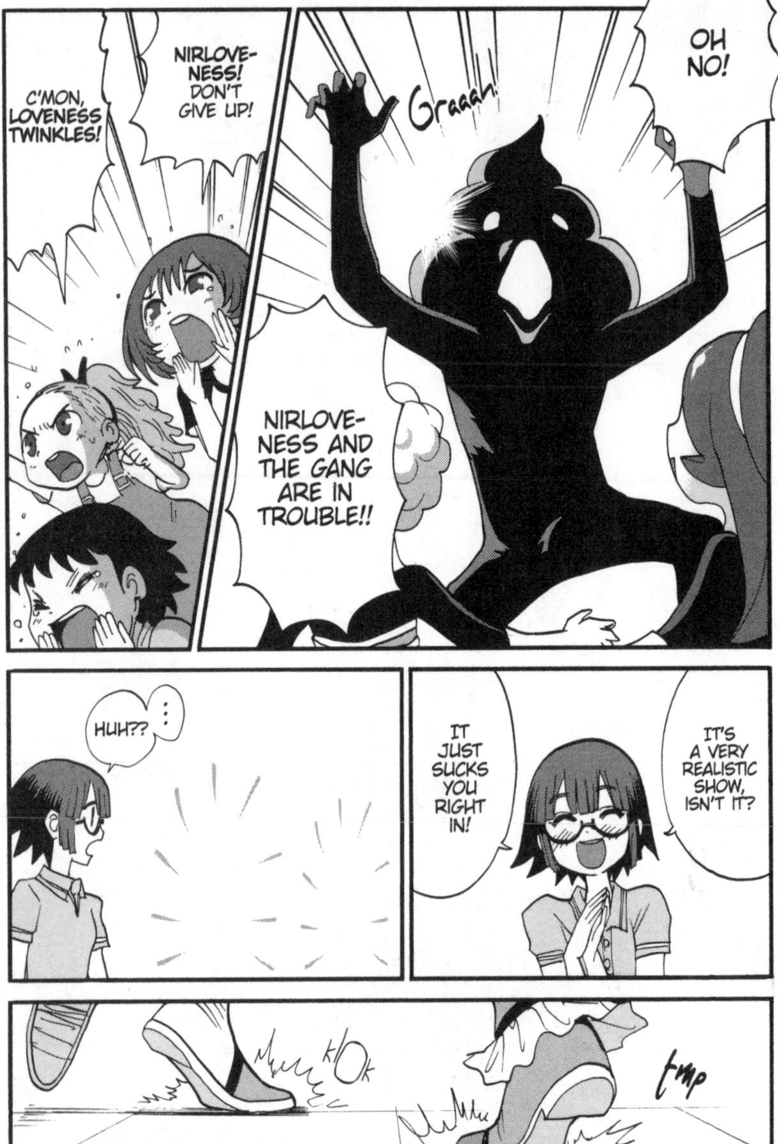
OH NO!
Graaah!
NIRLOVENESS AND THE GANG ARE IN TROUBLE!!
NIRLOVENESS! DON'T GIVE UP!
C'MON, LOVENESS TWINKLES!
IT'S A VERY REALISTIC SHOW, ISN'T IT?
IT JUST SUCKS YOU RIGHT IN!
HUH??
...
tmp
klOk

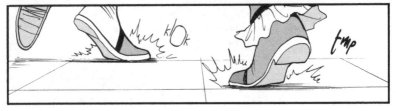

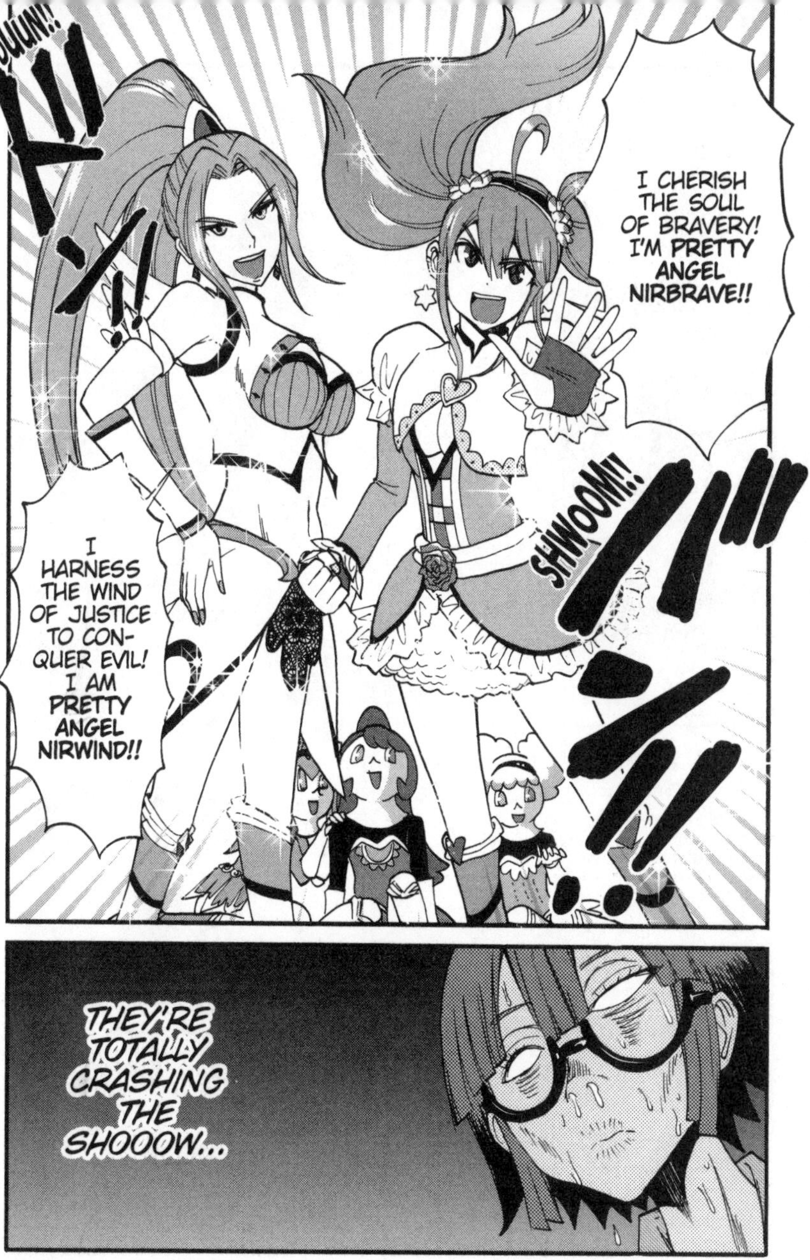
I CHERISH THE SOUL OF BRAVERY! I'M PRETTY ANGEL NIRBRAVE!!
DUUN!!
SHWOOM!!
I HARNESS THE WIND OF JUSTICE TO CON-QUER EVIL! I AM PRETTY ANGEL NIRWIND!!
THEY'RE TOTALLY CRASHING THE SHOOOW...

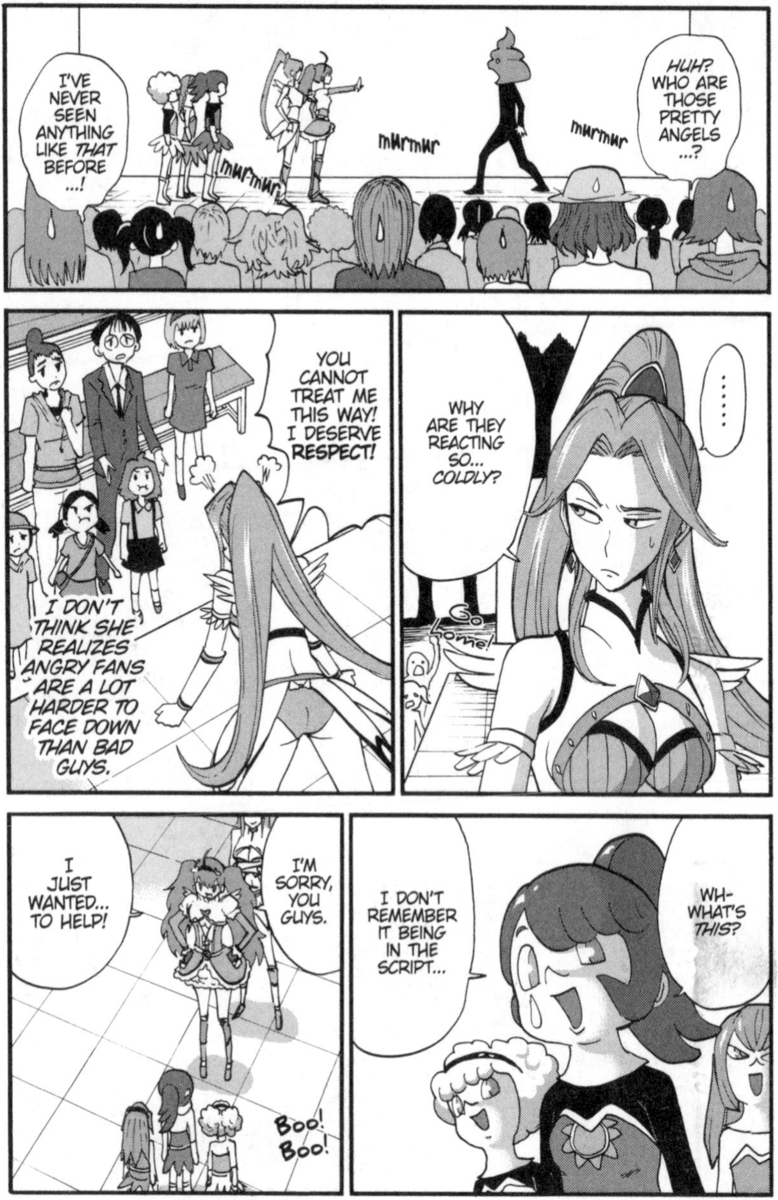
HUH? WHO ARE THOSE PRETTY ANGELS ...?
murmur
murmur
I'VE NEVER SEEN ANYTHING LIKE *THAT* BEFORE ...!
mur-mur
......
WHY ARE THEY REACTING SO... *COLDLY?*
Go home!
YOU CANNOT TREAT ME THIS WAY! I DESERVE **RESPECT!**
I DON'T THINK SHE REALIZES ANGRY FANS ARE A LOT HARDER TO FACE DOWN THAN BAD GUYS.
WH- WHAT'S *THIS?*
I DON'T REMEMBER IT BEING IN THE SCRIPT...
I'M SORRY, YOU GUYS.
I JUST WANTED... TO HELP!
Boo! Boo!

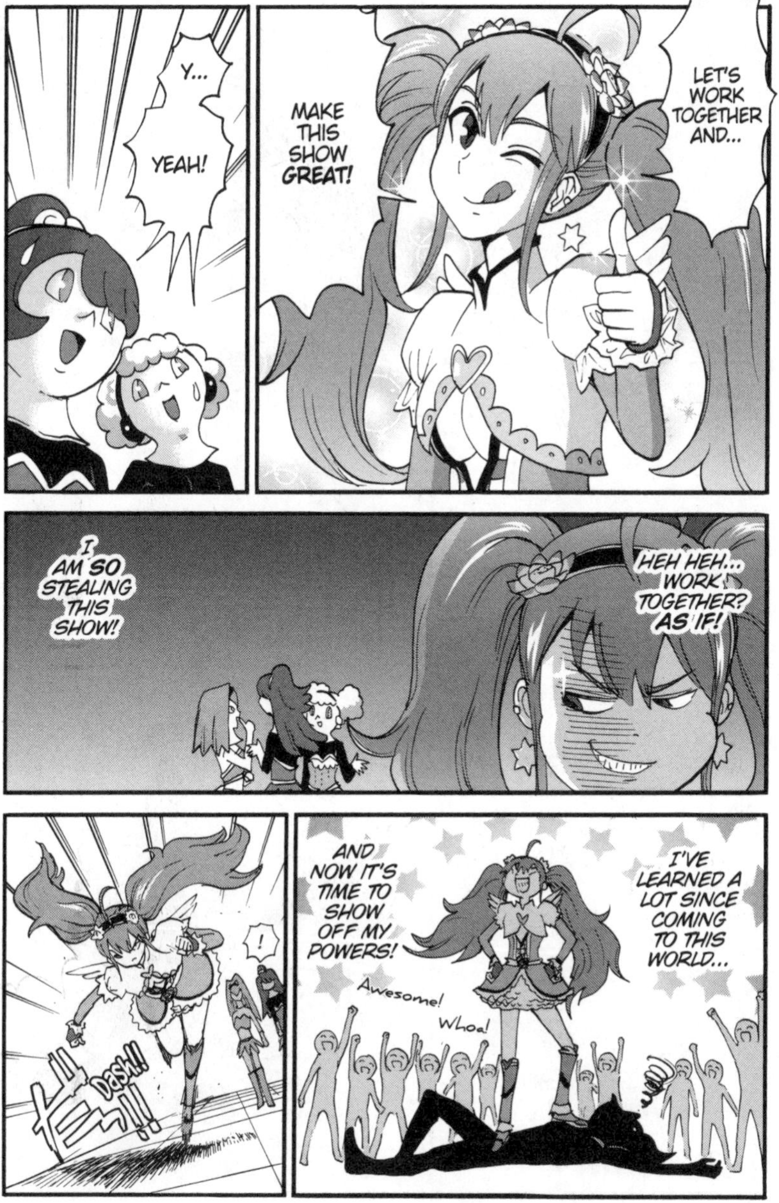
LET'S WORK TOGETHER AND...
MAKE THIS SHOW GREAT!
Y...
YEAH!
HEH HEH... WORK TOGETHER? AS IF!
I AM SO STEALING THIS SHOW!
I'VE LEARNED A LOT SINCE COMING TO THIS WORLD...
AND NOW IT'S TIME TO SHOW OFF MY POWERS!
Awesome!
Whoa!
!
Dash!!

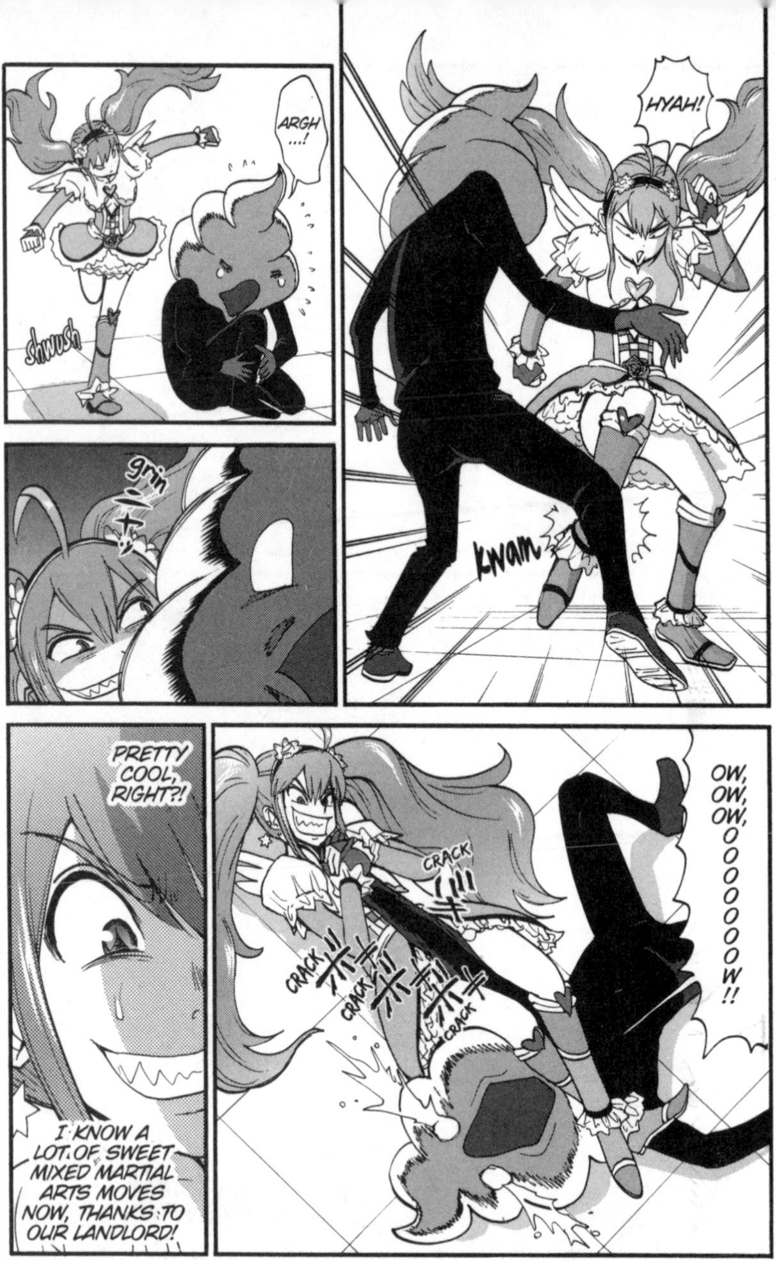
HYAH!
KWAM
ARGH ...!
shwush
grin
OW, OW, OW, OOOOOOOOOOOW!!
CRACK
CRACK
CRACK
CRACK
PRETTY COOL, RIGHT?!
I KNOW A LOT OF SWEET MIXED MARTIAL ARTS MOVES NOW, THANKS TO OUR LANDLORD!

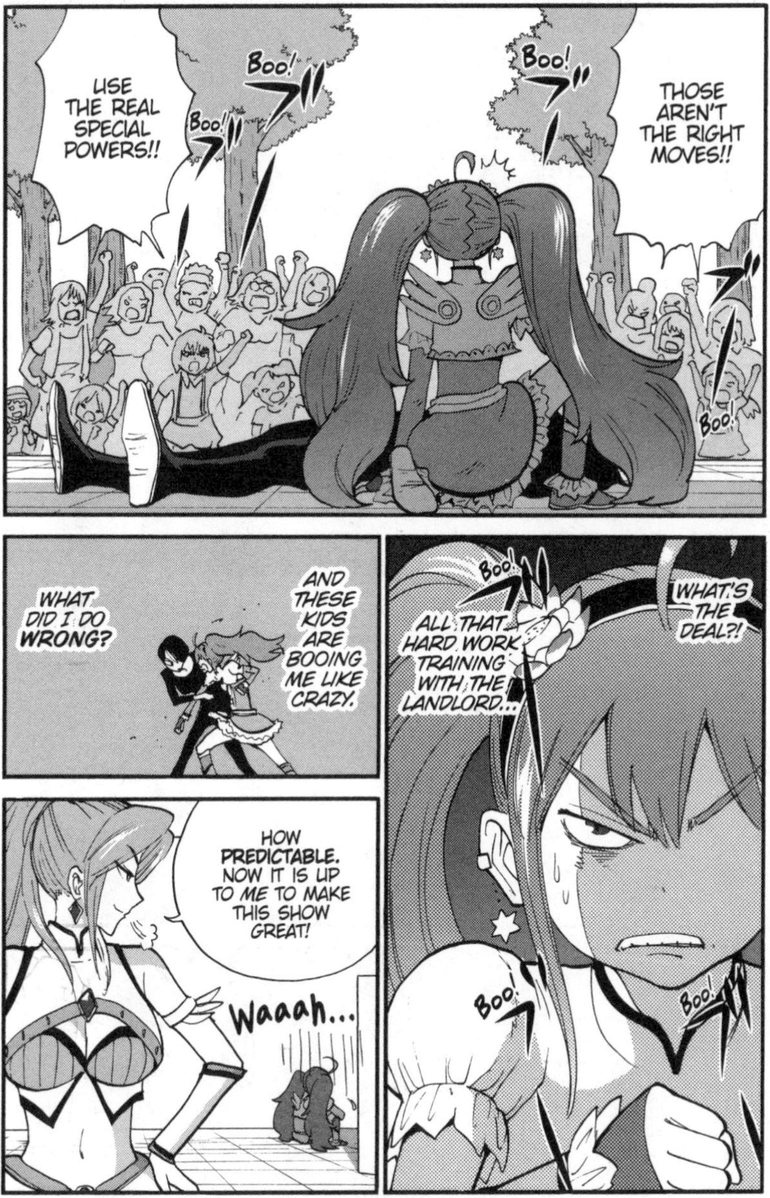

THOSE AREN'T THE RIGHT MOVES!!
Boo!
Boo!
Boo!
Boo!
USE THE REAL SPECIAL POWERS!!
WHAT'S THE DEAL?!
Boo!
ALL THAT HARD WORK TRAINING WITH THE LANDLORD...
Boo!
Boo!
AND THESE KIDS ARE BOOING ME LIKE CRAZY.
WHAT DID I DO WRONG?
HOW PREDICTABLE. NOW IT IS UP TO ME TO MAKE THIS SHOW GREAT!
Waaah...

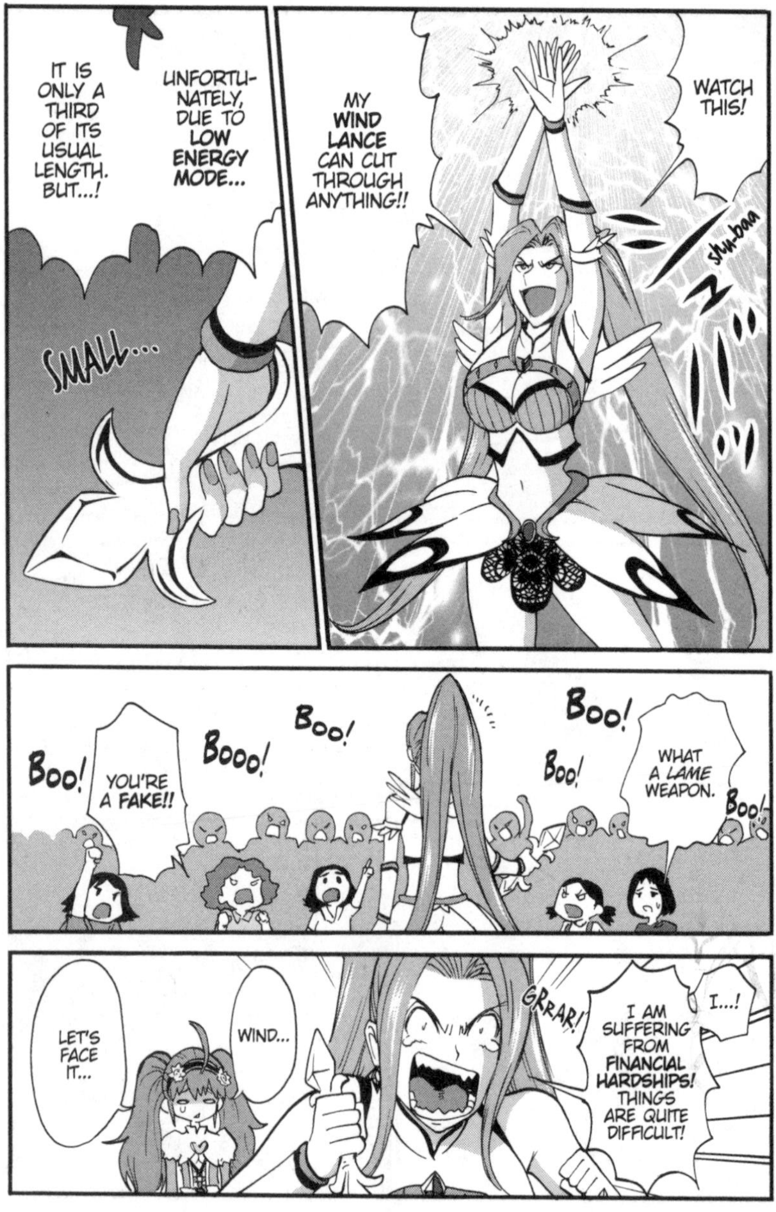
WATCH THIS!
MY WIND LANCE CAN CUT THROUGH ANYTHING!!
shu-baa
UNFORTUNATELY, DUE TO LOW ENERGY MODE...
IT IS ONLY A THIRD OF ITS USUAL LENGTH. BUT...!
SMALL...
Boo!
WHAT A LAME WEAPON.
Boo!
Boo!
Boo!
Booo!
YOU'RE A FAKE!!
Boo!
I...!
I AM SUFFERING FROM FINANCIAL HARDSHIPS! THINGS ARE QUITE DIFFICULT!
GRRAR!
WIND...
LET'S FACE IT...

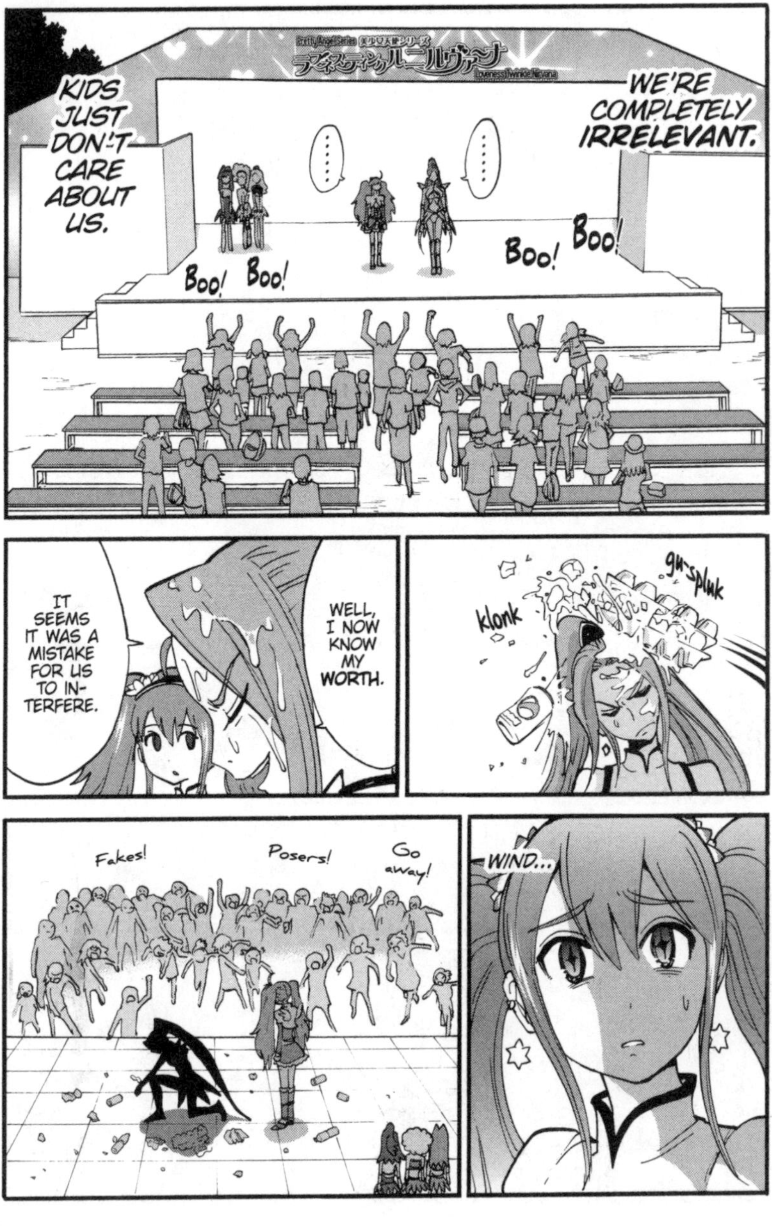

Pretty Angel Series 美少女天使シリーズ
ラブネスティンクルニルヴァ～ナ
Loveness Twinkle Nirvana
WE'RE COMPLETELY IRRELEVANT.
......
......
KIDS JUST DON'T CARE ABOUT US.
Boo! Boo!
Boo! Boo!
gu-splunk
klonk
WELL, I NOW KNOW MY WORTH.
IT SEEMS IT WAS A MISTAKE FOR US TO INTERFERE.
WIND...
Go away!
Posers!
Fakes!

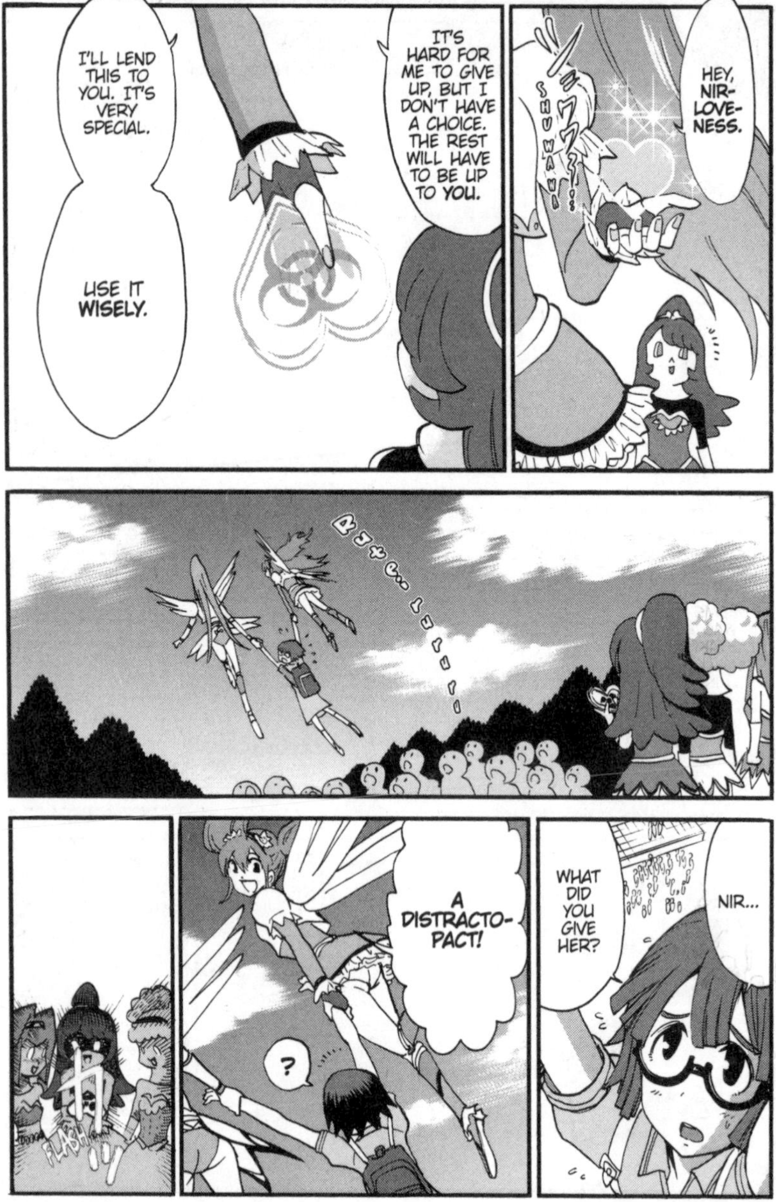
HEY, NIR-LOVENESS.
SHUWAWA
IT'S HARD FOR ME TO GIVE UP, BUT I DON'T HAVE A CHOICE. THE REST WILL HAVE TO BE UP TO YOU.
I'LL LEND THIS TO YOU. IT'S VERY SPECIAL.
USE IT WISELY.
NIR...
WHAT DID YOU GIVE HER?
A DISTRACTO-PACT!
?
FLASH

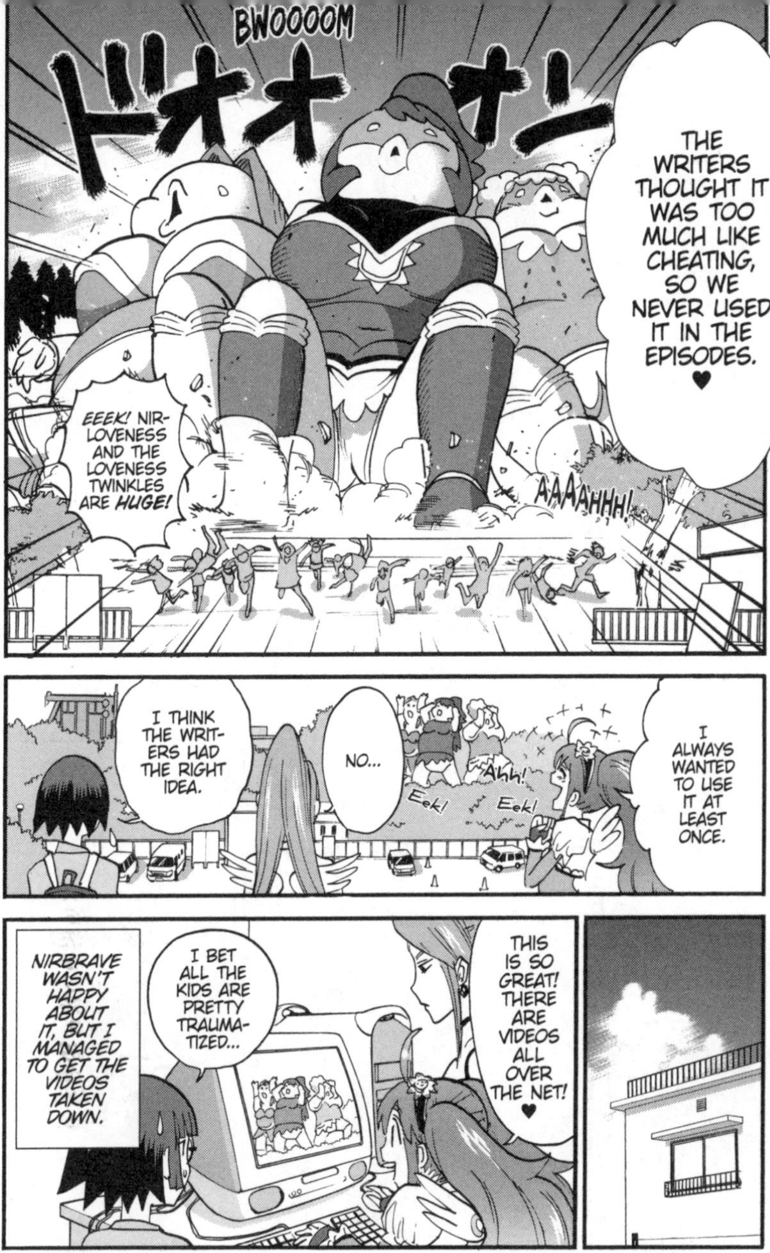
BWOOOOM
THE WRITERS THOUGHT IT WAS TOO MUCH LIKE CHEATING, SO WE NEVER USED IT IN THE EPISODES. ♥
EEEK! NIR-LOVENESS AND THE LOVENESS TWINKLES ARE *HUGE!*
AAAAHHH!
I ALWAYS WANTED TO USE IT AT LEAST ONCE.
Ahh!
Eek!
Eek!
NO...
I THINK THE WRIT-ERS HAD THE RIGHT IDEA.
THIS IS SO GREAT! THERE ARE VIDEOS ALL OVER THE NET! ♥
I BET ALL THE KIDS ARE PRETTY TRAUMA-TIZED...
NIRBRAVE WASN'T HAPPY ABOUT IT, BUT I MANAGED TO GET THE VIDEOS TAKEN DOWN.

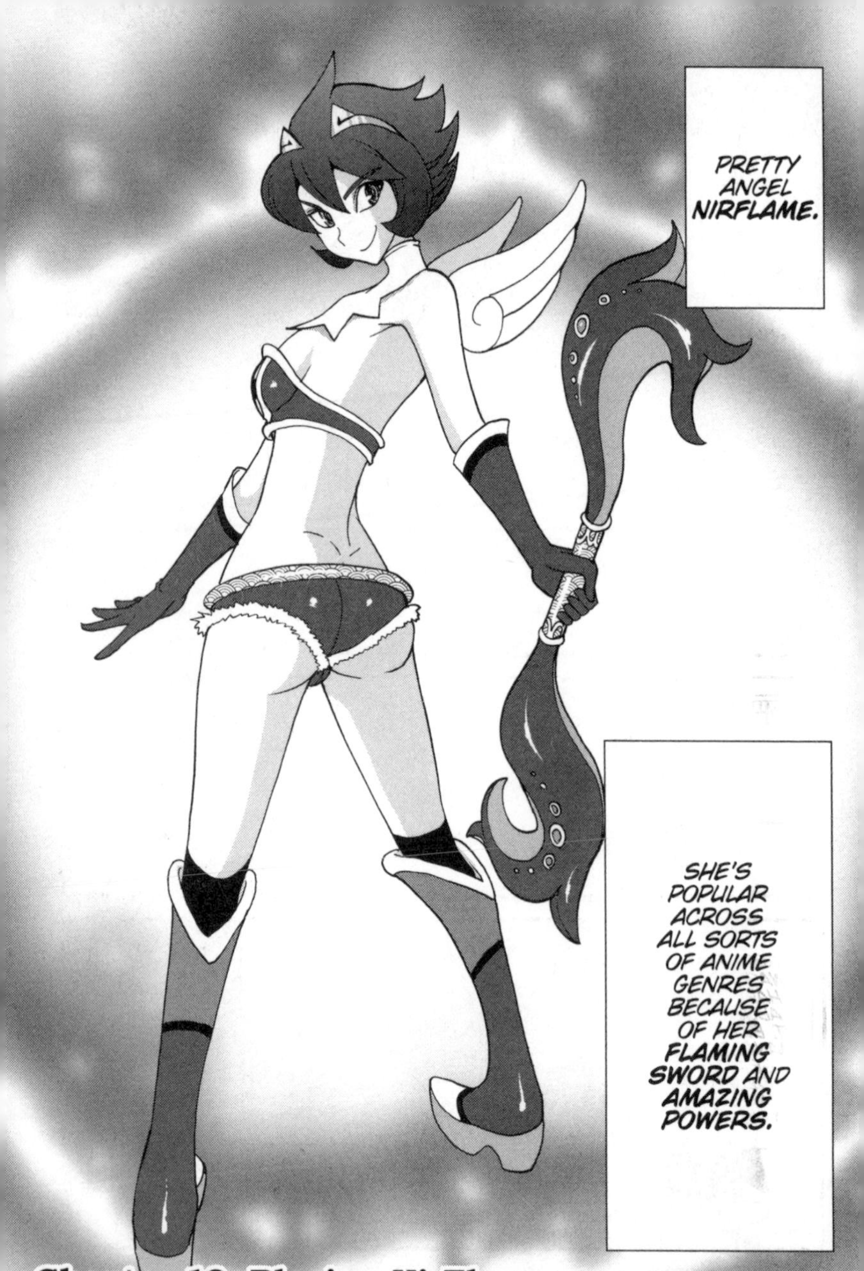
PRETTY ANGEL NIRFLAME.
SHE'S POPULAR ACROSS ALL SORTS OF ANIME GENRES BECAUSE OF HER FLAMING SWORD AND AMAZING POWERS.

Chapter 13: Blazing NirFlame

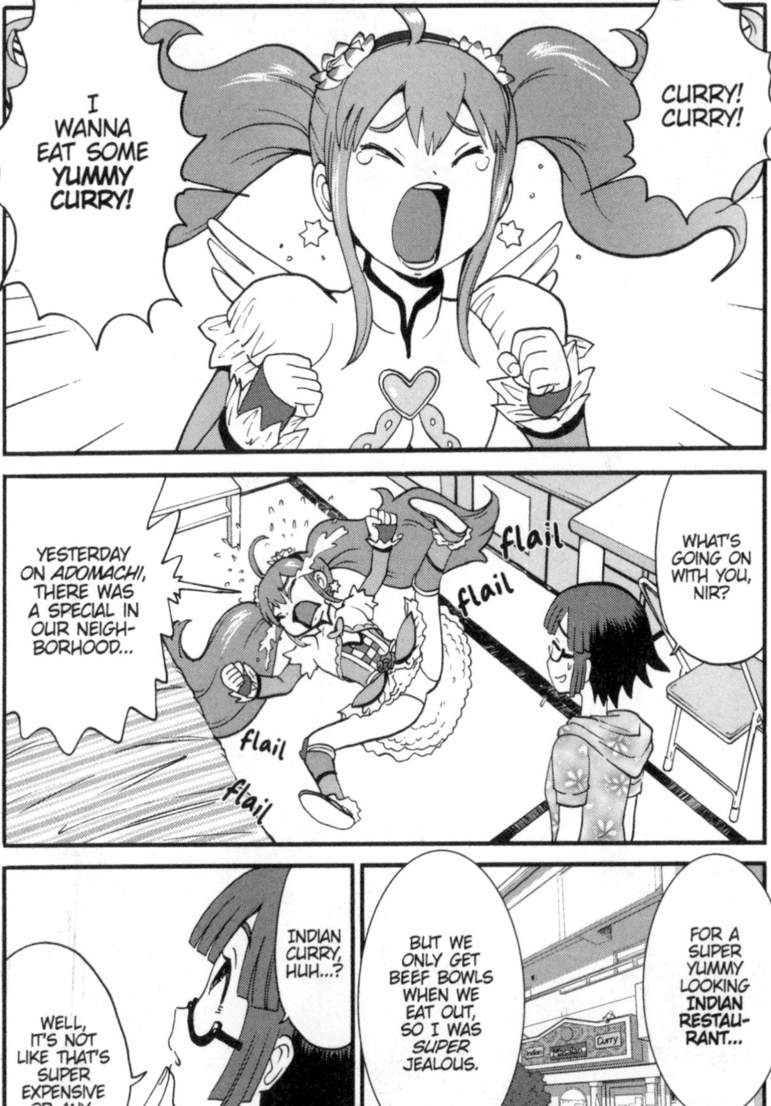
CURRY! CURRY!
I WANNA EAT SOME YUMMY CURRY!
WHAT'S GOING ON WITH YOU, NIR?
flail
flail
YESTERDAY ON *ADOMACHI*, THERE WAS A SPECIAL IN OUR NEIGHBORHOOD...
flail
flail
FOR A SUPER YUMMY LOOKING INDIAN RESTAURANT...
BUT WE ONLY GET BEEF BOWLS WHEN WE EAT OUT, SO I WAS *SUPER* JEALOUS.
Indian
Curry
INDIAN CURRY, HUH...?
WELL, IT'S NOT LIKE THAT'S SUPER EXPENSIVE OR ANYTHING...

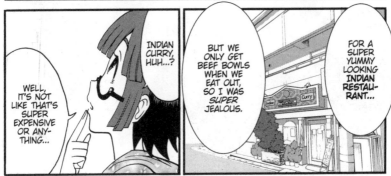

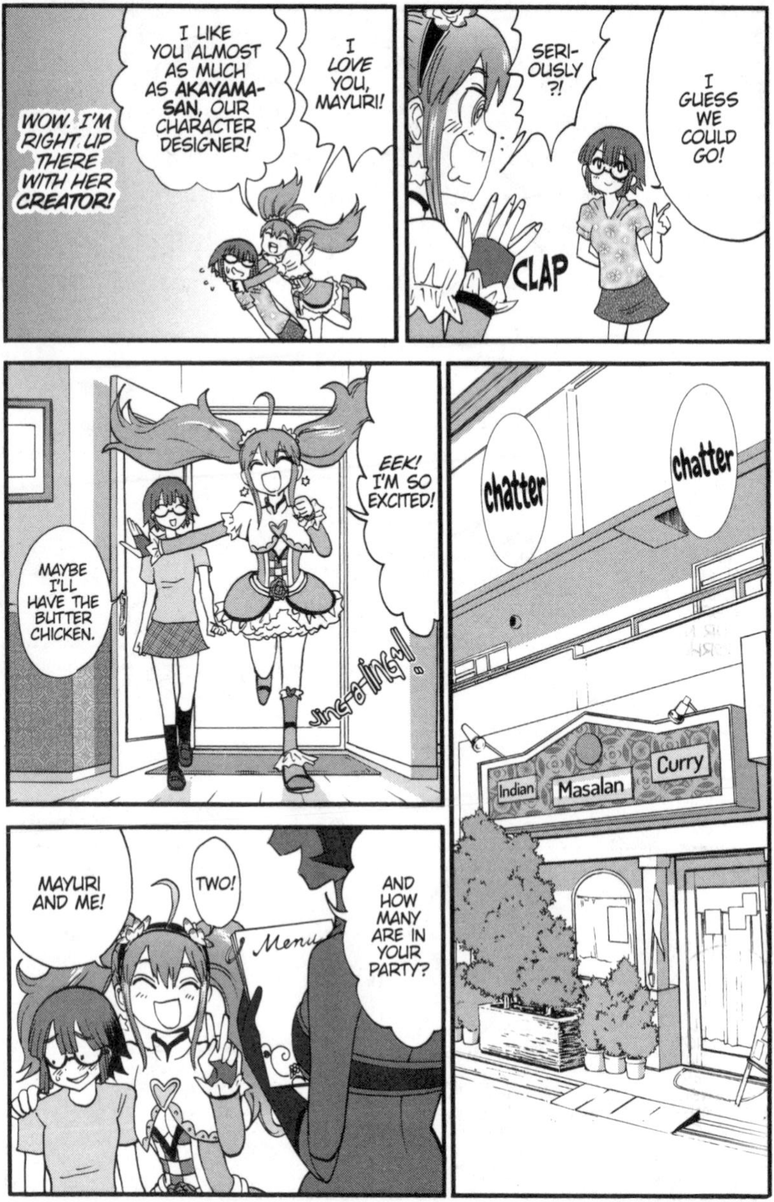
I GUESS WE COULD GO!
SERI-OUSLY?!
CLAP
I LOVE YOU, MAYURI!
I LIKE YOU ALMOST AS MUCH AS **AKAYAMA-SAN**, OUR CHARACTER DESIGNER!
*WOW. I'M RIGHT UP THERE WITH HER **CREATOR**!*
chatter
chatter
Indian Masalan Curry
EEK! I'M SO EXCITED!
Jing-a-ling!!
MAYBE I'LL HAVE THE BUTTER CHICKEN.
AND HOW MANY ARE IN YOUR PARTY?
TWO!
MAYURI AND ME!
Menu

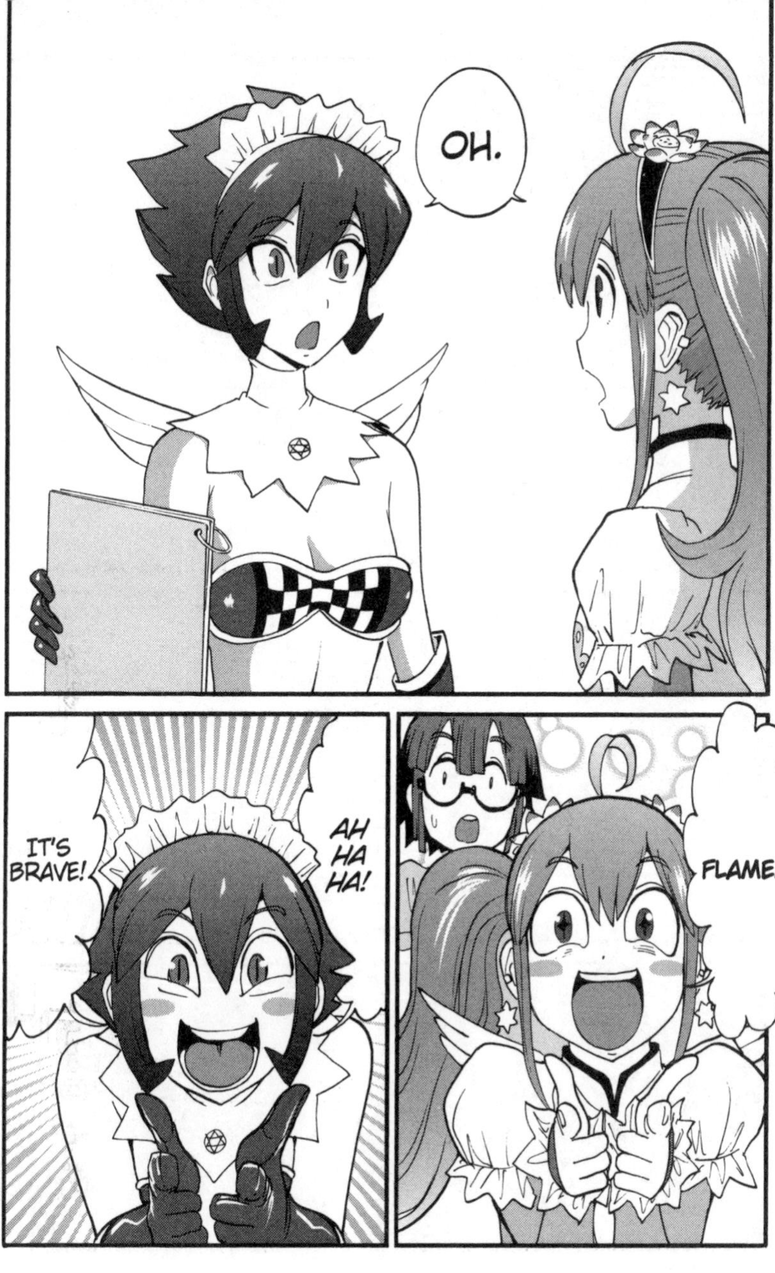
OH.
FLAME!
AH HA HA!
IT'S BRAVE!

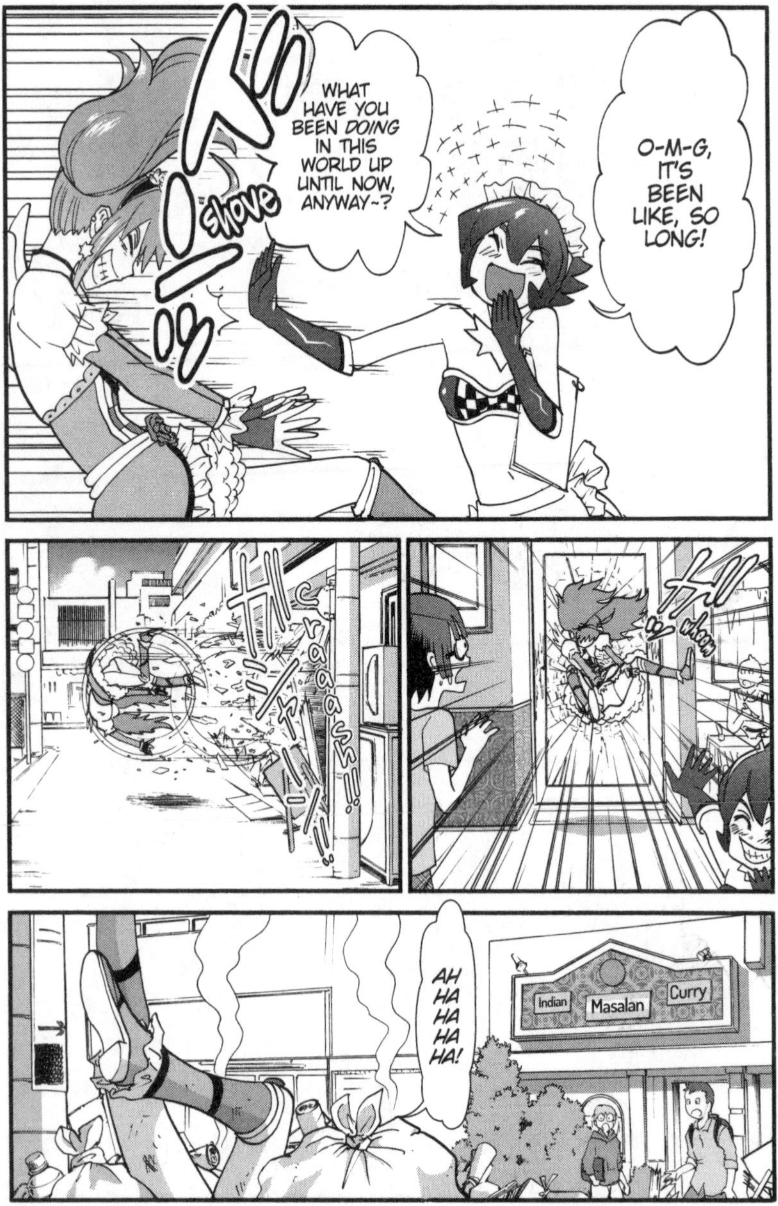
O-M-G, IT'S BEEN LIKE, SO LONG!
WHAT HAVE YOU BEEN *DOING* IN THIS WORLD UP UNTIL NOW, ANYWAY~?
shove
whoom
craaaash!!
AH HA HA HA HA!
Indian
Masalan
Curry

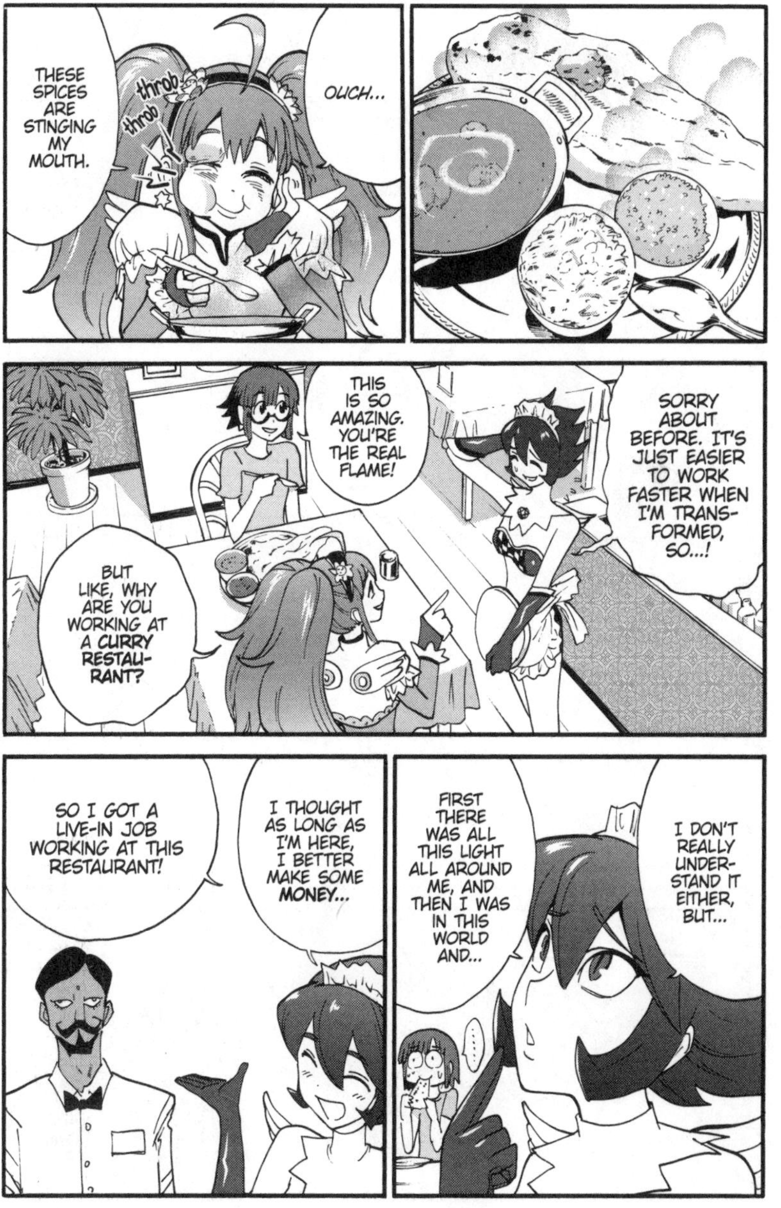
OUCH...
throb
throb
THESE SPICES ARE STINGING MY MOUTH.
SORRY ABOUT BEFORE. IT'S JUST EASIER TO WORK FASTER WHEN I'M TRANSFORMED, SO...!
THIS IS SO AMAZING. YOU'RE THE REAL FLAME!
BUT LIKE, WHY ARE YOU WORKING AT A **CURRY RESTAURANT?**
I DON'T REALLY UNDERSTAND IT EITHER, BUT...
FIRST THERE WAS ALL THIS LIGHT ALL AROUND ME, AND THEN I WAS IN THIS WORLD AND...
......
I THOUGHT AS LONG AS I'M HERE, I BETTER MAKE SOME **MONEY...**
SO I GOT A LIVE-IN JOB WORKING AT THIS RESTAURANT!

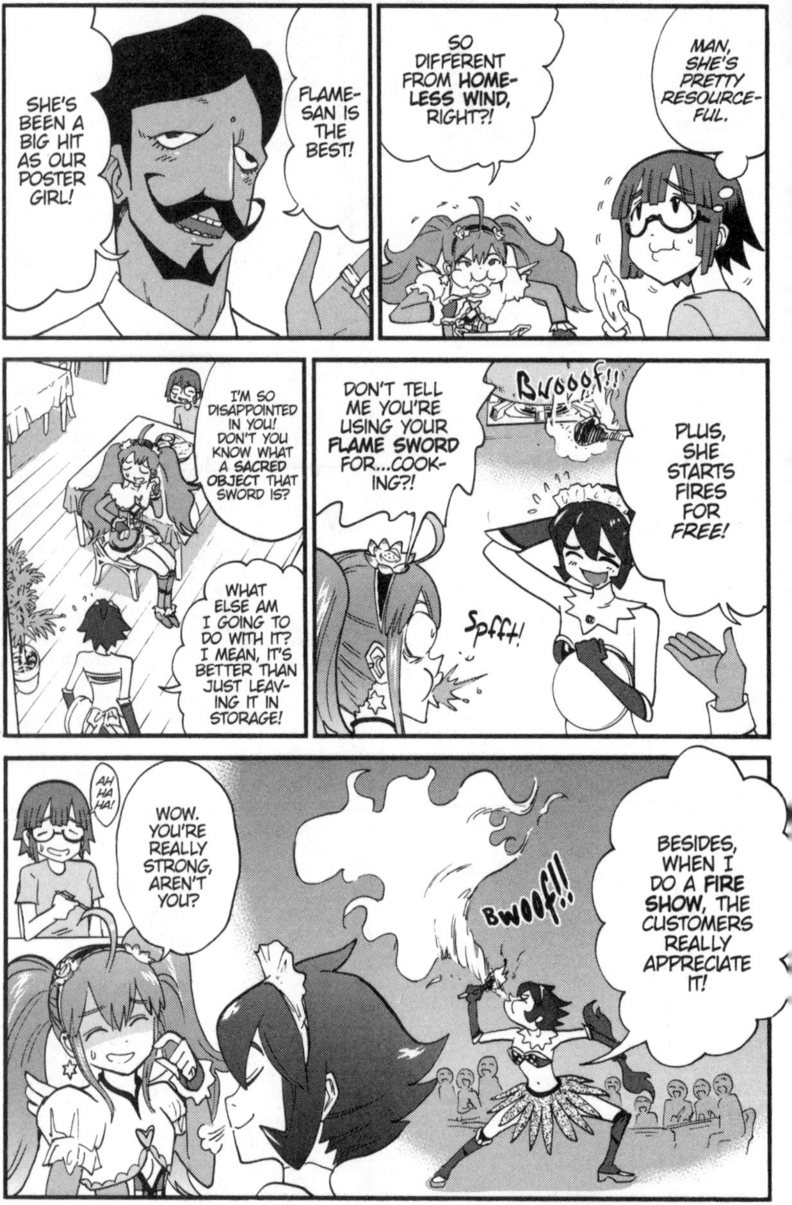
MAN, SHE'S PRETTY RESOURCEFUL.
SO DIFFERENT FROM HOMELESS WIND, RIGHT?!
FLAME-SAN IS THE BEST!
SHE'S BEEN A BIG HIT AS OUR POSTER GIRL!
PLUS, SHE STARTS FIRES FOR FREE!
BWOOOF!!
DON'T TELL ME YOU'RE USING YOUR FLAME SWORD FOR...COOKING?!
SPFFT!
I'M SO DISAPPOINTED IN YOU! DON'T YOU KNOW WHAT A SACRED OBJECT THAT SWORD IS?
WHAT ELSE AM I GOING TO DO WITH IT? I MEAN, IT'S BETTER THAN JUST LEAVING IT IN STORAGE!
BESIDES, WHEN I DO A FIRE SHOW, THE CUSTOMERS REALLY APPRECIATE IT!
BWOOF!!
WOW. YOU'RE REALLY STRONG, AREN'T YOU?
AH HA HA!

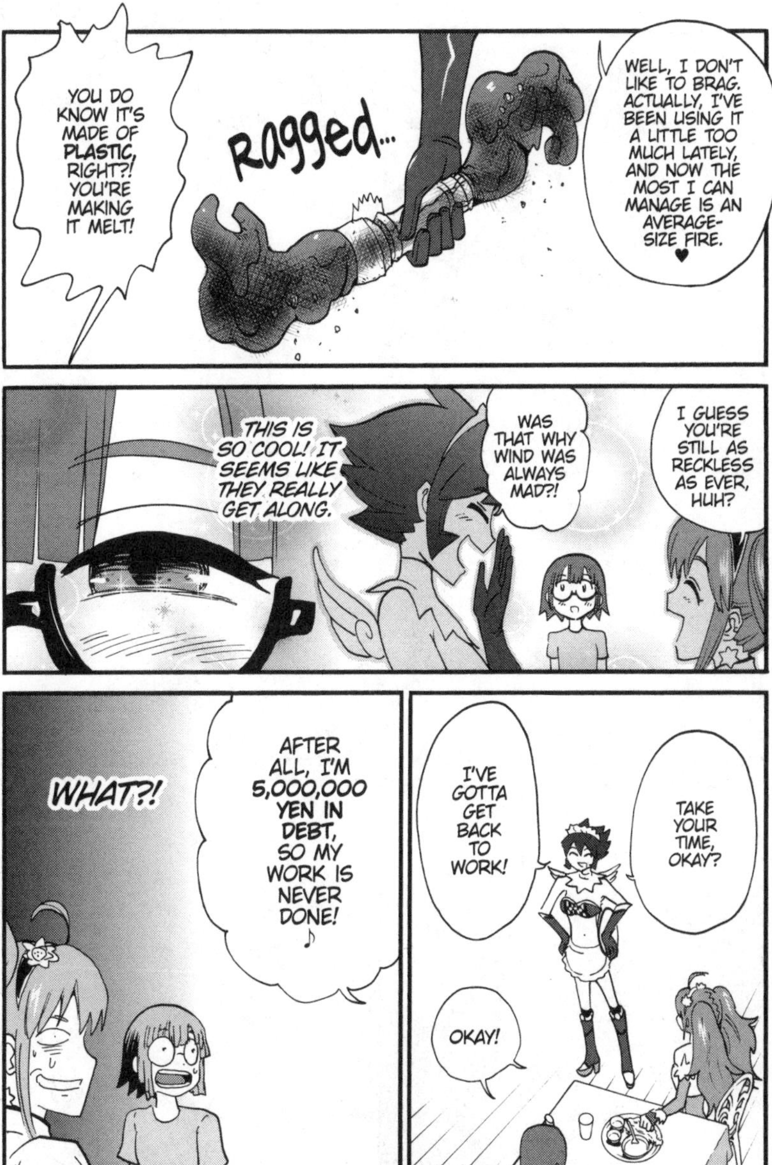
WELL, I DON'T LIKE TO BRAG. ACTUALLY, I'VE BEEN USING IT A LITTLE TOO MUCH LATELY, AND NOW THE MOST I CAN MANAGE IS AN AVERAGE-SIZE FIRE. ♥
Ragged...
YOU DO KNOW IT'S MADE OF PLASTIC, RIGHT?! YOU'RE MAKING IT MELT!
I GUESS YOU'RE STILL AS RECKLESS AS EVER, HUH?
WAS THAT WHY WIND WAS ALWAYS MAD?!
THIS IS SO COOL! IT SEEMS LIKE THEY REALLY GET ALONG.
TAKE YOUR TIME, OKAY?
I'VE GOTTA GET BACK TO WORK!
OKAY!
AFTER ALL, I'M 5,000,000 YEN IN DEBT, SO MY WORK IS NEVER DONE! ♪
WHAT?!

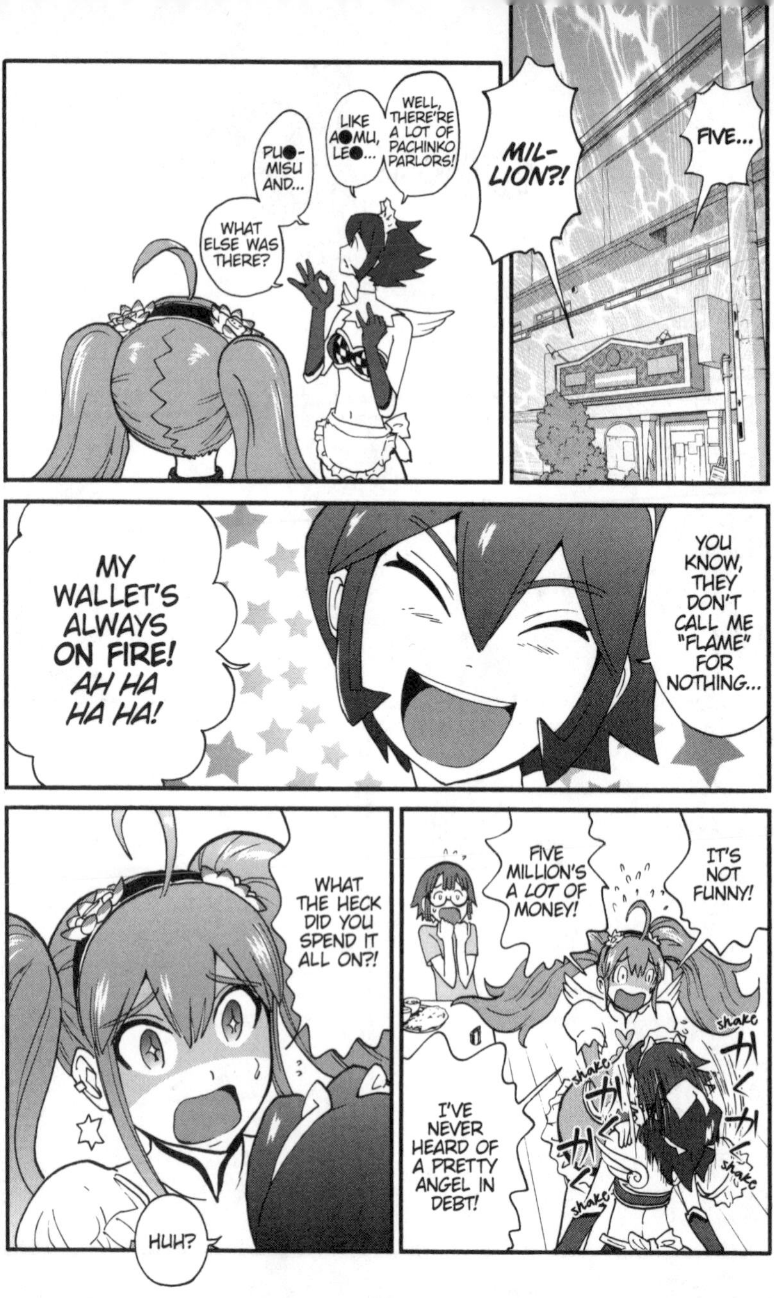
FIVE...
MIL-LION?!
WELL, THERE'RE A LOT OF PACHINKO PARLORS!
LIKE A●MU, LE●...
PU●-MISU AND...
WHAT ELSE WAS THERE?
YOU KNOW, THEY DON'T CALL ME "FLAME" FOR NOTHING...
MY WALLET'S ALWAYS ON FIRE! AH HA HA HA!
IT'S NOT FUNNY!
FIVE MILLION'S A LOT OF MONEY!
shake
shake
shake
shake
I'VE NEVER HEARD OF A PRETTY ANGEL IN DEBT!
WHAT THE HECK DID YOU SPEND IT ALL ON?!
HUH?

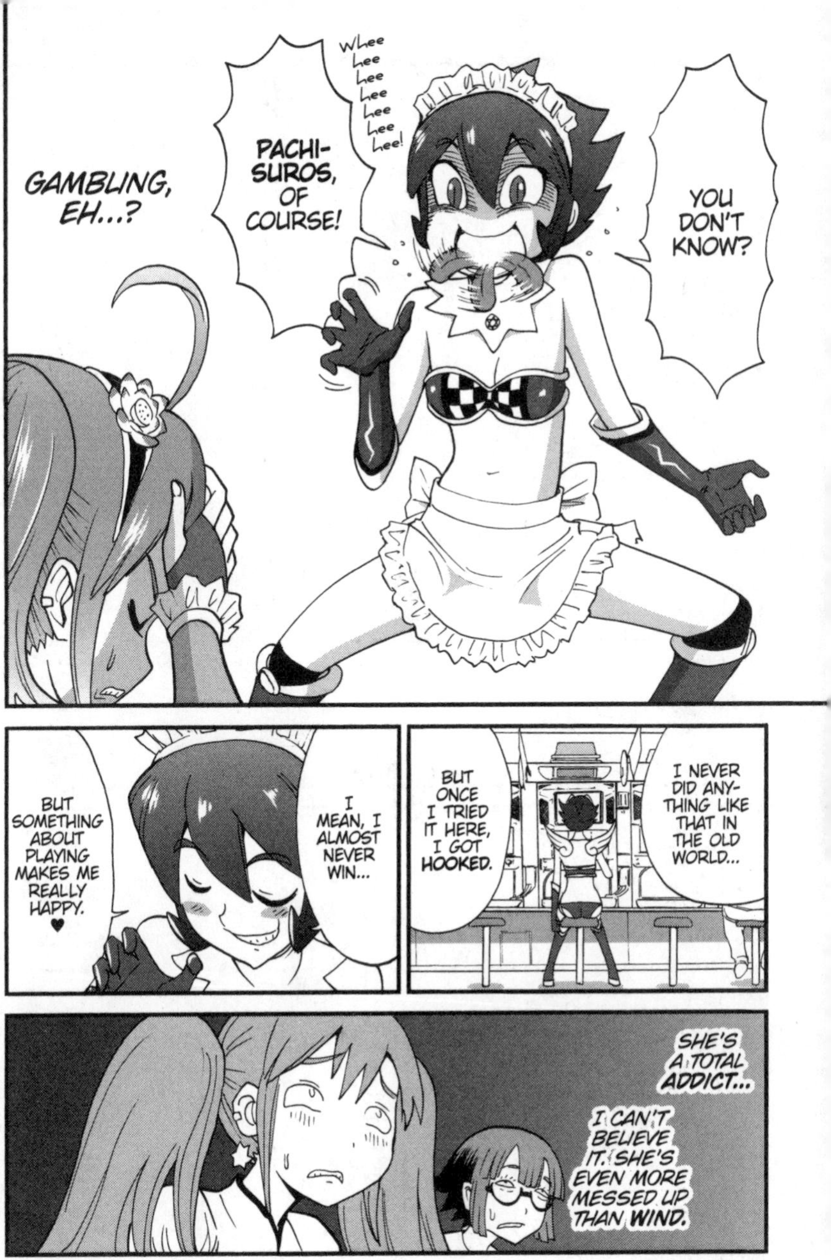
YOU DON'T KNOW?
Whee hee hee hee hee hee hee!
PACHI-SUROS, OF COURSE!
GAMBLING, EH...?
I NEVER DID ANYTHING LIKE THAT IN THE OLD WORLD...
BUT ONCE I TRIED IT HERE, I GOT HOOKED.
I MEAN, I ALMOST NEVER WIN...
BUT SOMETHING ABOUT PLAYING MAKES ME REALLY HAPPY. ♥
SHE'S A TOTAL ADDICT...
I CAN'T BELIEVE IT. SHE'S EVEN MORE MESSED UP THAN WIND.

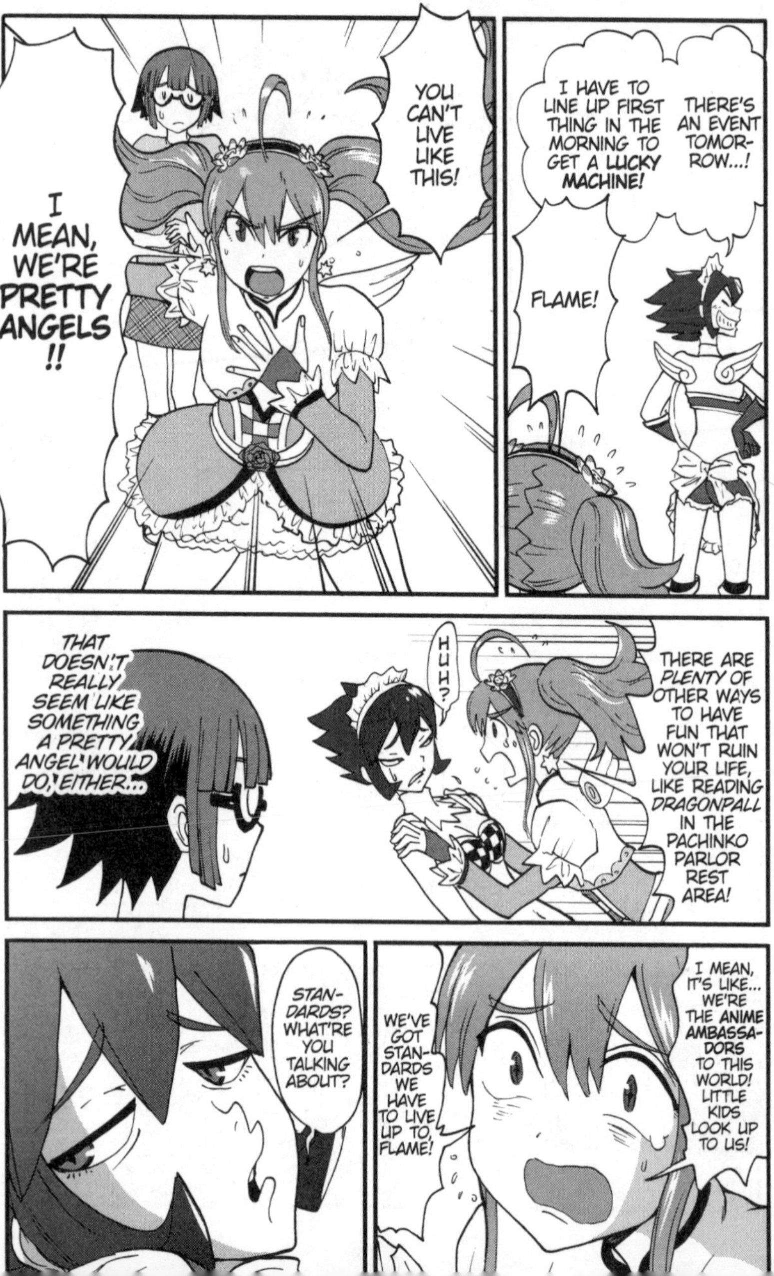
THERE'S AN EVENT TOMORROW...!
I HAVE TO LINE UP FIRST THING IN THE MORNING TO GET A LUCKY MACHINE!
FLAME!
YOU CAN'T LIVE LIKE THIS!
I MEAN, WE'RE PRETTY ANGELS!!
THERE ARE PLENTY OF OTHER WAYS TO HAVE FUN THAT WON'T RUIN YOUR LIFE, LIKE READING DRAGONPALL IN THE PACHINKO PARLOR REST AREA!
HUH?
THAT DOESN'T REALLY SEEM LIKE SOMETHING A PRETTY ANGEL WOULD DO, EITHER...
I MEAN, IT'S LIKE... WE'RE THE ANIME AMBASSADORS TO THIS WORLD! LITTLE KIDS LOOK UP TO US!
WE'VE GOT STANDARDS WE HAVE TO LIVE UP TO, FLAME!
STANDARDS? WHAT'RE YOU TALKING ABOUT?

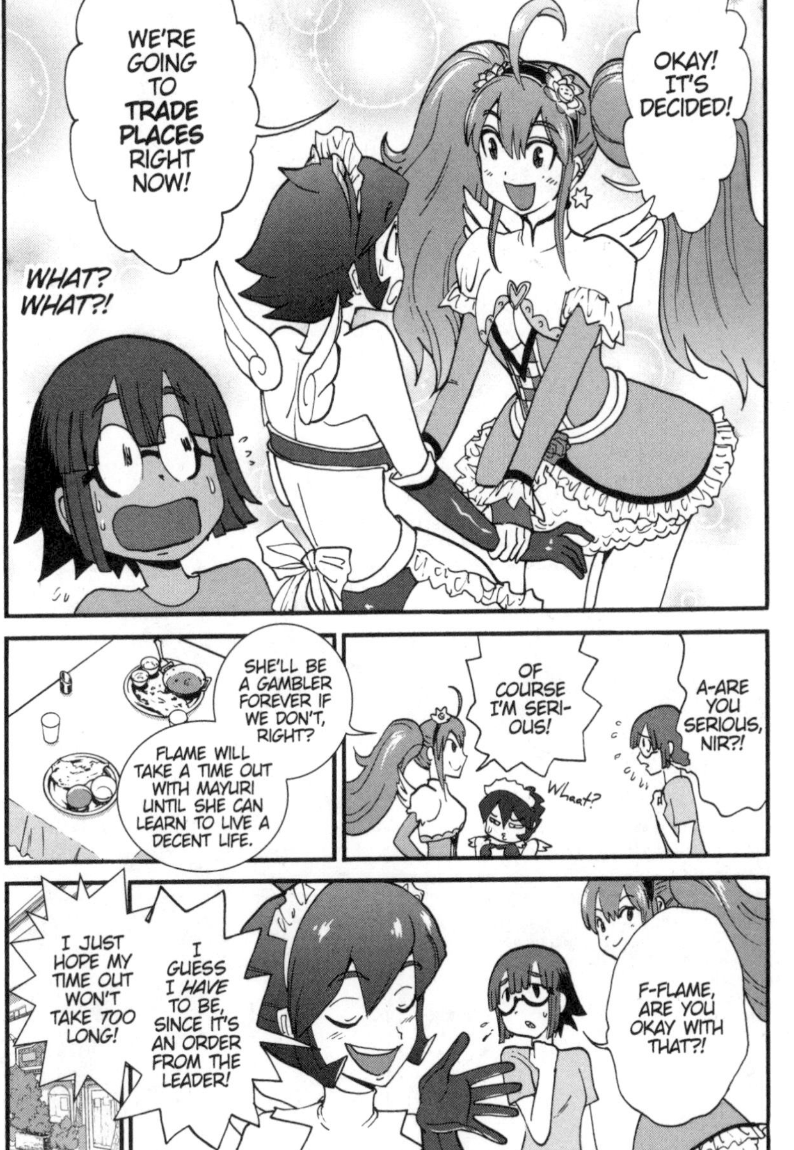
OKAY! IT'S DECIDED!
WE'RE GOING TO **TRADE PLACES** RIGHT NOW!
WHAT? WHAT?!
A-ARE YOU SERIOUS, NIR?!
OF COURSE I'M SERIOUS!
Whaat?
SHE'LL BE A GAMBLER FOREVER IF WE DON'T, RIGHT?
FLAME WILL TAKE A TIME OUT WITH MAYURI UNTIL SHE CAN LEARN TO LIVE A DECENT LIFE.
F-FLAME, ARE YOU OKAY WITH THAT?!
I GUESS I *HAVE* TO BE, SINCE IT'S AN ORDER FROM THE LEADER!
I JUST HOPE MY TIME OUT WON'T TAKE *TOO* LONG!

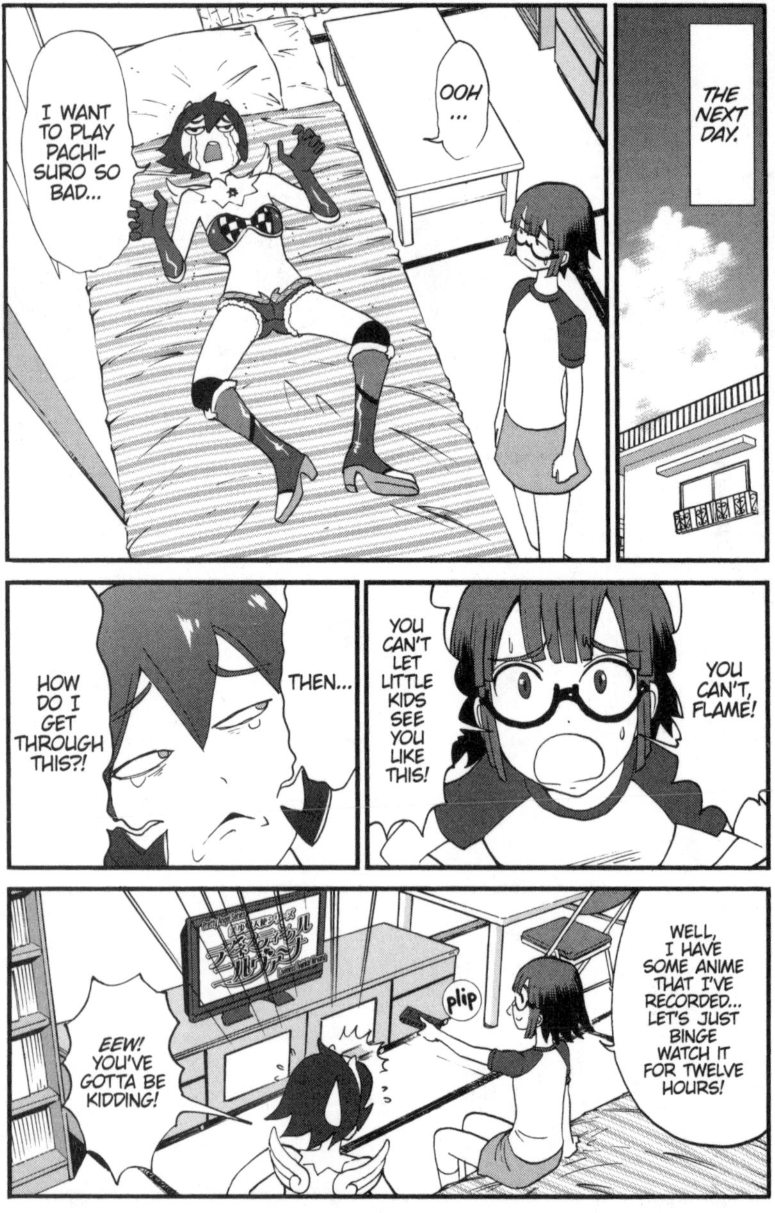
THE NEXT DAY.
OOH ...
I WANT TO PLAY PACHI-SURO SO BAD...
YOU CAN'T, FLAME!
YOU CAN'T LET LITTLE KIDS SEE YOU LIKE THIS!
THEN...
HOW DO I GET THROUGH THIS?!
WELL, I HAVE SOME ANIME THAT I'VE RECORDED... LET'S JUST BINGE WATCH IT FOR TWELVE HOURS!
plip
EEW! YOU'VE GOTTA BE KIDDING!

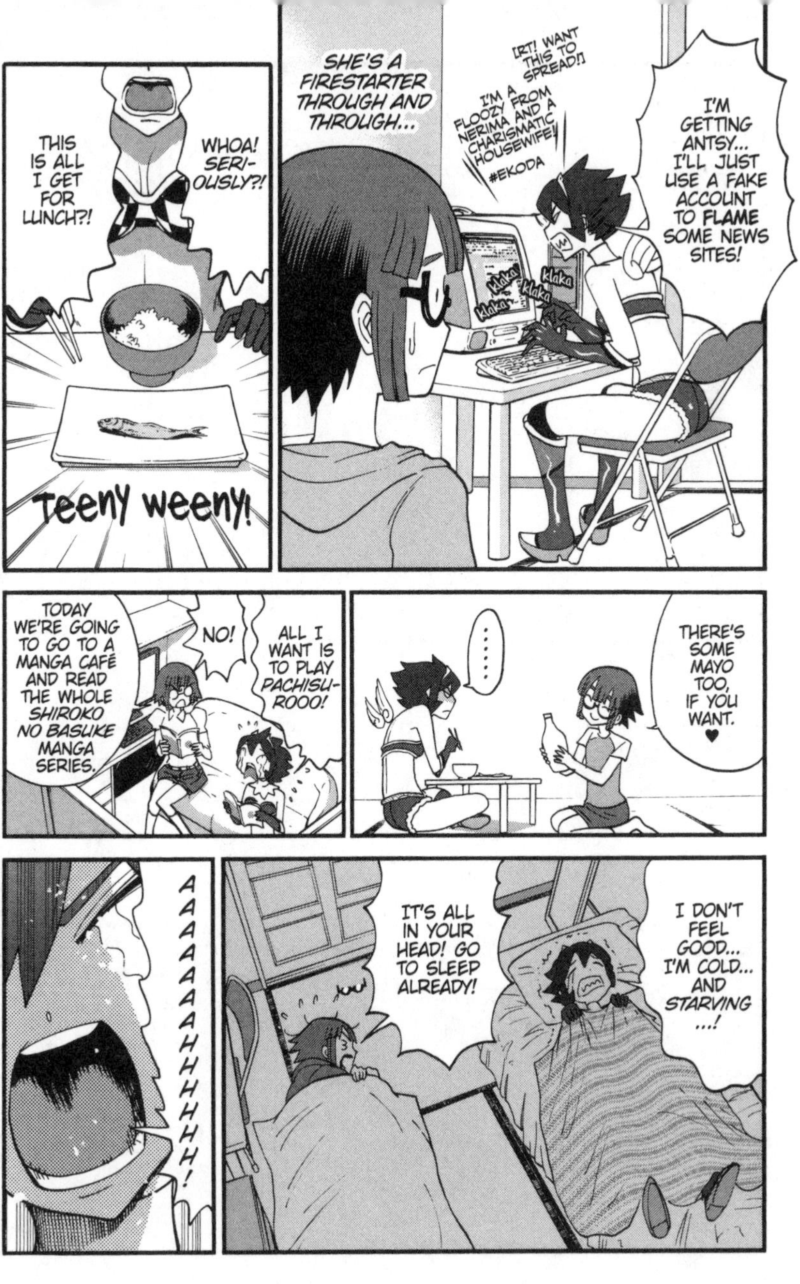
I'M GETTING ANTSY... I'LL JUST USE A FAKE ACCOUNT TO FLAME SOME NEWS SITES!
[RT! WANT THIS TO SPREAD!]
I'M A FLOOZY FROM NERIMA AND A CHARISMATIC HOUSEWIFE!!
#EKODA
klaka klaka klaka klaka
SHE'S A FIRESTARTER THROUGH AND THROUGH...
WHOA! SERI-OUSLY?!
THIS IS ALL I GET FOR LUNCH?!
Teeny weeny!
THERE'S SOME MAYO TOO, IF YOU WANT. ♥
......
ALL I WANT IS TO PLAY PACHISU-ROOO!
NO!
TODAY WE'RE GOING TO GO TO A MANGA CAFÉ AND READ THE WHOLE SHIROKO NO BASUKE MANGA SERIES.
I DON'T FEEL GOOD... I'M COLD... AND STARVING ...!
IT'S ALL IN YOUR HEAD! GO TO SLEEP ALREADY!
AAAAAAAHHHHHH!

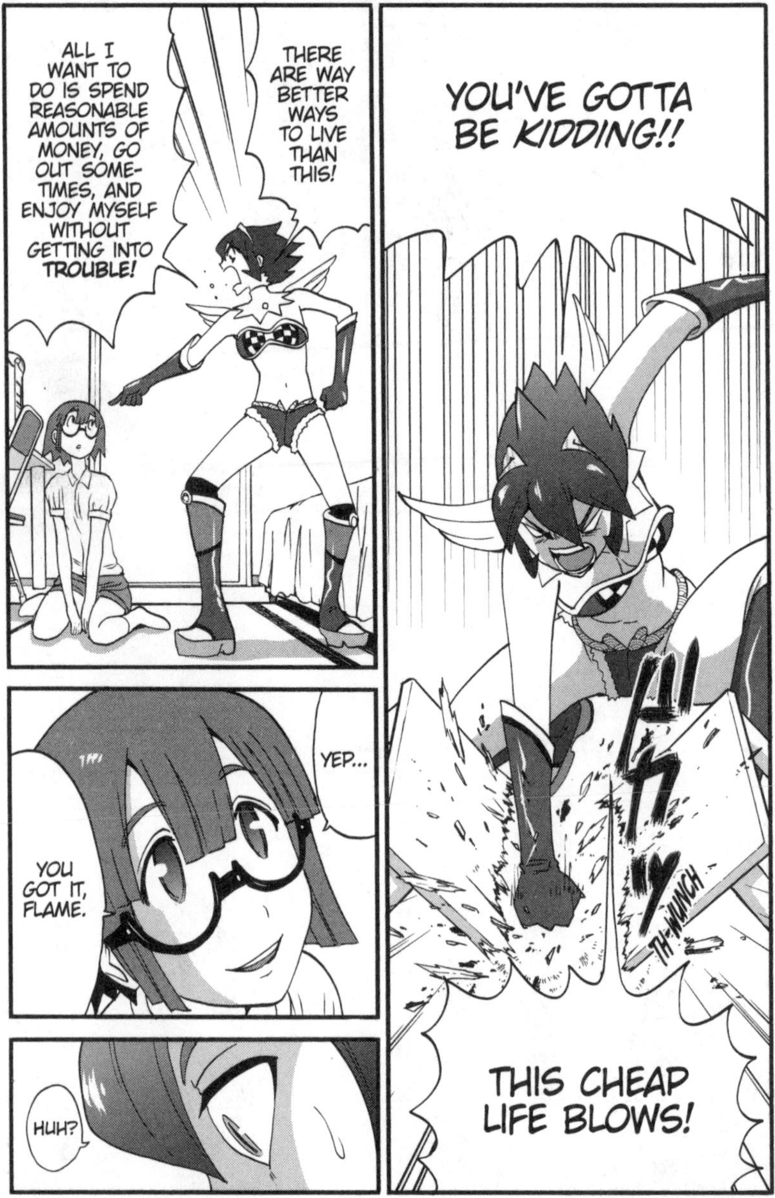
YOU'VE GOTTA BE KIDDING!!
TH-WUNCH
THIS CHEAP LIFE BLOWS!
THERE ARE WAY BETTER WAYS TO LIVE THAN THIS!
ALL I WANT TO DO IS SPEND REASONABLE AMOUNTS OF MONEY, GO OUT SOME-TIMES, AND ENJOY MYSELF WITHOUT GETTING INTO TROUBLE!
YEP...
YOU GOT IT, FLAME.
HUH?

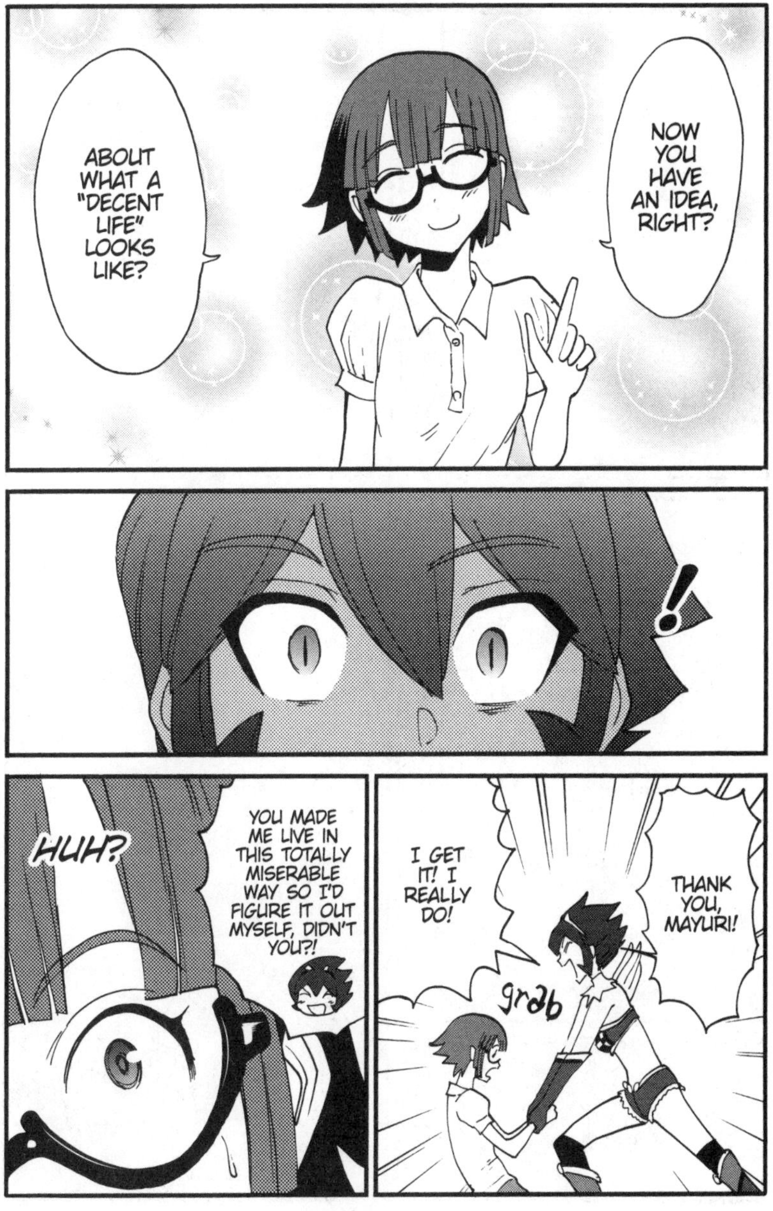
NOW YOU HAVE AN IDEA, RIGHT?
ABOUT WHAT A "DECENT LIFE" LOOKS LIKE?
!
THANK YOU, MAYURI!
I GET IT! I REALLY DO!
grab
YOU MADE ME LIVE IN THIS TOTALLY MISERABLE WAY SO I'D FIGURE IT OUT MYSELF, DIDN'T YOU?!
HUH?

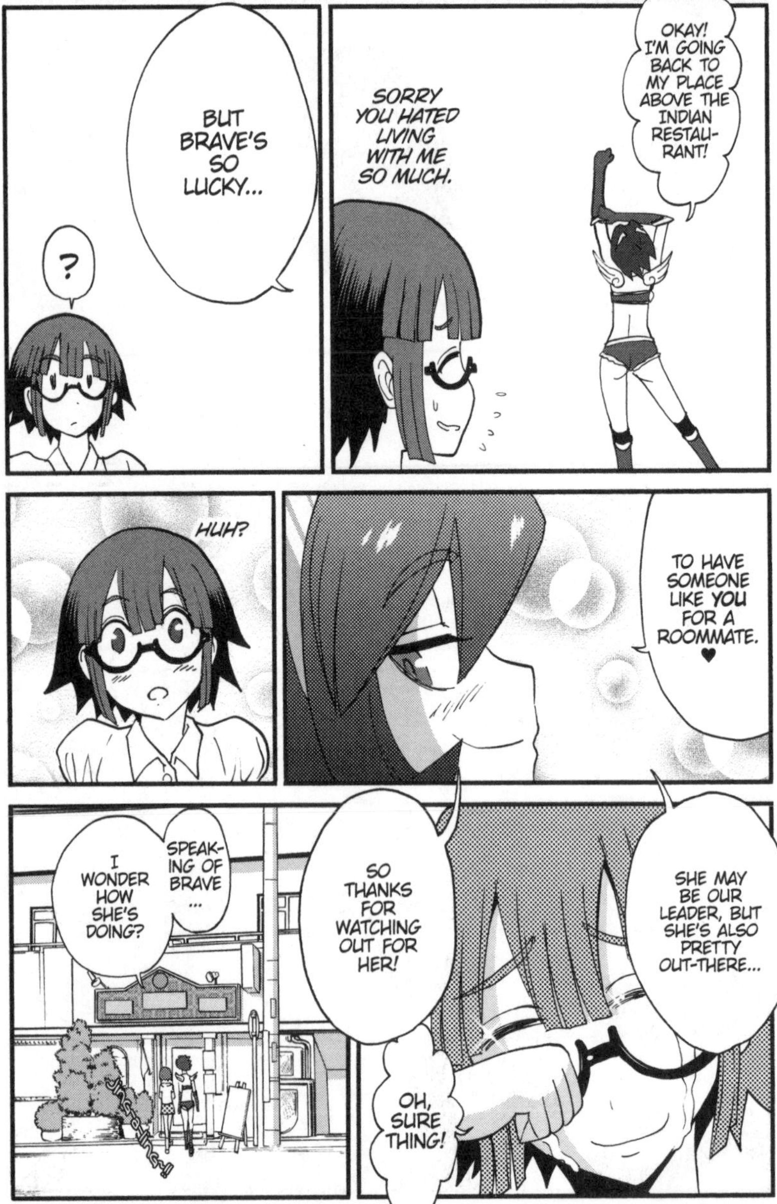
OKAY! I'M GOING BACK TO MY PLACE ABOVE THE INDIAN RESTAURANT!
SORRY YOU HATED LIVING WITH ME SO MUCH.
BUT BRAVE'S SO LUCKY...
?
TO HAVE SOMEONE LIKE YOU FOR A ROOMMATE. ♥
HUH?
SHE MAY BE OUR LEADER, BUT SHE'S ALSO PRETTY OUT-THERE...
SO THANKS FOR WATCHING OUT FOR HER!
OH, SURE THING!
SPEAKING OF BRAVE...
I WONDER HOW SHE'S DOING?
Jing-a-ling~!

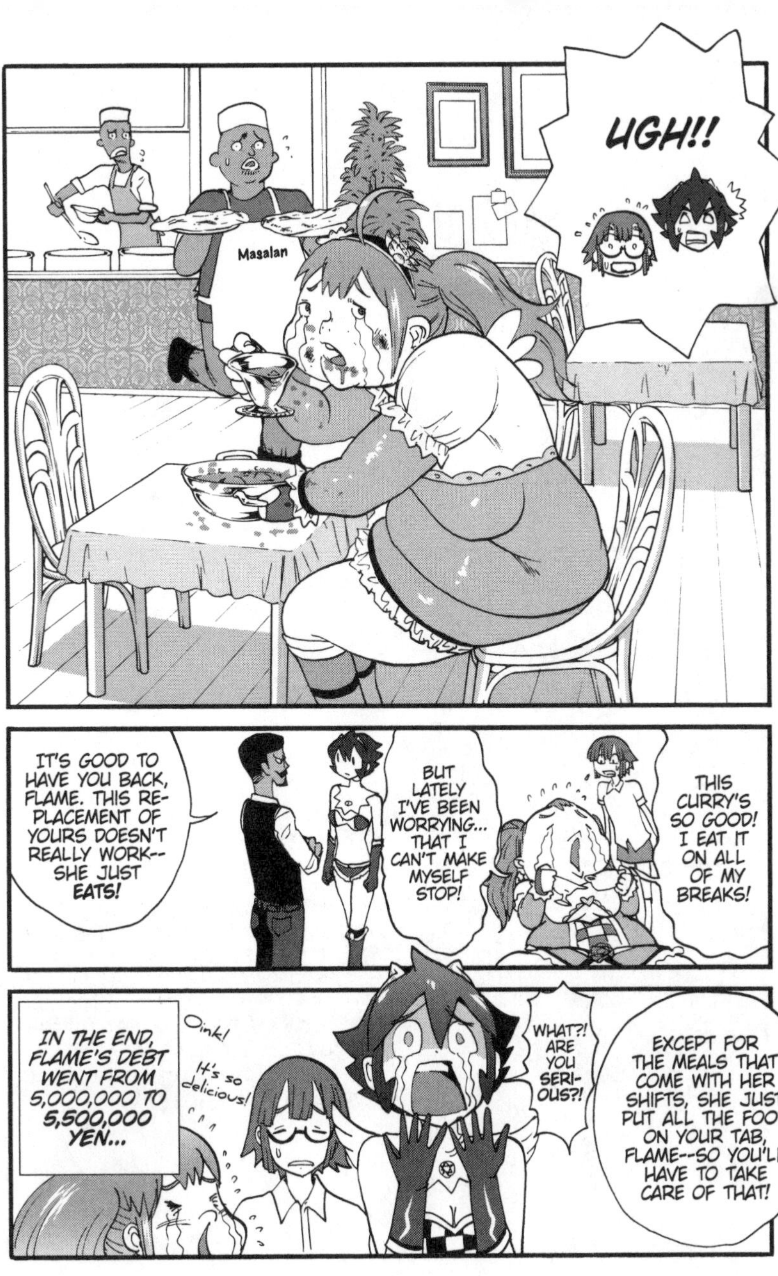
UGH!!
Masalan
THIS CURRY'S SO GOOD! I EAT IT ON ALL OF MY BREAKS!
BUT LATELY I'VE BEEN WORRYING... THAT I CAN'T MAKE MYSELF STOP!
IT'S GOOD TO HAVE YOU BACK, FLAME. THIS REPLACEMENT OF YOURS DOESN'T REALLY WORK--SHE JUST EATS!
EXCEPT FOR THE MEALS THAT COME WITH HER SHIFTS, SHE JUST PUT ALL THE FOOD ON YOUR TAB, FLAME--SO YOU'LL HAVE TO TAKE CARE OF THAT!
WHAT?! ARE YOU SERIOUS?!
Oink!
It's so delicious!
IN THE END, FLAME'S DEBT WENT FROM 5,000,000 TO 5,500,000 YEN...

NirFlame

The Pretty Angel who controls the powers of fire. Her reckless personality tends to get her into trouble; recently, she's become addicted to gambling and is now heavily in debt. Although there's something about her spitfire persona that men can't resist, NirFlame is actually really shy when it comes to romantic relationships.

Unmagical Girl

The melancholy days
of a has-been magical girl (2)

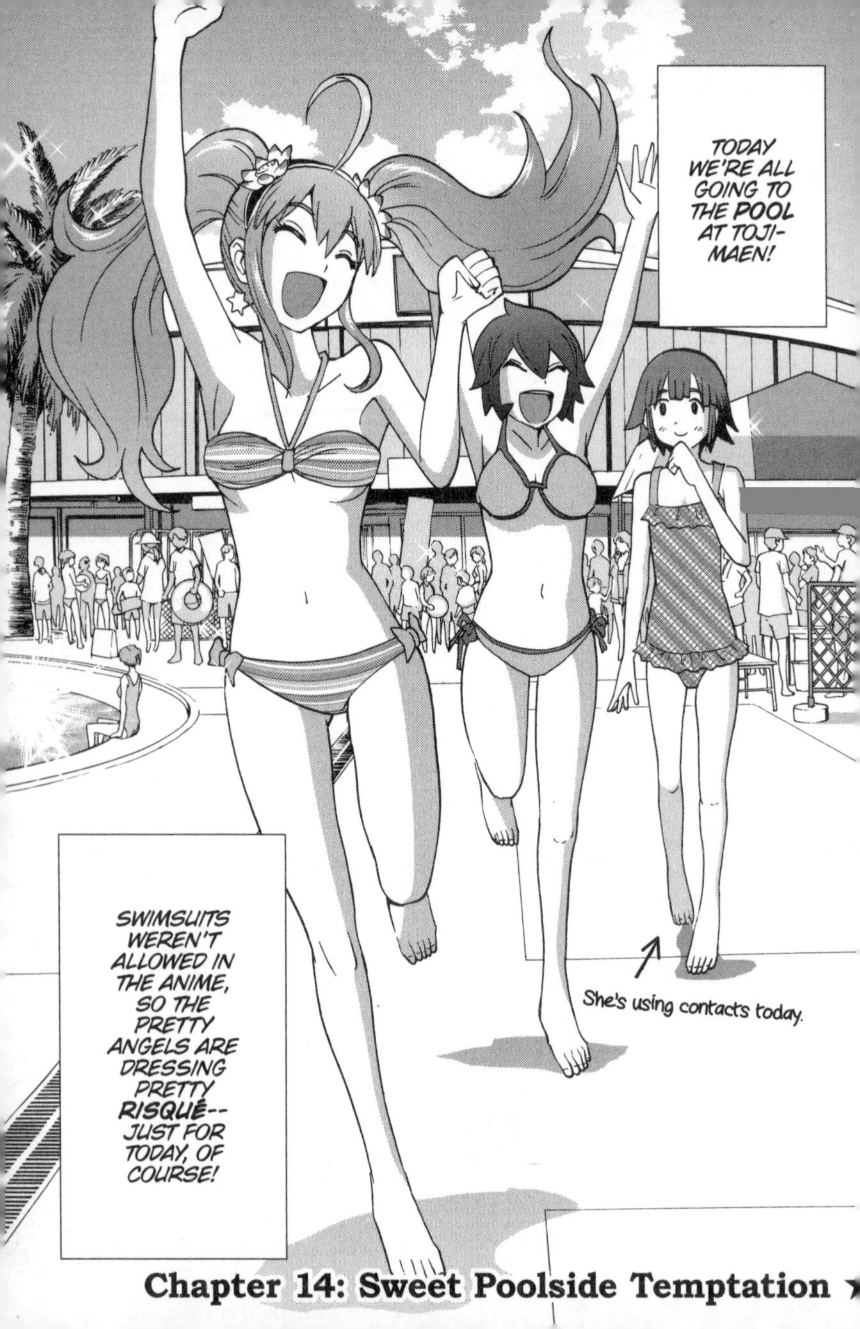
TODAY WE'RE ALL GOING TO THE POOL AT TOJI-MAEN!
She's using contacts today.
SWIMSUITS WEREN'T ALLOWED IN THE ANIME, SO THE PRETTY ANGELS ARE DRESSING PRETTY RISQUÉ-- JUST FOR TODAY, OF COURSE!
Chapter 14: Sweet Poolside Temptation ★

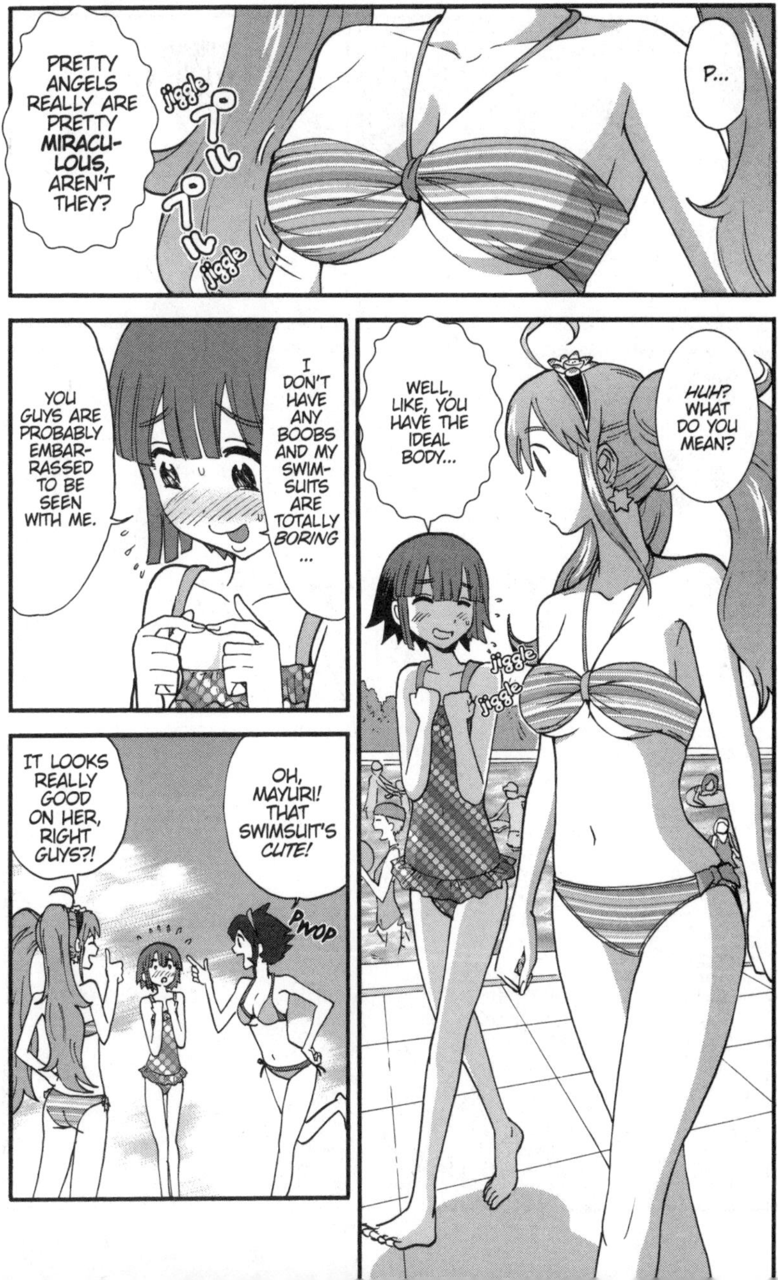
P...
PRETTY ANGELS REALLY ARE PRETTY **MIRACULOUS,** AREN'T THEY?
jiggle プル
プル jiggle
HUH? WHAT DO YOU MEAN?
WELL, LIKE, YOU HAVE THE IDEAL BODY...
jiggle
jiggle
I DON'T HAVE ANY BOOBS AND MY SWIMSUITS ARE TOTALLY *BORING*...
YOU GUYS ARE PROBABLY EMBARRASSED TO BE SEEN WITH ME.
OH, MAYURI! THAT SWIMSUIT'S *CUTE!*
PWOP
IT LOOKS REALLY GOOD ON HER, RIGHT GUYS?!

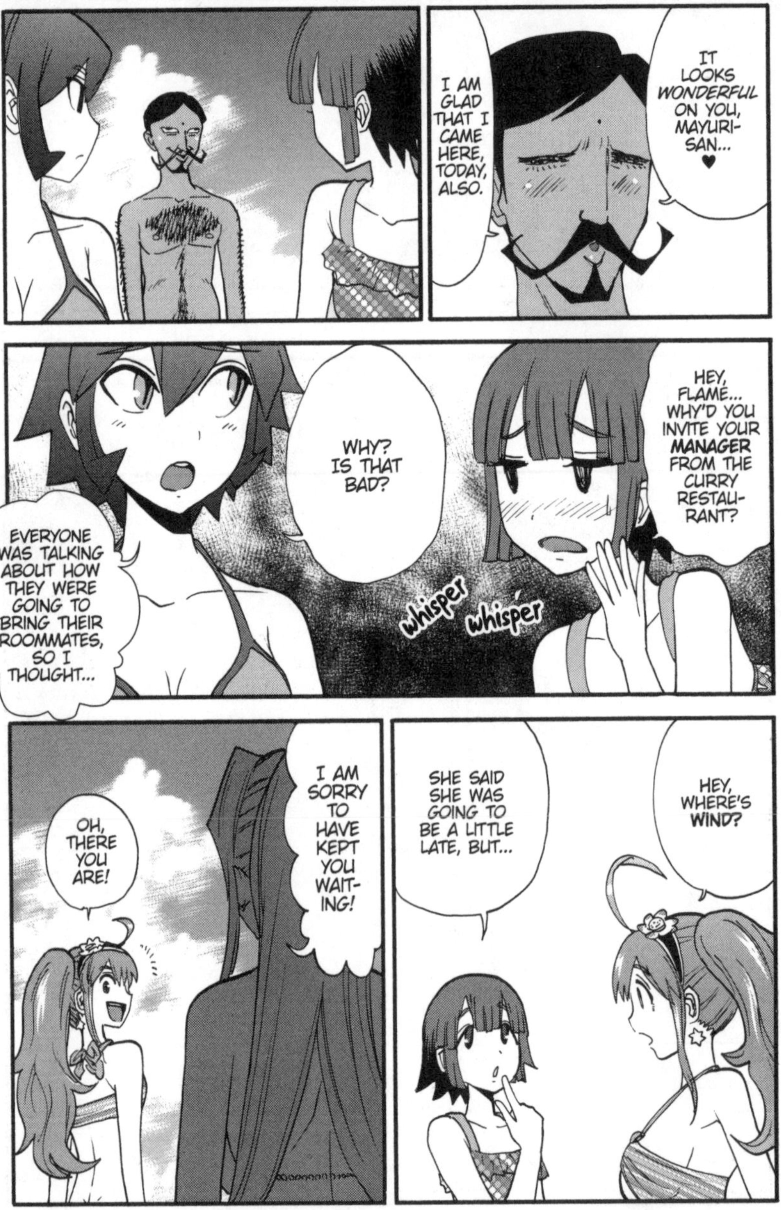
IT LOOKS WONDERFUL ON YOU, MAYURI-SAN... ♥
I AM GLAD THAT I CAME HERE, TODAY, ALSO.
HEY, FLAME... WHY'D YOU INVITE YOUR MANAGER FROM THE CURRY RESTAURANT?
whisper whisper
WHY? IS THAT BAD?
EVERYONE WAS TALKING ABOUT HOW THEY WERE GOING TO BRING THEIR ROOMMATES, SO I THOUGHT...
HEY, WHERE'S WIND?
SHE SAID SHE WAS GOING TO BE A LITTLE LATE, BUT...
I AM SORRY TO HAVE KEPT YOU WAITING!
OH, THERE YOU ARE!

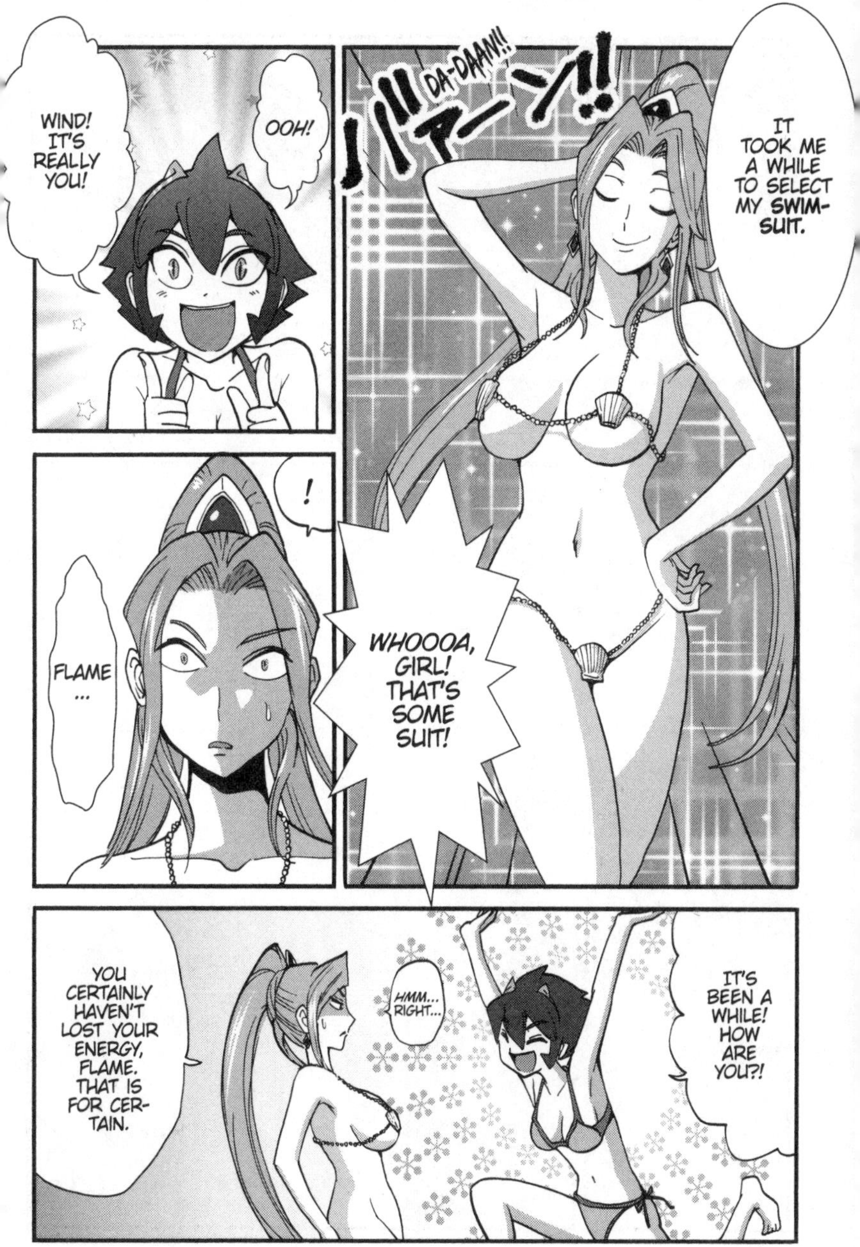
バアーン!!
DA-DAAN!!
IT TOOK ME A WHILE TO SELECT MY SWIMSUIT.
WHOOOA, GIRL! THAT'S SOME SUIT!
OOH!
WIND! IT'S REALLY YOU!
!
FLAME...
IT'S BEEN A WHILE! HOW ARE YOU?!
HMM... RIGHT...
YOU CERTAINLY HAVEN'T LOST YOUR ENERGY, FLAME. THAT IS FOR CERTAIN.

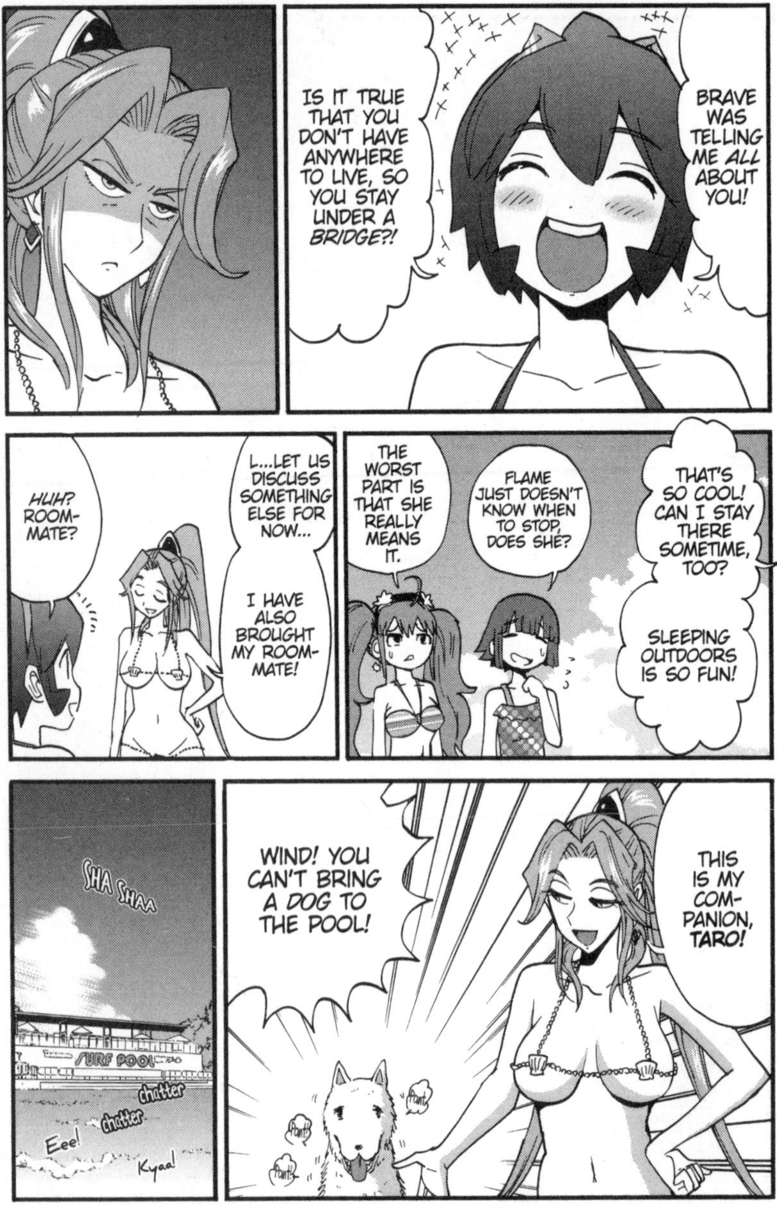
BRAVE WAS TELLING ME ALL ABOUT YOU!
IS IT TRUE THAT YOU DON'T HAVE ANYWHERE TO LIVE, SO YOU STAY UNDER A BRIDGE?!
THAT'S SO COOL! CAN I STAY THERE SOMETIME, TOO?
SLEEPING OUTDOORS IS SO FUN!
FLAME JUST DOESN'T KNOW WHEN TO STOP, DOES SHE?
THE WORST PART IS THAT SHE REALLY MEANS IT.
L...LET US DISCUSS SOMETHING ELSE FOR NOW...
I HAVE ALSO BROUGHT MY ROOMMATE!
HUH? ROOMMATE?
THIS IS MY COMPANION, TARO!
WIND! YOU CAN'T BRING A DOG TO THE POOL!
Pant!
Pant!
Pant!
SHA SHAA
SURF POOL
chatter
chatter
Eee!
Kyaa!

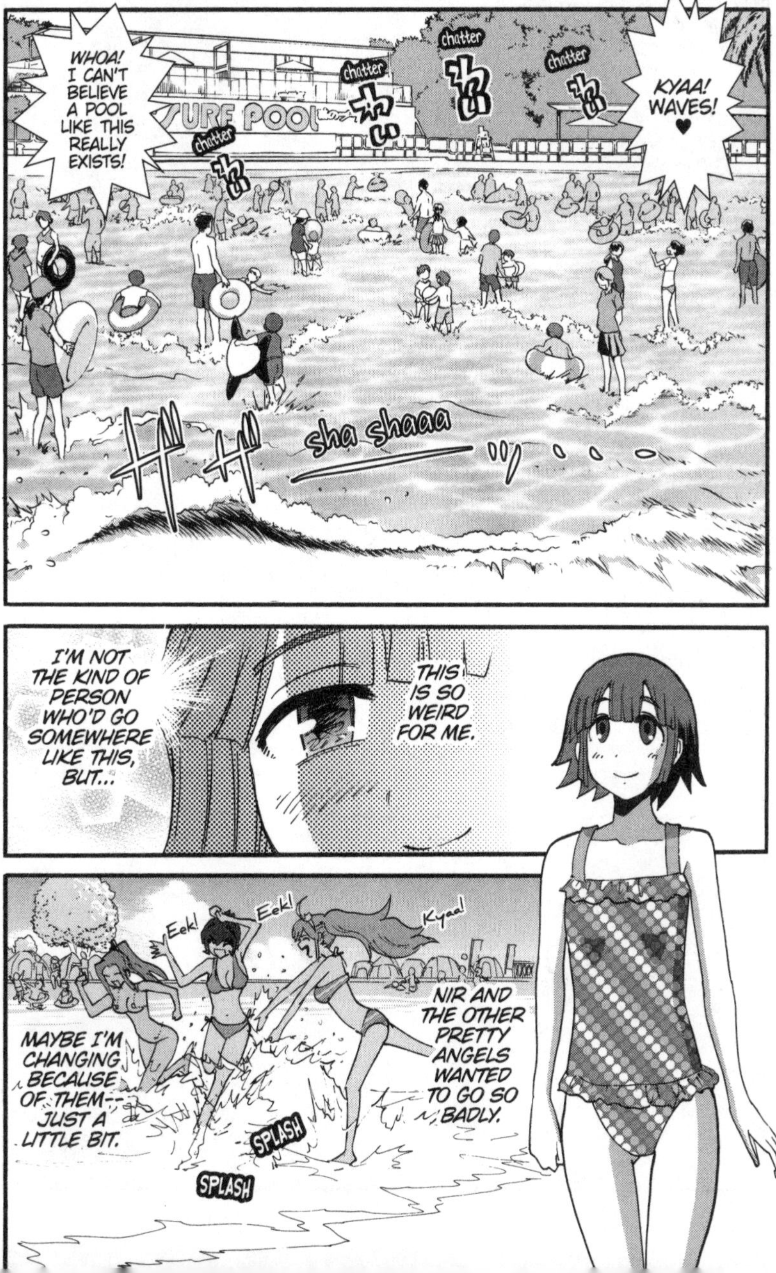
KYAA! WAVES! ♥
chatter
chatter
chatter
chatter
SURF POOL
WHOA! I CAN'T BELIEVE A POOL LIKE THIS REALLY EXISTS!
sha shaaa
THIS IS SO WEIRD FOR ME.
I'M NOT THE KIND OF PERSON WHO'D GO SOMEWHERE LIKE THIS, BUT...
NIR AND THE OTHER PRETTY ANGELS WANTED TO GO SO BADLY.
Kyaa!
Eek!
Eek!
MAYBE I'M CHANGING BECAUSE OF THEM-- JUST A LITTLE BIT.
SPLASH
SPLASH

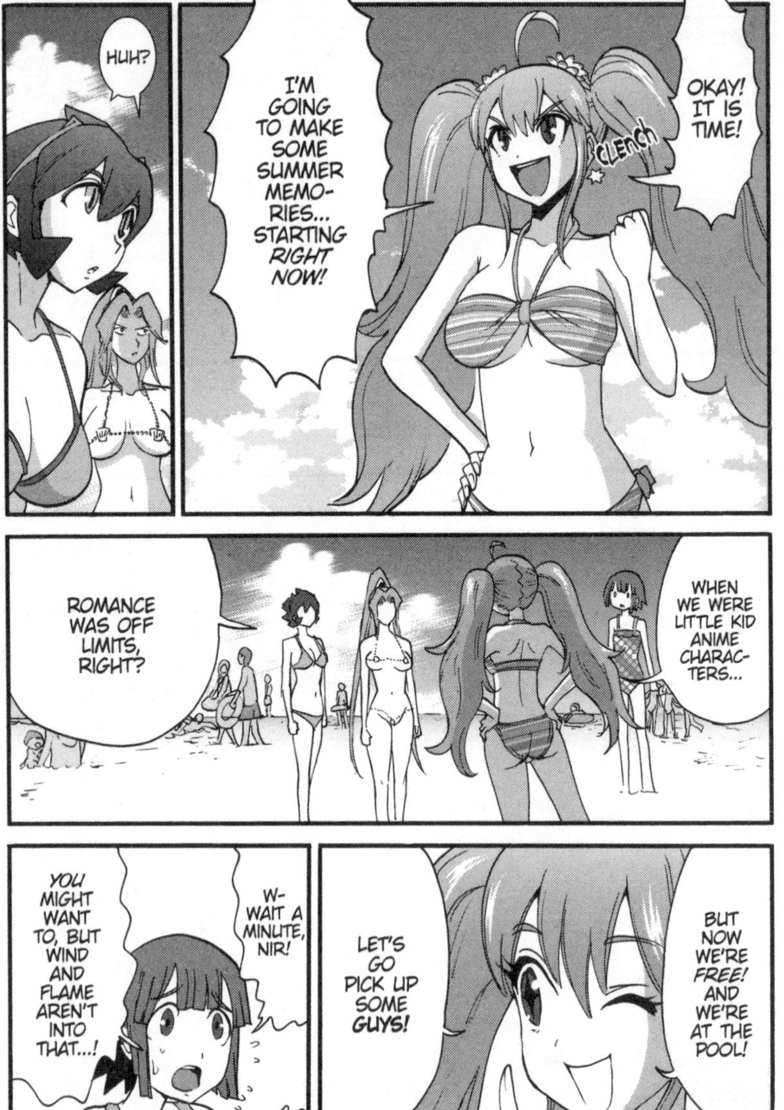
OKAY! IT IS TIME!
CLENCH
I'M GOING TO MAKE SOME SUMMER MEMO-RIES... STARTING *RIGHT* NOW!
HUH?
WHEN WE WERE LITTLE KID ANIME CHARAC-TERS...
ROMANCE WAS OFF LIMITS, RIGHT?
BUT NOW WE'RE *FREE!* AND WE'RE AT THE POOL!
LET'S GO PICK UP SOME **GUYS!**
W-WAIT A MINUTE, NIR!
YOU MIGHT WANT TO, BUT WIND AND FLAME AREN'T INTO THAT...!

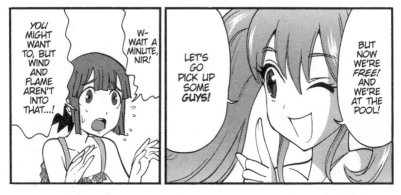

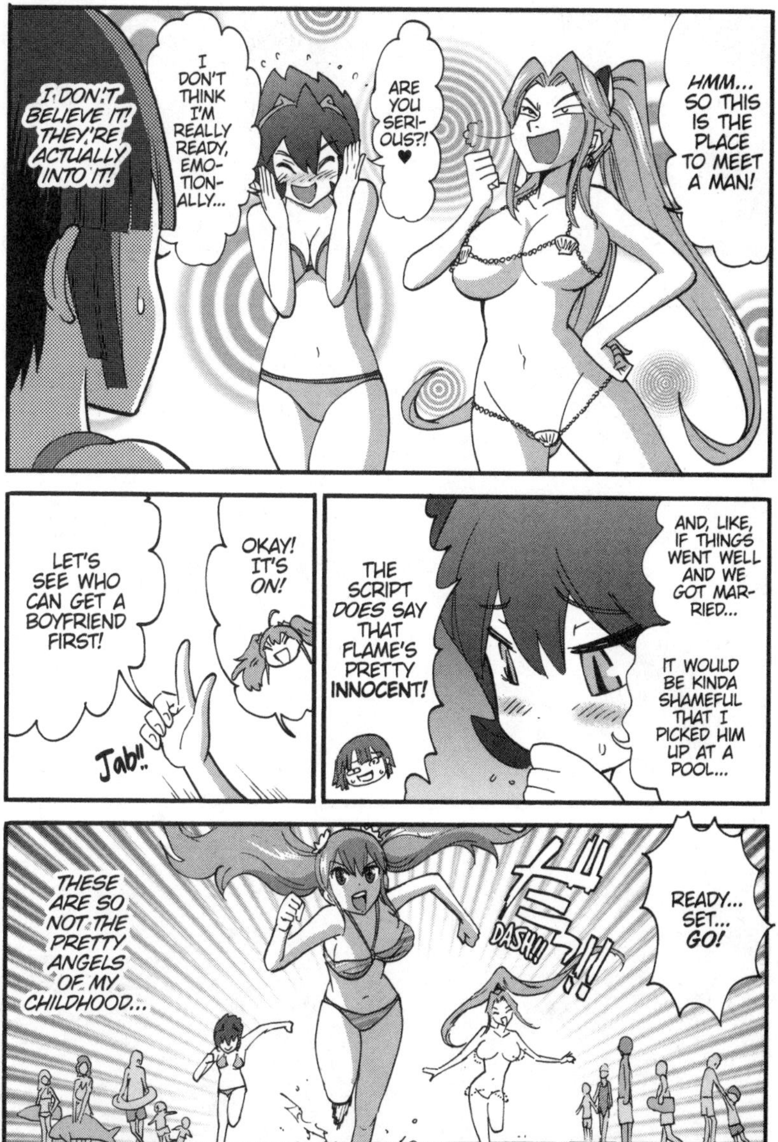
HMM... SO THIS IS THE PLACE TO MEET A MAN!
ARE YOU SERIOUS?! ♥
I DON'T THINK I'M REALLY READY, EMOTIONALLY...
I DON'T BELIEVE IT! THEY'RE ACTUALLY INTO IT!
AND, LIKE, IF THINGS WENT WELL AND WE GOT MARRIED...
IT WOULD BE KINDA SHAMEFUL THAT I PICKED HIM UP AT A POOL...
THE SCRIPT DOES SAY THAT FLAME'S PRETTY INNOCENT!
OKAY! IT'S ON!
LET'S SEE WHO CAN GET A BOYFRIEND FIRST!
Jab!!
READY... SET... GO!
DASH!!
THESE ARE SO NOT THE PRETTY ANGELS OF MY CHILDHOOD...

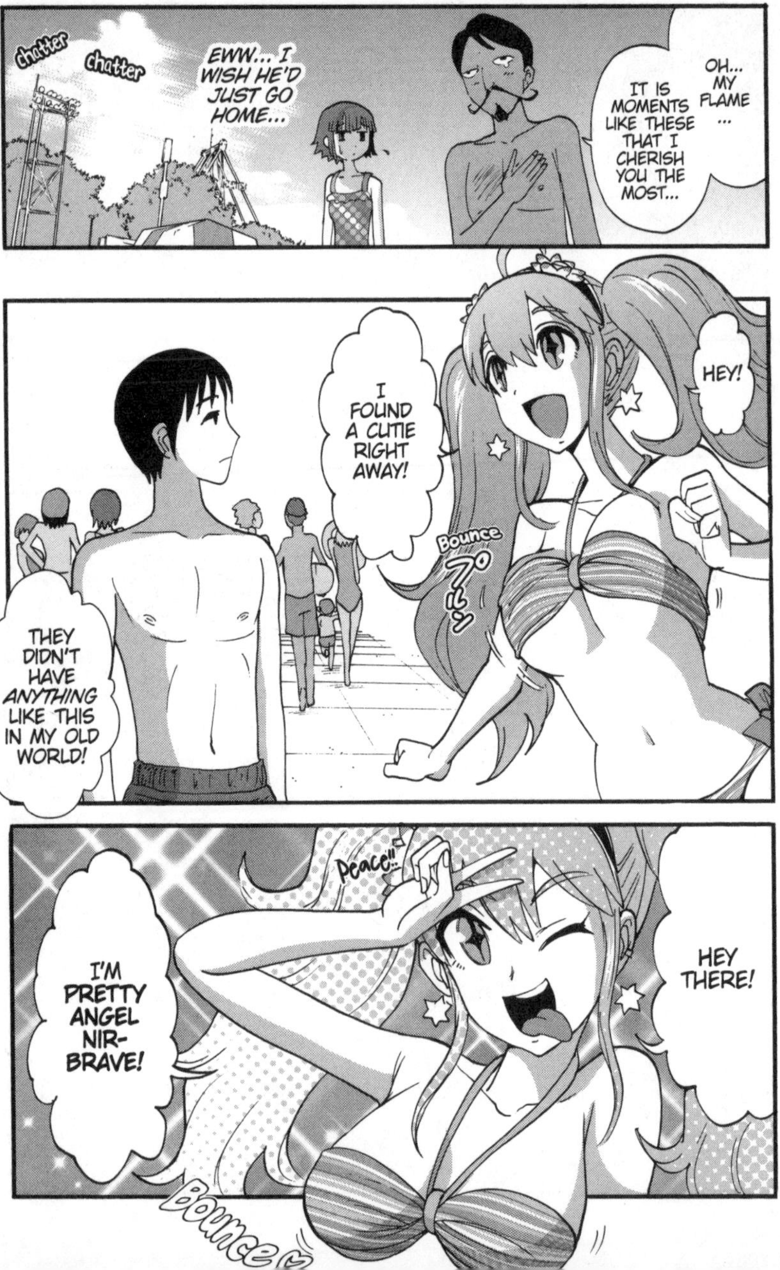
OH... MY FLAME ...
IT IS MOMENTS LIKE THESE THAT I CHERISH YOU THE MOST...
EWW... I WISH HE'D JUST GO HOME...
chatter
chatter
HEY!
I FOUND A CUTIE RIGHT AWAY!
Bounce
THEY DIDN'T HAVE ANYTHING LIKE THIS IN MY OLD WORLD!
HEY THERE!
Peace!!
I'M PRETTY ANGEL NIR-BRAVE!
Bounce

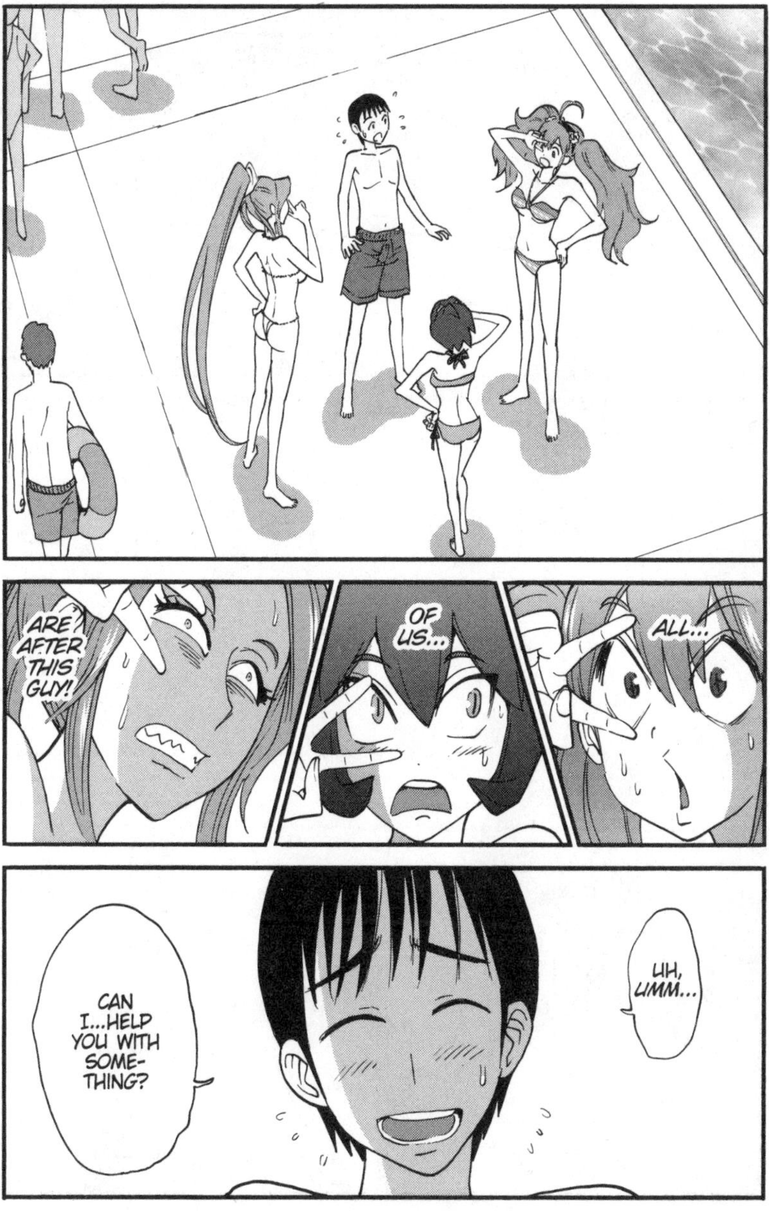
ALL...
OF US...
ARE AFTER THIS GUY!
UH, UMM...
CAN I...HELP YOU WITH SOME-THING?

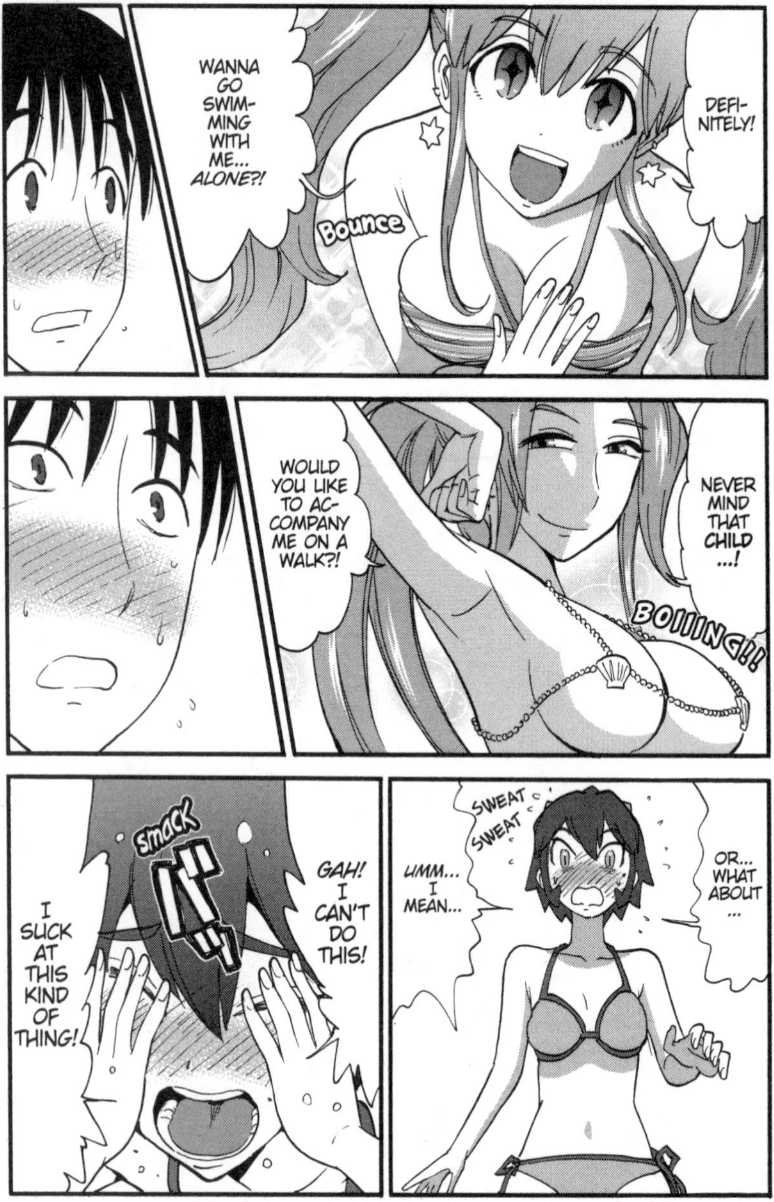
WANNA GO SWIMMING WITH ME... ALONE?!
DEFI-NITELY!
Bounce
NEVER MIND THAT CHILD ...!
WOULD YOU LIKE TO AC-COMPANY ME ON A WALK?!
BOIIING!!
OR... WHAT ABOUT ...
SWEAT SWEAT
UMM... I MEAN...
GAH! I CAN'T DO THIS!
smack
I SUCK AT THIS KIND OF THING!

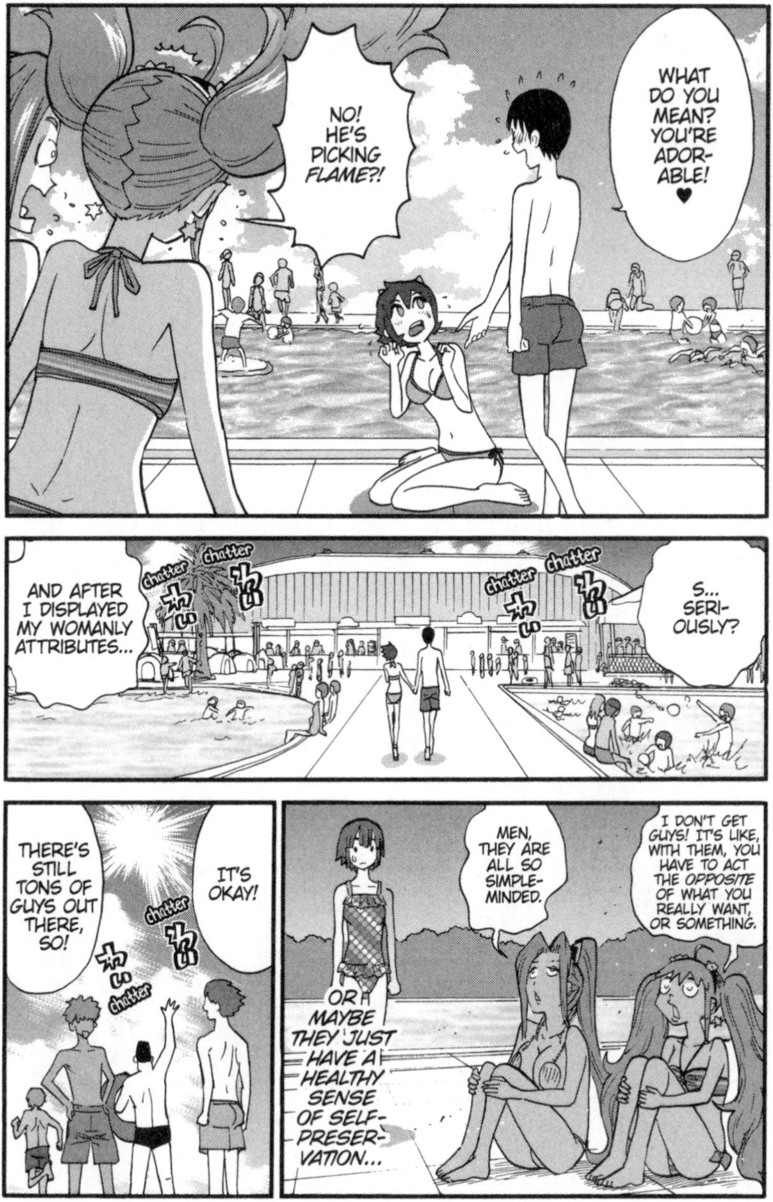
WHAT DO YOU MEAN? YOU'RE ADORABLE! ♥
NO! HE'S PICKING *FLAME*?!
S... SERIOUSLY?
chatter
chatter
chatter
chatter
AND AFTER I DISPLAYED MY WOMANLY ATTRIBUTES...
I DON'T GET GUYS! IT'S LIKE, WITH THEM, YOU HAVE TO ACT THE *OPPOSITE* OF WHAT YOU REALLY WANT, OR SOMETHING.
MEN, THEY ARE ALL SO SIMPLE-MINDED.
OR MAYBE THEY JUST HAVE A HEALTHY SENSE OF SELF-PRESERVATION...
IT'S OKAY!
THERE'S STILL TONS OF GUYS OUT THERE, SO!
chatter
chatter

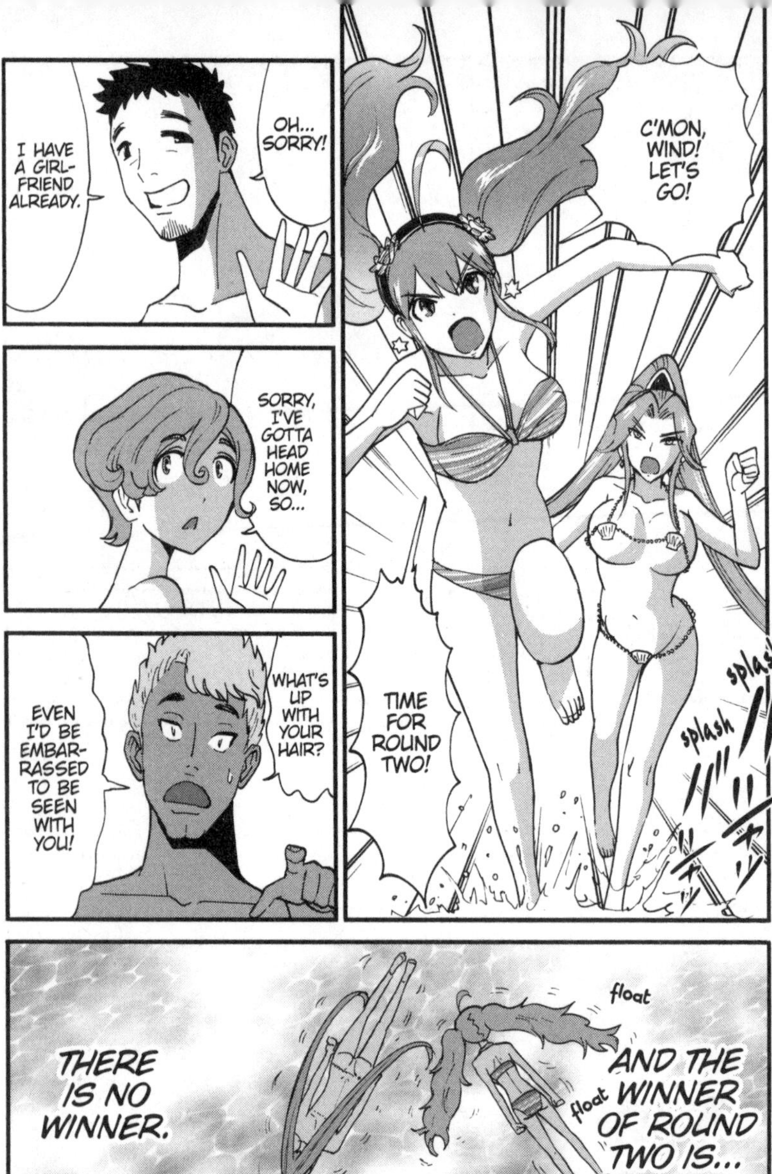
C'MON, WIND! LET'S GO!
TIME FOR ROUND TWO!
splash
splash
OH... SORRY!
I HAVE A GIRL-FRIEND ALREADY.
SORRY, I'VE GOTTA HEAD HOME NOW, SO...
WHAT'S UP WITH YOUR HAIR?
EVEN I'D BE EMBAR-RASSED TO BE SEEN WITH YOU!
float
AND THE WINNER OF ROUND TWO IS...
float
THERE IS NO WINNER.

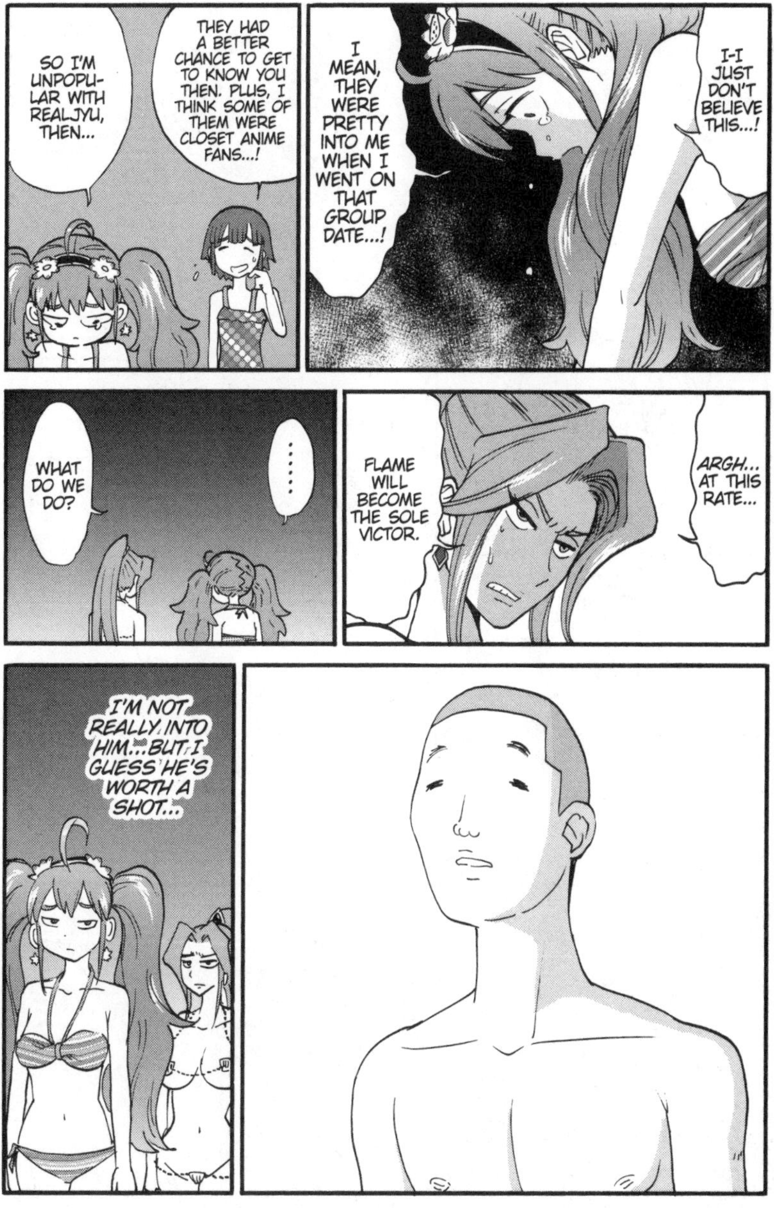
I-I JUST DON'T BELIEVE THIS...!
I MEAN, THEY WERE PRETTY INTO ME WHEN I WENT ON THAT GROUP DATE...!
THEY HAD A BETTER CHANCE TO GET TO KNOW YOU THEN. PLUS, I THINK SOME OF THEM WERE CLOSET ANIME FANS...!
SO I'M UNPOPULAR WITH REALJYU, THEN...
ARGH... AT THIS RATE...
FLAME WILL BECOME THE SOLE VICTOR.
......
WHAT DO WE DO?
I'M NOT REALLY INTO HIM...BUT I GUESS HE'S WORTH A SHOT...

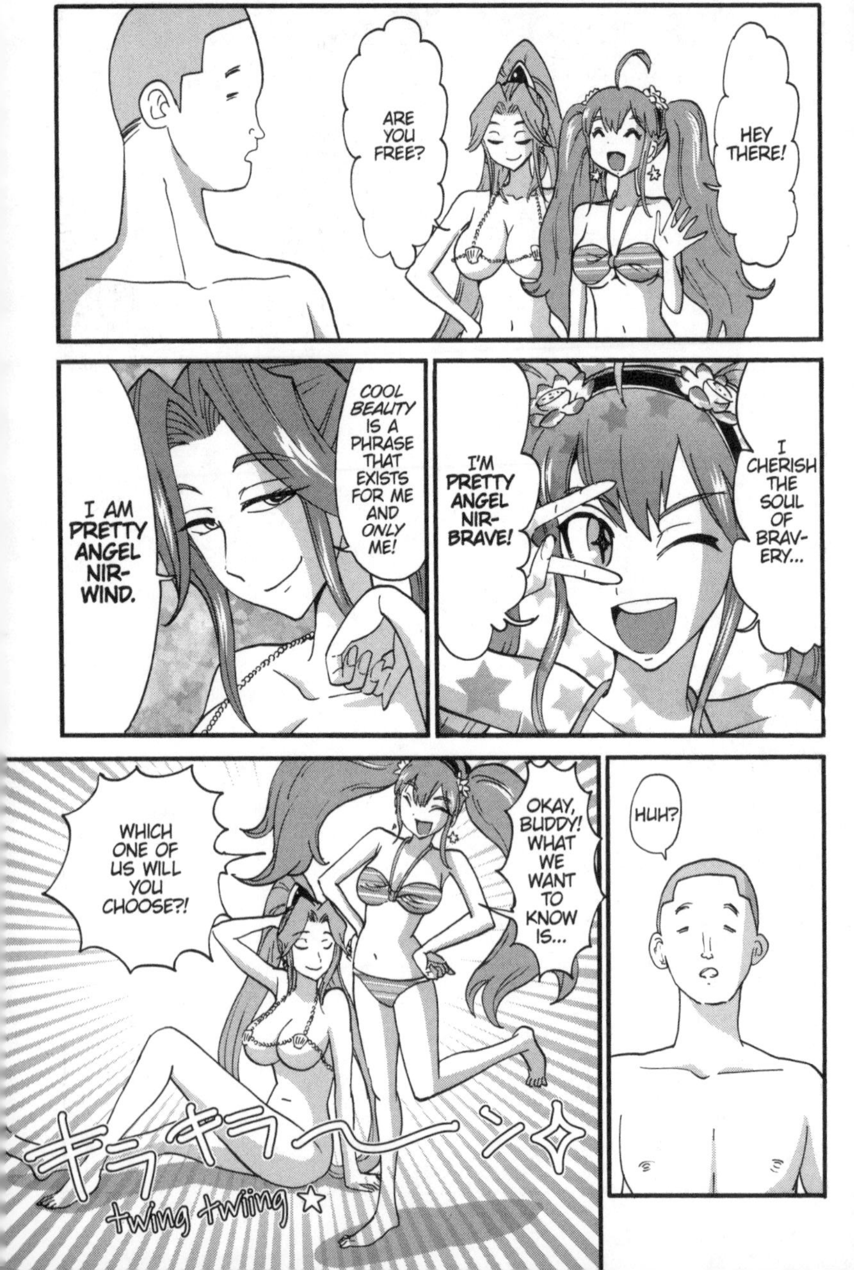
HEY THERE!
ARE YOU FREE?
I CHERISH THE SOUL OF BRAVERY...
I'M PRETTY ANGEL NIR-BRAVE!
COOL BEAUTY IS A PHRASE THAT EXISTS FOR ME AND ONLY ME!
I AM PRETTY ANGEL NIR-WIND.
HUH?
OKAY, BUDDY! WHAT WE WANT TO KNOW IS...
WHICH ONE OF US WILL YOU CHOOSE?!
twing twiing ☆

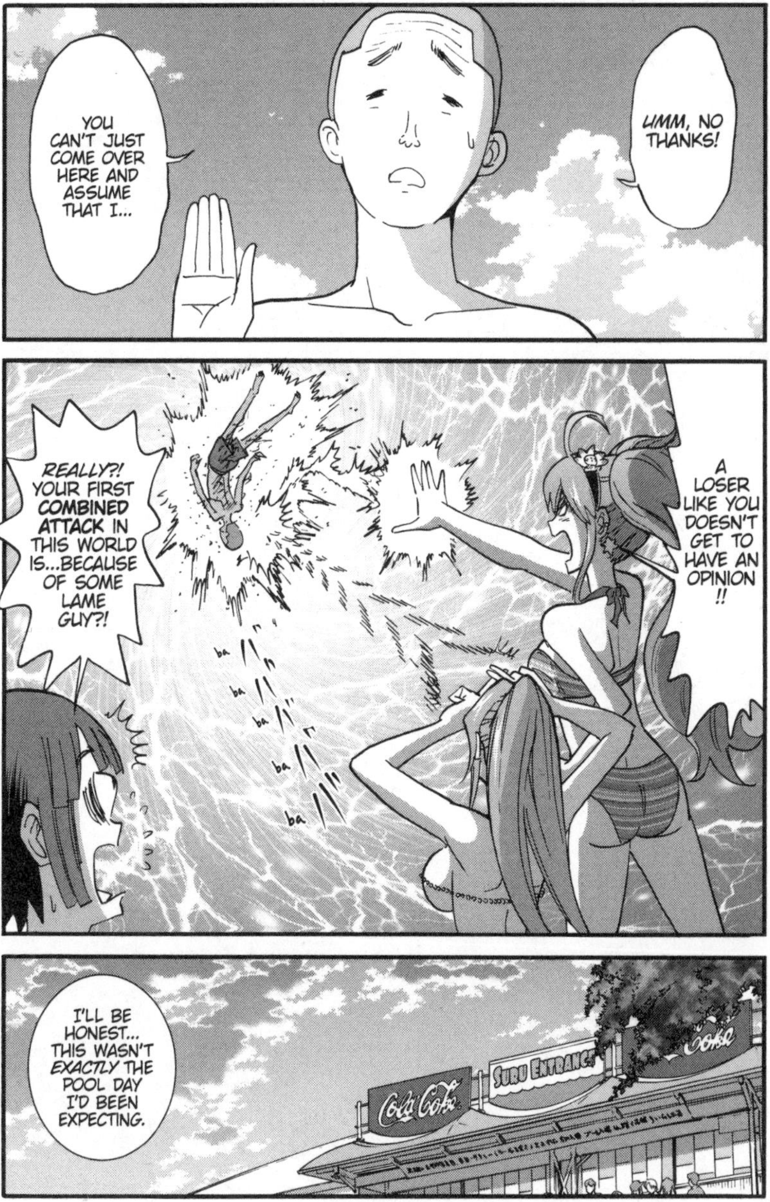
UMM, NO THANKS!
YOU CAN'T JUST COME OVER HERE AND ASSUME THAT I...
A LOSER LIKE YOU DOESN'T GET TO HAVE AN OPINION !!
REALLY?! YOUR FIRST COMBINED ATTACK IN THIS WORLD IS...BECAUSE OF SOME LAME GUY?!
ba
ba
ba
ba
ba
I'LL BE HONEST... THIS WASN'T EXACTLY THE POOL DAY I'D BEEN EXPECTING.
SURU ENTRANC
Cola Coke

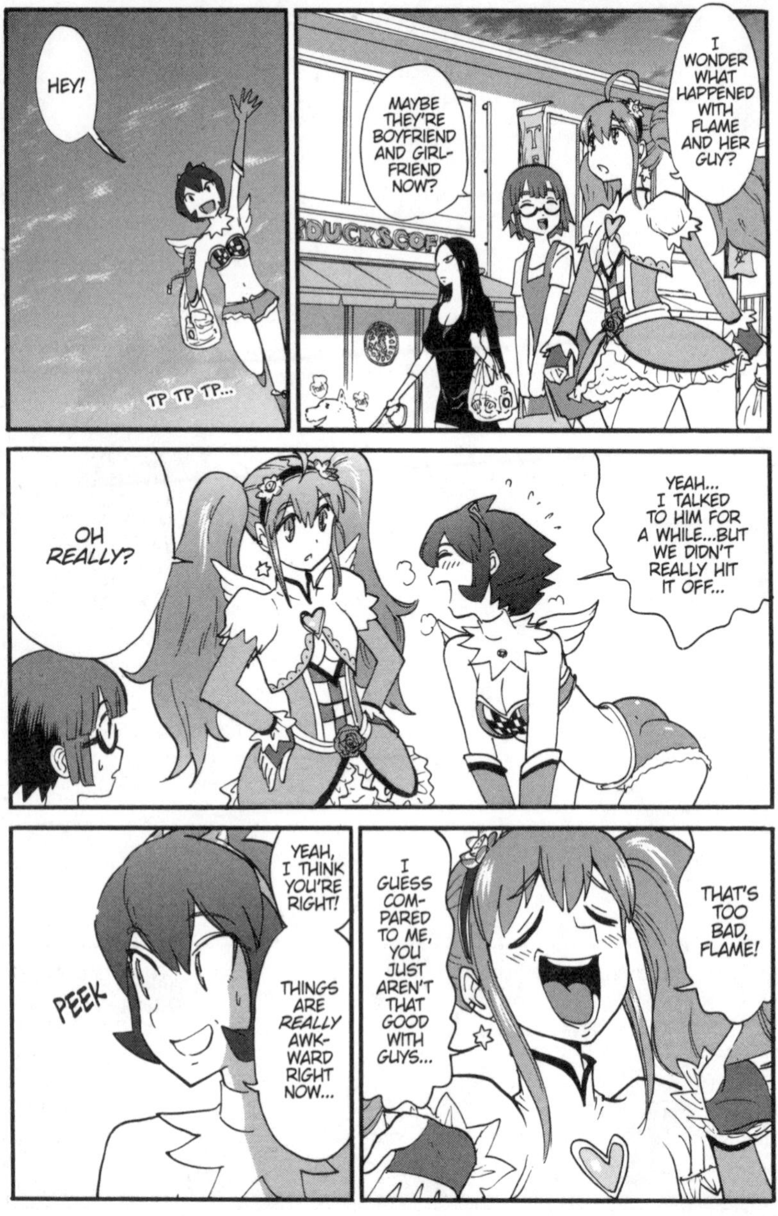
I WONDER WHAT HAPPENED WITH FLAME AND HER GUY?
MAYBE THEY'RE BOYFRIEND AND GIRL-FRIEND NOW?
HEY!
TP TP TP...
YEAH... I TALKED TO HIM FOR A WHILE...BUT WE DIDN'T REALLY HIT IT OFF...
OH *REALLY?*
THAT'S TOO BAD, FLAME!
I GUESS COM-PARED TO ME, YOU JUST AREN'T THAT GOOD WITH GUYS...
YEAH, I THINK YOU'RE RIGHT!
THINGS ARE *REALLY* AWK-WARD RIGHT NOW...
PEEK

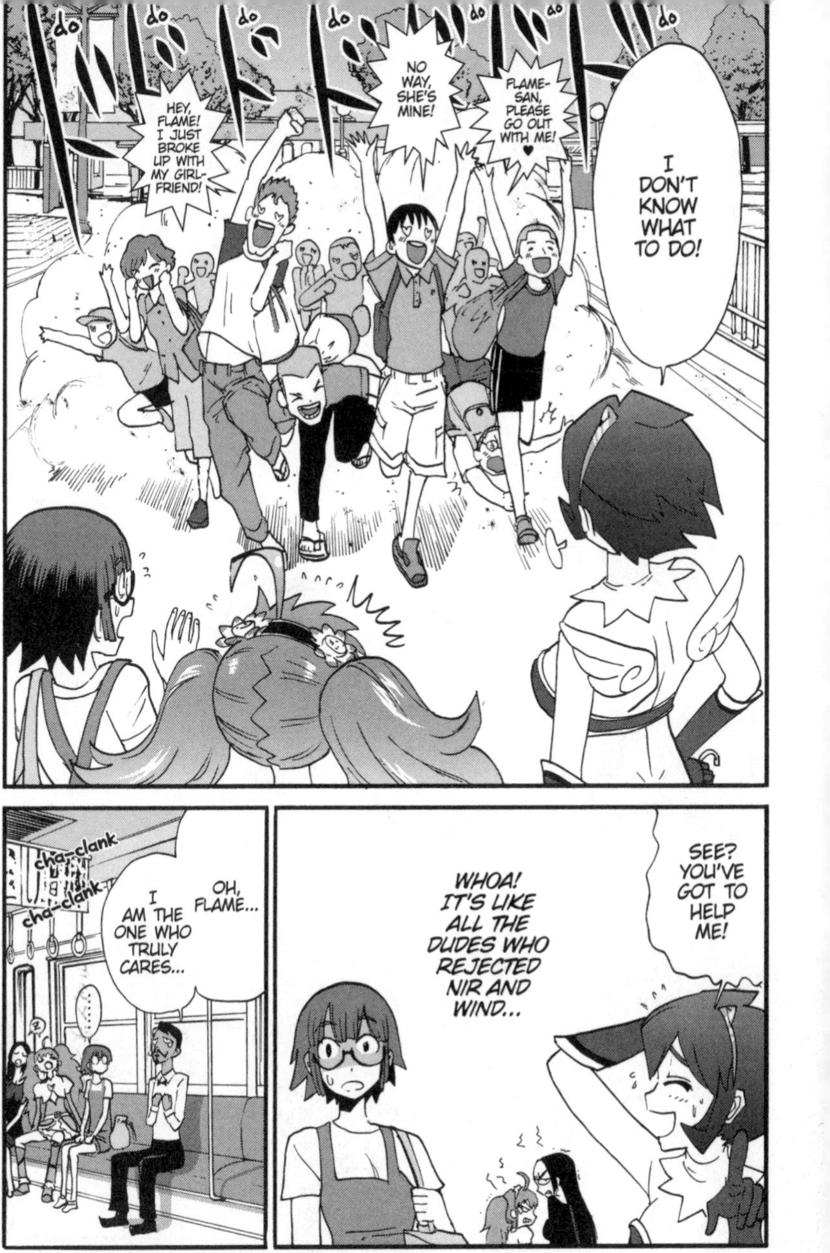
do do do do do do do
I DON'T KNOW WHAT TO DO!
FLAME-SAN, PLEASE GO OUT WITH ME! ♥
NO WAY, SHE'S MINE!
HEY, FLAME! I JUST BROKE UP WITH MY GIRL-FRIEND!
SEE? YOU'VE GOT TO HELP ME!
WHOA! IT'S LIKE ALL THE DUDES WHO REJECTED NIR AND WIND...
OH, FLAME...
I AM THE ONE WHO TRULY CARES...
cha-clank
cha-clank

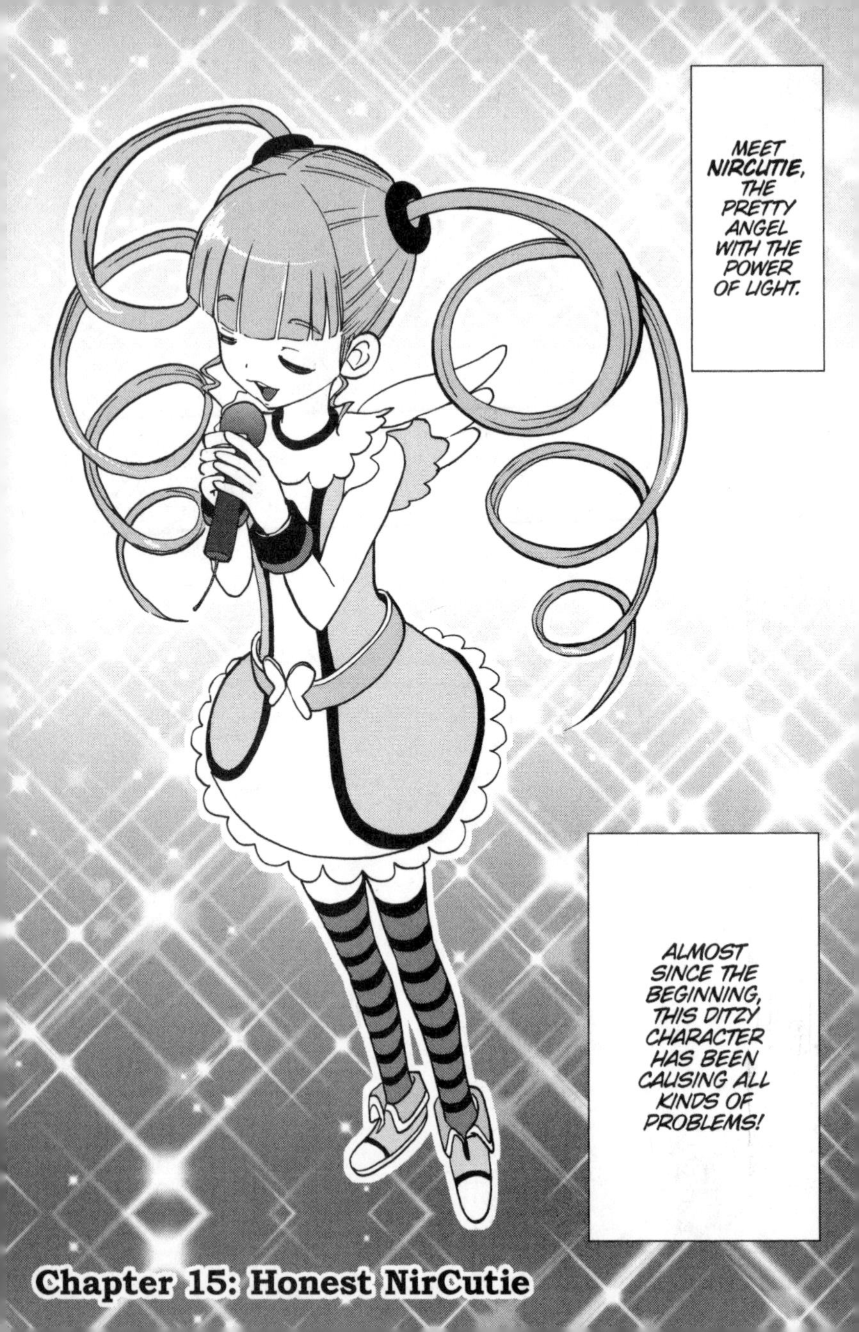
MEET NIRCUTIE, THE PRETTY ANGEL WITH THE POWER OF LIGHT.
ALMOST SINCE THE BEGINNING, THIS DITZY CHARACTER HAS BEEN CAUSING ALL KINDS OF PROBLEMS!

Chapter 15: Honest NirCutie

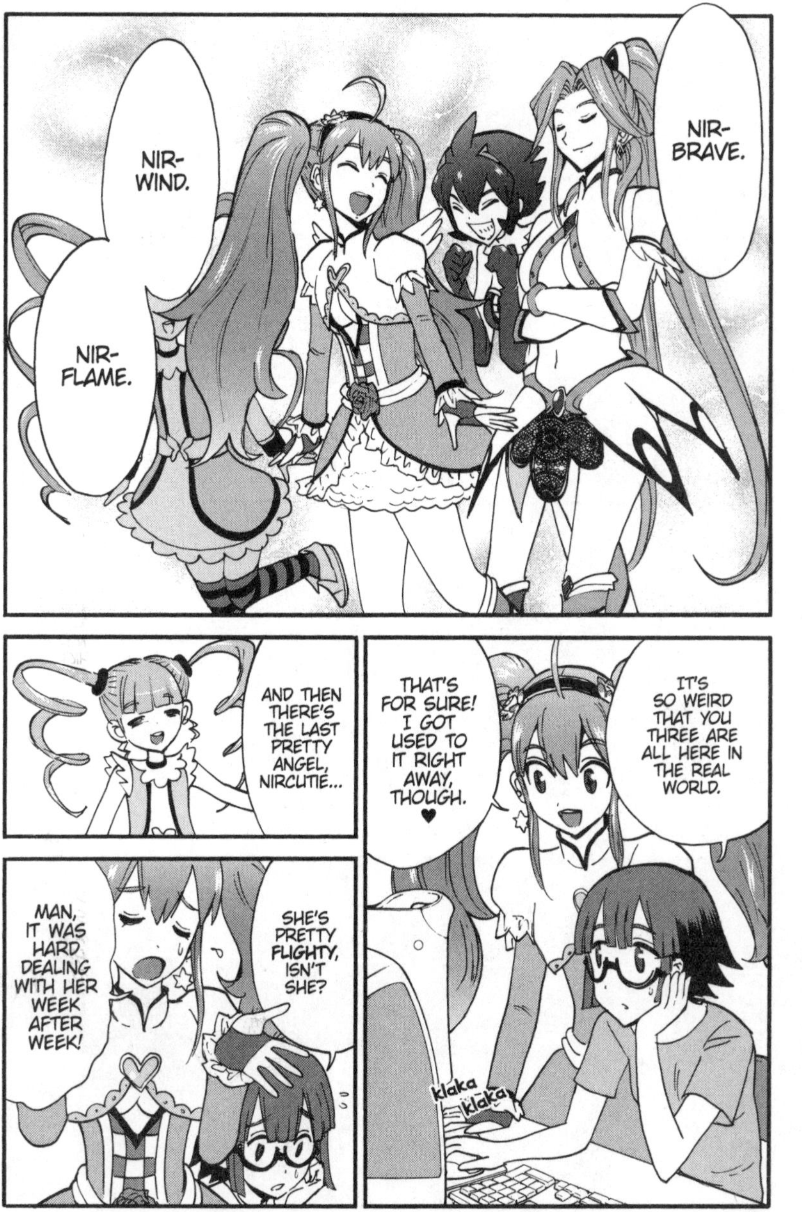
NIR-BRAVE.
NIR-WIND.
NIR-FLAME.
IT'S SO WEIRD THAT YOU THREE ARE ALL HERE IN THE REAL WORLD.
THAT'S FOR SURE! I GOT USED TO IT RIGHT AWAY, THOUGH. ♥
klaka klaka
AND THEN THERE'S THE LAST PRETTY ANGEL, NIRCUTIE...
SHE'S PRETTY FLIGHTY, ISN'T SHE?
MAN, IT WAS HARD DEALING WITH HER WEEK AFTER WEEK!

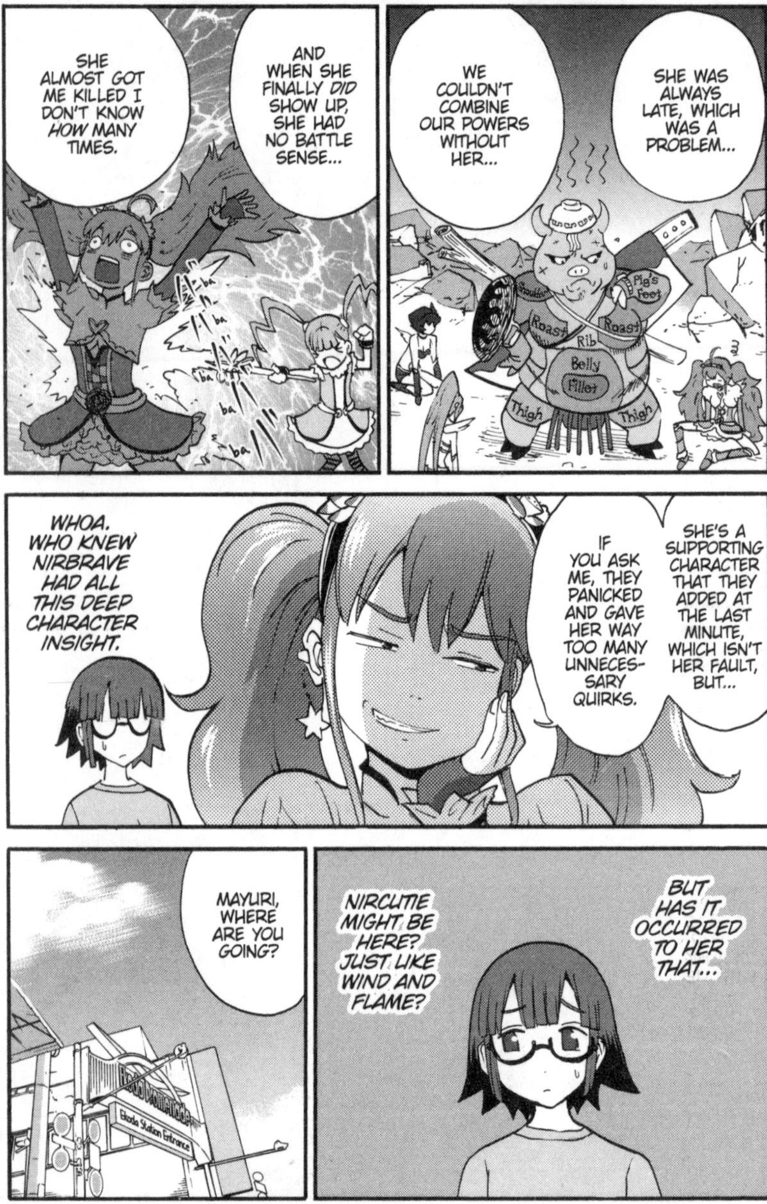
SHE WAS ALWAYS LATE, WHICH WAS A PROBLEM...
WE COULDN'T COMBINE OUR POWERS WITHOUT HER...
Pig's Feet
Roast
Roast
Rib
Belly
Fillet
Thigh
Thigh
AND WHEN SHE FINALLY *DID* SHOW UP, SHE HAD NO BATTLE SENSE...
SHE ALMOST GOT ME KILLED I DON'T KNOW *HOW* MANY TIMES.
ba
ba
ba
ba
ba
SHE'S A SUPPORTING CHARACTER THAT THEY ADDED AT THE LAST MINUTE, WHICH ISN'T HER FAULT, BUT...
IF YOU ASK ME, THEY PANICKED AND GAVE HER WAY TOO MANY UNNECES-SARY QUIRKS.
WHOA. WHO KNEW NIRBRAVE HAD ALL THIS DEEP CHARACTER INSIGHT.
BUT HAS IT OCCURRED TO HER THAT...
NIRCUTIE MIGHT BE HERE? JUST LIKE WIND AND FLAME?
MAYURI, WHERE ARE YOU GOING?
Ekoda Station Entrance

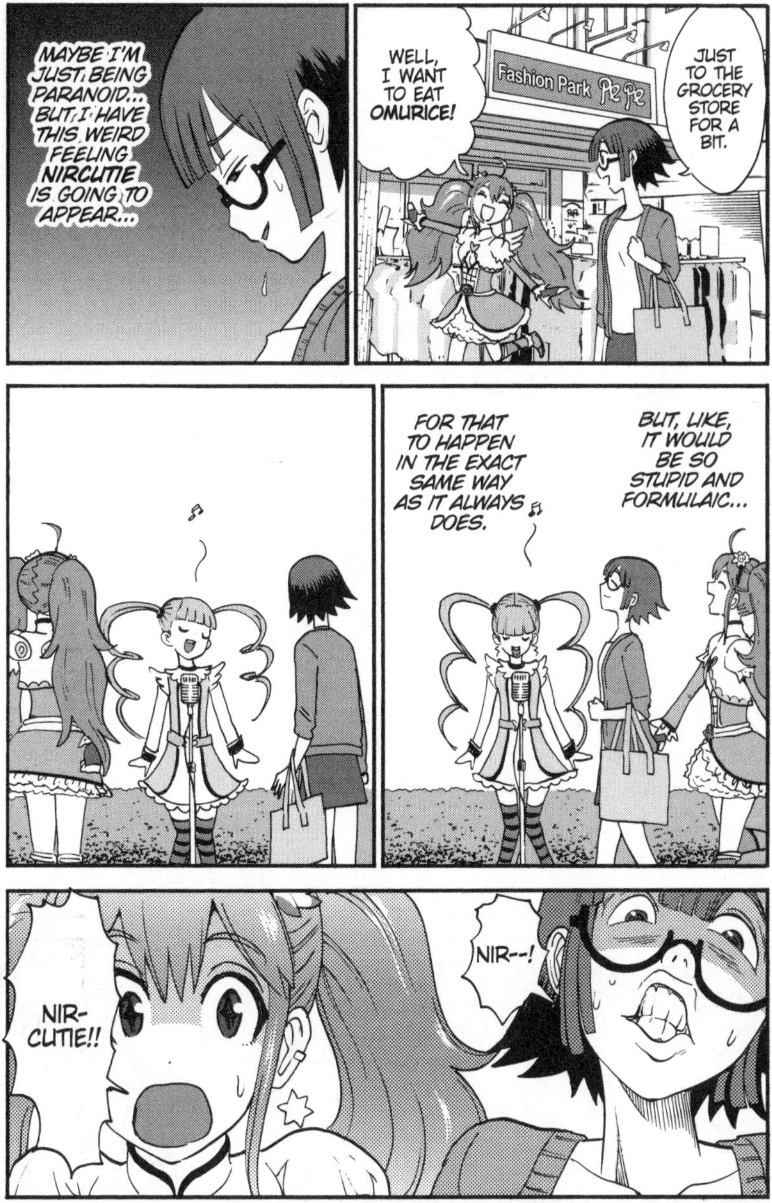
JUST TO THE GROCERY STORE FOR A BIT.
Fashion Park PePe
WELL, I WANT TO EAT OMURICE!
MAYBE I'M JUST BEING PARANOID... BUT I HAVE THIS WEIRD FEELING NIRCUTIE IS GOING TO APPEAR...
BUT, LIKE, IT WOULD BE SO STUPID AND FORMULAIC...
FOR THAT TO HAPPEN IN THE EXACT SAME WAY AS IT ALWAYS DOES.
NIR--!
NIR-CUTIE!!

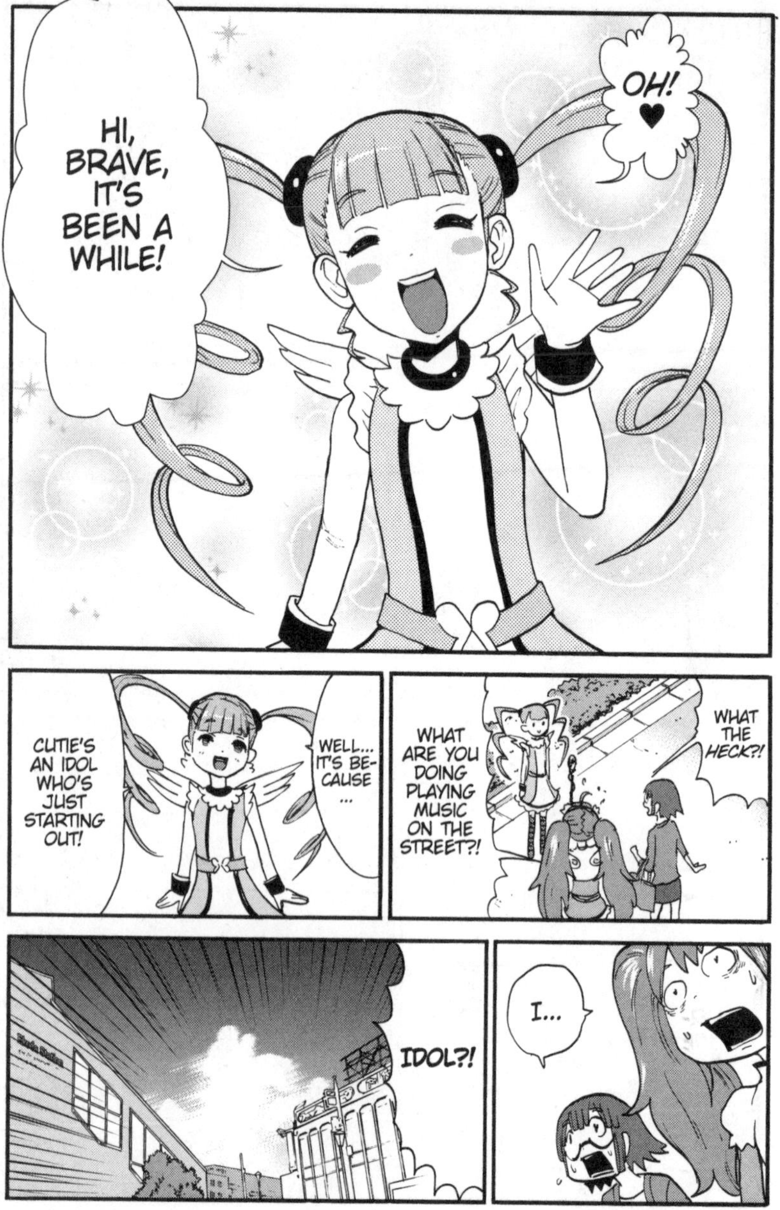
OH! ♥
HI, BRAVE, IT'S BEEN A WHILE!
WHAT THE HECK?!
WHAT ARE YOU DOING PLAYING MUSIC ON THE STREET?!
WELL... IT'S BE-CAUSE ...
CUTIE'S AN IDOL WHO'S JUST STARTING OUT!
I...
IDOL?!

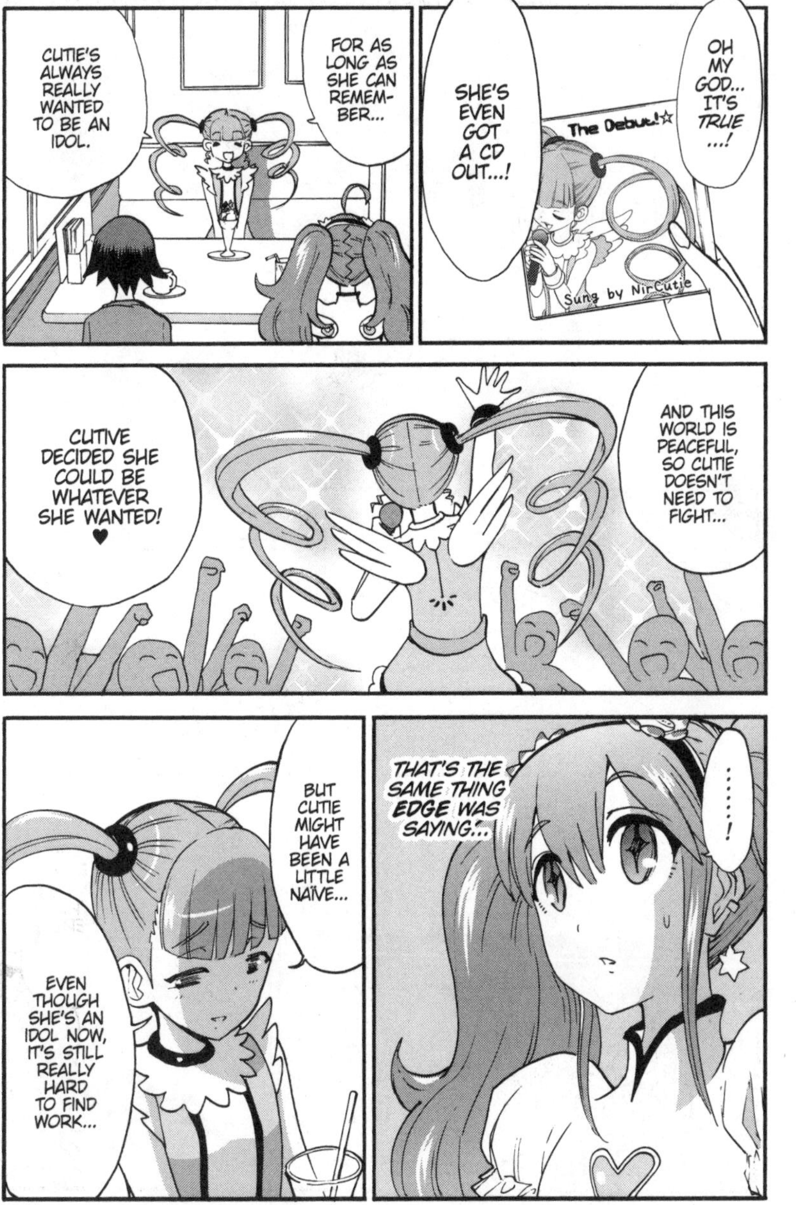
OH MY GOD... IT'S *TRUE* ...!
SHE'S EVEN GOT A CD OUT...!
The Debut!☆
Sung by NirCutie
FOR AS LONG AS SHE CAN REMEMBER...
CUTIE'S ALWAYS REALLY WANTED TO BE AN IDOL.
AND THIS WORLD IS PEACEFUL, SO CUTIE DOESN'T NEED TO FIGHT...
CUTIVE DECIDED SHE COULD BE WHATEVER SHE WANTED! ♥
......!
THAT'S THE SAME THING ***EDGE*** *WAS SAYING...*
BUT CUTIE MIGHT HAVE BEEN A LITTLE NAÏVE...
EVEN THOUGH SHE'S AN IDOL NOW, IT'S STILL REALLY HARD TO FIND WORK...

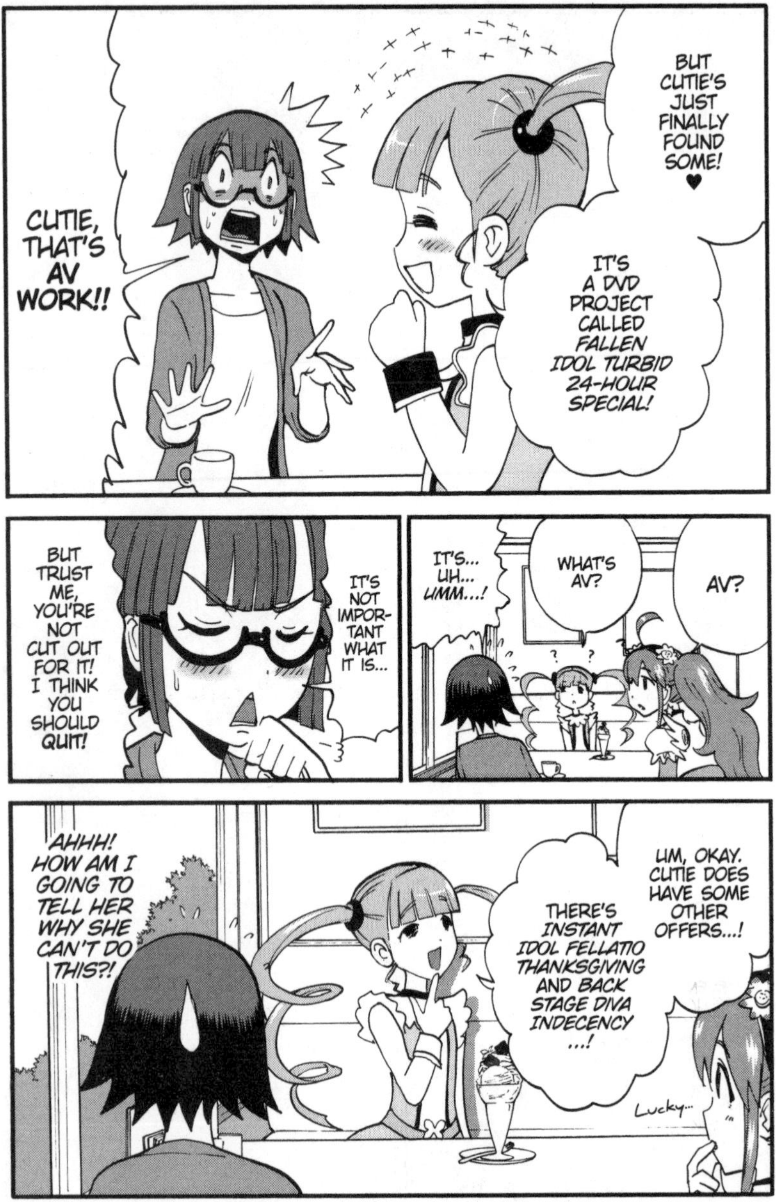
BUT CUTIE'S JUST FINALLY FOUND SOME! ♥
IT'S A DVD PROJECT CALLED FALLEN IDOL TURBID 24-HOUR SPECIAL!
CUTIE, THAT'S AV WORK!!
AV?
WHAT'S AV?
IT'S... UH... UMM...!
IT'S NOT IMPORTANT WHAT IT IS...
BUT TRUST ME, YOU'RE NOT CUT OUT FOR IT! I THINK YOU SHOULD QUIT!
UM, OKAY. CUTIE DOES HAVE SOME OTHER OFFERS...!
THERE'S INSTANT IDOL FELLATIO THANKSGIVING AND BACK STAGE DIVA INDECENCY ...!
Lucky...
AHHH! HOW AM I GOING TO TELL HER WHY SHE CAN'T DO THIS?!

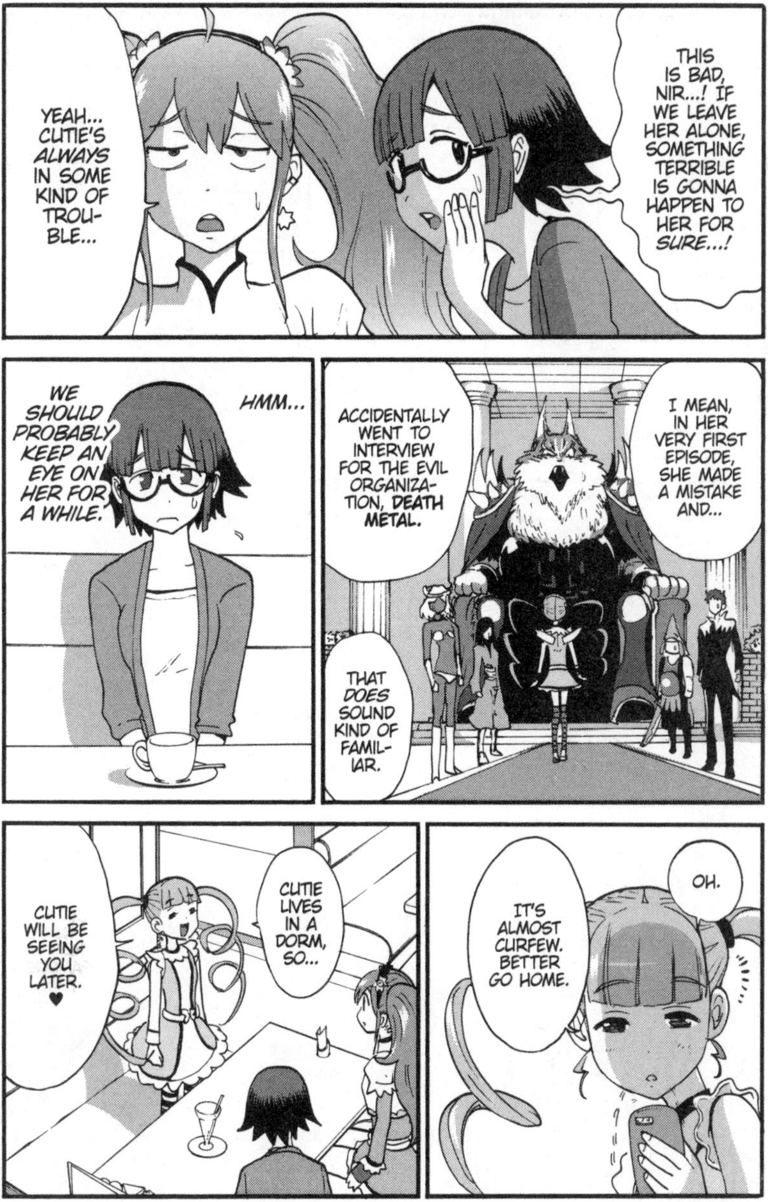
THIS IS BAD, NIR...! IF WE LEAVE HER ALONE, SOMETHING TERRIBLE IS GONNA HAPPEN TO HER FOR *SURE*...!
YEAH... CUTIE'S *ALWAYS* IN SOME KIND OF TROUBLE...
I MEAN, IN HER VERY FIRST EPISODE, SHE MADE A MISTAKE AND...
ACCIDENTALLY WENT TO INTERVIEW FOR THE EVIL ORGANIZATION, **DEATH METAL.**
THAT *DOES* SOUND KIND OF FAMILIAR.
HMM...
WE SHOULD PROBABLY KEEP AN EYE ON HER FOR A WHILE.
OH.
IT'S ALMOST CURFEW. BETTER GO HOME.
CUTIE LIVES IN A DORM, SO...
CUTIE WILL BE SEEING YOU LATER. ♥

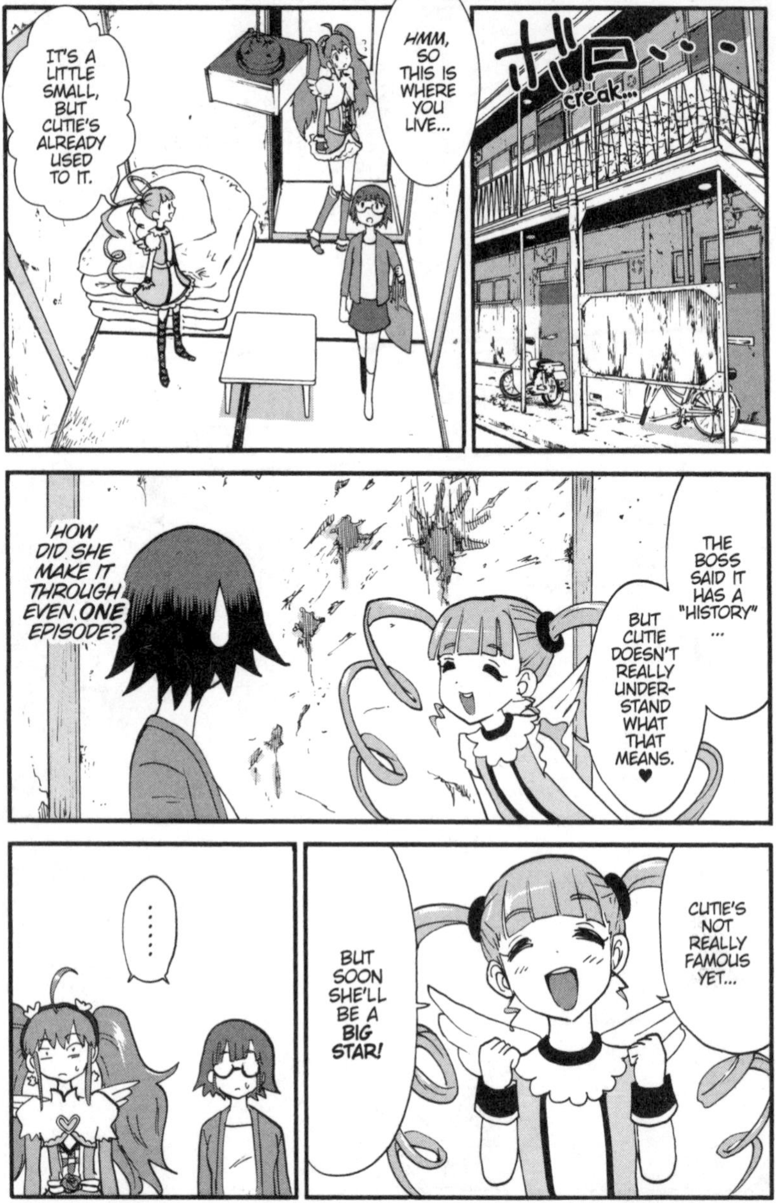
ボロ・・・
creak...
HMM, SO THIS IS WHERE YOU LIVE...
IT'S A LITTLE SMALL, BUT CUTIE'S ALREADY USED TO IT.
THE BOSS SAID IT HAS A "HISTORY"...
BUT CUTIE DOESN'T REALLY UNDER-STAND WHAT THAT MEANS. ♥
HOW DID SHE MAKE IT THROUGH EVEN ONE EPISODE?
CUTIE'S NOT REALLY FAMOUS YET...
BUT SOON SHE'LL BE A BIG STAR!
......

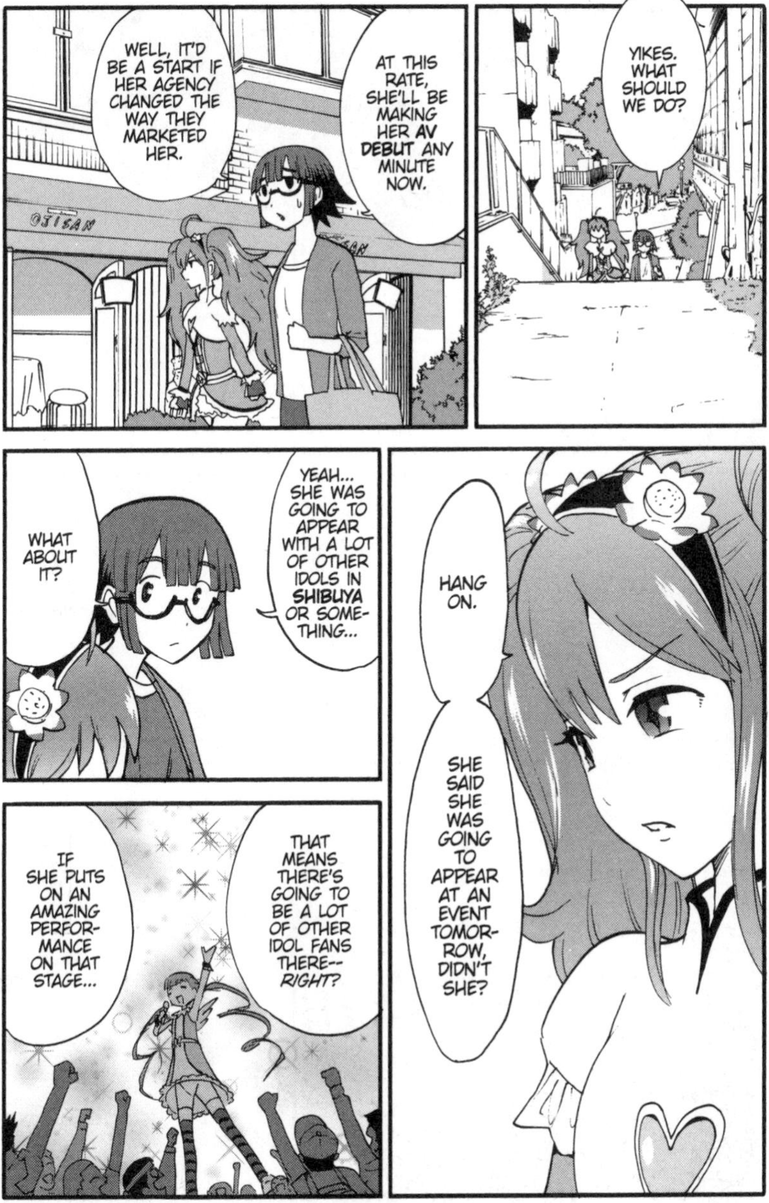
YIKES. WHAT SHOULD WE DO?
AT THIS RATE, SHE'LL BE MAKING HER **AV DEBUT** ANY MINUTE NOW.
WELL, IT'D BE A START IF HER AGENCY CHANGED THE WAY THEY MARKETED HER.
OJISAN
HANG ON.
SHE SAID SHE WAS GOING TO APPEAR AT AN EVENT TOMORROW, DIDN'T SHE?
YEAH... SHE WAS GOING TO APPEAR WITH A LOT OF OTHER IDOLS IN **SHIBUYA** OR SOMETHING...
WHAT ABOUT IT?
THAT MEANS THERE'S GOING TO BE A LOT OF OTHER IDOL FANS THERE--*RIGHT?*
IF SHE PUTS ON AN AMAZING PERFORMANCE ON THAT STAGE...

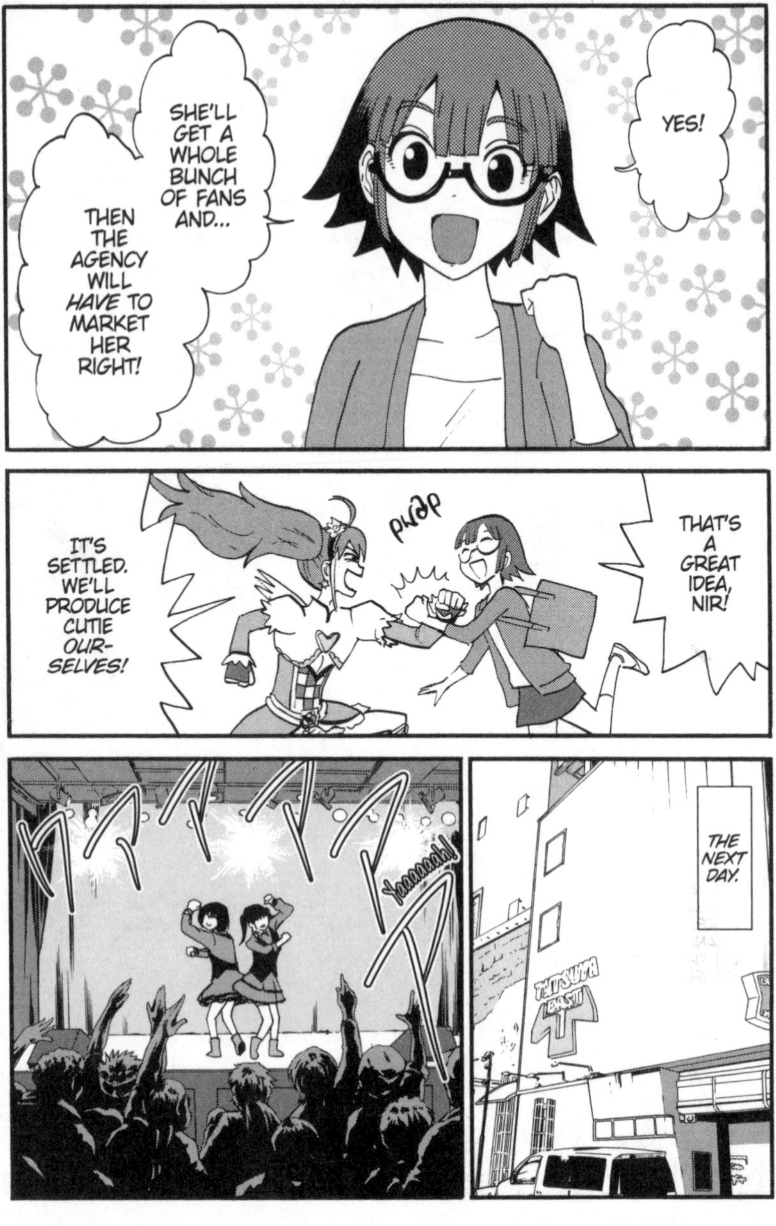
YES!
SHE'LL GET A WHOLE BUNCH OF FANS AND...
THEN THE AGENCY WILL *HAVE* TO MARKET HER RIGHT!
THAT'S A GREAT IDEA, NIR!
IT'S SETTLED. WE'LL PRODUCE CUTIE OUR-SELVES!
THE NEXT DAY.
Yaaaaaah!

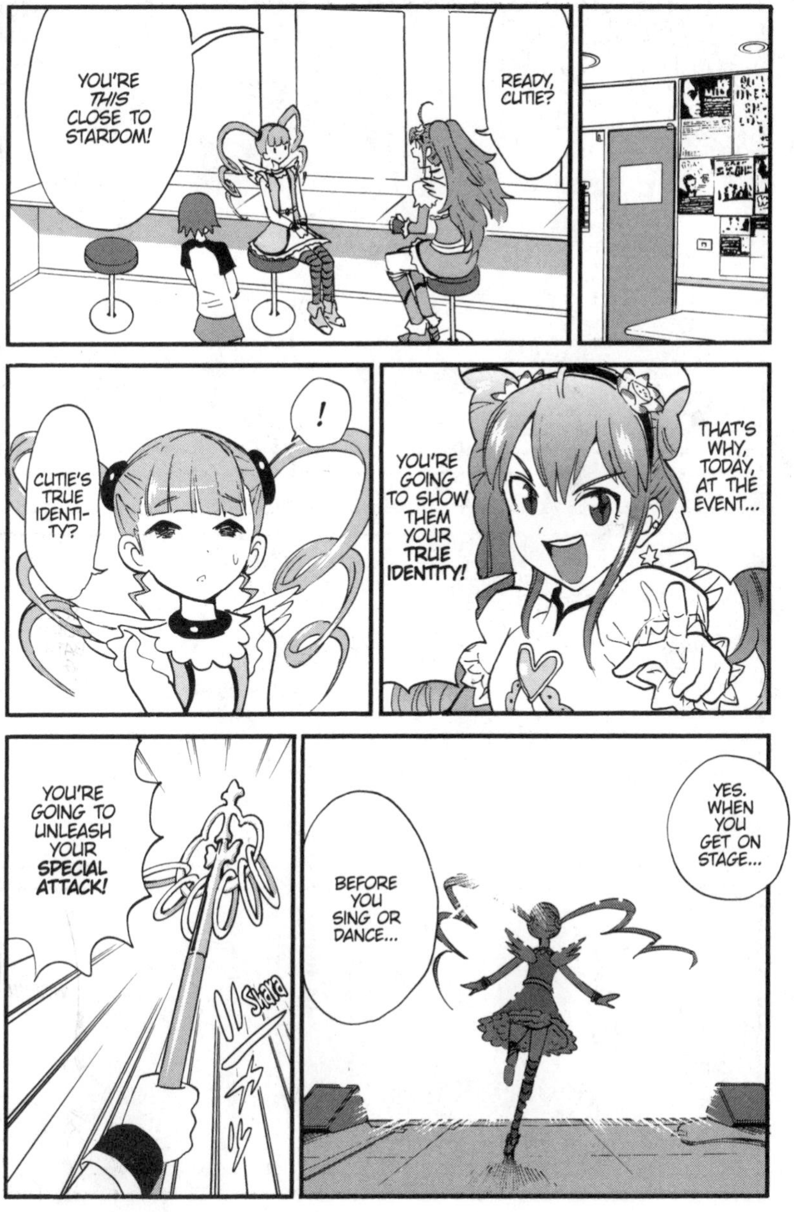
READY, CUTIE?
YOU'RE THIS CLOSE TO STARDOM!
THAT'S WHY, TODAY, AT THE EVENT...
YOU'RE GOING TO SHOW THEM YOUR TRUE IDENTITY!
!
CUTIE'S TRUE IDENTITY?
YES. WHEN YOU GET ON STAGE...
BEFORE YOU SING OR DANCE...
YOU'RE GOING TO UNLEASH YOUR SPECIAL ATTACK!
Shara

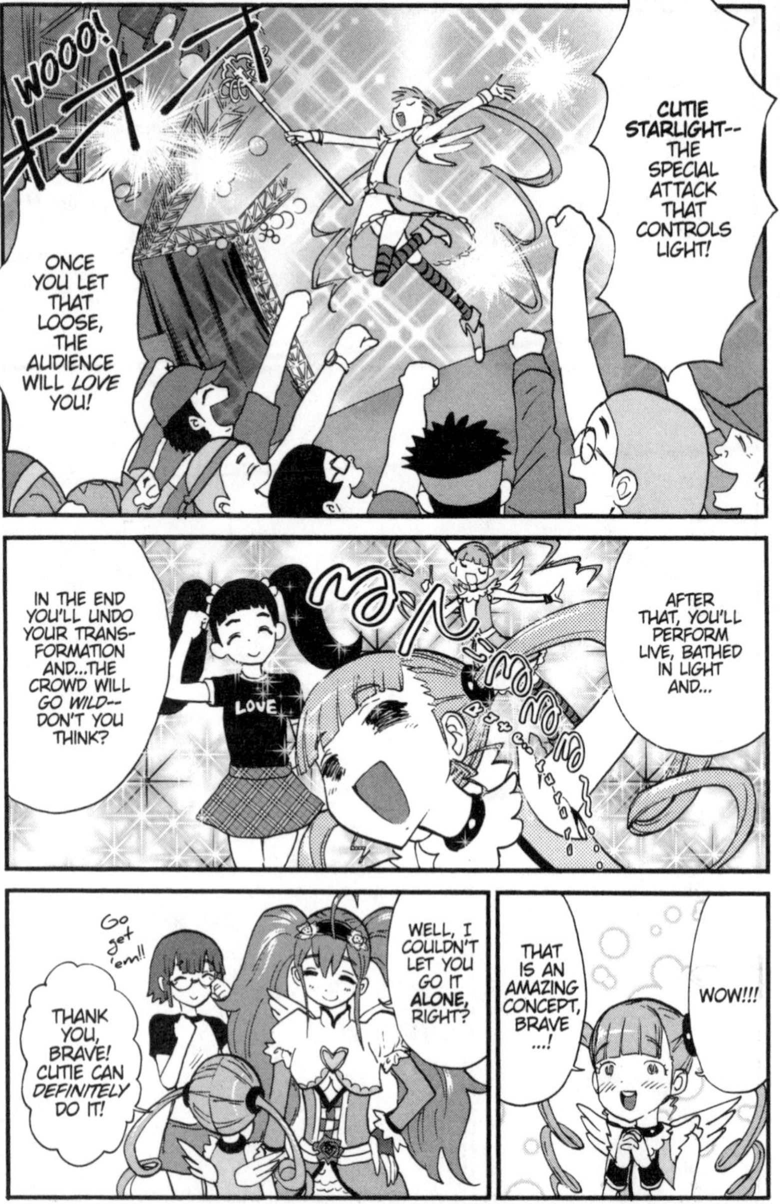
CUTIE STARLIGHT-- THE SPECIAL ATTACK THAT CONTROLS LIGHT!
WOOO!
ONCE YOU LET THAT LOOSE, THE AUDIENCE WILL *LOVE* YOU!
AFTER THAT, YOU'LL PERFORM LIVE, BATHED IN LIGHT AND...
IN THE END YOU'LL UNDO YOUR TRANS-FORMATION AND...THE CROWD WILL GO *WILD*-- DON'T YOU THINK?
LOVE
WOW!!!
THAT IS AN AMAZING CONCEPT, BRAVE ...!
WELL, I COULDN'T LET YOU GO IT *ALONE*, RIGHT?
Go get 'em!!
THANK YOU, BRAVE! CUTIE CAN *DEFINITELY* DO IT!

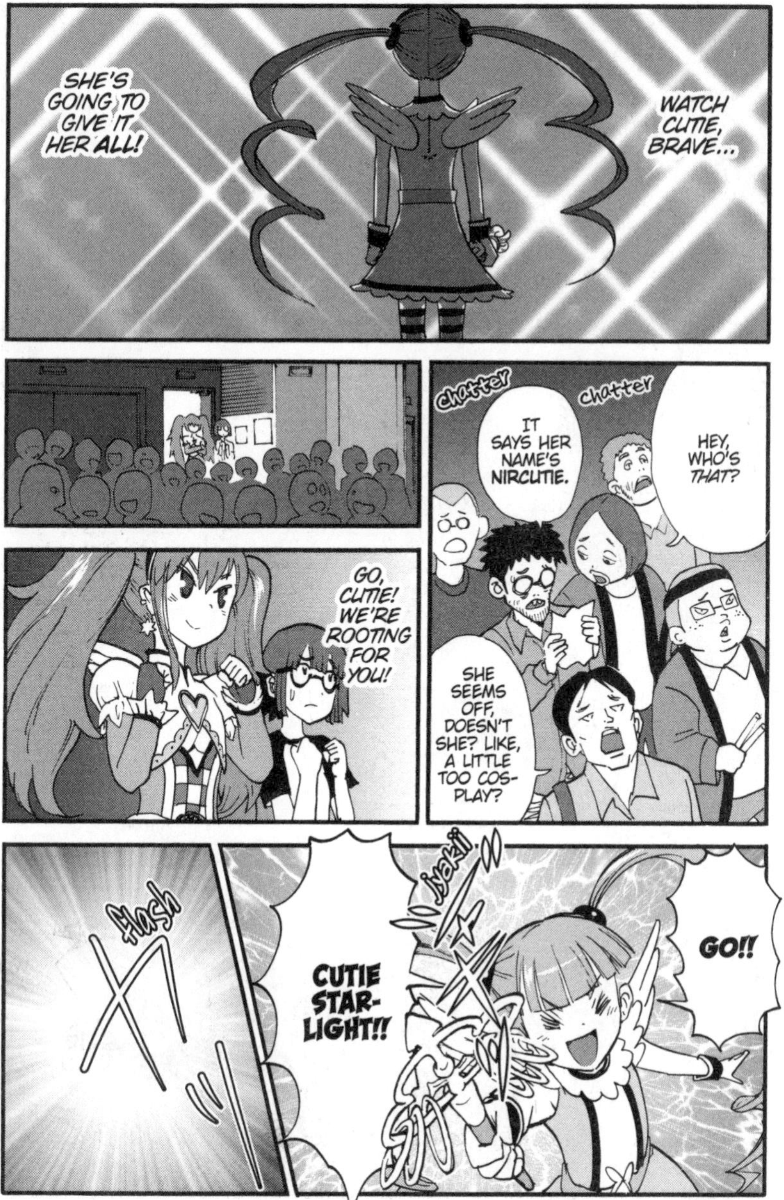
WATCH CUTIE, BRAVE...
SHE'S GOING TO GIVE IT HER ALL!
chatter
chatter
HEY, WHO'S THAT?
IT SAYS HER NAME'S NIRCUTIE.
SHE SEEMS OFF, DOESN'T SHE? LIKE, A LITTLE TOO COS-PLAY?
GO, CUTIE! WE'RE ROOTING FOR YOU!
GO!!
jyaki!!
CUTIE STAR-LIGHT!!
flash

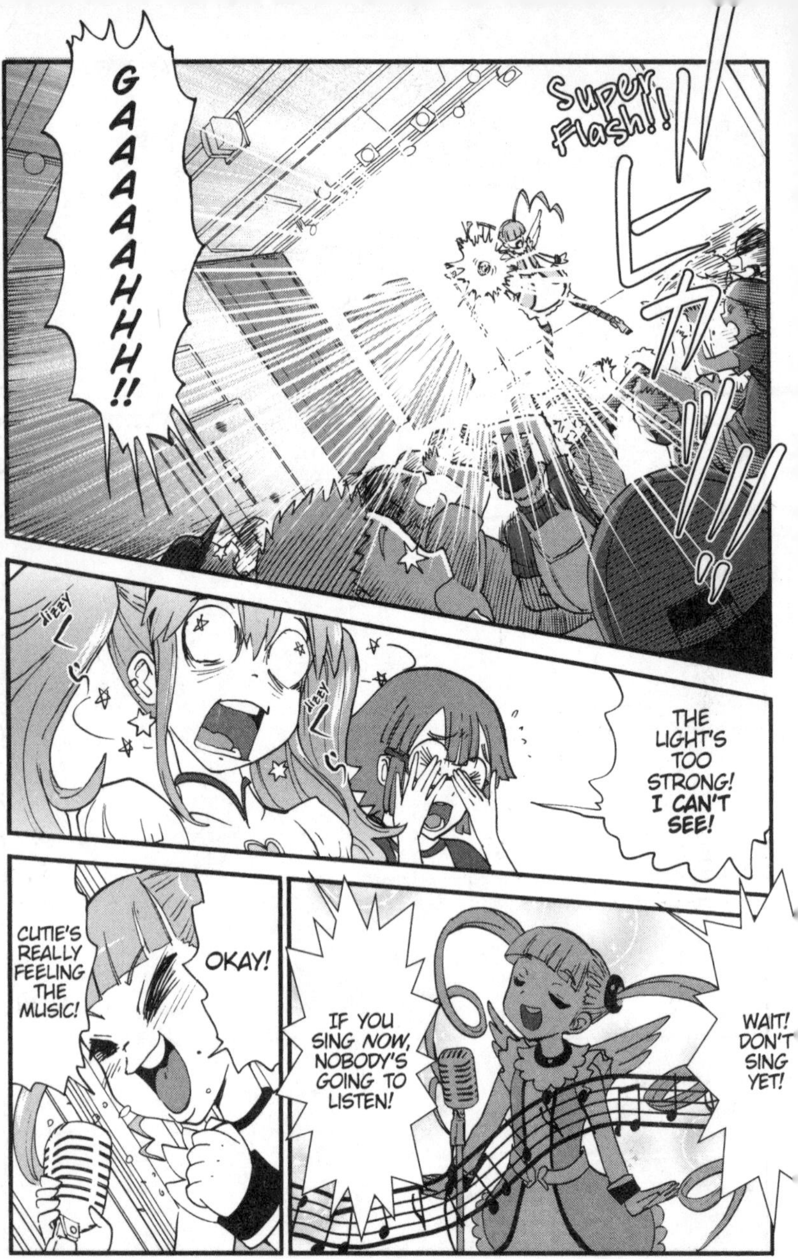
Super Flash!!
GAAAAAHHH!!
dizzy
dizzy
THE LIGHT'S TOO STRONG! I CAN'T SEE!
WAIT! DON'T SING YET!
IF YOU SING NOW, NOBODY'S GOING TO LISTEN!
OKAY!
CUTIE'S REALLY FEELING THE MUSIC!

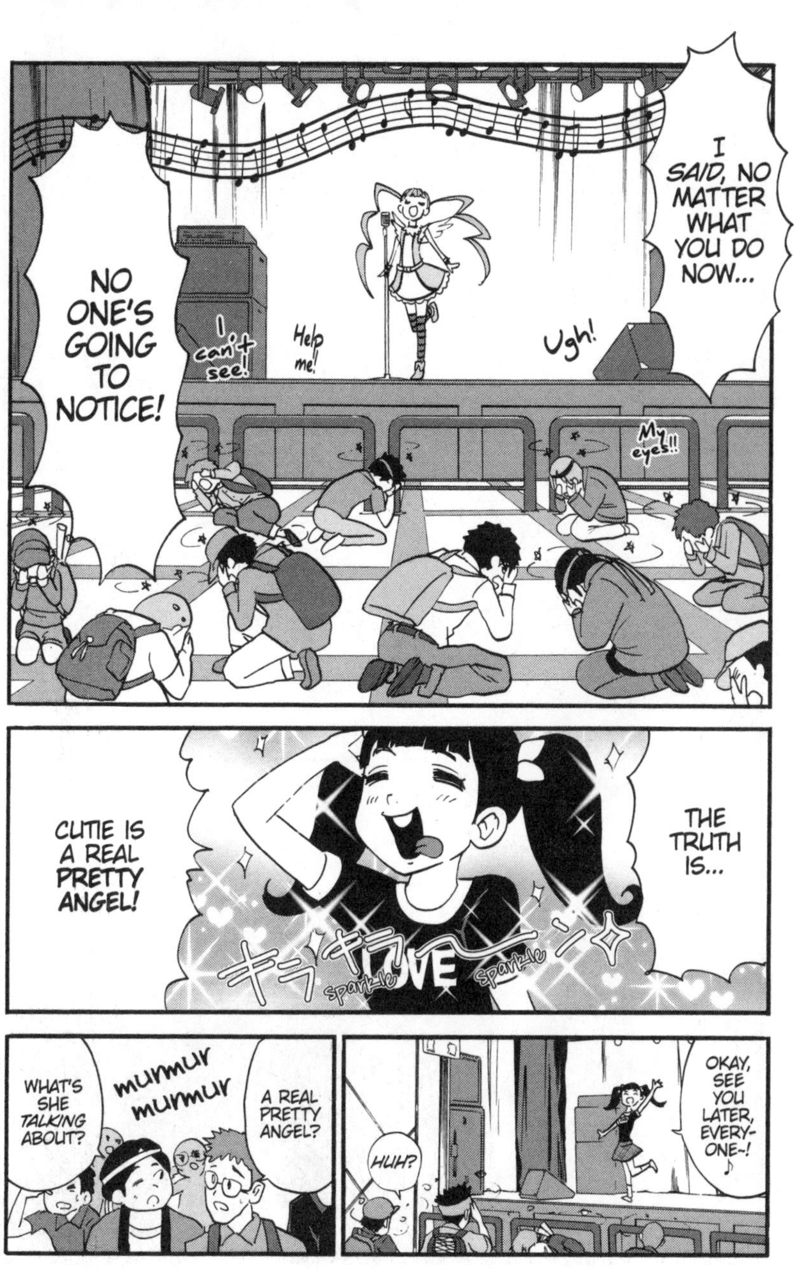
I SAID, NO MATTER WHAT YOU DO NOW...
Ugh!
Help me!
I can't see!
NO ONE'S GOING TO NOTICE!
My eyes!!
THE TRUTH IS...
CUTIE IS A REAL PRETTY ANGEL!
sparkle sparkle
OKAY, SEE YOU LATER, EVERY-ONE~! ♪
HUH?
A REAL PRETTY ANGEL?
murmur murmur
WHAT'S SHE TALKING ABOUT?

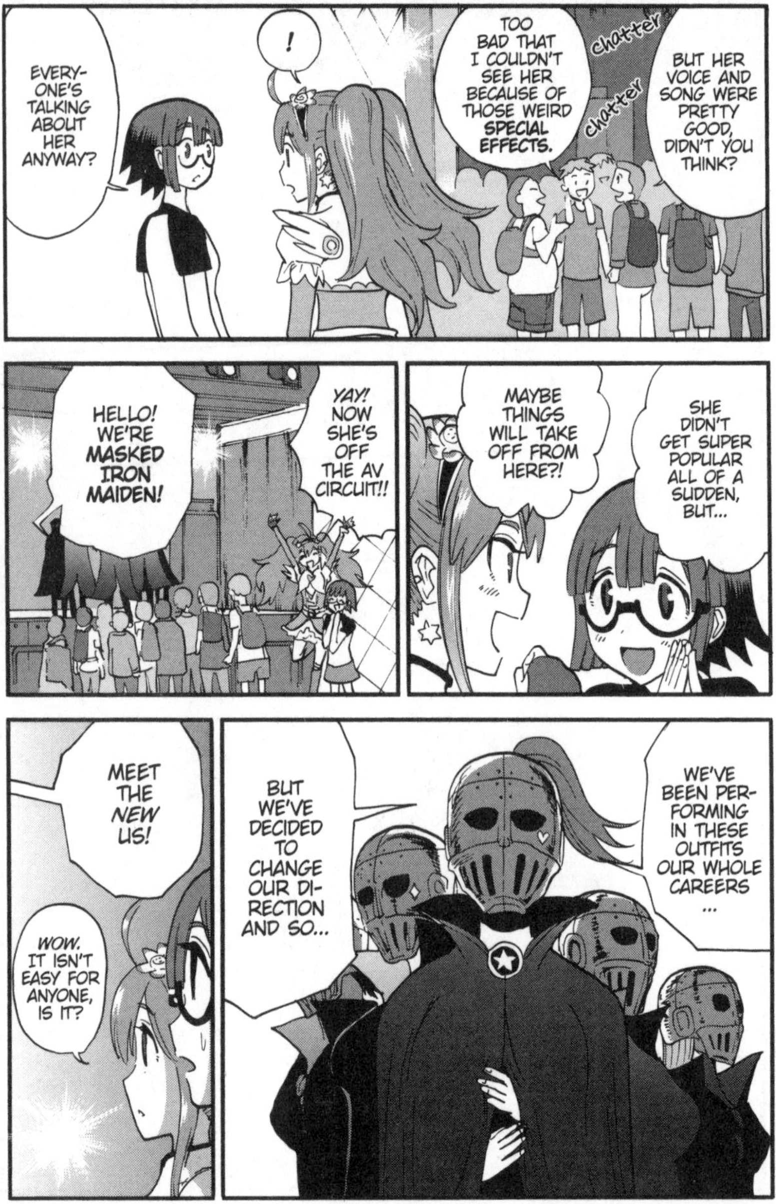
BUT HER VOICE AND SONG WERE PRETTY GOOD, DIDN'T YOU THINK?
chatter
chatter
TOO BAD THAT I COULDN'T SEE HER BECAUSE OF THOSE WEIRD **SPECIAL EFFECTS.**
!
EVERY-ONE'S TALKING ABOUT HER ANYWAY?
SHE DIDN'T GET SUPER POPULAR ALL OF A SUDDEN, BUT...
MAYBE THINGS WILL TAKE OFF FROM HERE?!
YAY! NOW SHE'S OFF THE AV CIRCUIT!!
HELLO! WE'RE **MASKED IRON MAIDEN!**
WE'VE BEEN PER-FORMING IN THESE OUTFITS OUR WHOLE CAREERS ...
BUT WE'VE DECIDED TO CHANGE OUR DI-RECTION AND SO...
MEET THE *NEW* US!
WOW. IT ISN'T EASY FOR ANYONE, IS IT?

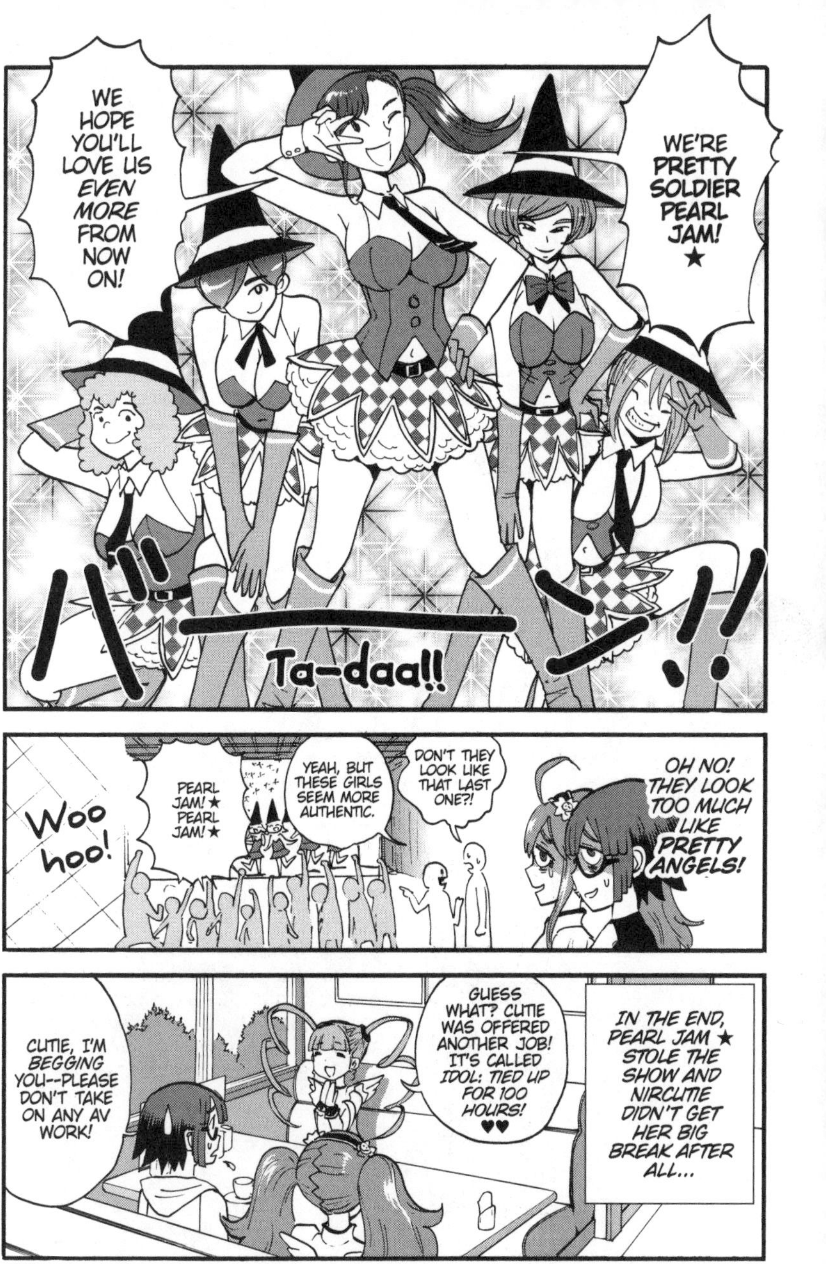
WE'RE PRETTY SOLDIER PEARL JAM! ★
WE HOPE YOU'LL LOVE US EVEN MORE FROM NOW ON!
Ta-daa!!
OH NO! THEY LOOK TOO MUCH LIKE PRETTY ANGELS!
DON'T THEY LOOK LIKE THAT LAST ONE?!
YEAH, BUT THESE GIRLS SEEM MORE AUTHENTIC.
PEARL JAM! ★ PEARL JAM! ★
Woo hoo!
IN THE END, PEARL JAM ★ STOLE THE SHOW AND NIRCUTIE DIDN'T GET HER BIG BREAK AFTER ALL...
GUESS WHAT? CUTIE WAS OFFERED ANOTHER JOB! IT'S CALLED IDOL: TIED UP FOR 100 HOURS! ♥♥
CUTIE, I'M BEGGING YOU--PLEASE DON'T TAKE ON ANY AV WORK!

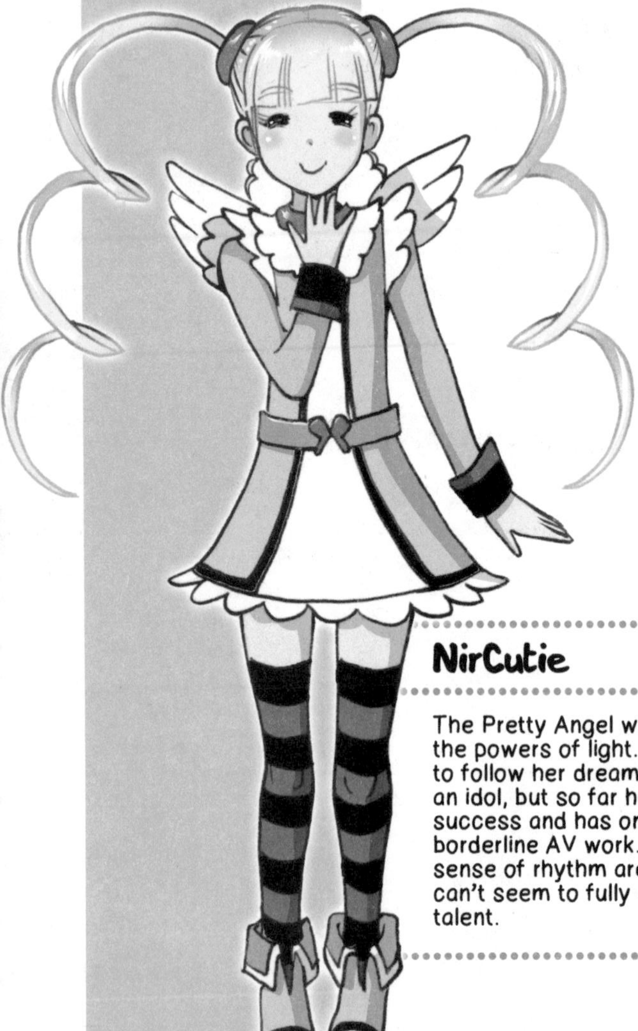

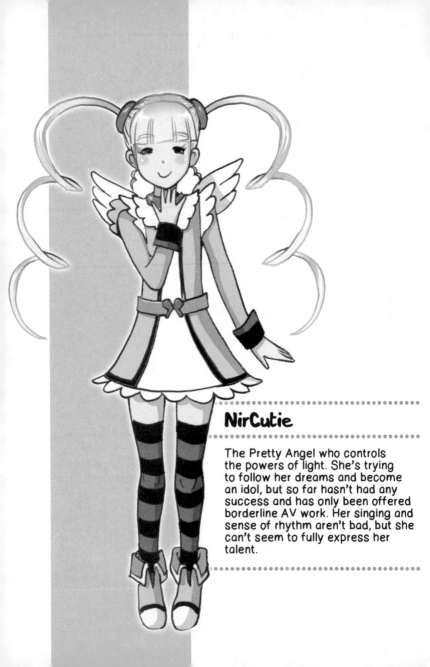

NirCutie

The Pretty Angel who controls the powers of light. She's trying to follow her dreams and become an idol, but so far hasn't had any success and has only been offered borderline AV work. Her singing and sense of rhythm aren't bad, but she can't seem to fully express her talent.

Unmagical Girl

The melancholy days
of a has-been magical girl (2)

Chapter 16: Mayuri's Confession

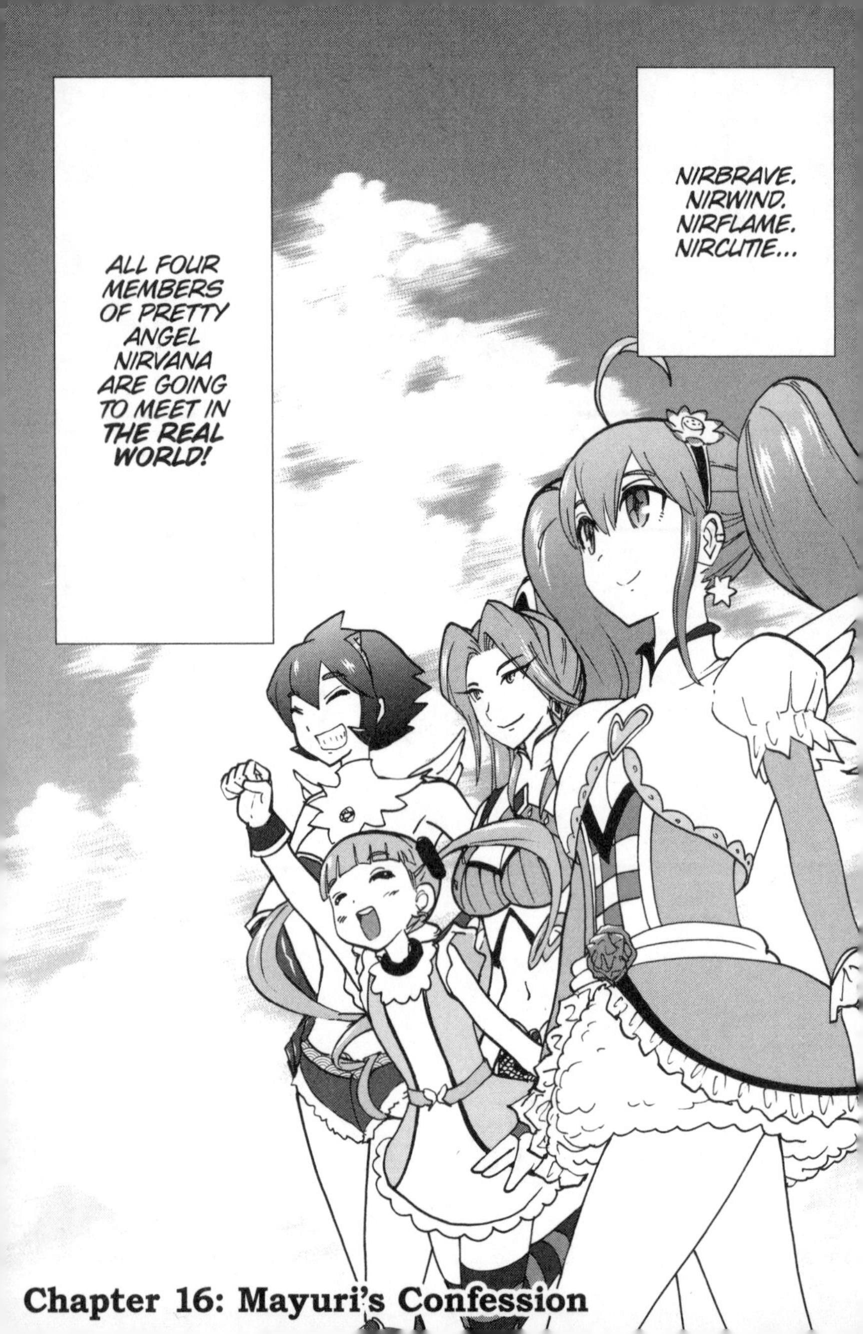
NIRBRAVE. NIRWIND. NIRFLAME. NIRCUTIE...
ALL FOUR MEMBERS OF PRETTY ANGEL NIRVANA ARE GOING TO MEET IN THE REAL WORLD!

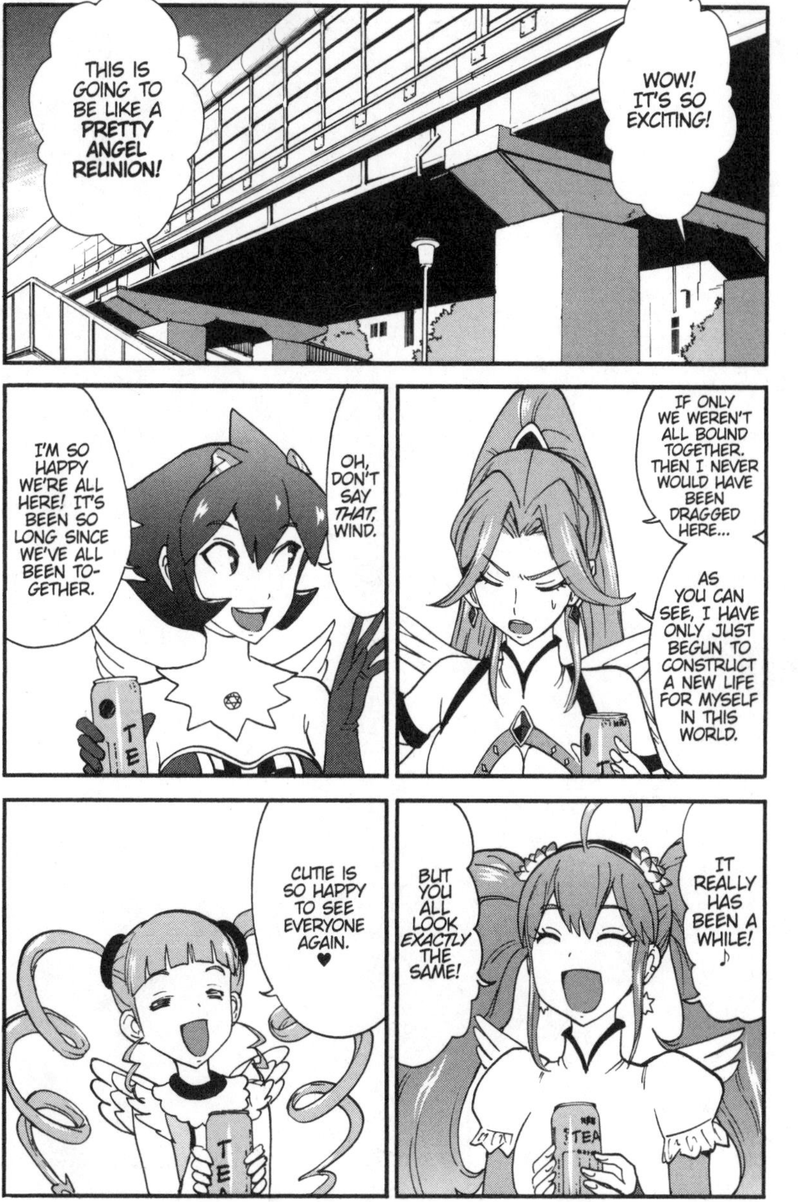
WOW! IT'S SO EXCITING!
THIS IS GOING TO BE LIKE A PRETTY ANGEL REUNION!
IF ONLY WE WEREN'T ALL BOUND TOGETHER. THEN I NEVER WOULD HAVE BEEN DRAGGED HERE...
AS YOU CAN SEE, I HAVE ONLY JUST BEGUN TO CONSTRUCT A NEW LIFE FOR MYSELF IN THIS WORLD.
OH, DON'T SAY *THAT*, WIND.
I'M SO HAPPY WE'RE ALL HERE! IT'S BEEN SO LONG SINCE WE'VE ALL BEEN TO-GETHER.
IT REALLY HAS BEEN A WHILE! ♪
BUT YOU ALL LOOK *EXACTLY* THE SAME!
CUTIE IS SO HAPPY TO SEE EVERYONE AGAIN. ♥

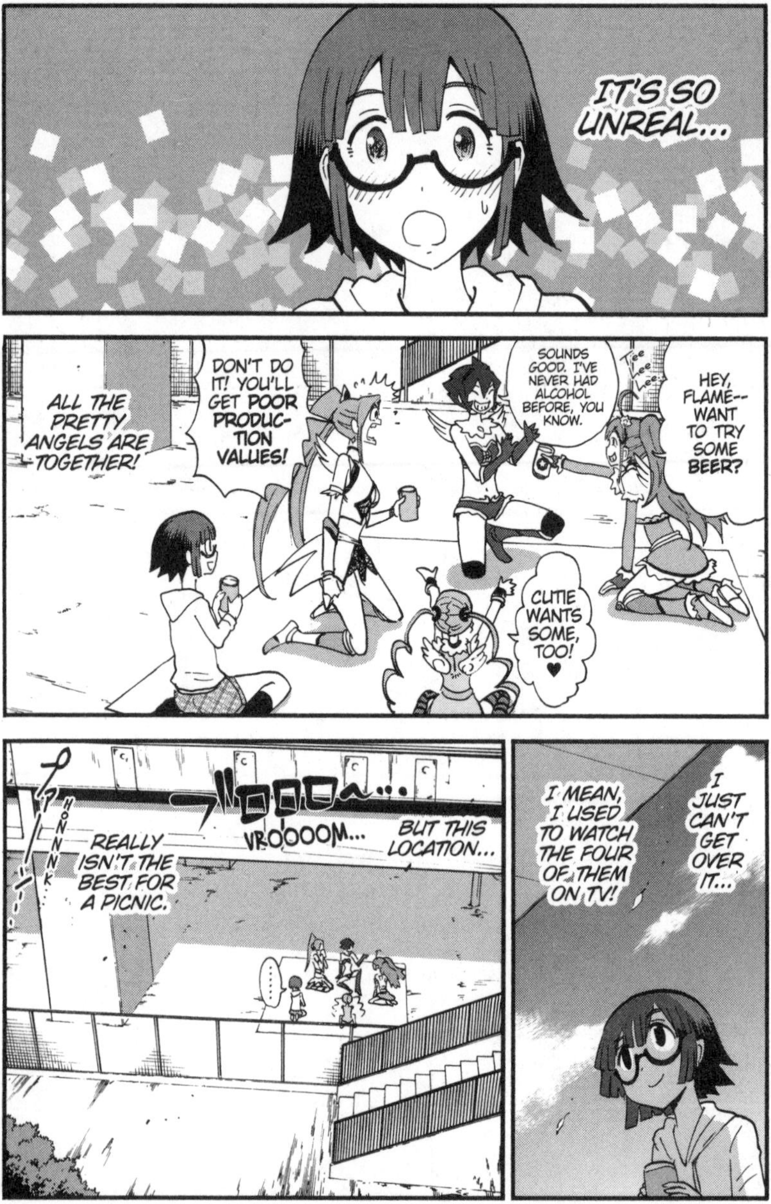
IT'S SO UNREAL...
HEY, FLAME--WANT TO TRY SOME BEER?
Tee Lee Lee
SOUNDS GOOD. I'VE NEVER HAD ALCOHOL BEFORE, YOU KNOW.
DON'T DO IT! YOU'LL GET POOR PRODUCTION VALUES!
ALL THE PRETTY ANGELS ARE TOGETHER!
CUTIE WANTS SOME, TOO! ♥
I JUST CAN'T GET OVER IT...
I MEAN, I USED TO WATCH THE FOUR OF THEM ON TV!
BUT THIS LOCATION...
VROOOOM...
REALLY ISN'T THE BEST FOR A PICNIC.
HONNNK...
......

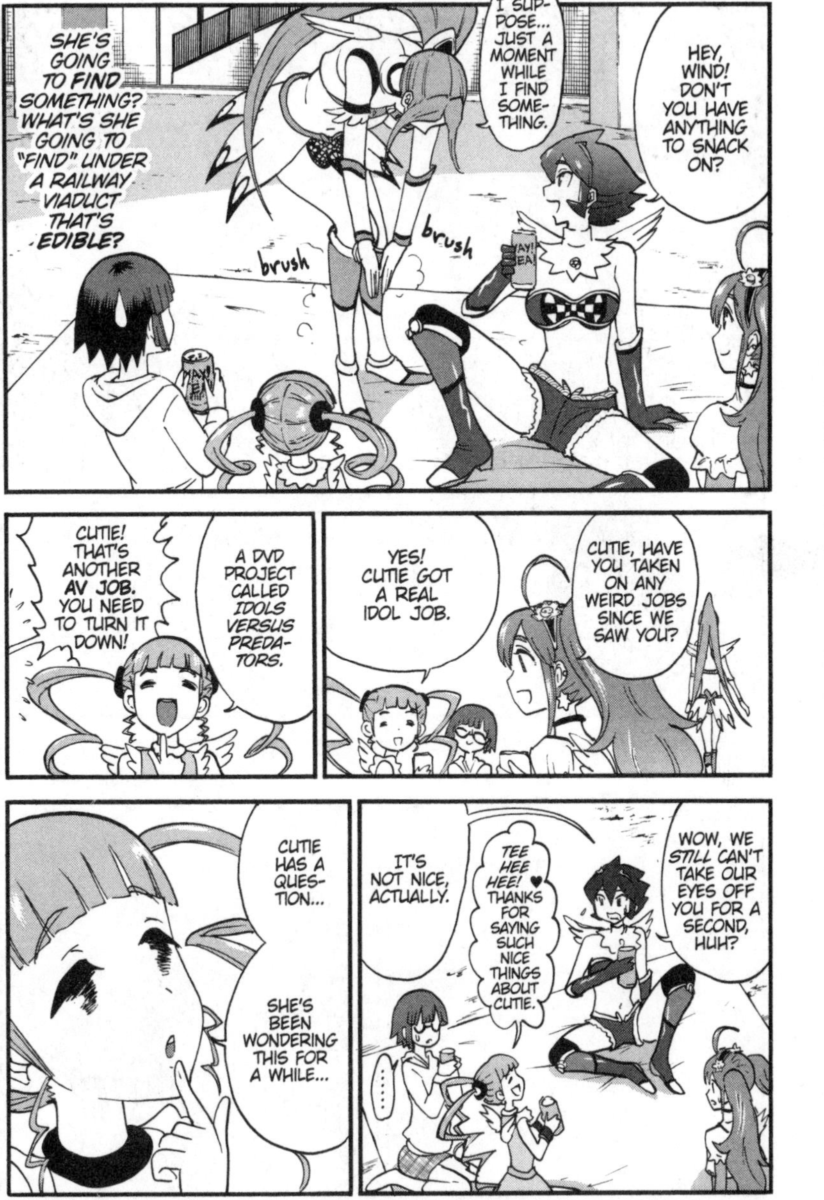
HEY, WIND! DON'T YOU HAVE ANYTHING TO SNACK ON?
I SUPPOSE... JUST A MOMENT WHILE I FIND SOMETHING.
SHE'S GOING TO **FIND** SOMETHING? WHAT'S SHE GOING TO "FIND" UNDER A RAILWAY VIADUCT THAT'S **EDIBLE**?
brush
brush
CUTIE, HAVE YOU TAKEN ON ANY WEIRD JOBS SINCE WE SAW YOU?
YES! CUTIE GOT A REAL IDOL JOB.
A DVD PROJECT CALLED *IDOLS VERSUS PREDATORS*.
CUTIE! THAT'S ANOTHER **AV JOB**. YOU NEED TO TURN IT DOWN!
WOW, WE *STILL* CAN'T TAKE OUR EYES OFF YOU FOR A SECOND, HUH?
TEE HEE HEE! ♥ THANKS FOR SAYING SUCH NICE THINGS ABOUT CUTIE.
IT'S NOT NICE, ACTUALLY.
......
CUTIE HAS A QUESTION...
SHE'S BEEN WONDERING THIS FOR A WHILE...

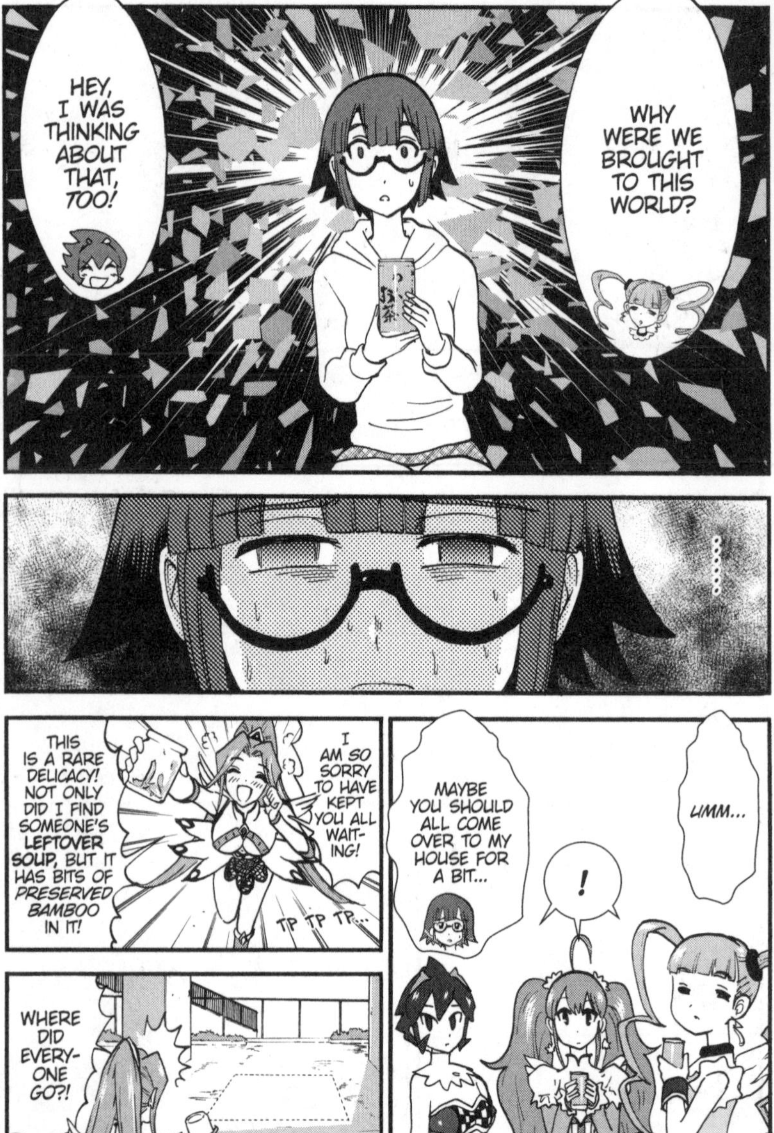
WHY WERE WE BROUGHT TO THIS WORLD?
HEY, I WAS THINKING ABOUT THAT, TOO!
......
UMM...
MAYBE YOU SHOULD ALL COME OVER TO MY HOUSE FOR A BIT...
!
I AM SO SORRY TO HAVE KEPT YOU ALL WAIT-ING!
THIS IS A RARE DELICACY! NOT ONLY DID I FIND SOMEONE'S LEFTOVER SOUP, BUT IT HAS BITS OF PRESERVED BAMBOO IN IT!
TP TP TP...
WHERE DID EVERY-ONE GO?!

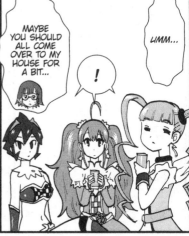

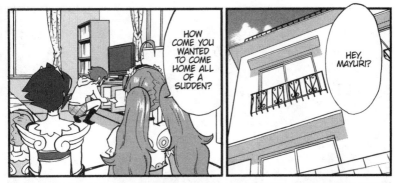

HEY, MAYURI?

HOW COME YOU WANTED TO COME HOME ALL OF A SUDDEN?

THERE'S SOME-THING I HAVE TO SAY...

TO ALL OF YOU.

THIS IS MY ANIME FIGURE COLLECTION-- BUT LOOK...!

MY NEVER-RELEASED-TO-THE-PUBLIC PRETTY ANGEL FIGURES ARE MISSING.

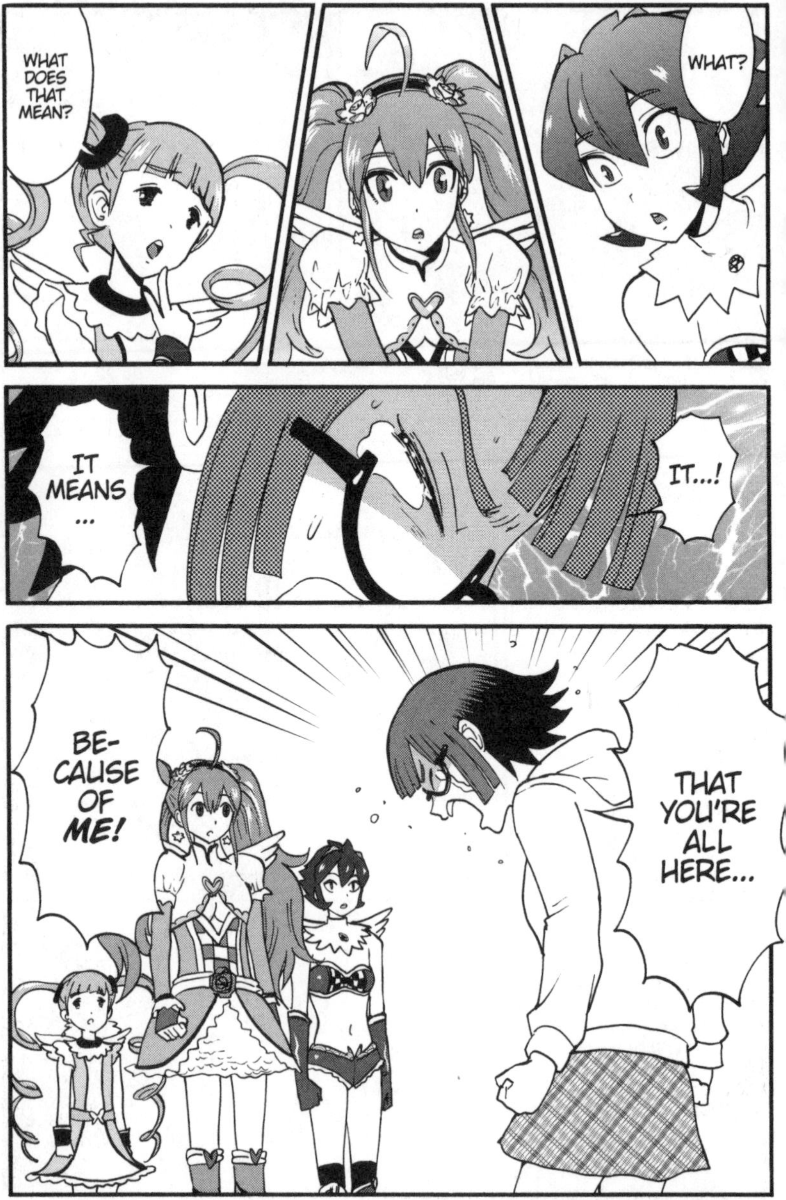
WHAT?
WHAT DOES THAT MEAN?
IT...!
IT MEANS...
THAT YOU'RE ALL HERE...
BE-CAUSE OF *ME!*

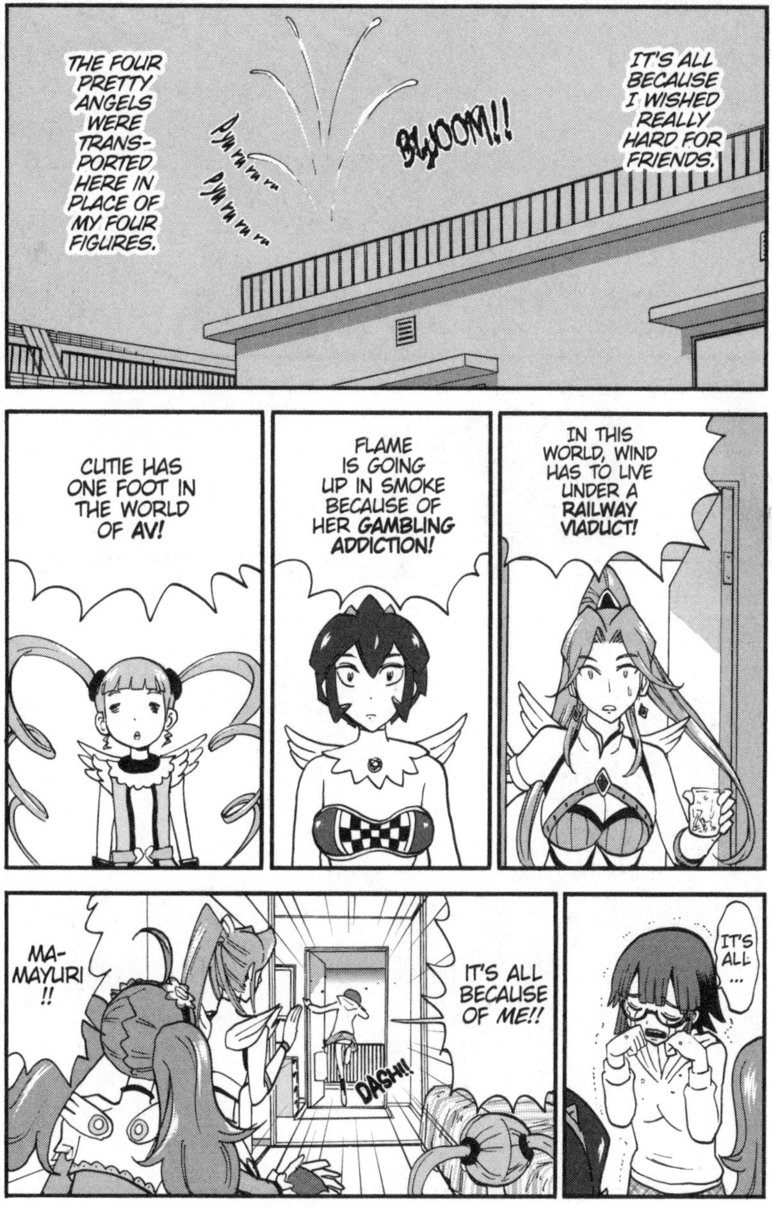
IT'S ALL BECAUSE I WISHED REALLY HARD FOR FRIENDS.
BLOOM!!
Pyu ru ru ru
Pyu ru ru ru
THE FOUR PRETTY ANGELS WERE TRANS-PORTED HERE IN PLACE OF MY FOUR FIGURES.
IN THIS WORLD, WIND HAS TO LIVE UNDER A **RAILWAY VIADUCT!**
FLAME IS GOING UP IN SMOKE BECAUSE OF HER **GAMBLING ADDICTION!**
CUTIE HAS ONE FOOT IN THE WORLD OF **AV!**
IT'S ALL ...
IT'S ALL BECAUSE OF ME!!
DASH!!
MA-MAYURI!!

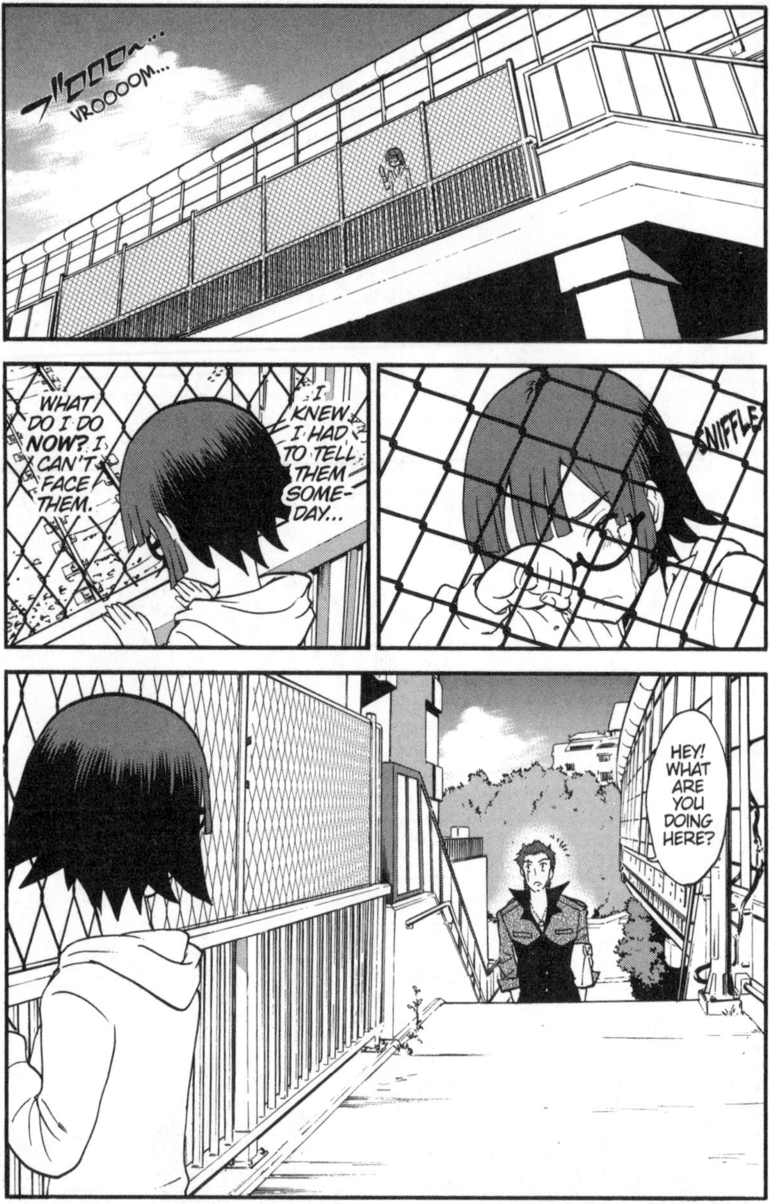
ブロロロ〜...
VROOOOM...
SNIFFLE
I KNEW I HAD TO TELL THEM SOME-DAY...
WHAT DO I DO NOW? I CAN'T FACE THEM.
HEY! WHAT ARE YOU DOING HERE?

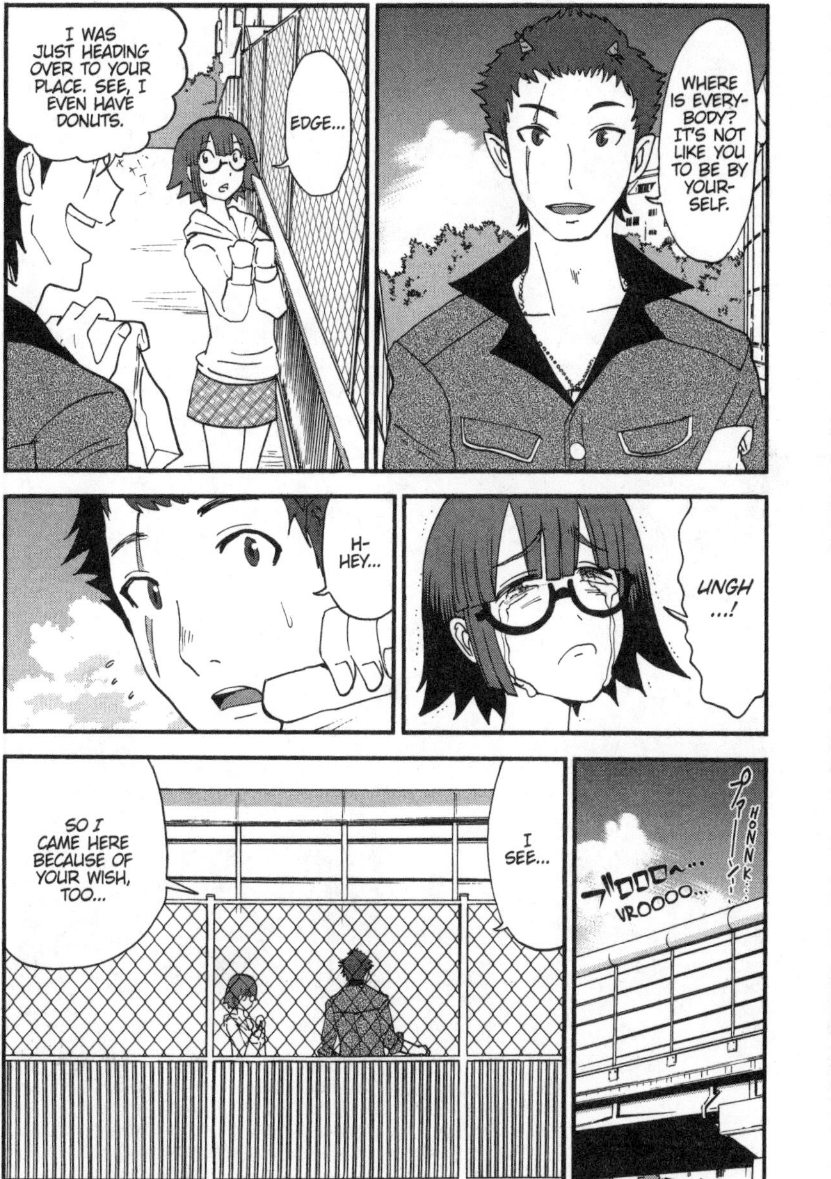
WHERE IS EVERYBODY? IT'S NOT LIKE YOU TO BE BY YOURSELF.
EDGE...
I WAS JUST HEADING OVER TO YOUR PLACE. SEE, I EVEN HAVE DONUTS.
UNGH ...!
H-HEY...
HONNK...
VROOOO...
I SEE...
SO I CAME HERE BECAUSE OF YOUR WISH, TOO...

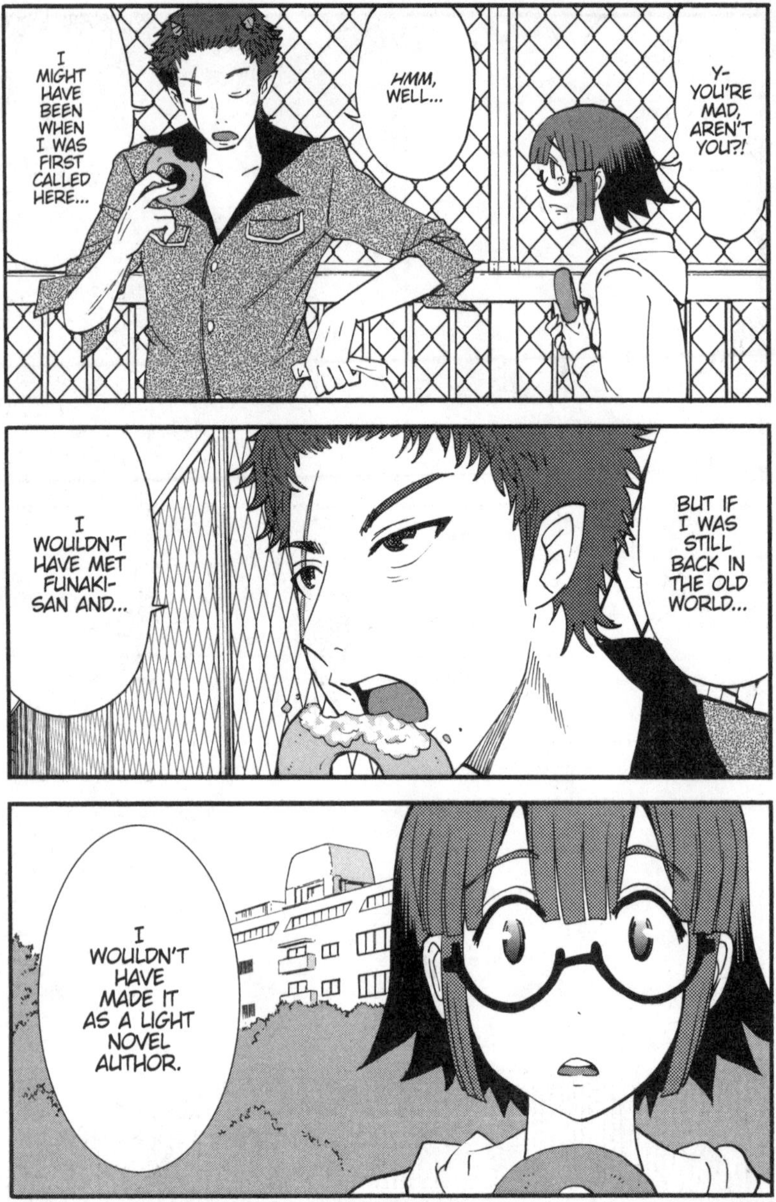
Y- YOU'RE MAD, AREN'T YOU?!
HMM, WELL...
I MIGHT HAVE BEEN WHEN I WAS FIRST CALLED HERE...
BUT IF I WAS STILL BACK IN THE OLD WORLD...
I WOULDN'T HAVE MET FUNAKI-SAN AND...
I WOULDN'T HAVE MADE IT AS A LIGHT NOVEL AUTHOR.

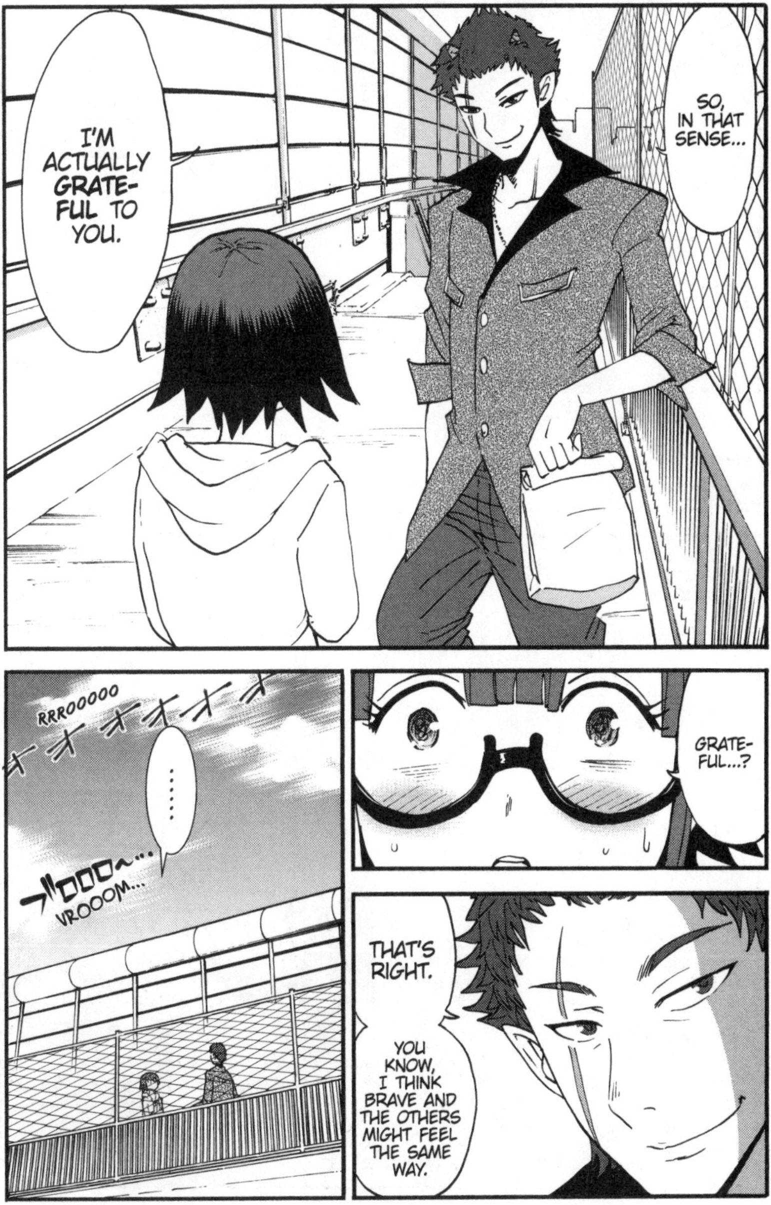
SO, IN THAT SENSE...
I'M ACTUALLY GRATE-FUL TO YOU.
GRATE-FUL...?
THAT'S RIGHT.
YOU KNOW, I THINK BRAVE AND THE OTHERS MIGHT FEEL THE SAME WAY.
RRROOOOO
......
ブロロロ~...
VROOOM...

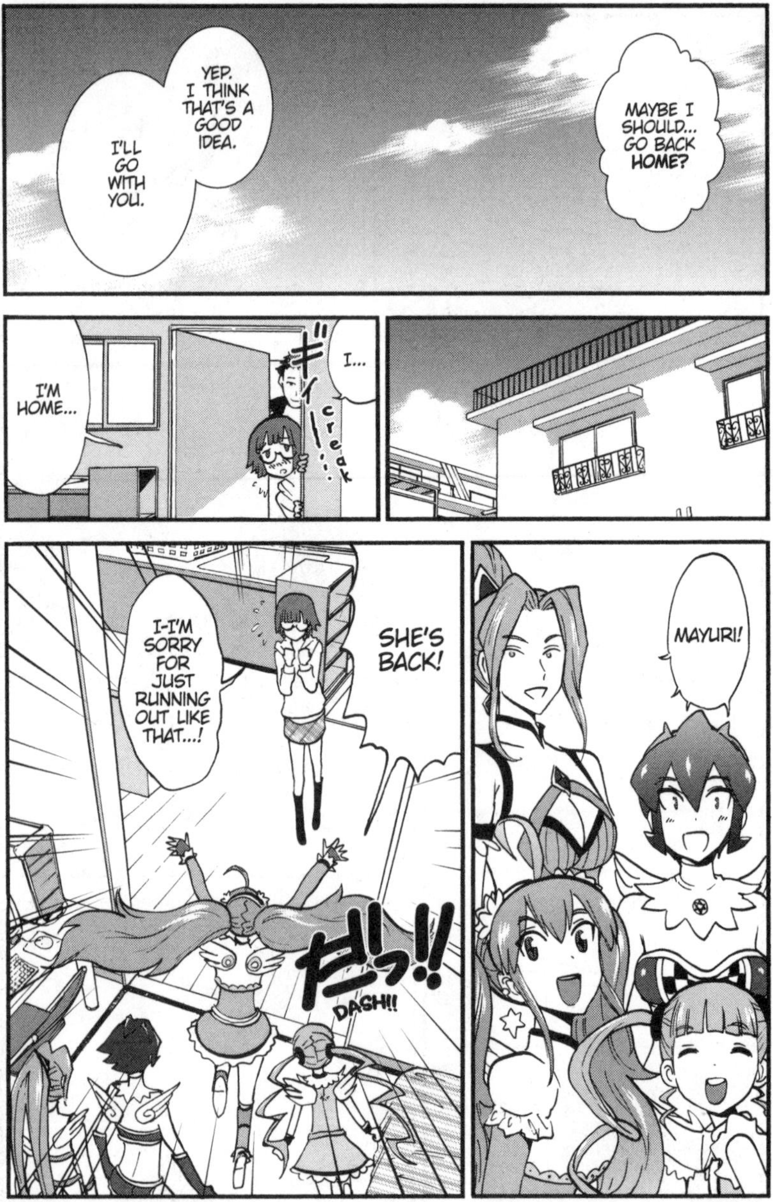
MAYBE I SHOULD... GO BACK HOME?
YEP. I THINK THAT'S A GOOD IDEA.
I'LL GO WITH YOU.
I...
creak
I'M HOME...
MAYURI!
SHE'S BACK!
I-I'M SORRY FOR JUST RUNNING OUT LIKE THAT...!
だっ!!
DASH!!

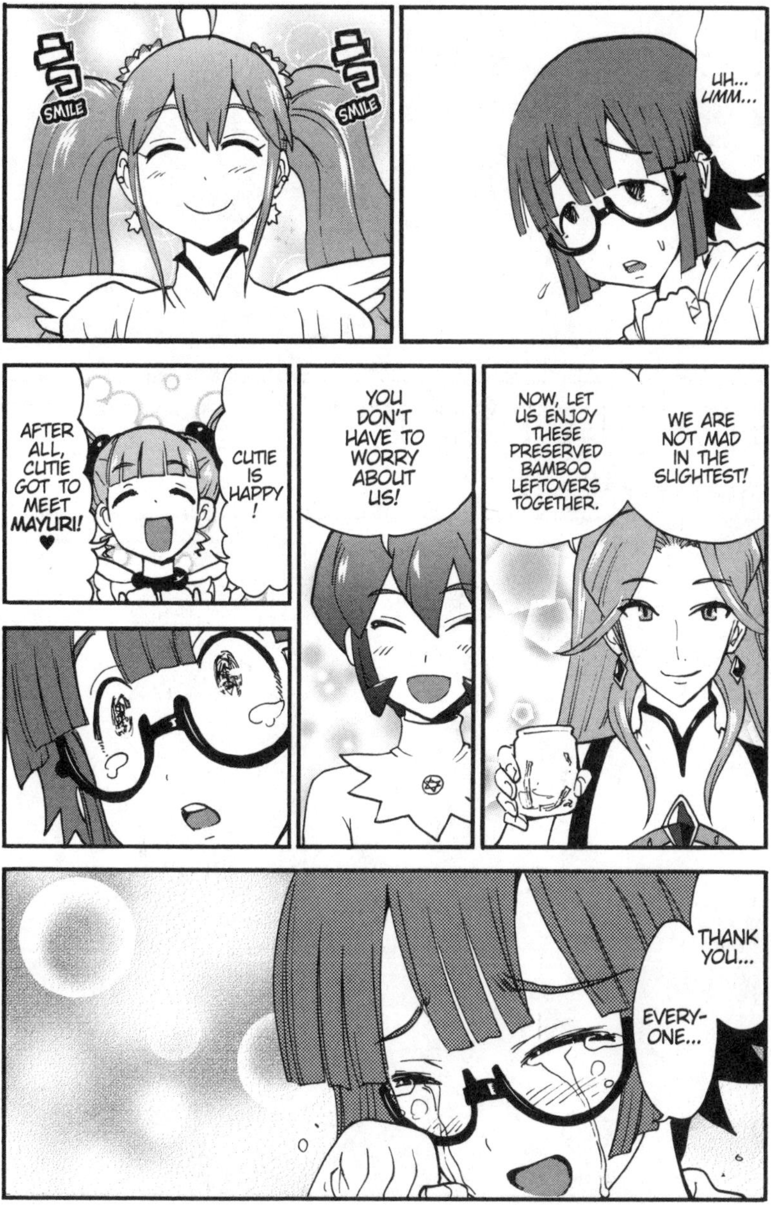
UH... UMM...
SMILE
SMILE
WE ARE NOT MAD IN THE SLIGHTEST!
NOW, LET US ENJOY THESE PRESERVED BAMBOO LEFTOVERS TOGETHER.
YOU DON'T HAVE TO WORRY ABOUT US!
CUTIE IS HAPPY!
AFTER ALL, CUTIE GOT TO MEET MAYURI! ♥
THANK YOU...
EVERY-ONE...

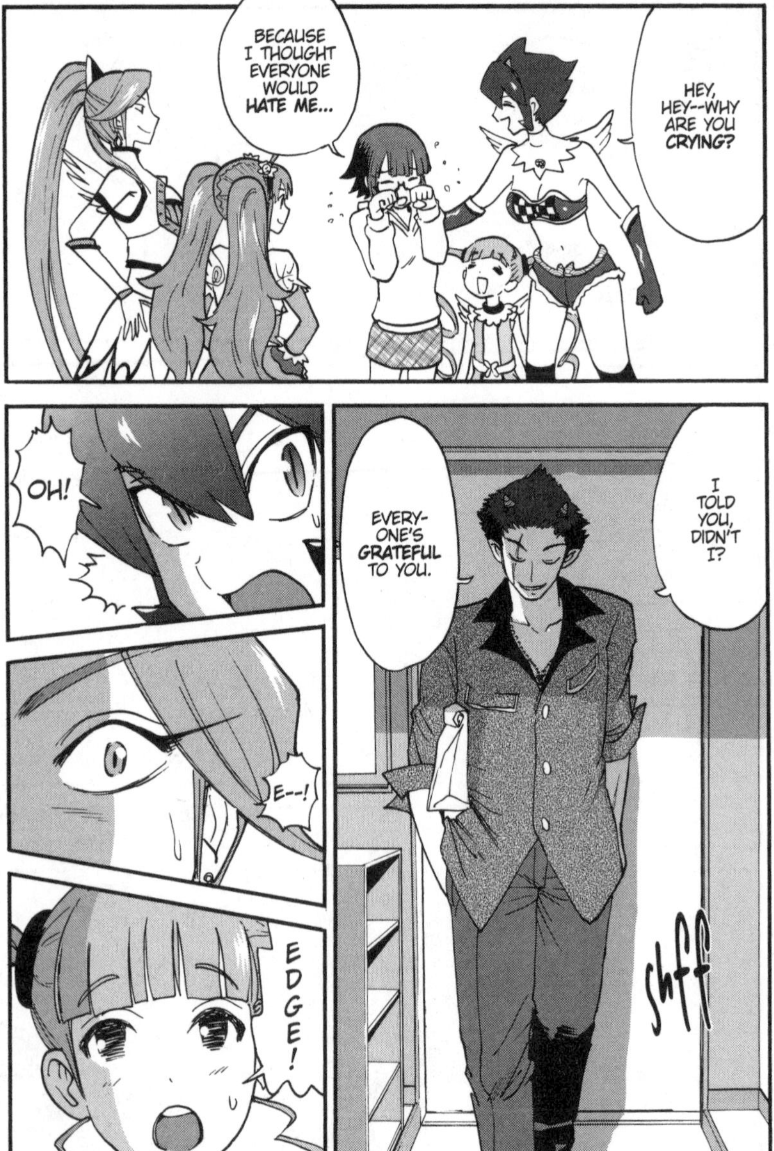
HEY, HEY--WHY ARE YOU CRYING?
BECAUSE I THOUGHT EVERYONE WOULD HATE ME...
I TOLD YOU, DIDN'T I?
EVERY-ONE'S GRATEFUL TO YOU.
shff
OH!
E--!
EDGE!

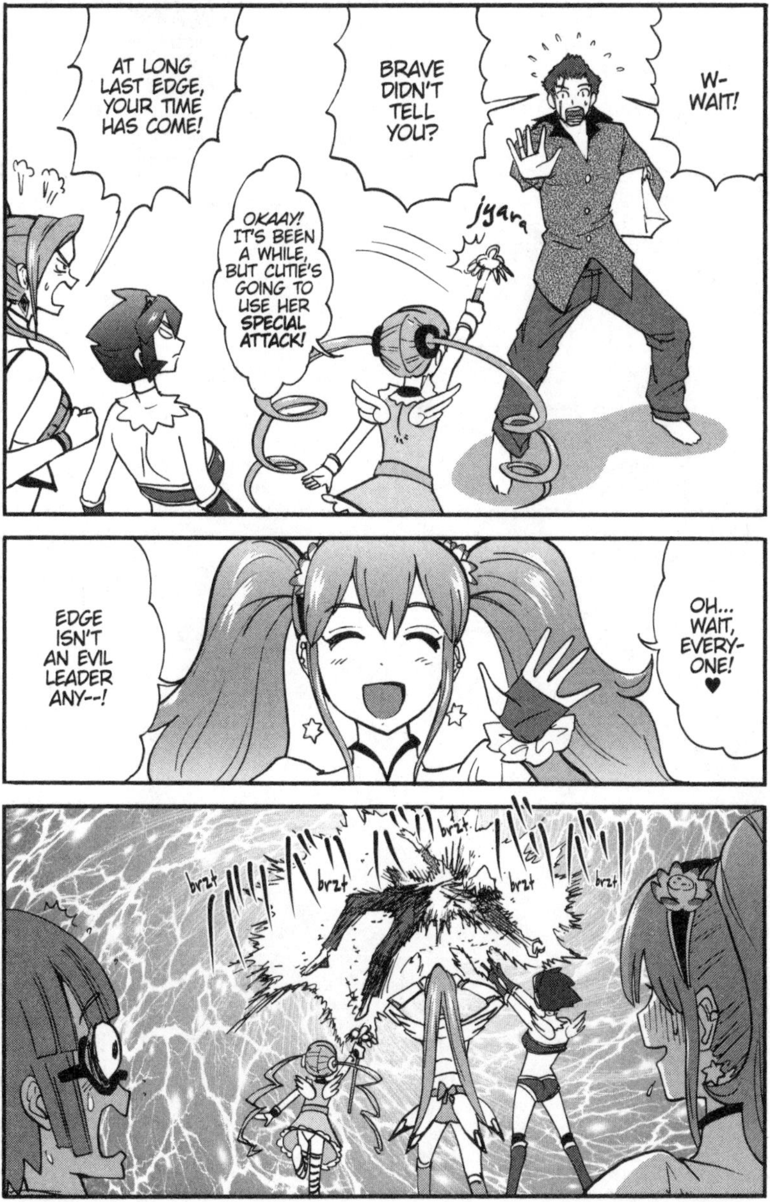
W-
WAIT!
BRAVE DIDN'T TELL YOU?
AT LONG LAST EDGE, YOUR TIME HAS COME!
jyara
OKAAY! IT'S BEEN A WHILE, BUT CUTIE'S GOING TO USE HER SPECIAL ATTACK!
OH... WAIT, EVERY-ONE! ♥
EDGE ISN'T AN EVIL LEADER ANY--!
brzt
brzt
brzt
brzt
brzt

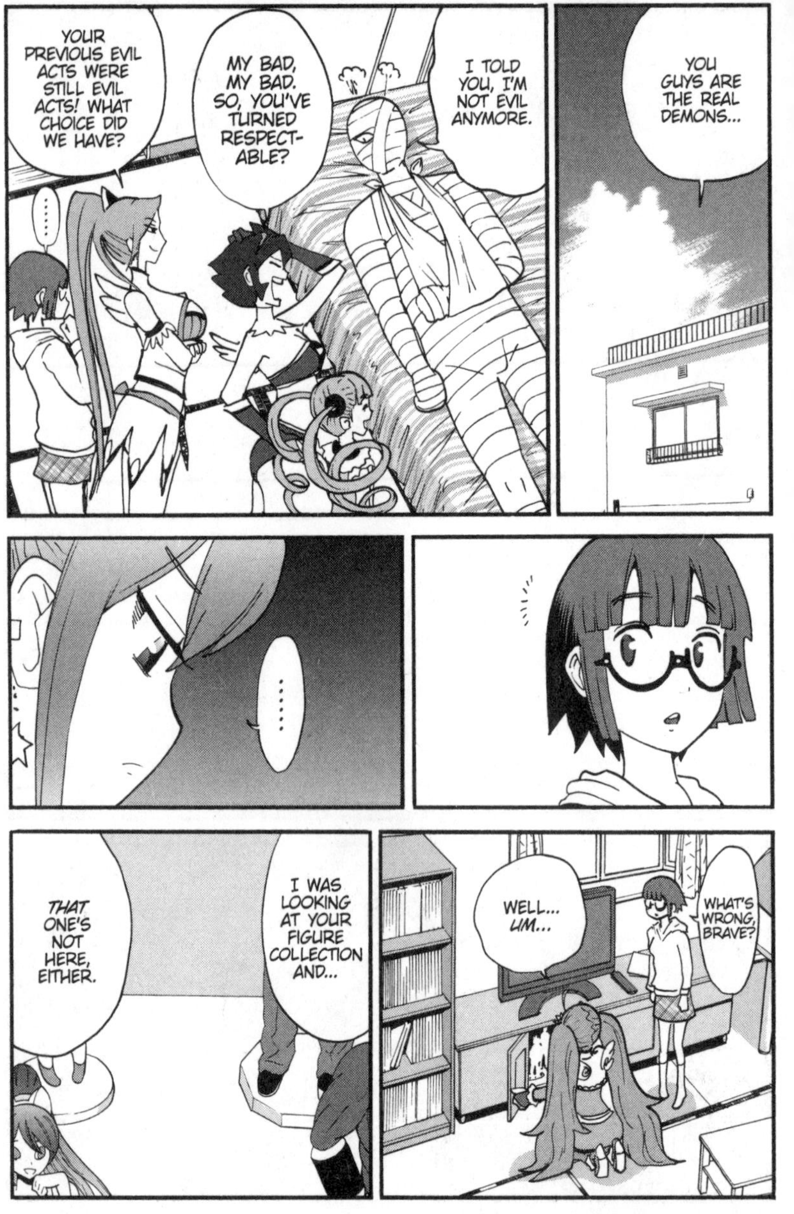
YOU GUYS ARE THE REAL DEMONS...
I TOLD YOU, I'M NOT EVIL ANYMORE.
MY BAD, MY BAD. SO, YOU'VE TURNED RESPECTABLE?
YOUR PREVIOUS EVIL ACTS WERE STILL EVIL ACTS! WHAT CHOICE DID WE HAVE?
......
......
WHAT'S WRONG, BRAVE?
WELL... *UM*...
I WAS LOOKING AT YOUR FIGURE COLLECTION AND...
THAT ONE'S NOT HERE, EITHER.

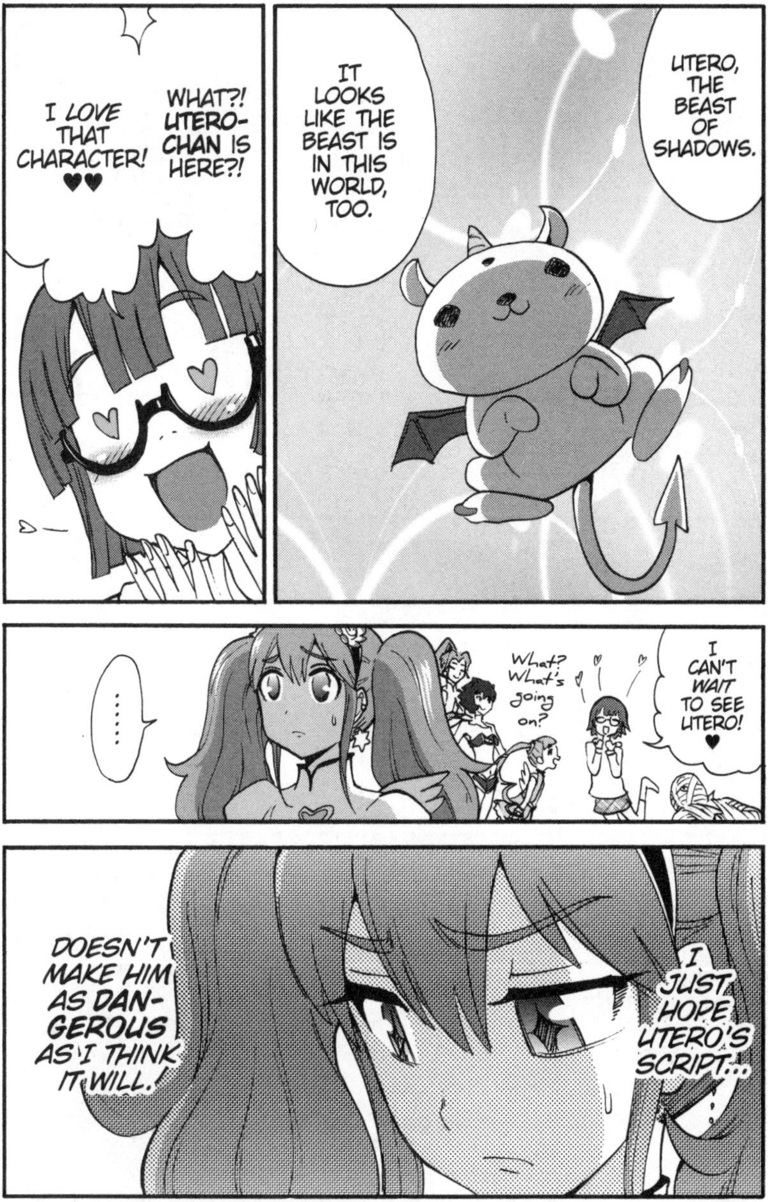
UTERO, THE BEAST OF SHADOWS.
IT LOOKS LIKE THE BEAST IS IN THIS WORLD, TOO.
WHAT?! UTERO-CHAN IS HERE?!
I LOVE THAT CHARACTER! ♥♥
I CAN'T WAIT TO SEE UTERO! ♥
What? What's going on?
......
I JUST HOPE UTERO'S SCRIPT...
DOESN'T MAKE HIM AS DAN-GEROUS AS I THINK IT WILL.

Chapter 17: The Dreadful Utero

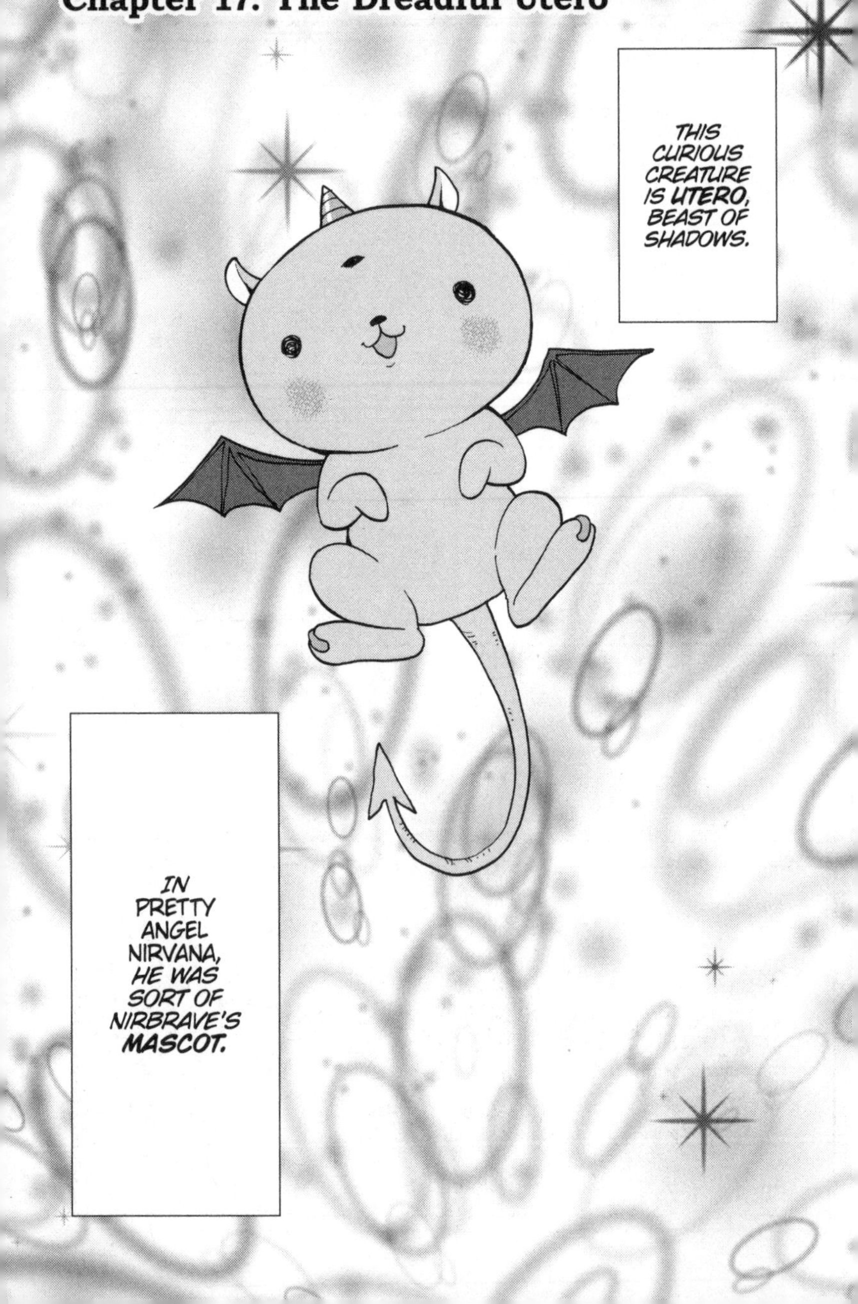
THIS CURIOUS CREATURE IS **UTERO**, BEAST OF SHADOWS.
IN PRETTY ANGEL NIRVANA, *HE WAS SORT OF NIRBRAVE'S* **MASCOT.**

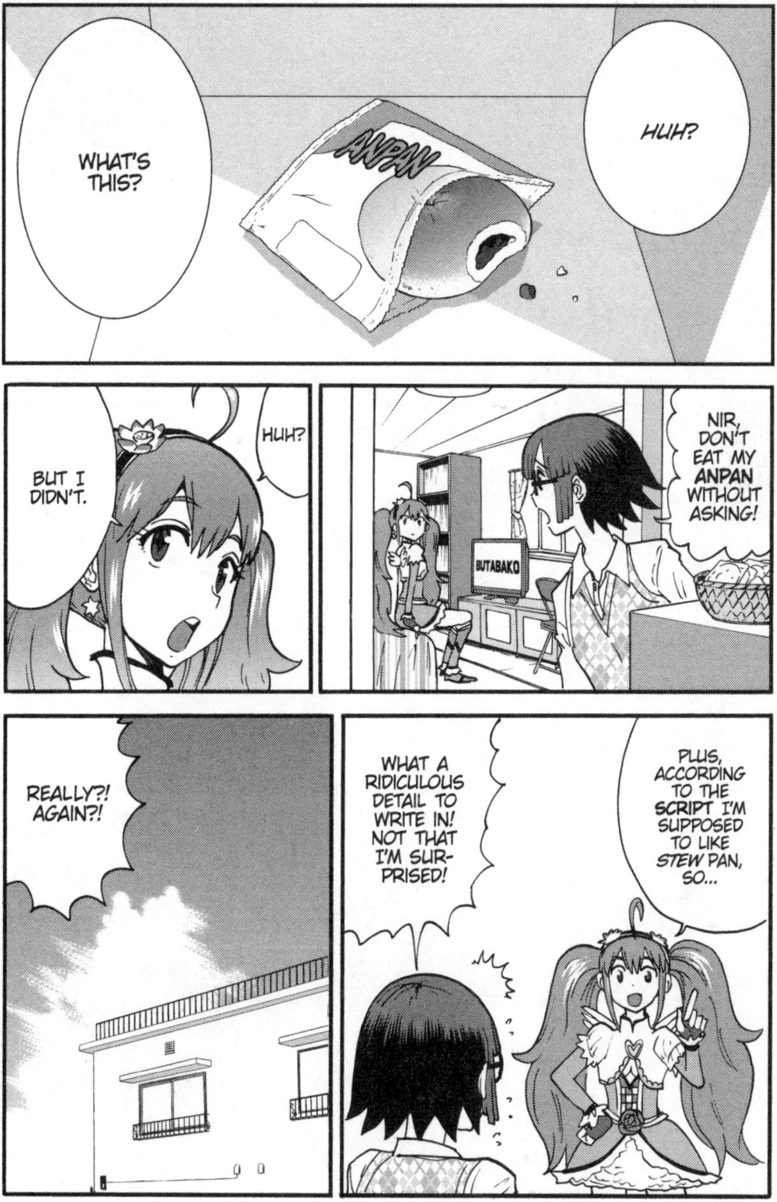
HUH?
WHAT'S THIS?
ANPAN
NIR, DON'T EAT MY ANPAN WITHOUT ASKING!
BUTABAKO
HUH?
BUT I DIDN'T.
PLUS, ACCORDING TO THE SCRIPT I'M SUPPOSED TO LIKE STEW PAN, SO...
WHAT A RIDICULOUS DETAIL TO WRITE IN! NOT THAT I'M SURPRISED!
REALLY?! AGAIN?!

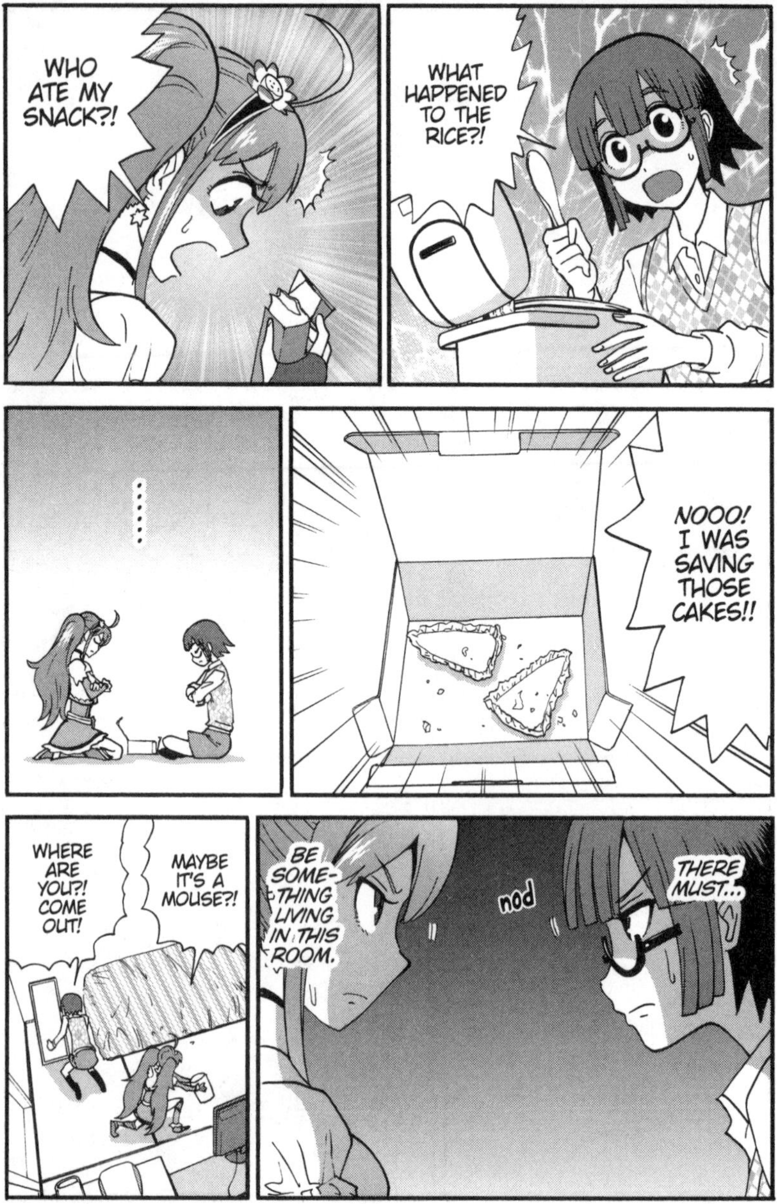
WHAT HAPPENED TO THE RICE?!
WHO ATE MY SNACK?!
NOOO! I WAS SAVING THOSE CAKES!!
......
THERE MUST...
nod
BE SOME-THING LIVING IN THIS ROOM.
MAYBE IT'S A MOUSE?!
WHERE ARE YOU?! COME OUT!

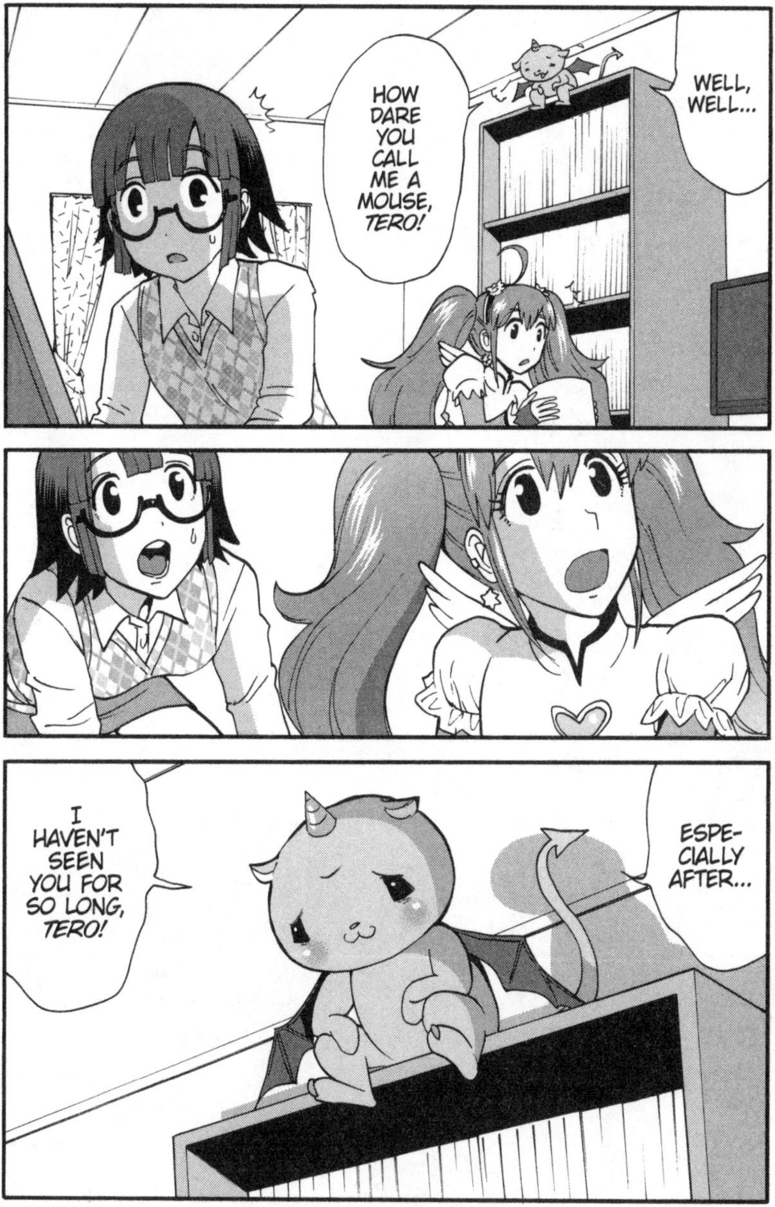
WELL, WELL...
HOW DARE YOU CALL ME A MOUSE, TERO!
ESPE-CIALLY AFTER...
I HAVEN'T SEEN YOU FOR SO LONG, TERO!

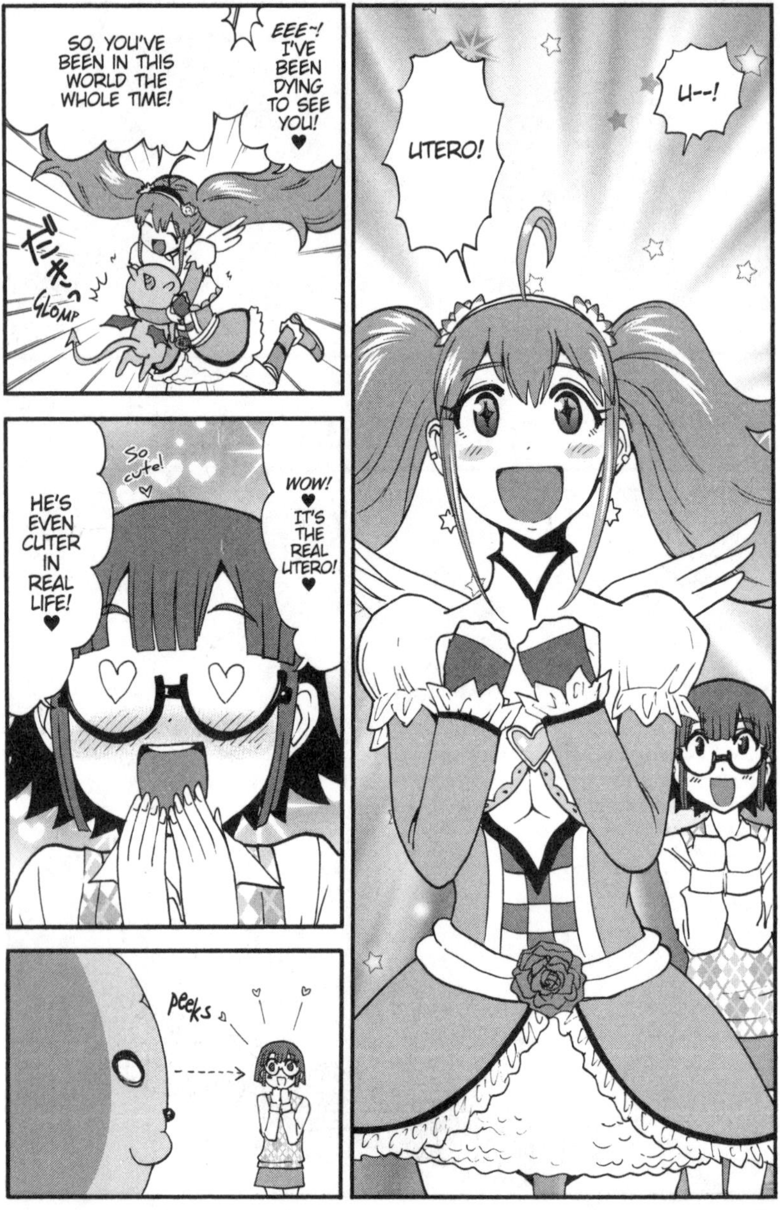
U--!
UTERO!
EEE~! I'VE BEEN DYING TO SEE YOU! ♥
SO, YOU'VE BEEN IN THIS WORLD THE WHOLE TIME!
GLOMP
WOW! ♥ IT'S THE REAL UTERO! ♥
So cute! ♥
HE'S EVEN CUTER IN REAL LIFE! ♥
peeks

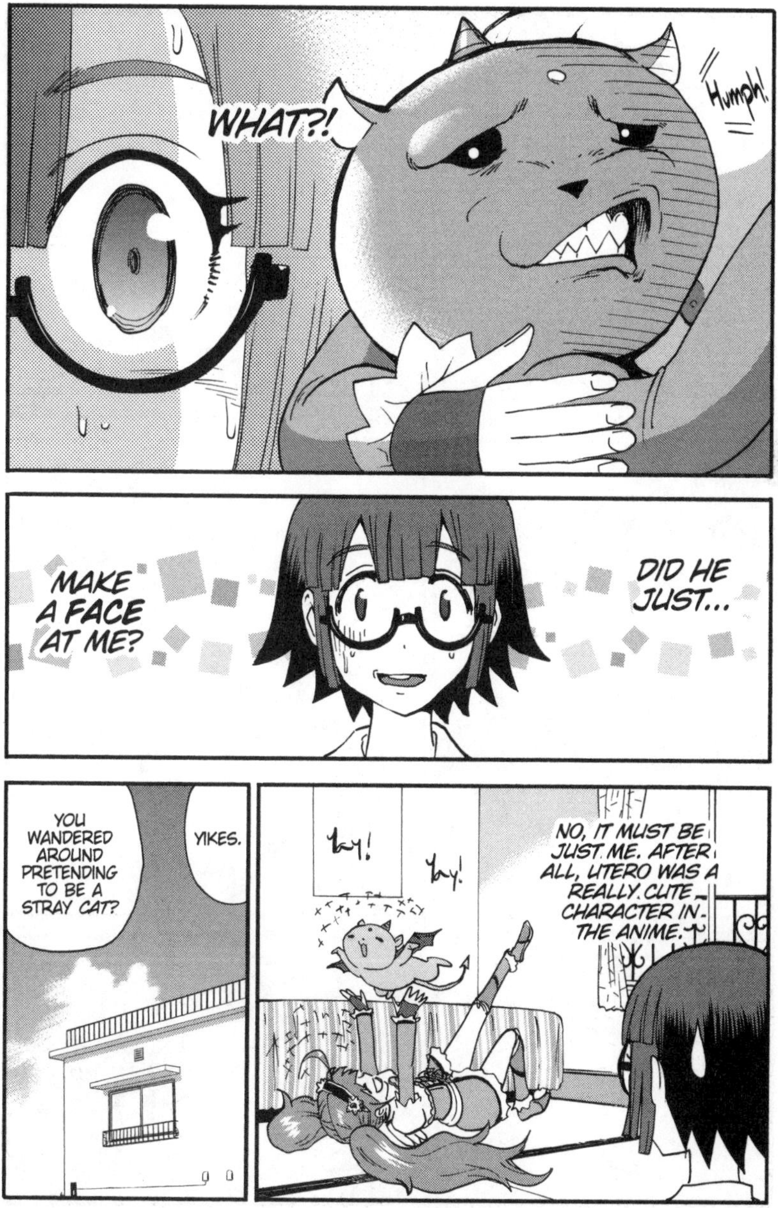
Humph!
WHAT?!
DID HE JUST...
MAKE A FACE AT ME?
NO, IT MUST BE JUST ME. AFTER ALL, UTERO WAS A REALLY CUTE CHARACTER IN THE ANIME.
Yay!
Yay!
YIKES.
YOU WANDERED AROUND PRETENDING TO BE A STRAY CAT?

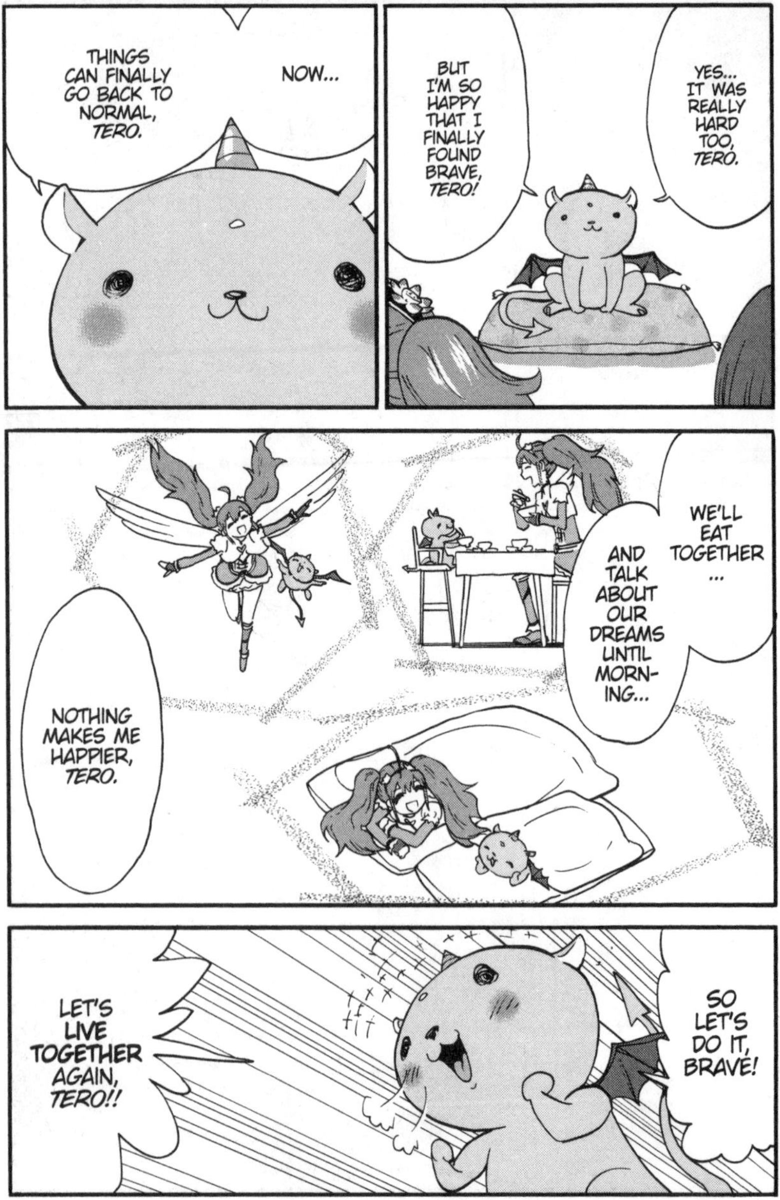
YES... IT WAS REALLY HARD TOO, *TERO.*
BUT I'M SO HAPPY THAT I FINALLY FOUND BRAVE, *TERO!*
NOW...
THINGS CAN FINALLY GO BACK TO NORMAL, *TERO.*
WE'LL EAT TOGETHER ...
AND TALK ABOUT OUR DREAMS UNTIL MORN-ING...
NOTHING MAKES ME HAPPIER, *TERO.*
SO LET'S DO IT, BRAVE!
LET'S LIVE TOGETHER AGAIN, *TERO!!*

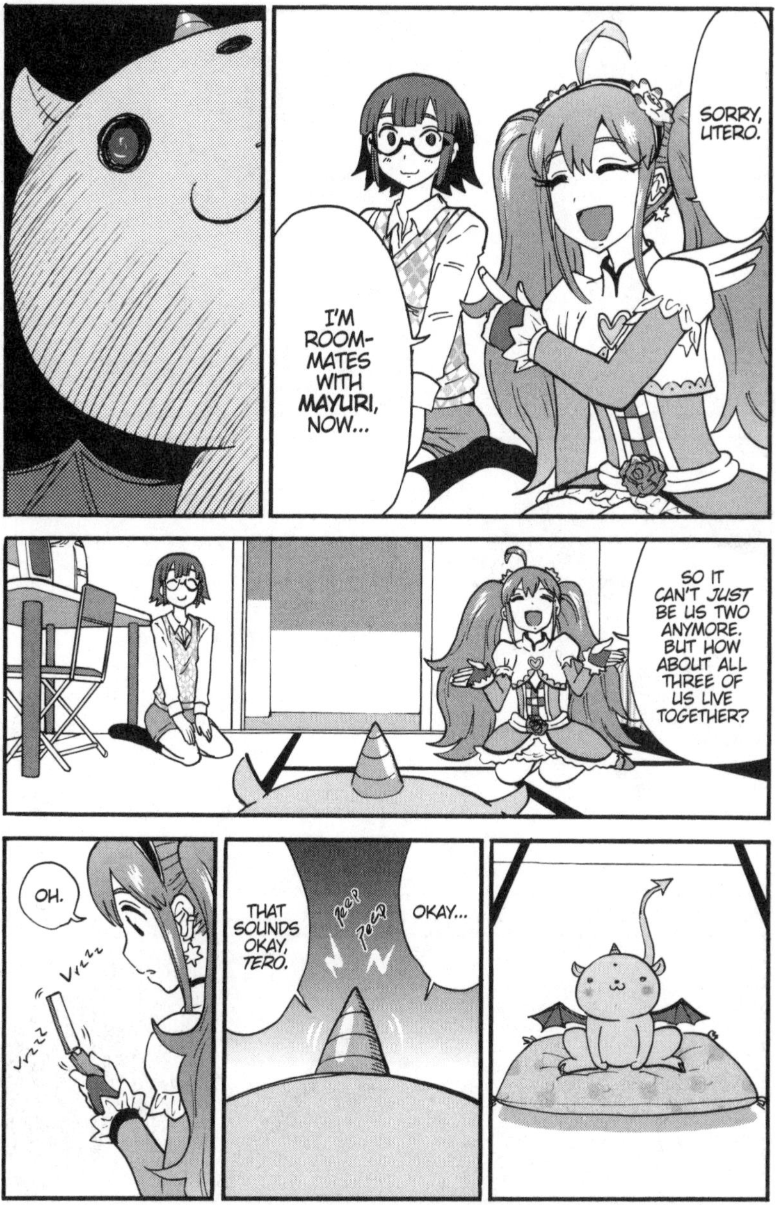
SORRY, UTERO.
I'M ROOMMATES WITH MAYURI, NOW...
SO IT CAN'T *JUST* BE US TWO ANYMORE. BUT HOW ABOUT ALL THREE OF US LIVE TOGETHER?
OKAY...
THAT SOUNDS OKAY, TERO.
OH.

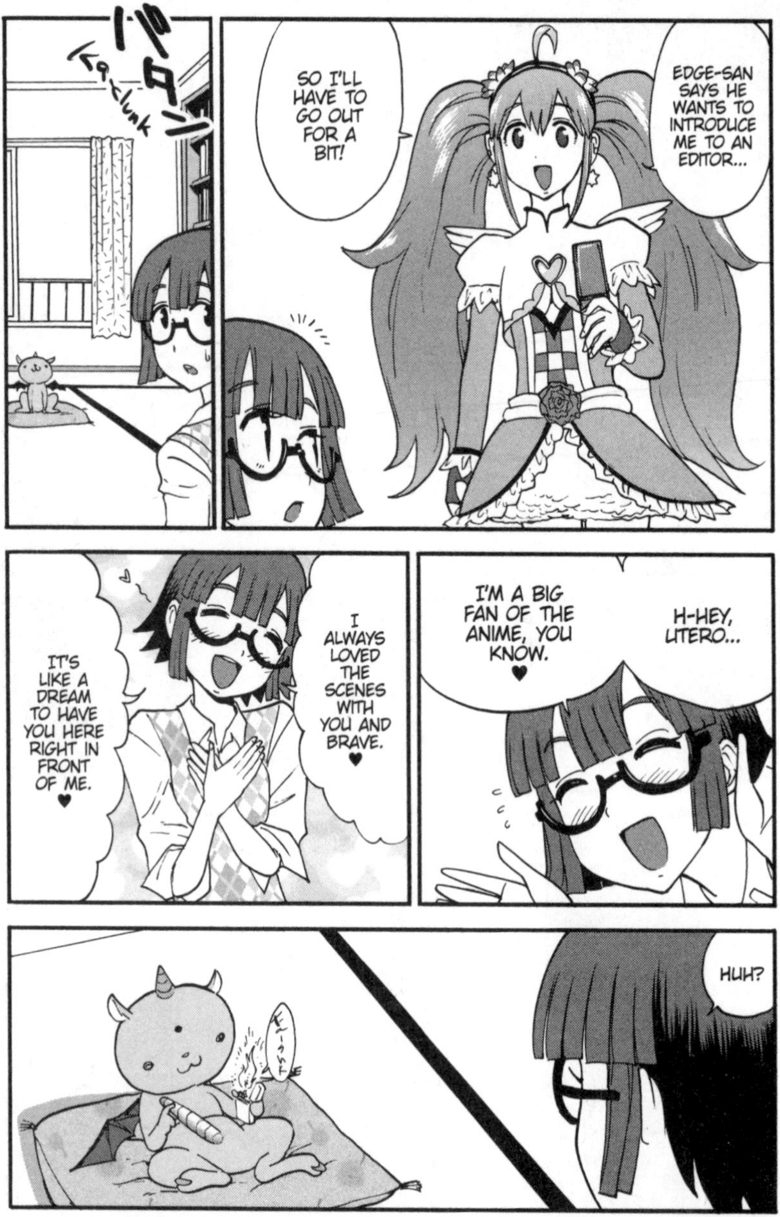
EDGE-SAN SAYS HE WANTS TO INTRODUCE ME TO AN EDITOR...
SO I'LL HAVE TO GO OUT FOR A BIT!
ka-clunk
H-HEY, UTERO...
I'M A BIG FAN OF THE ANIME, YOU KNOW. ♥
I ALWAYS LOVED THE SCENES WITH YOU AND BRAVE. ♥
IT'S LIKE A DREAM TO HAVE YOU HERE RIGHT IN FRONT OF ME. ♥
HUH?

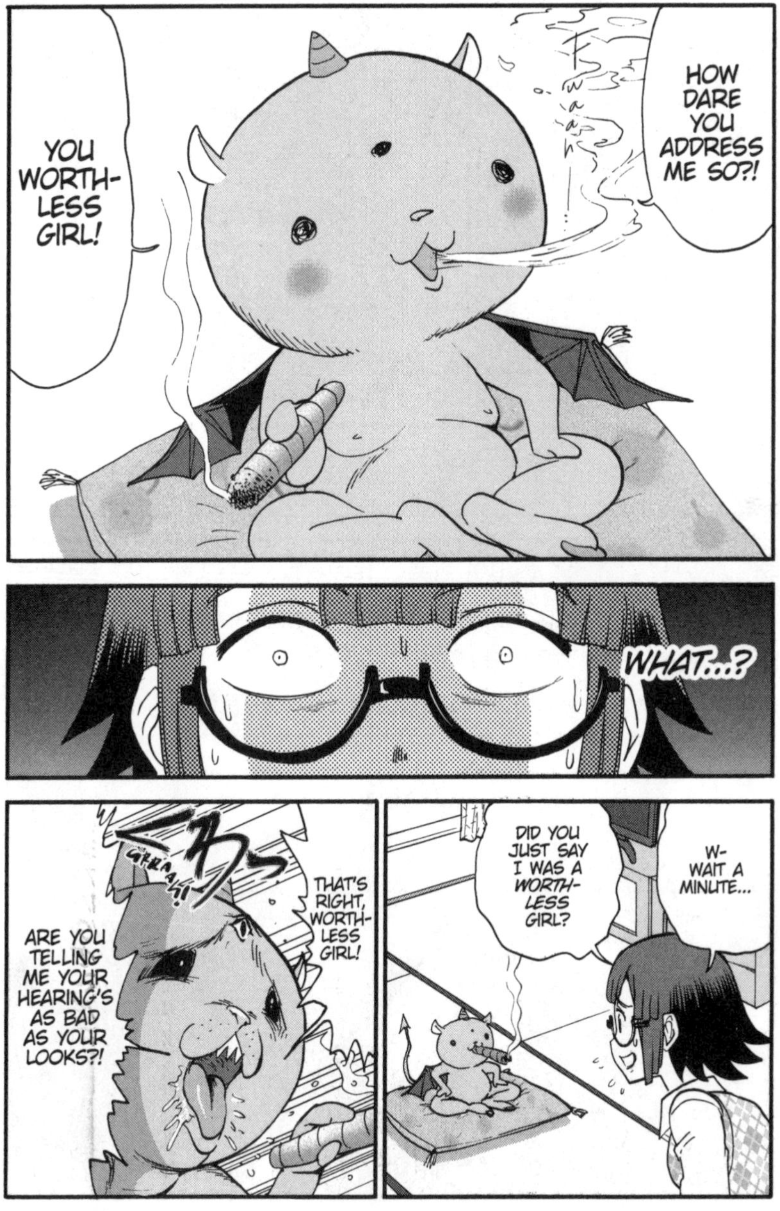
HOW DARE YOU ADDRESS ME SO?!
YOU WORTH-LESS GIRL!
WHAT...?
W-WAIT A MINUTE...
DID YOU JUST SAY I WAS A WORTH-LESS GIRL?
THAT'S RIGHT, WORTH-LESS GIRL!
ARE YOU TELLING ME YOUR HEARING'S AS BAD AS YOUR LOOKS?!

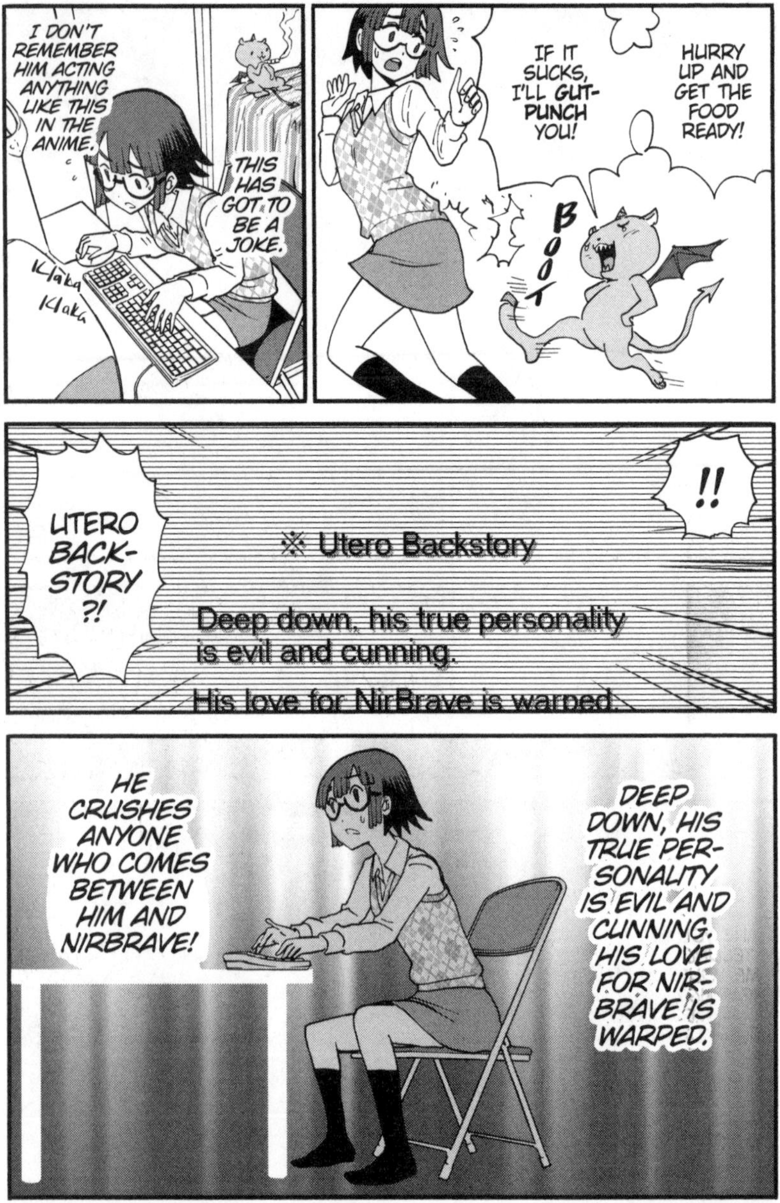
HURRY UP AND GET THE FOOD READY!
IF IT SUCKS, I'LL GUT-PUNCH YOU!
BOOT
I DON'T REMEMBER HIM ACTING ANYTHING LIKE THIS IN THE ANIME.
THIS HAS GOT TO BE A JOKE.
Klaka Klaka
!!
※ Utero Backstory
Deep down, his true personality is evil and cunning.
His love for NirBrave is warped.
UTERO BACK-STORY ?!
DEEP DOWN, HIS TRUE PER-SONALITY IS EVIL AND CUNNING. HIS LOVE FOR NIR-BRAVE IS WARPED.
HE CRUSHES ANYONE WHO COMES BETWEEN HIM AND NIRBRAVE!

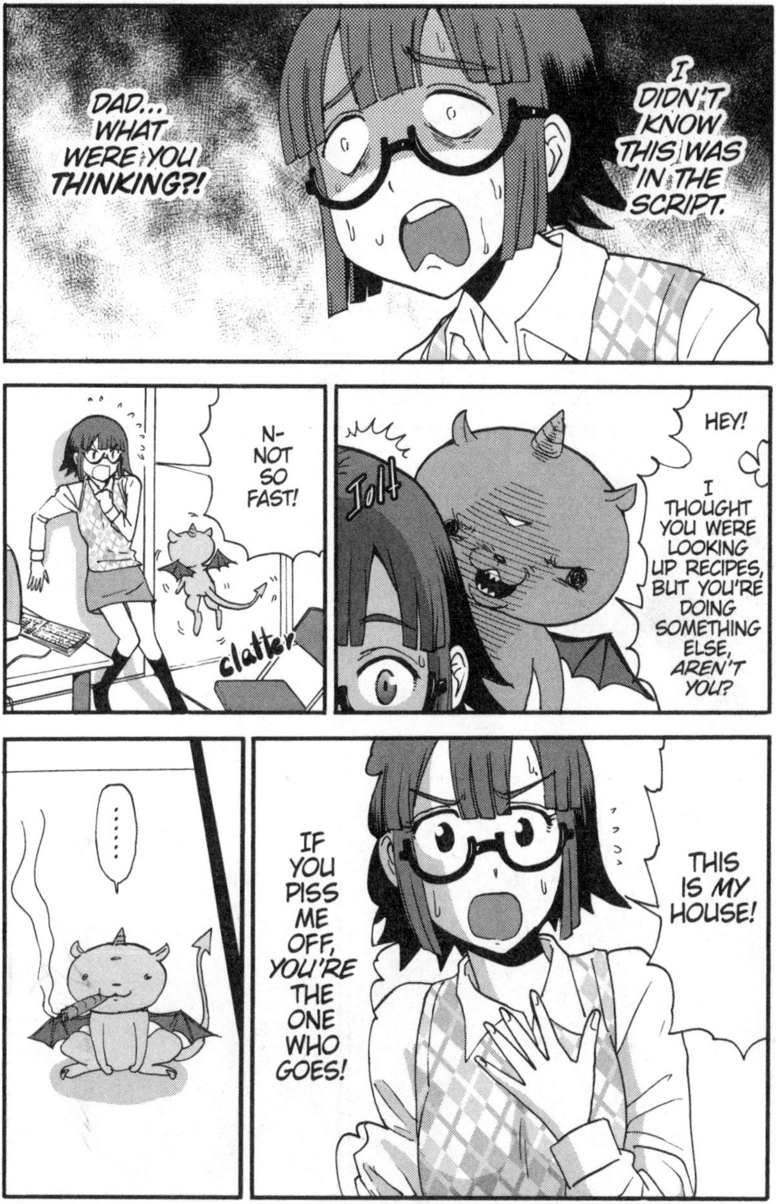
I DIDN'T KNOW THIS WAS IN THE SCRIPT.
DAD... WHAT WERE YOU THINKING?!
HEY!
I THOUGHT YOU WERE LOOKING UP RECIPES, BUT YOU'RE DOING SOMETHING ELSE, *AREN'T* YOU?
Jolt
N-NOT SO FAST!
clatter
THIS IS *MY* HOUSE!
IF YOU PISS ME OFF, *YOU'RE* THE ONE WHO GOES!
......

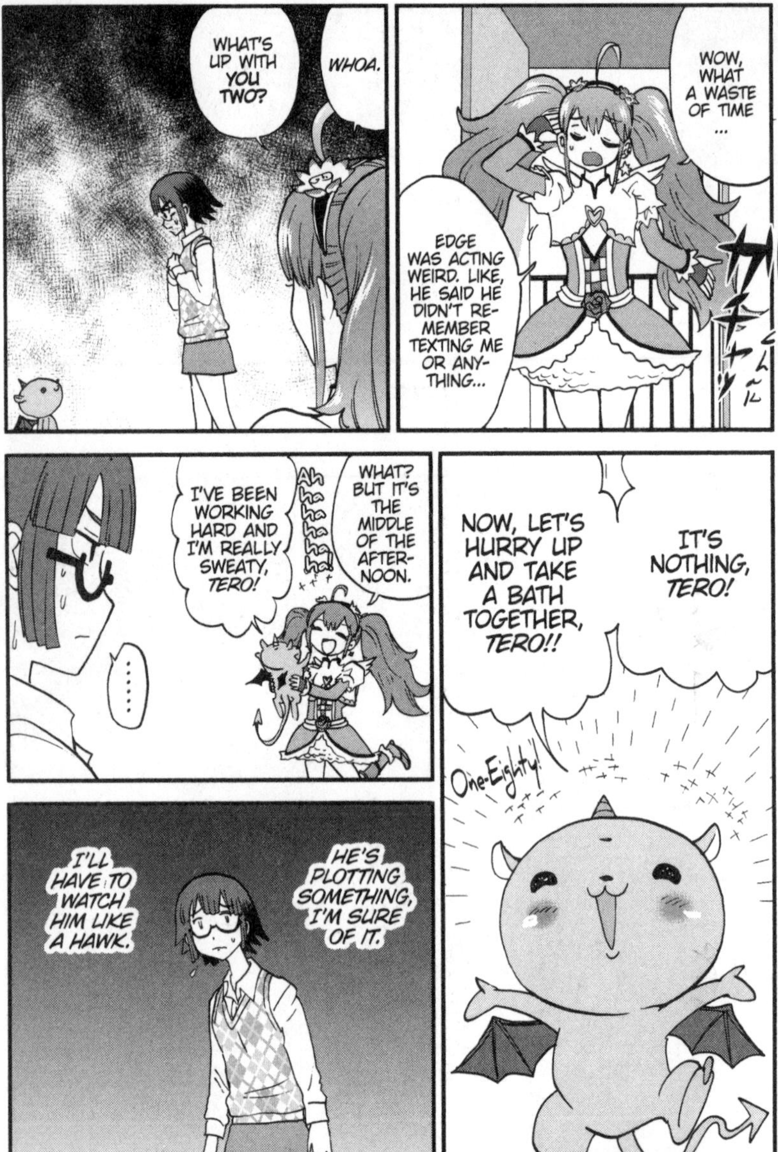
WOW, WHAT A WASTE OF TIME ...
EDGE WAS ACTING WEIRD. LIKE, HE SAID HE DIDN'T RE-MEMBER TEXTING ME OR ANY-THING...
WHOA.
WHAT'S UP WITH YOU TWO?
IT'S NOTHING, TERO!
NOW, LET'S HURRY UP AND TAKE A BATH TOGETHER, TERO!!
One-Eighty!
WHAT? BUT IT'S THE MIDDLE OF THE AFTER-NOON.
Ahahahahaha!
I'VE BEEN WORKING HARD AND I'M REALLY SWEATY, TERO!
......
HE'S PLOTTING SOMETHING, I'M SURE OF IT.
I'LL HAVE TO WATCH HIM LIKE A HAWK.

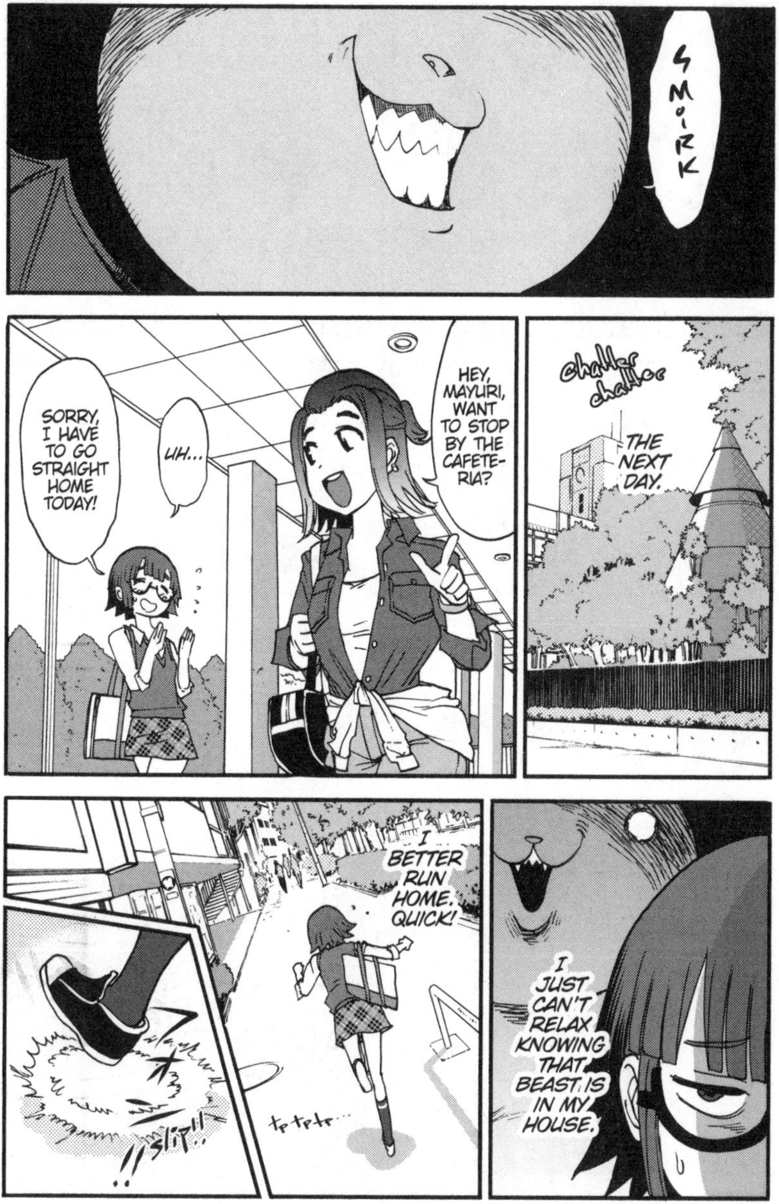
SMIRK
chatter chatter
THE NEXT DAY.
HEY, MAYURI, WANT TO STOP BY THE CAFETERIA?
UH...
SORRY, I HAVE TO GO STRAIGHT HOME TODAY!
I JUST CAN'T RELAX KNOWING THAT BEAST IS IN MY HOUSE.
I BETTER RUN HOME. QUICK!
tp tp tp tp...
slip!!
!!

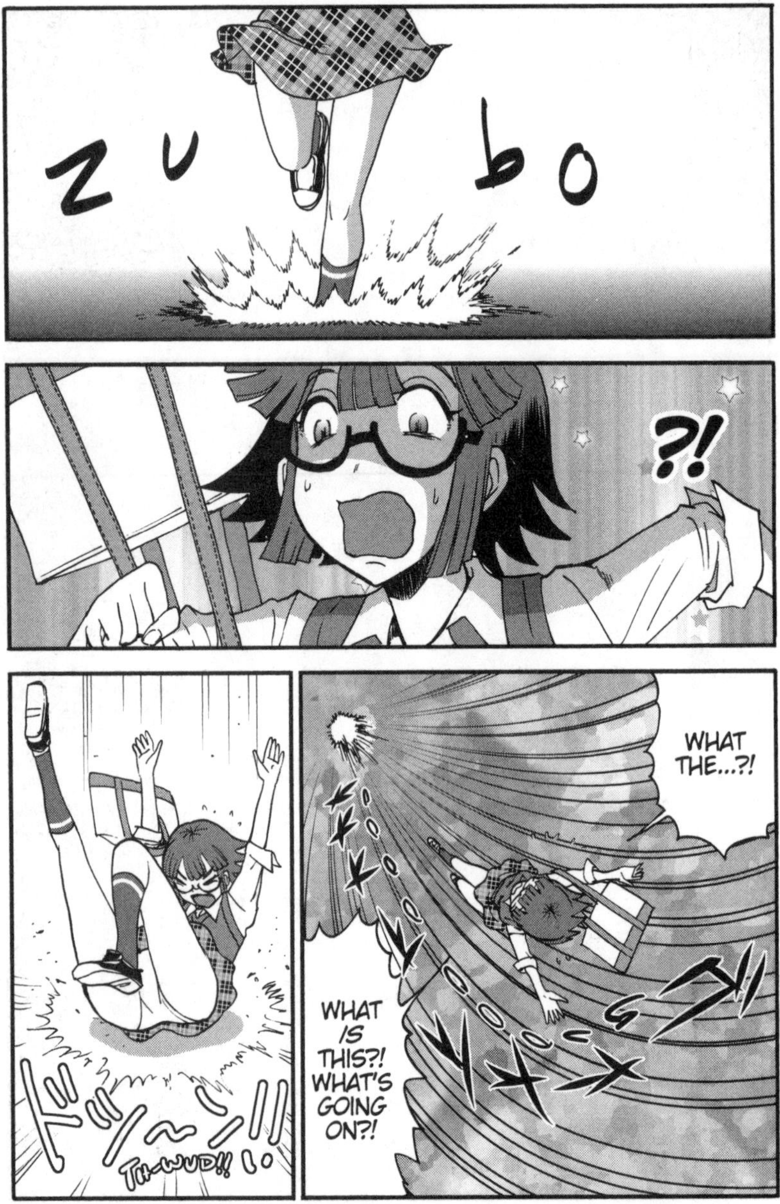
ZU bo
?!
WHAT THE...?!
WHAT IS THIS?! WHAT'S GOING ON?!
TH-WUD!!

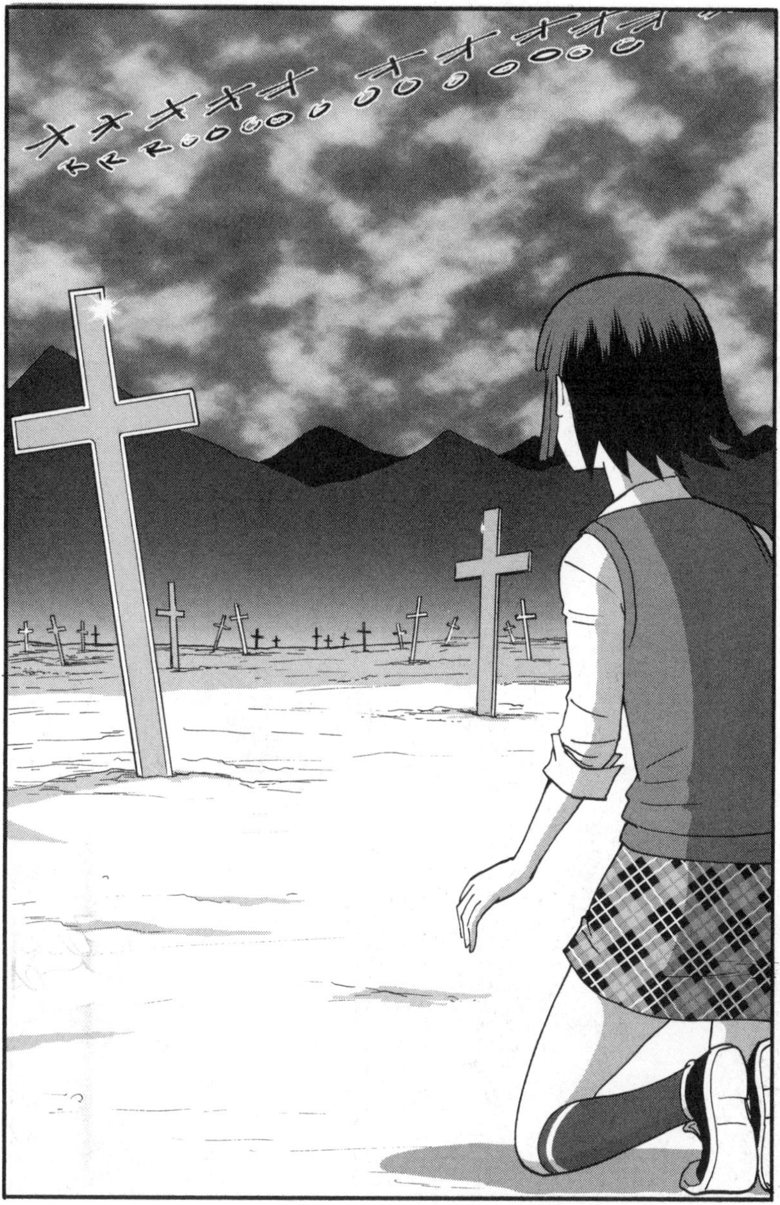
KRRROOOOOOOOOOOOO

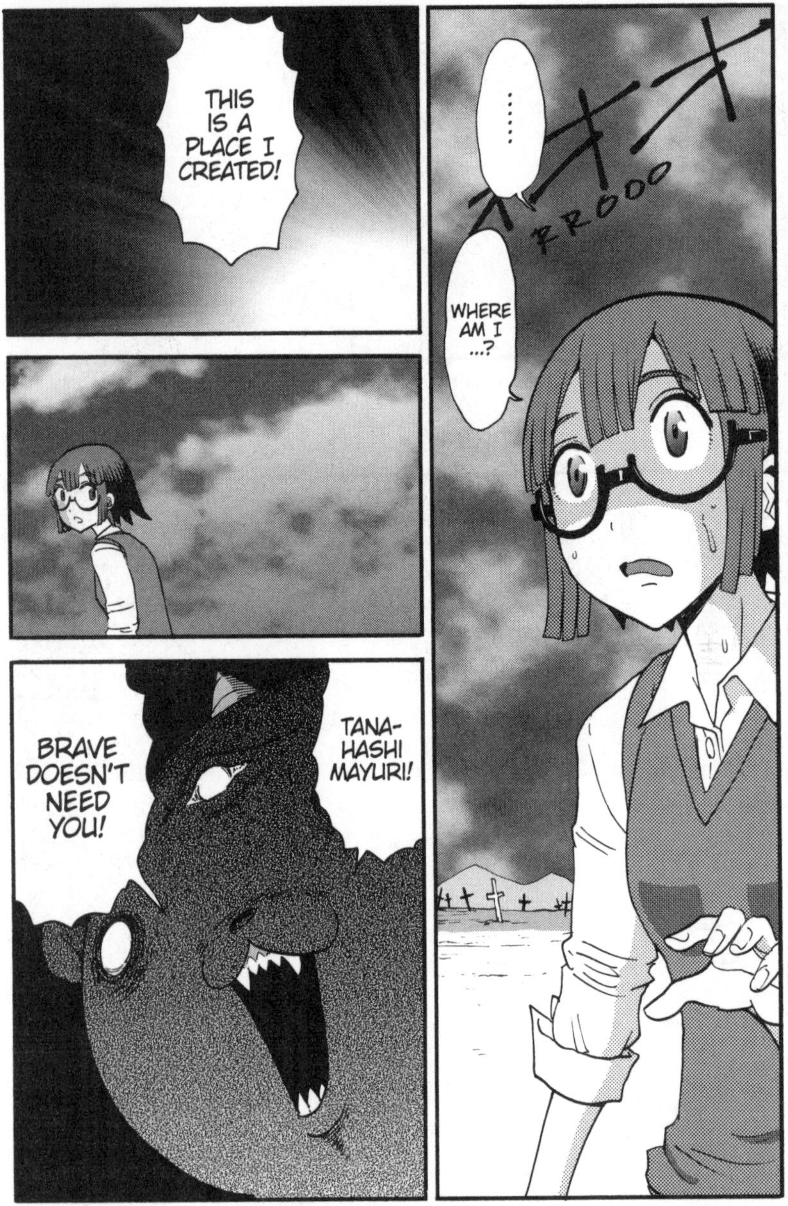
......
RROOO
WHERE AM I ...?
THIS IS A PLACE I CREATED!
TANA-HASHI MAYURI!
BRAVE DOESN'T NEED YOU!

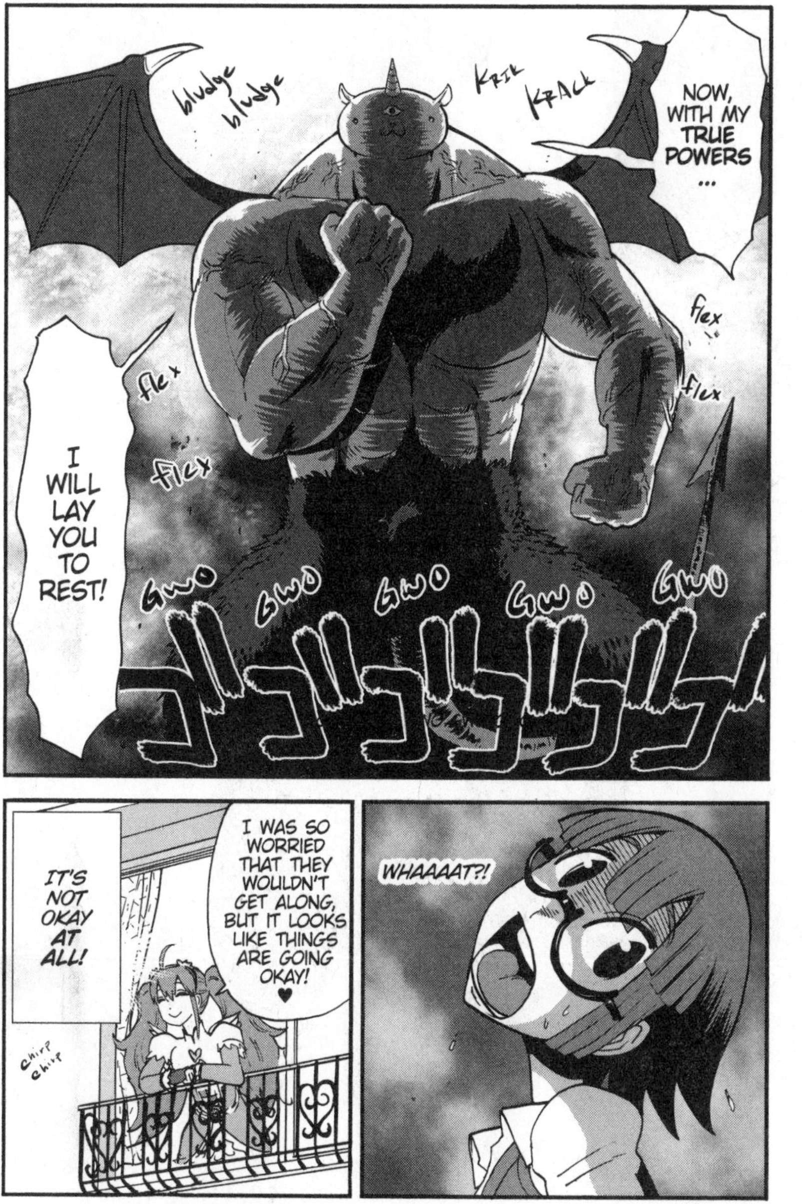

NOW, WITH MY TRUE POWERS ...
KRIK KRACK
bludge bludge
flex
flex
flex
flex
I WILL LAY YOU TO REST!
GWO GWO GWO GWO GWO
WHAAAAT?!
I WAS SO WORRIED THAT THEY WOULDN'T GET ALONG, BUT IT LOOKS LIKE THINGS ARE GOING OKAY! ♥
IT'S NOT OKAY AT ALL!
chirp chirp

Chapter 18: The Otherworldly Battle ★

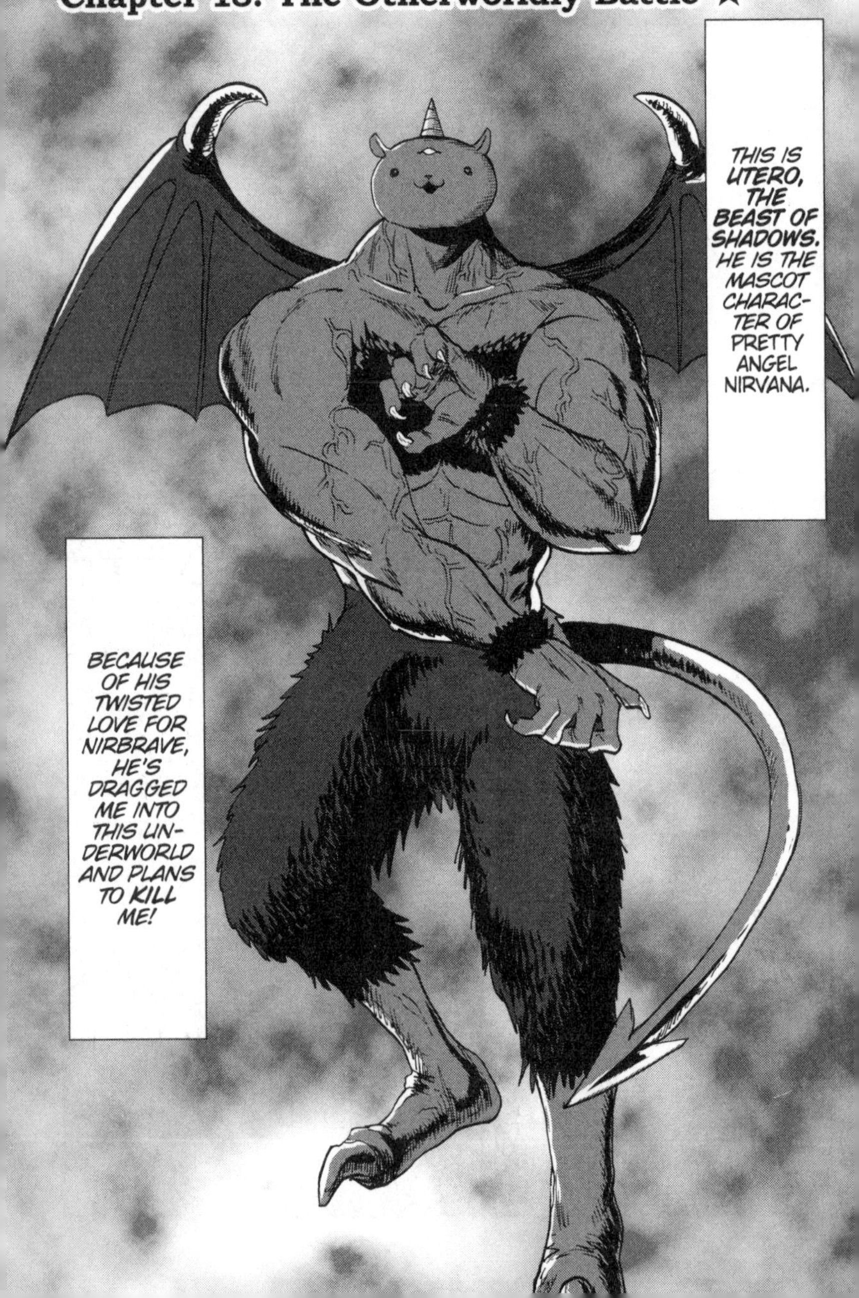
THIS IS UTERO, THE BEAST OF SHADOWS. HE IS THE MASCOT CHARACTER OF PRETTY ANGEL NIRVANA.
BECAUSE OF HIS TWISTED LOVE FOR NIRBRAVE, HE'S DRAGGED ME INTO THIS UNDERWORLD AND PLANS TO KILL ME!

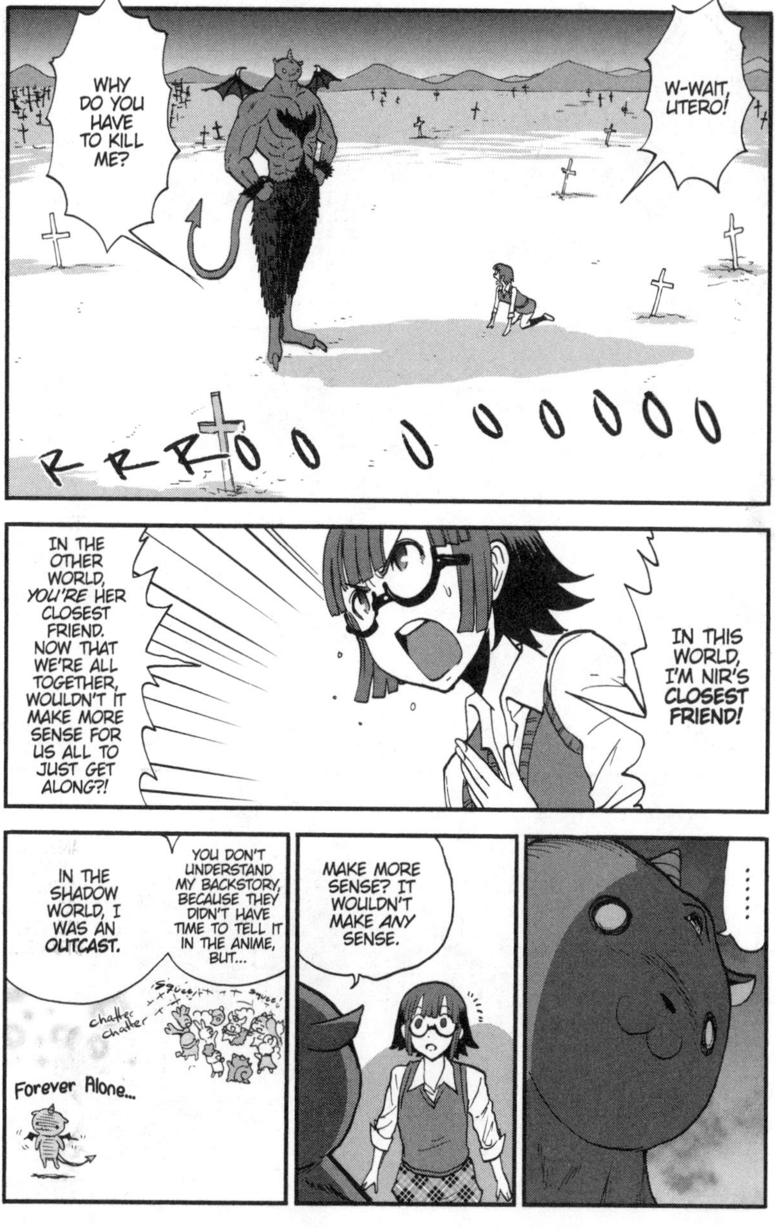

W-WAIT, UTERO!
WHY DO YOU HAVE TO KILL ME?
RRROOOOOOOO
IN THIS WORLD, I'M NIR'S **CLOSEST FRIEND!**
IN THE OTHER WORLD, *YOU'RE* HER CLOSEST FRIEND. NOW THAT WE'RE ALL TOGETHER, WOULDN'T IT MAKE MORE SENSE FOR US ALL TO JUST GET ALONG?!
......
MAKE MORE SENSE? IT WOULDN'T MAKE *ANY* SENSE.
YOU DON'T UNDERSTAND MY BACKSTORY, BECAUSE THEY DIDN'T HAVE TIME TO TELL IT IN THE ANIME, BUT...
IN THE SHADOW WORLD, I WAS AN **OUTCAST.**
chatter chatter
Forever Alone...

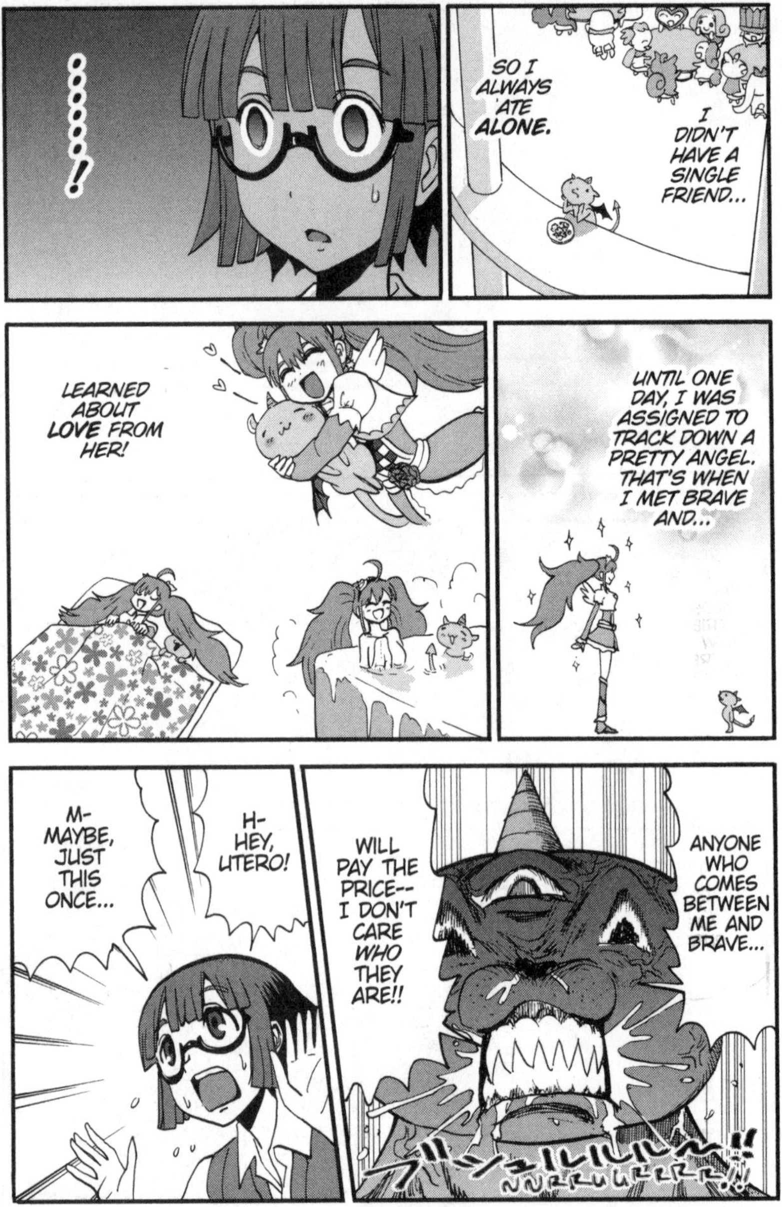

I DIDN'T HAVE A SINGLE FRIEND...
SO I ALWAYS ATE ALONE.
......!
UNTIL ONE DAY, I WAS ASSIGNED TO TRACK DOWN A PRETTY ANGEL. THAT'S WHEN I MET BRAVE AND...
LEARNED ABOUT LOVE FROM HER!
ANYONE WHO COMES BETWEEN ME AND BRAVE...
WILL PAY THE PRICE-- I DON'T CARE WHO THEY ARE!!
NNRRUURRRR!!
H-HEY, UTERO!
M-MAYBE, JUST THIS ONCE...

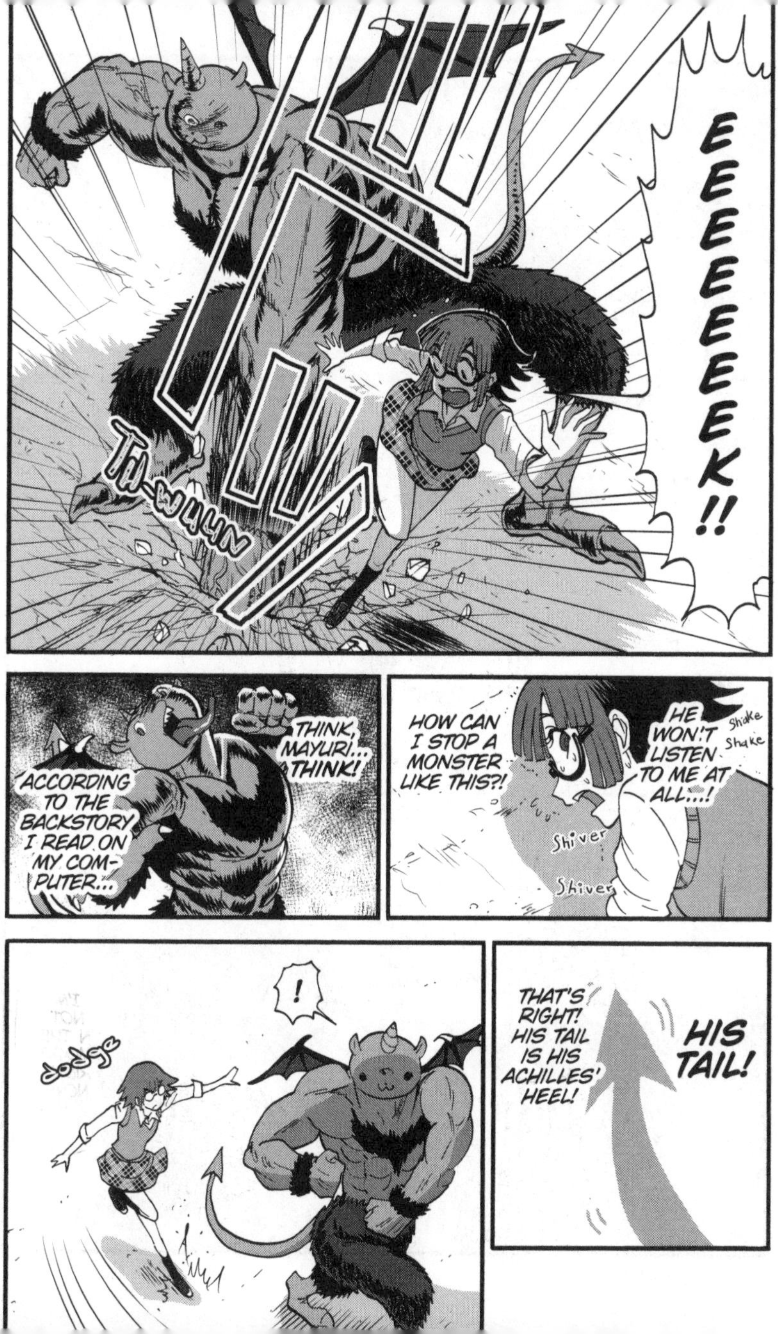
EEEEEEEEEK!!
TH-WUYUN
HE WON'T LISTEN TO ME AT ALL...!
Shake Shake
HOW CAN I STOP A MONSTER LIKE THIS?!
Shiver
Shiver
THINK, MAYURI... THINK!
ACCORDING TO THE BACKSTORY I READ ON MY COMPUTER...
HIS TAIL!
THAT'S RIGHT! HIS TAIL IS HIS ACHILLES' HEEL!
!
dodge

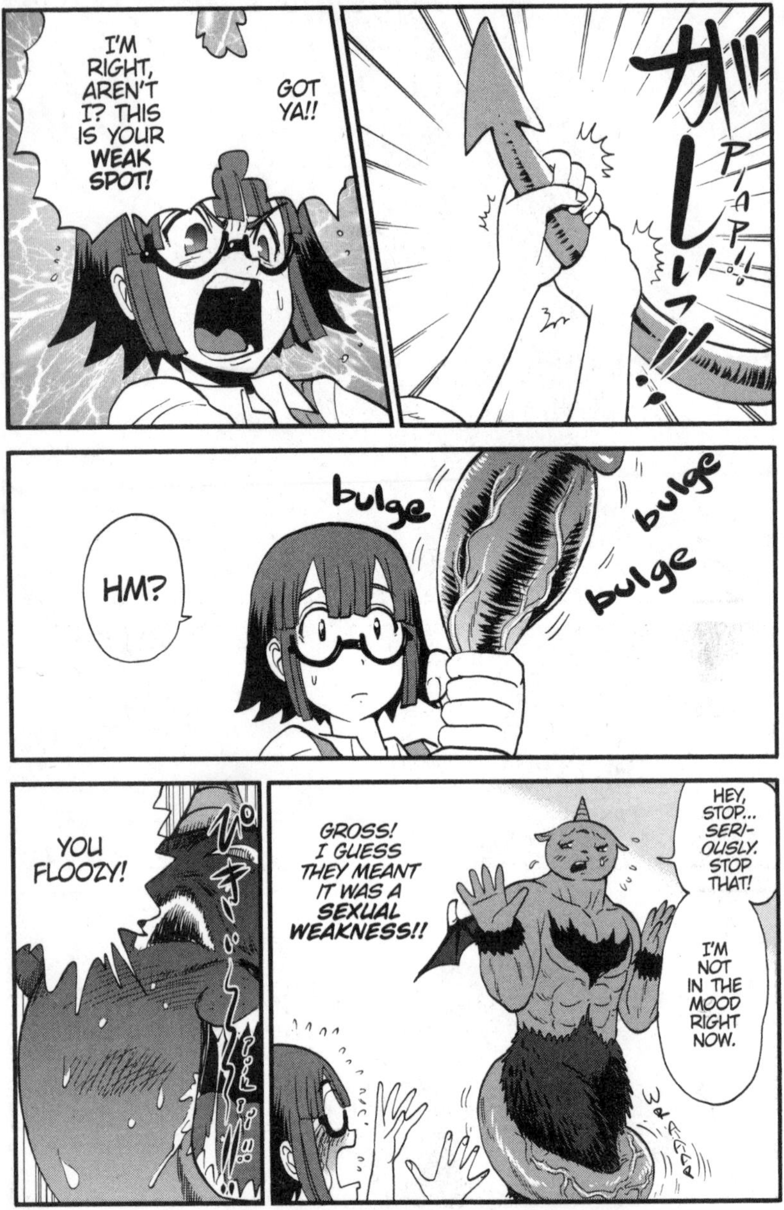
ガシッ
PAP!!
GOT YA!!
I'M RIGHT, AREN'T I? THIS IS YOUR WEAK SPOT!
bulge
bulge
bulge
HM?
HEY, STOP... SERI-OUSLY. STOP THAT!
I'M NOT IN THE MOOD RIGHT NOW.
GROSS! I GUESS THEY MEANT IT WAS A SEXUAL WEAKNESS!!
WRAAAP
YOU FLOOZY!

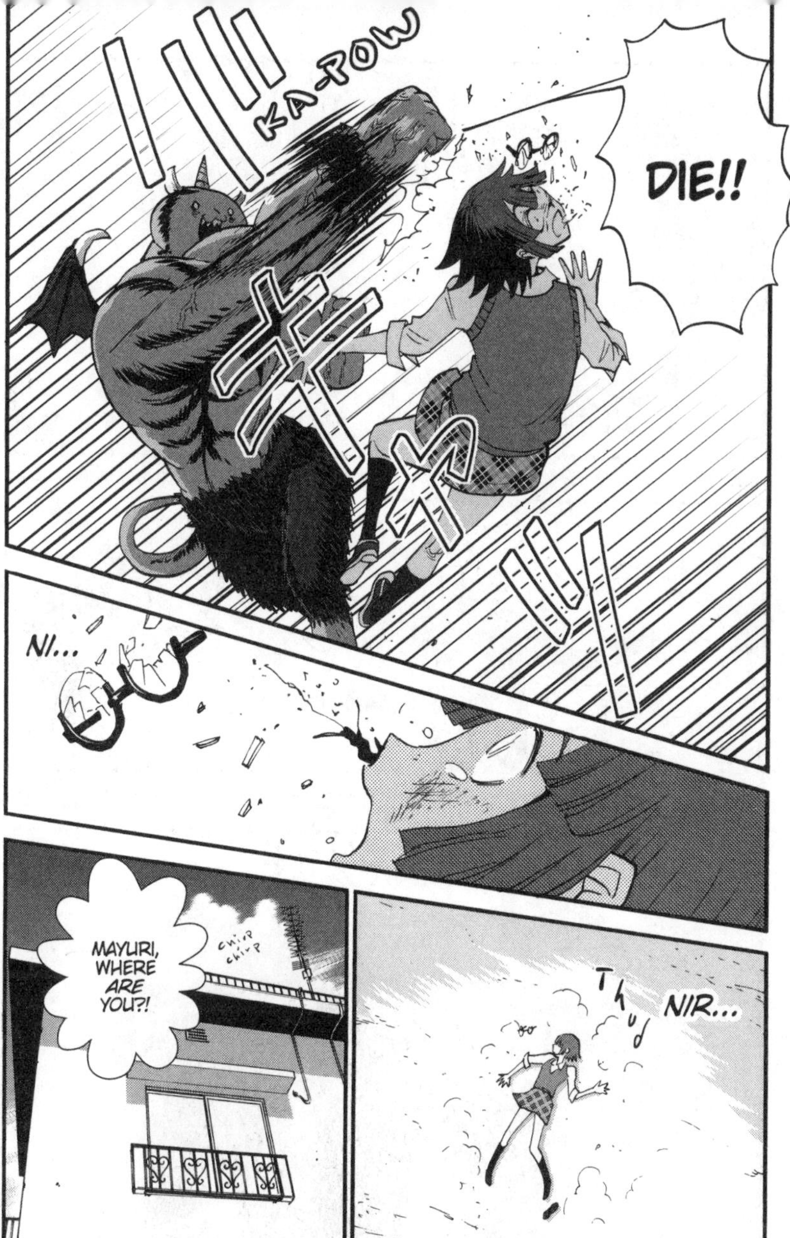
DIE!!
KA-POW
NI...
NIR...
Thud
MAYURI, WHERE ARE YOU?!
chirp chirp

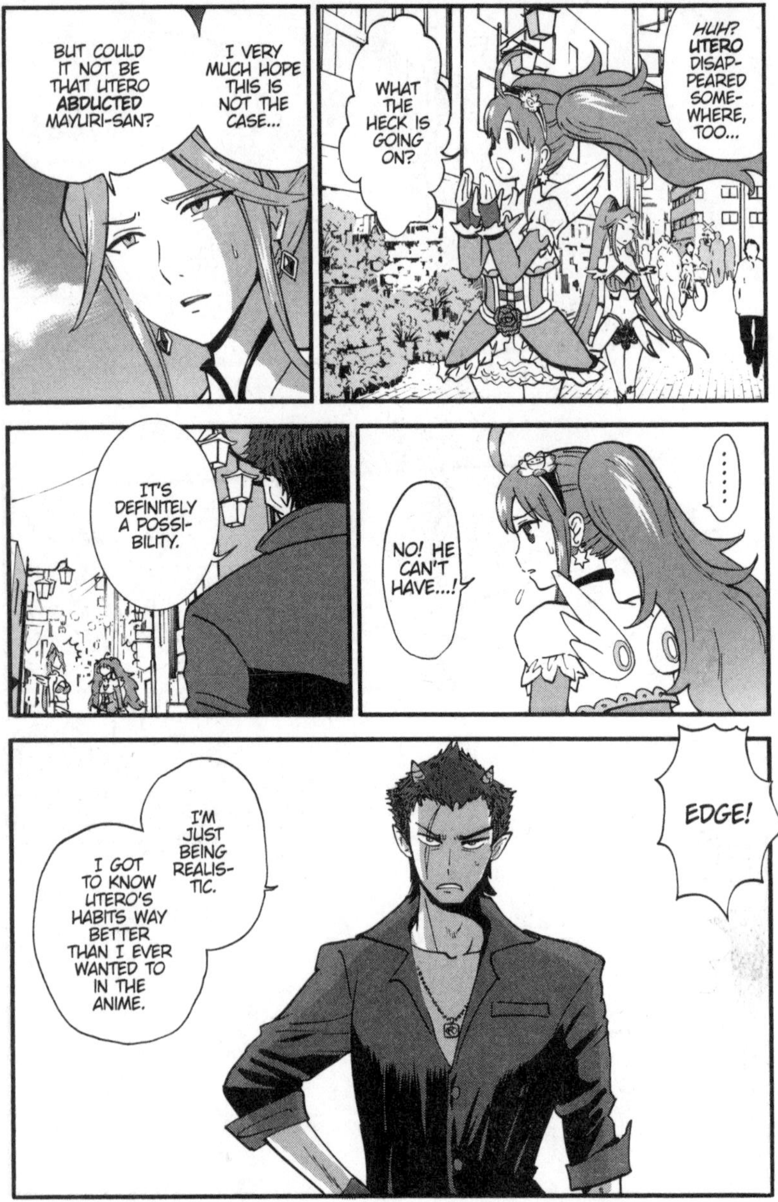
HUH? UTERO DISAPPEARED SOMEWHERE, TOO...
WHAT THE HECK IS GOING ON?
I VERY MUCH HOPE THIS IS NOT THE CASE...
BUT COULD IT NOT BE THAT UTERO ABDUCTED MAYURI-SAN?
......
NO! HE CAN'T HAVE...!
IT'S DEFINITELY A POSSIBILITY.
EDGE!
I'M JUST BEING REALISTIC.
I GOT TO KNOW UTERO'S HABITS WAY BETTER THAN I EVER WANTED TO IN THE ANIME.

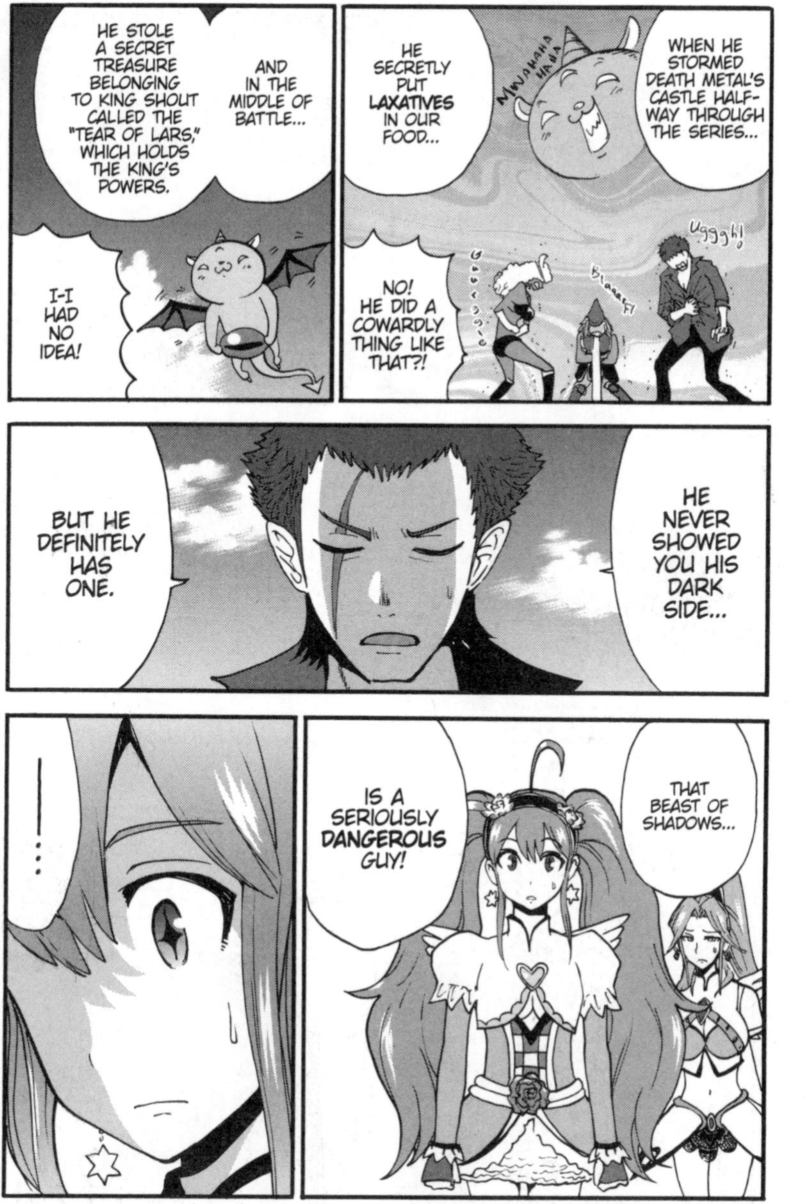
WHEN HE STORMED DEATH METAL'S CASTLE HALF-WAY THROUGH THE SERIES...
HE SECRETLY PUT **LAXATIVES** IN OUR FOOD...
Ugggh!
NO! HE DID A COWARDLY THING LIKE THAT?!
AND IN THE MIDDLE OF BATTLE...
HE STOLE A SECRET TREASURE BELONGING TO KING SHOUT CALLED THE "TEAR OF LARS," WHICH HOLDS THE KING'S POWERS.
I-I HAD NO IDEA!
HE NEVER SHOWED YOU HIS DARK SIDE...
BUT HE DEFINITELY HAS ONE.
THAT BEAST OF SHADOWS...
IS A SERIOUSLY **DANGEROUS** GUY!
......!

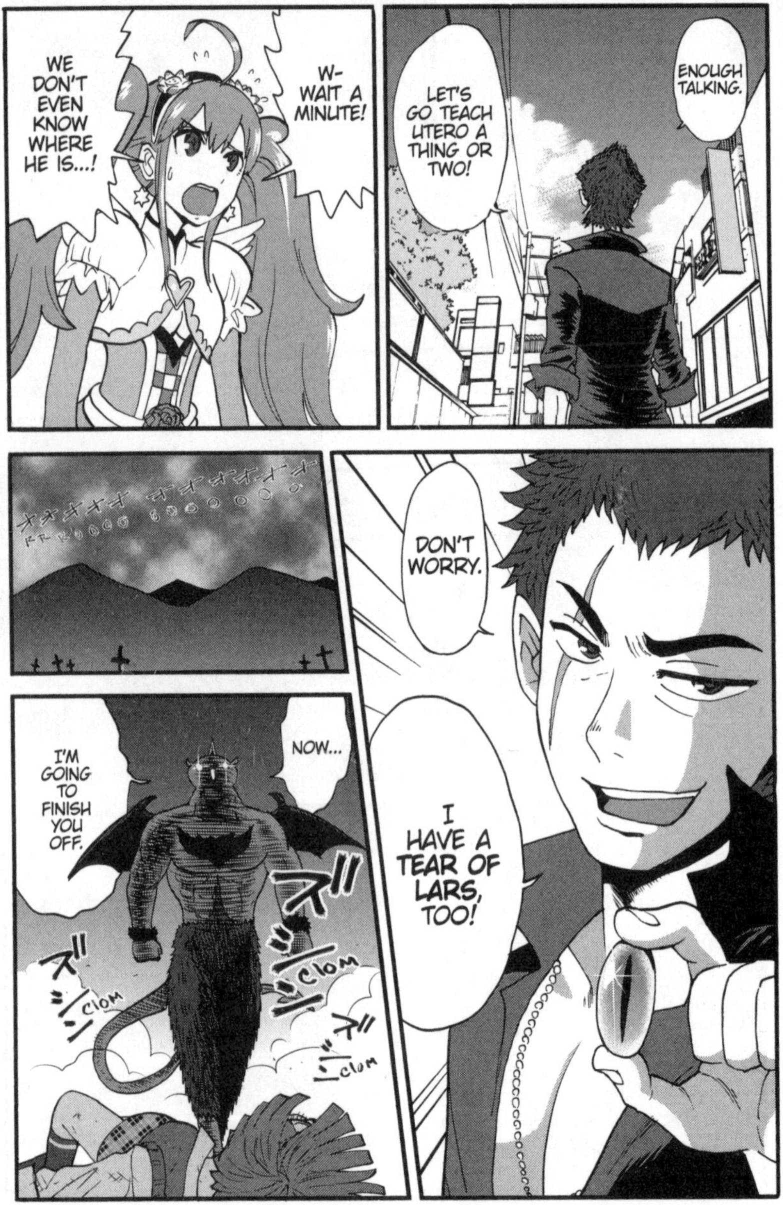
ENOUGH TALKING.
LET'S GO TEACH UTERO A THING OR TWO!
W-WAIT A MINUTE!
WE DON'T EVEN KNOW WHERE HE IS...!
DON'T WORRY.
I HAVE A TEAR OF LARS, TOO!
NOW...
I'M GOING TO FINISH YOU OFF.
CLOM
CLOM
CLOM

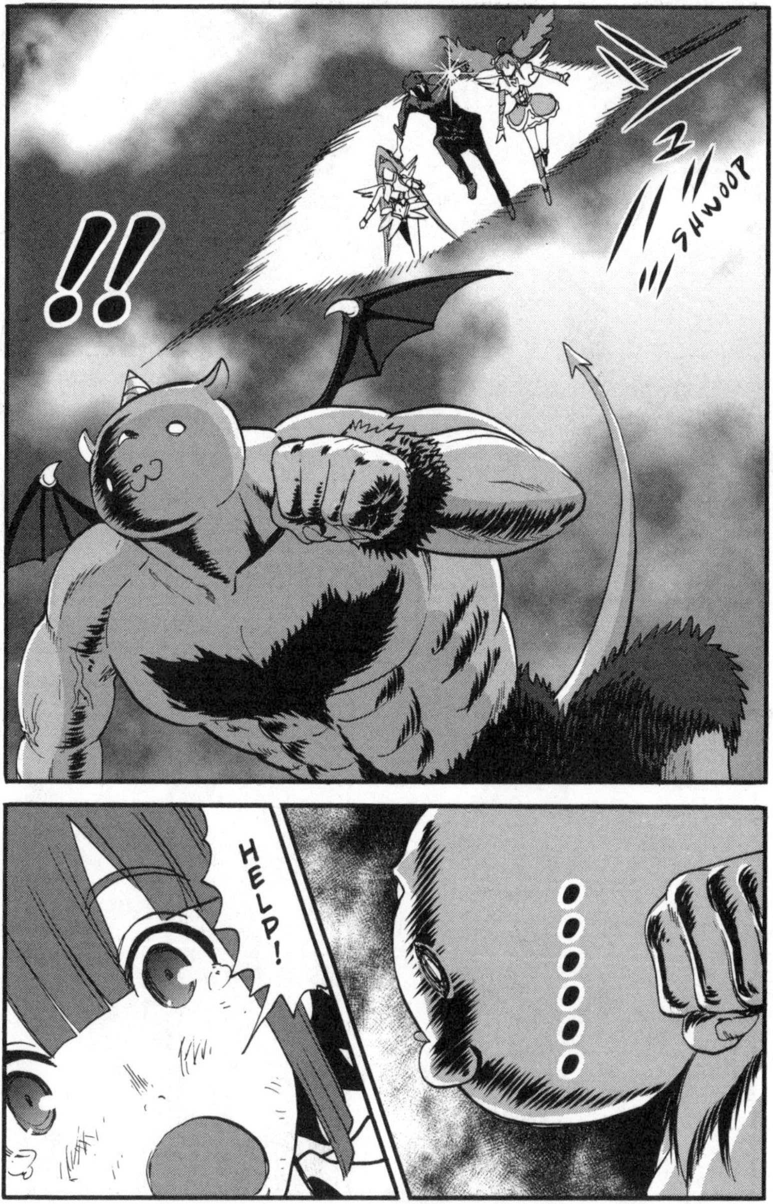
!!
SHWOOP
HELP!
......

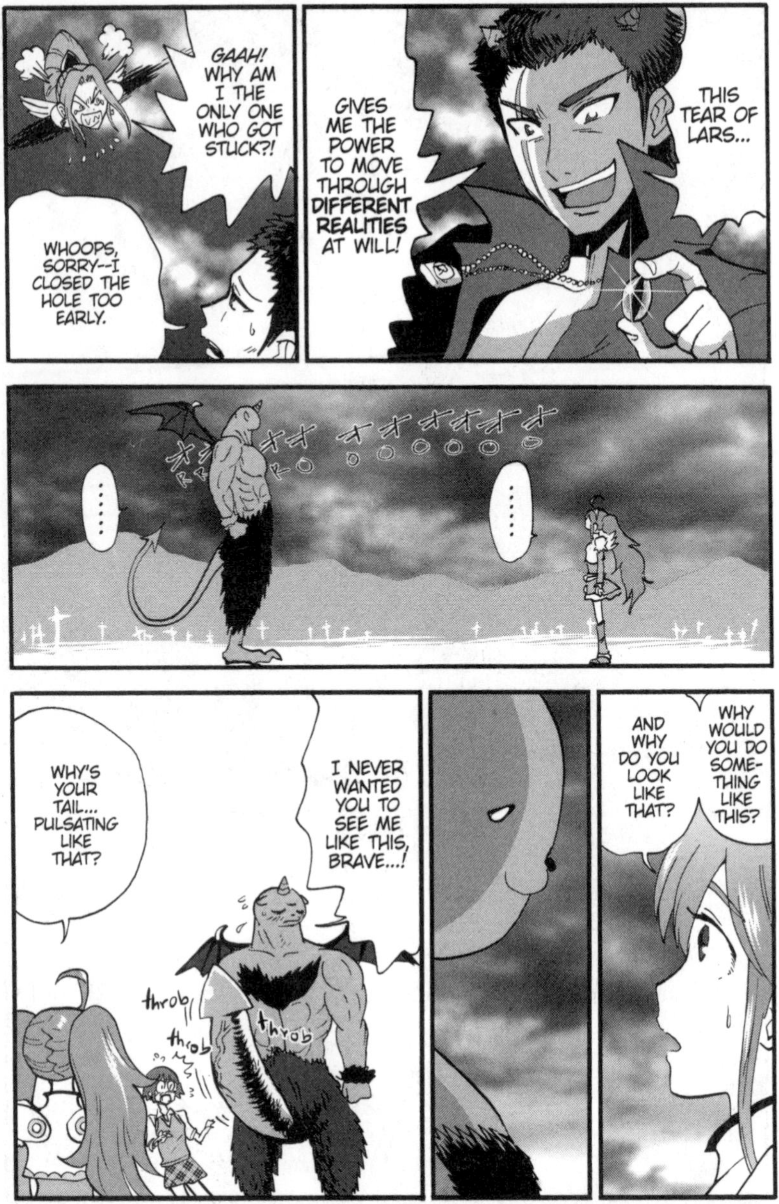
THIS TEAR OF LARS...
GIVES ME THE POWER TO MOVE THROUGH DIFFERENT REALITIES AT WILL!
GAAH! WHY AM I THE ONLY ONE WHO GOT STUCK?!
WHOOPS, SORRY--I CLOSED THE HOLE TOO EARLY.
......
......
WHY WOULD YOU DO SOME-THING LIKE THIS?
AND WHY DO YOU LOOK LIKE THAT?
I NEVER WANTED YOU TO SEE ME LIKE THIS, BRAVE...!
WHY'S YOUR TAIL... PULSATING LIKE THAT?
throb
throb
throb

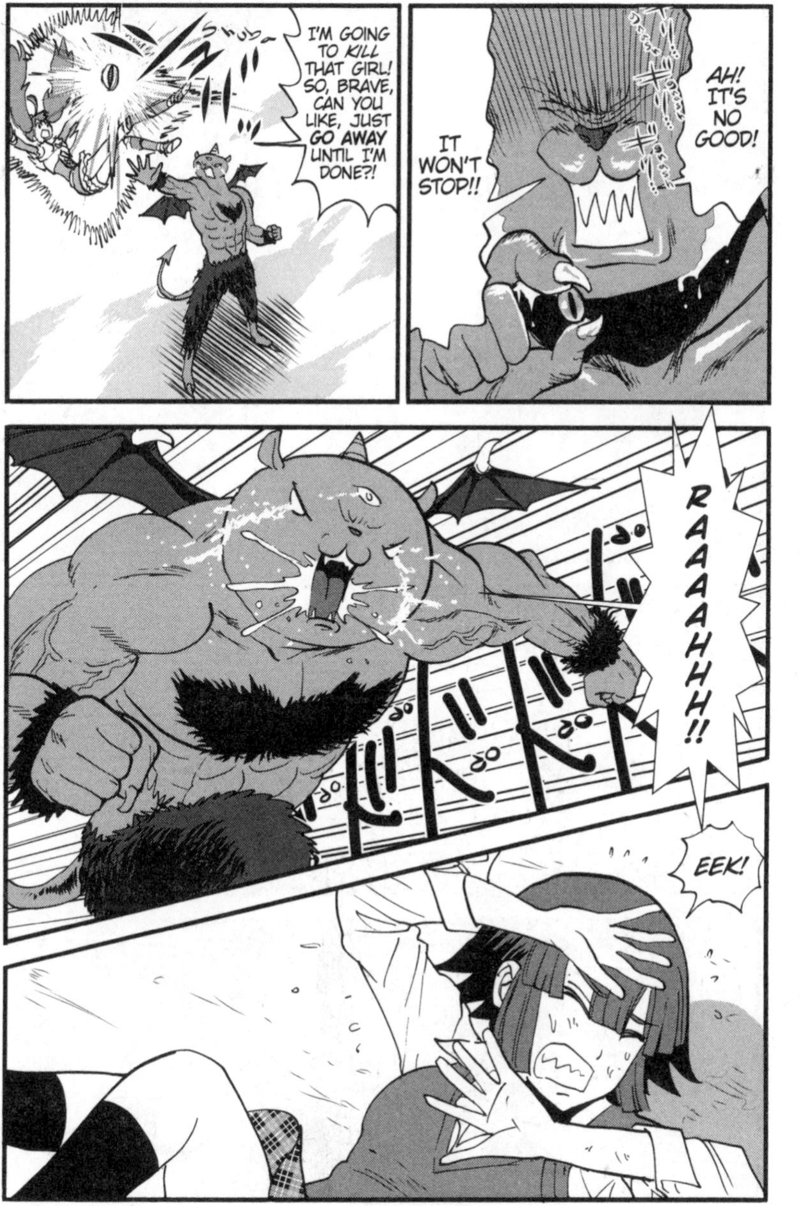
AH! IT'S NO GOOD!
IT WON'T STOP!!
I'M GOING TO KILL THAT GIRL! SO, BRAVE, CAN YOU LIKE, JUST GO AWAY UNTIL I'M DONE?!
RAAAAAHHH!!
EEK!

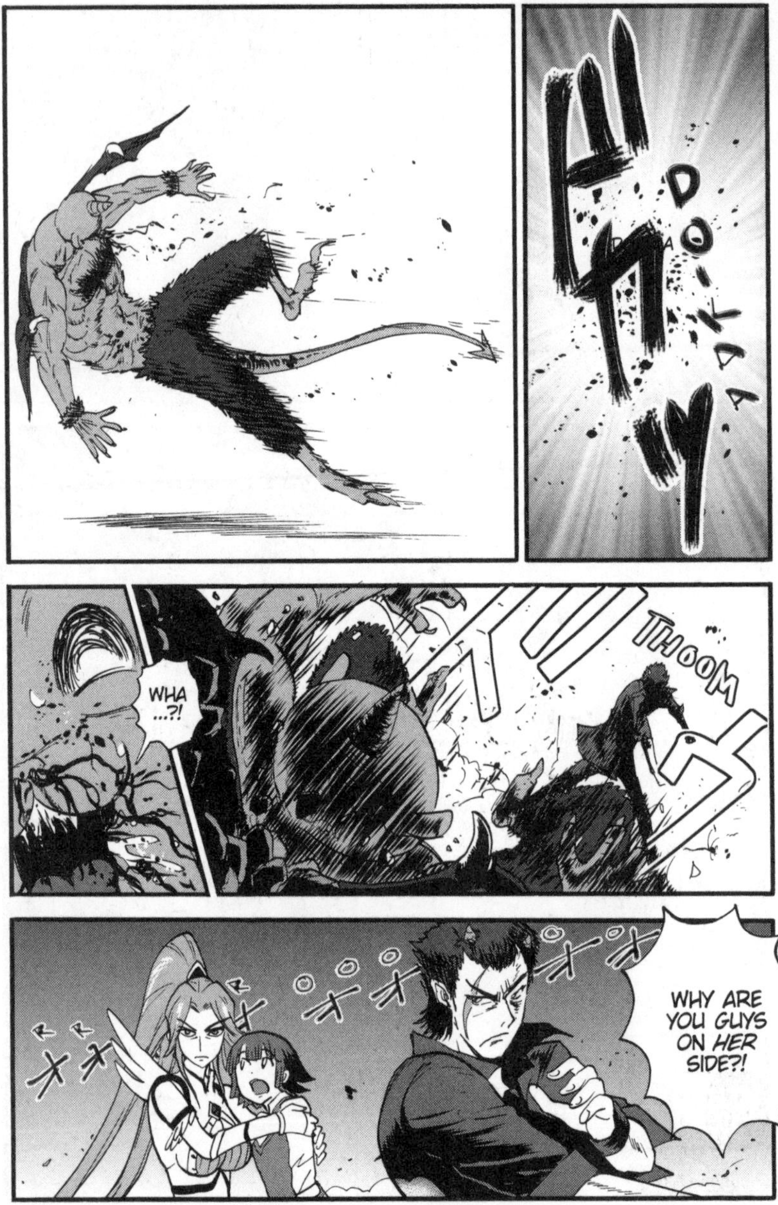
DO-KAA
DA
THOOM
D
WHA ...?!
WHY ARE YOU GUYS ON *HER* SIDE?!
R R R
O O O O O O

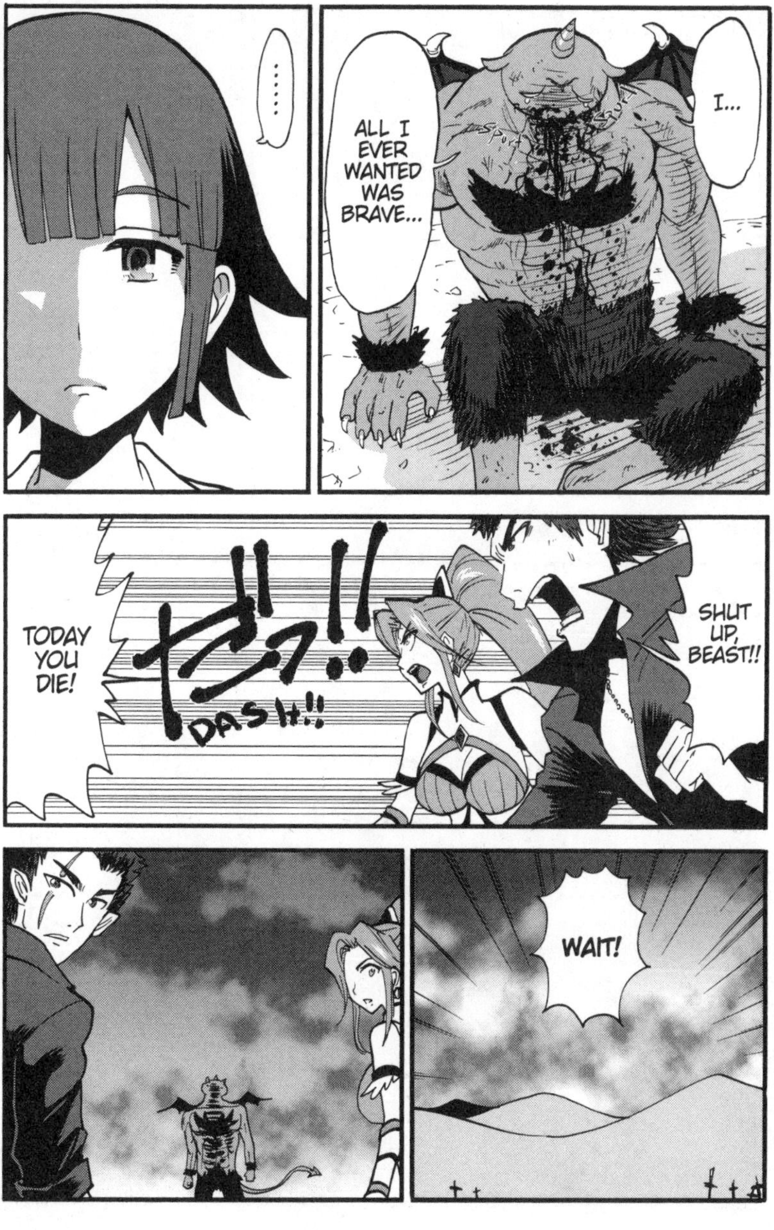
I...
ALL I EVER WANTED WAS BRAVE...
......
SHUT UP, BEAST!!
DASH!!
TODAY YOU DIE!
WAIT!

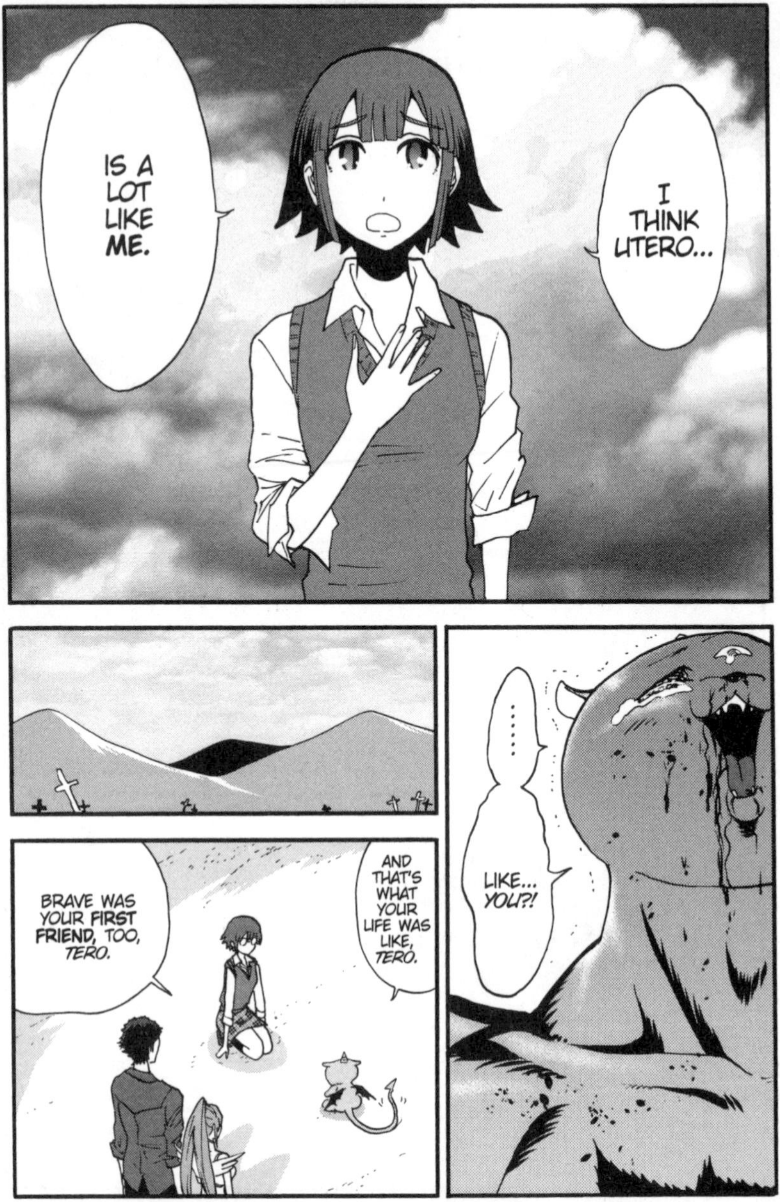
I THINK UTERO...
IS A LOT LIKE **ME.**
......
LIKE... *YOU?!*
AND THAT'S WHAT YOUR LIFE WAS LIKE, *TERO.*
BRAVE WAS YOUR **FIRST FRIEND,** TOO, *TERO.*

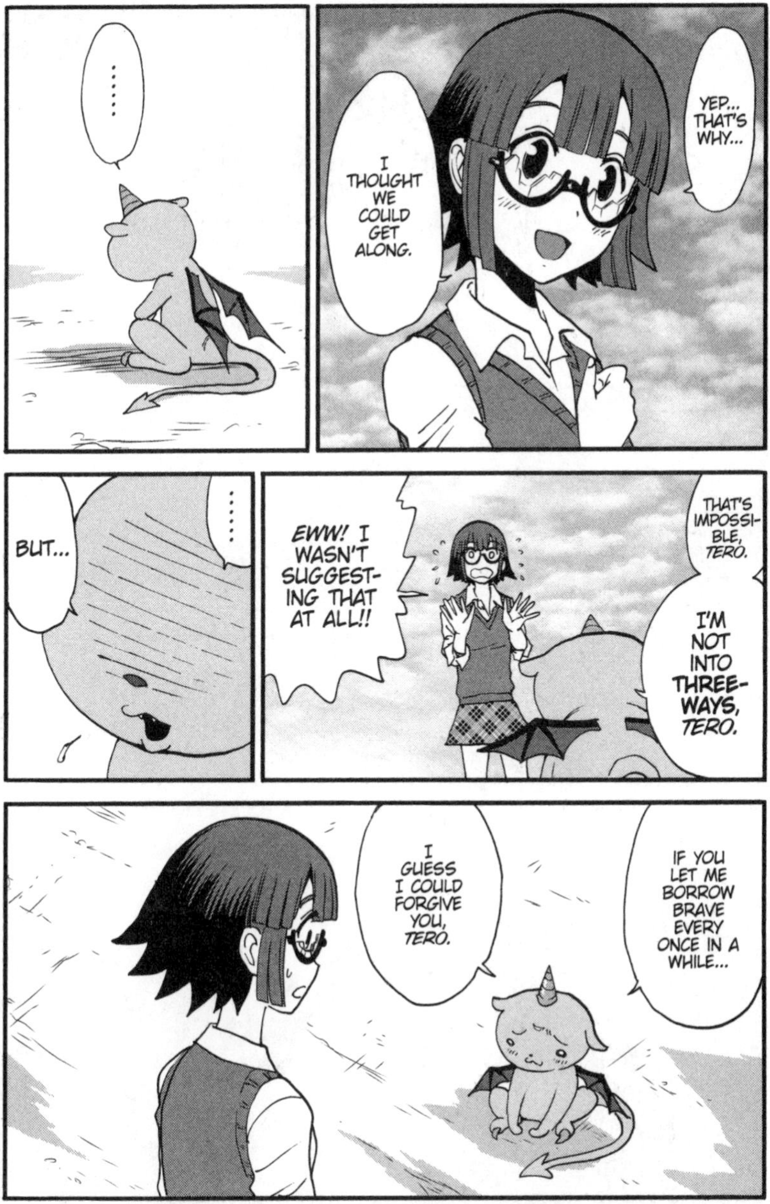
YEP... THAT'S WHY...
I THOUGHT WE COULD GET ALONG.
......
THAT'S IMPOSSIBLE, *TERO.*
I'M NOT INTO **THREE-WAYS,** *TERO.*
EWW! I WASN'T SUGGESTING THAT AT ALL!!
......
BUT...
IF YOU LET ME BORROW BRAVE EVERY ONCE IN A WHILE...
I GUESS I COULD FORGIVE YOU, *TERO.*

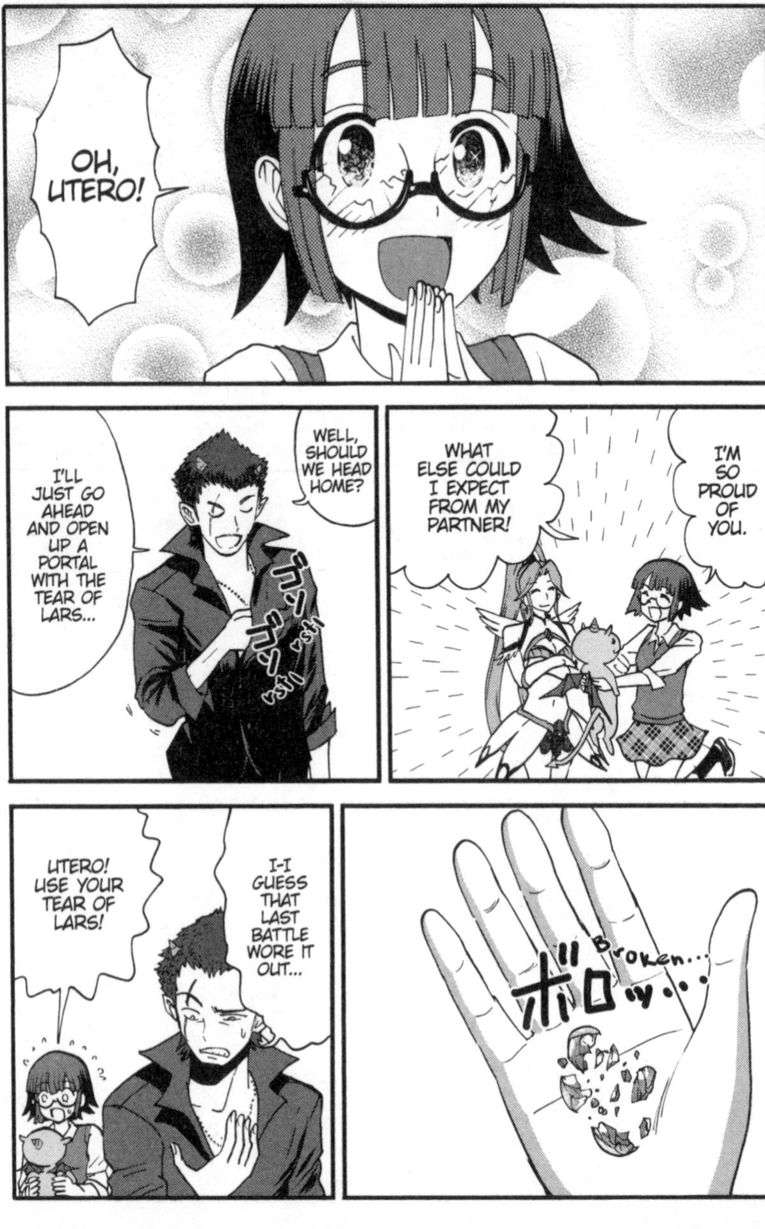
OH, UTERO!
I'M SO PROUD OF YOU.
WHAT ELSE COULD I EXPECT FROM MY PARTNER!
WELL, SHOULD WE HEAD HOME?
I'LL JUST GO AHEAD AND OPEN UP A PORTAL WITH THE TEAR OF LARS...
ゴソ rstl
ゴソ rstl
ボロッ... Broken...
I-I GUESS THAT LAST BATTLE WORE IT OUT...
UTERO! USE YOUR TEAR OF LARS!

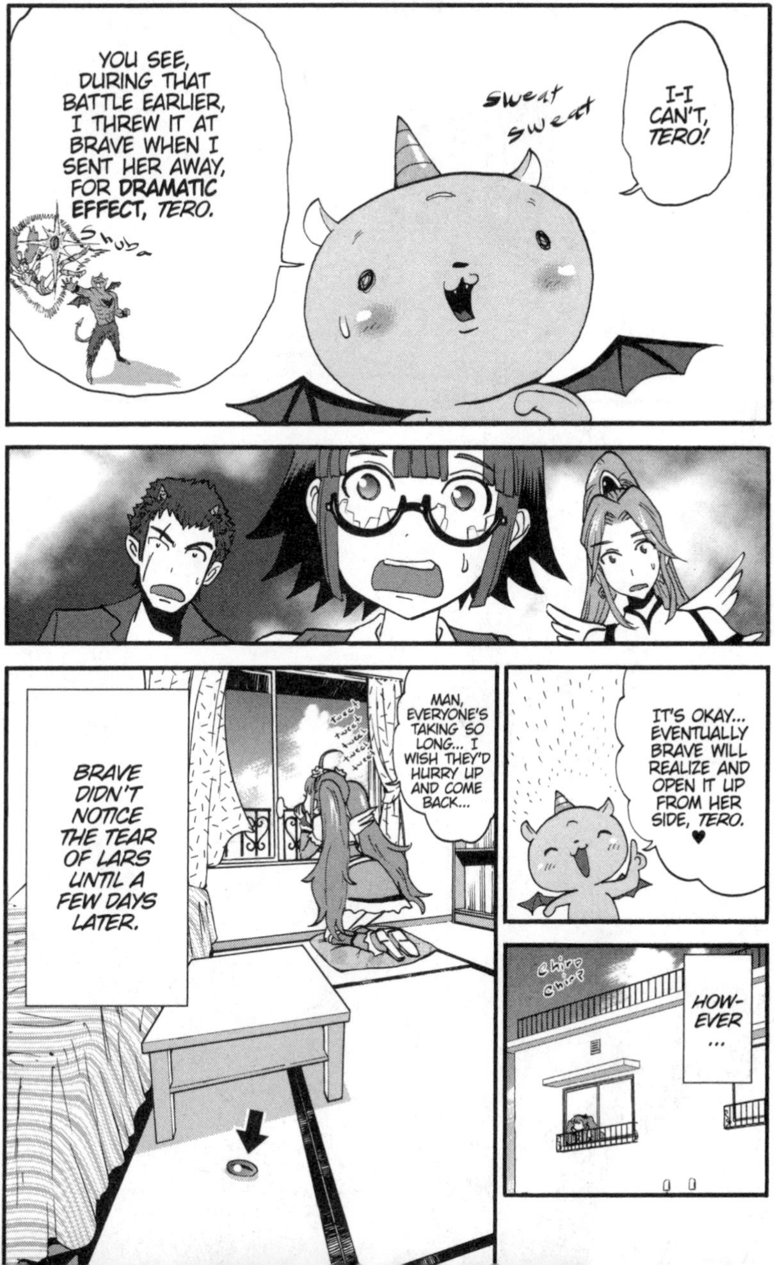
I-I CAN'T, TERO!
SWEAT SWEAT
YOU SEE, DURING THAT BATTLE EARLIER, I THREW IT AT BRAVE WHEN I SENT HER AWAY, FOR DRAMATIC EFFECT, TERO.
SHUBA
IT'S OKAY... EVENTUALLY BRAVE WILL REALIZE AND OPEN IT UP FROM HER SIDE, TERO. ♥
CHIRP CHIRP
HOW-EVER...
MAN, EVERYONE'S TAKING SO LONG... I WISH THEY'D HURRY UP AND COME BACK...
BRAVE DIDN'T NOTICE THE TEAR OF LARS UNTIL A FEW DAYS LATER.

Chapter 19: The Evil King Shout

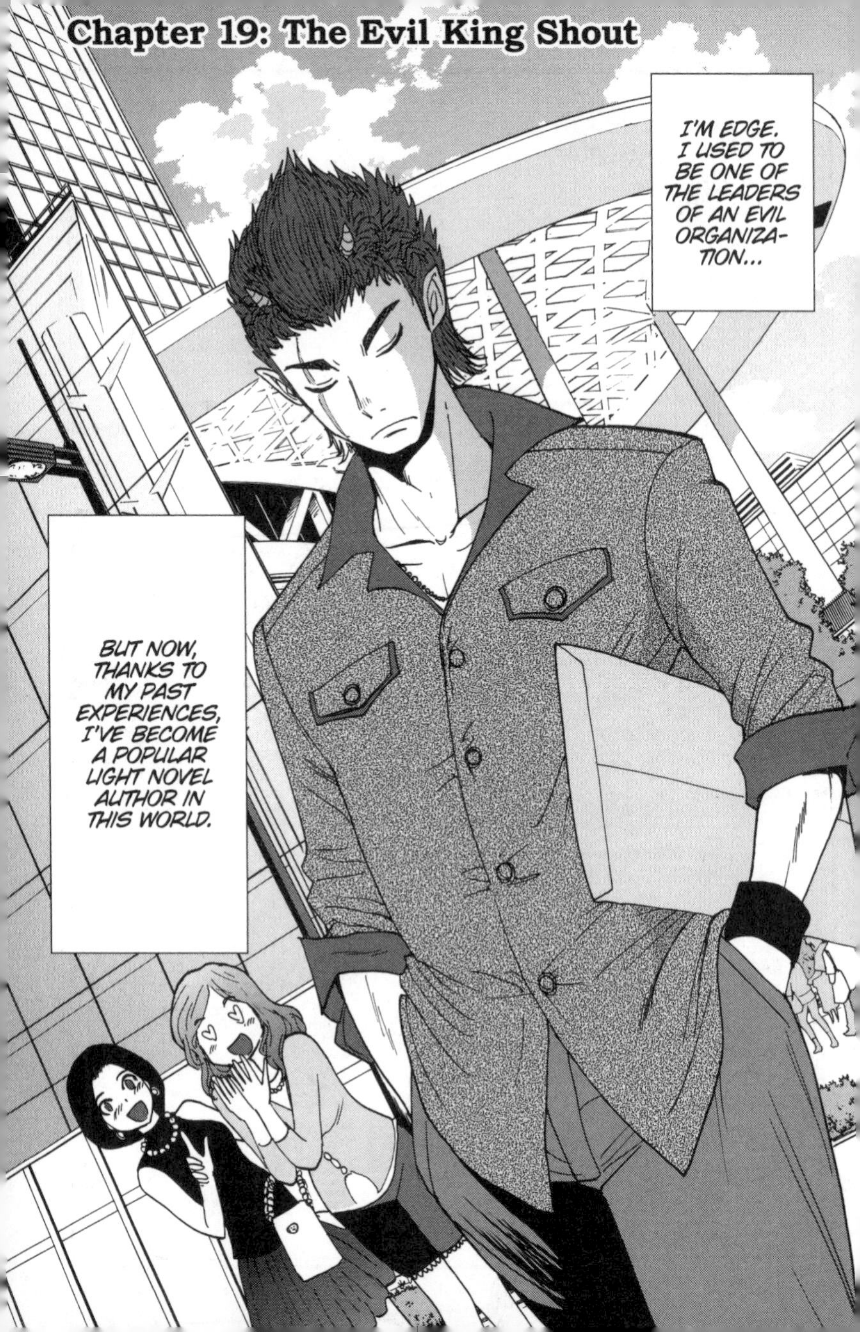
I'M EDGE. I USED TO BE ONE OF THE LEADERS OF AN EVIL ORGANIZA-TION...
BUT NOW, THANKS TO MY PAST EXPERIENCES, I'VE BECOME A POPULAR LIGHT NOVEL AUTHOR IN THIS WORLD.

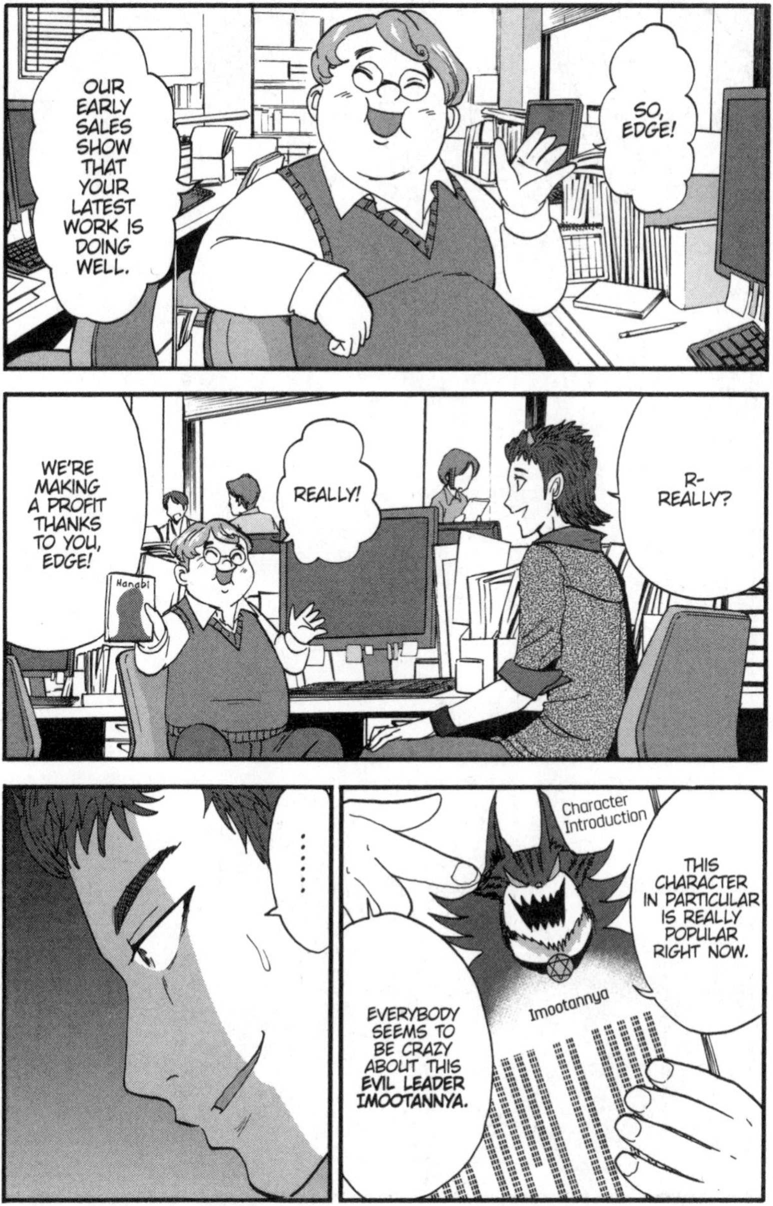
SO, EDGE!
OUR EARLY SALES SHOW THAT YOUR LATEST WORK IS DOING WELL.
R- REALLY?
REALLY!
WE'RE MAKING A PROFIT THANKS TO YOU, EDGE!
Hanabi
Character Introduction
THIS CHARACTER IN PARTICULAR IS REALLY POPULAR RIGHT NOW.
Imootannya
EVERYBODY SEEMS TO BE CRAZY ABOUT THIS **EVIL LEADER IMOOTANNYA.**
......

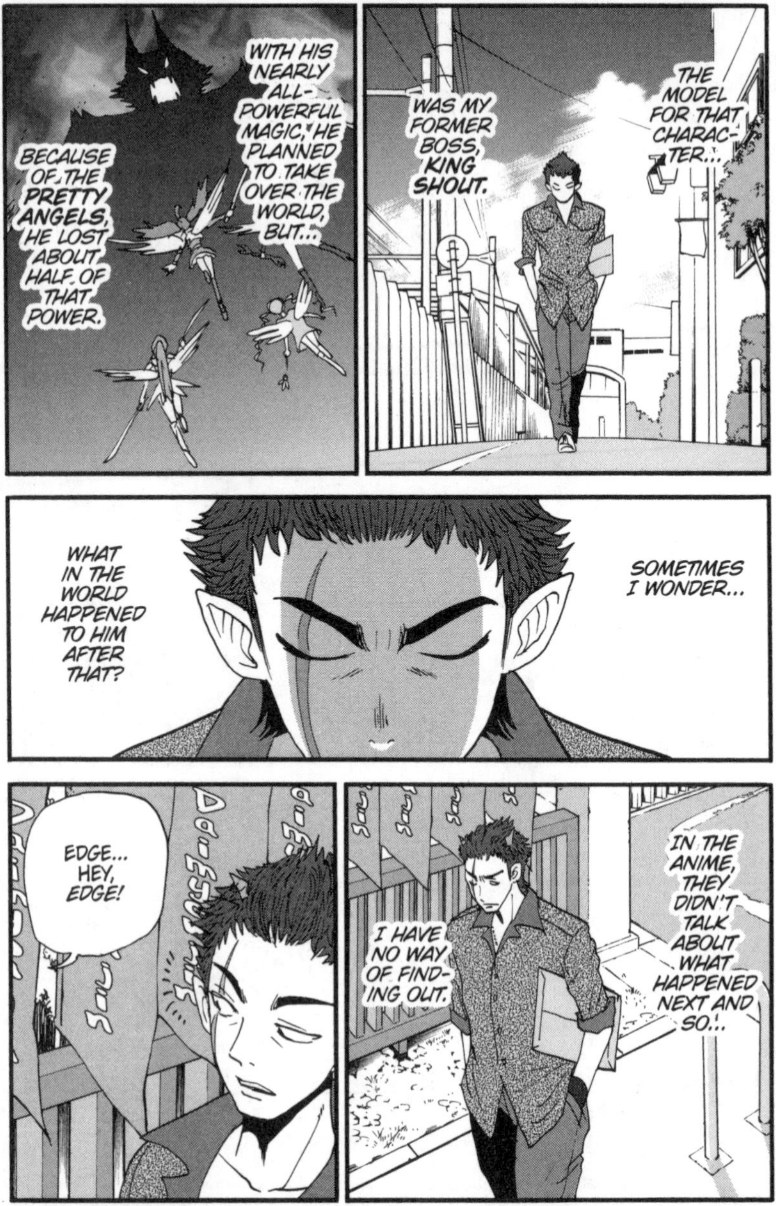
THE MODEL FOR THAT CHARAC-TER...
WAS MY FORMER BOSS, KING SHOUT.
WITH HIS NEARLY ALL-POWERFUL MAGIC, HE PLANNED TO TAKE OVER THE WORLD, BUT...
BECAUSE OF THE PRETTY ANGELS, HE LOST ABOUT HALF OF THAT POWER.
SOMETIMES I WONDER...
WHAT IN THE WORLD HAPPENED TO HIM AFTER THAT?
IN THE ANIME, THEY DIDN'T TALK ABOUT WHAT HAPPENED NEXT AND SO...
I HAVE NO WAY OF FIND-ING OUT.
EDGE... HEY, EDGE!

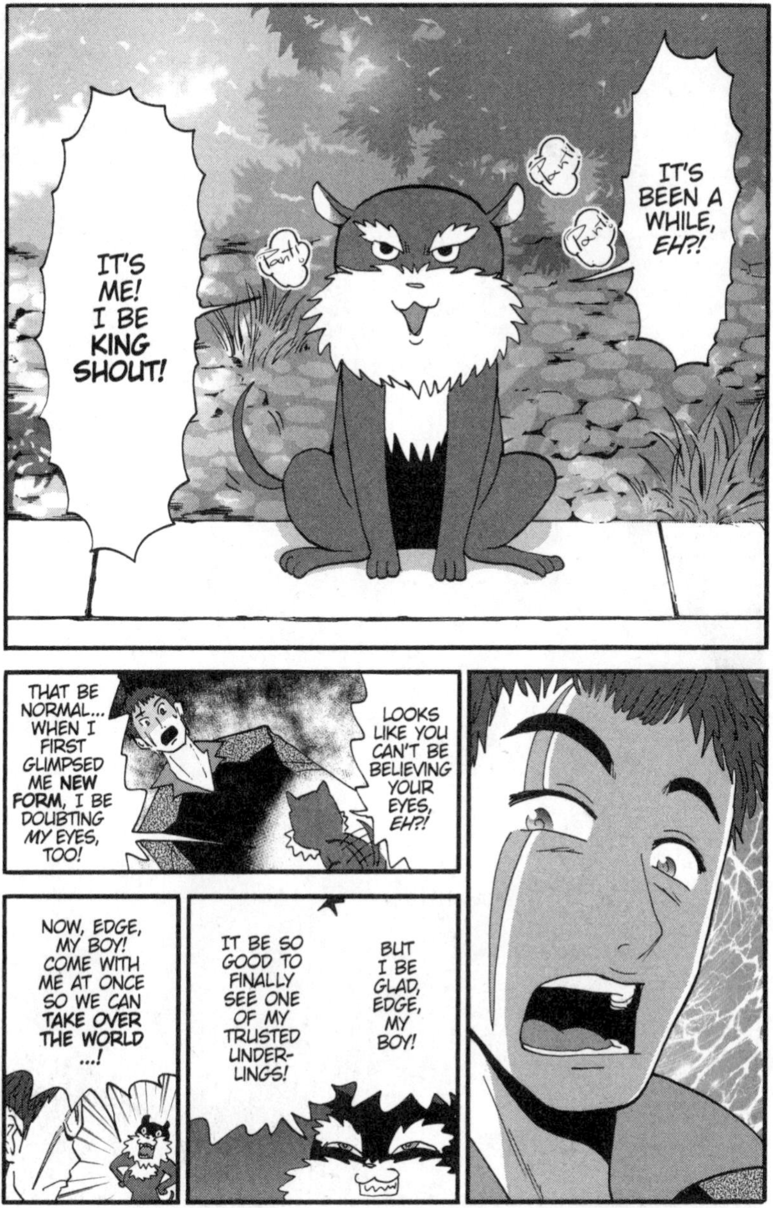
IT'S BEEN A WHILE, EH?!
Pant!
Pant!
Pant!
IT'S ME! I BE KING SHOUT!
LOOKS LIKE YOU CAN'T BE BELIEVING YOUR EYES, EH?!
THAT BE NORMAL... WHEN I FIRST GLIMPSED ME NEW FORM, I BE DOUBTING MY EYES, TOO!
BUT I BE GLAD, EDGE, MY BOY!
IT BE SO GOOD TO FINALLY SEE ONE OF MY TRUSTED UNDER-LINGS!
NOW, EDGE, MY BOY! COME WITH ME AT ONCE SO WE CAN TAKE OVER THE WORLD ...!

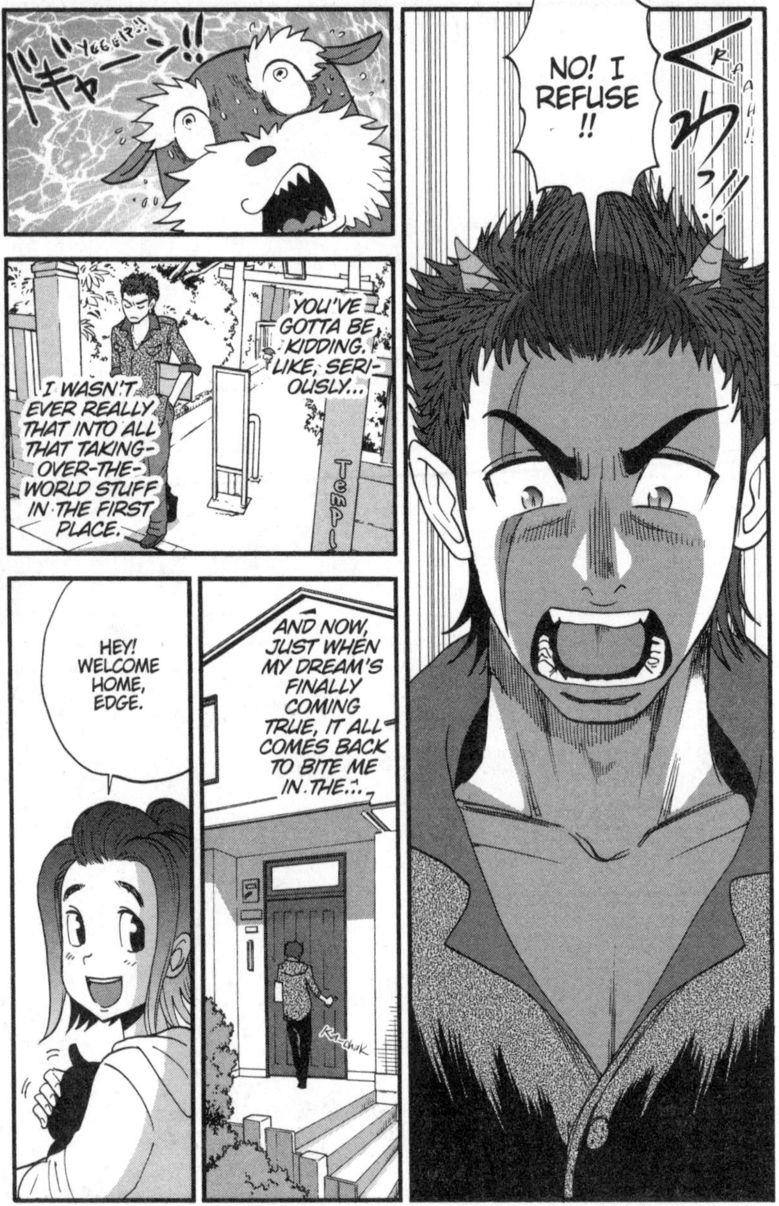
NO! I REFUSE !!
RAAH!!
ドキャーン!!
YOU'VE GOTTA BE KIDDING. LIKE, SERIOUSLY...
I WASN'T EVER REALLY THAT INTO ALL THAT TAKING-OVER-THE-WORLD STUFF IN THE FIRST PLACE.
AND NOW, JUST WHEN MY DREAM'S FINALLY COMING TRUE, IT ALL COMES BACK TO BITE ME IN THE...
KA-CHAK
HEY! WELCOME HOME, EDGE.

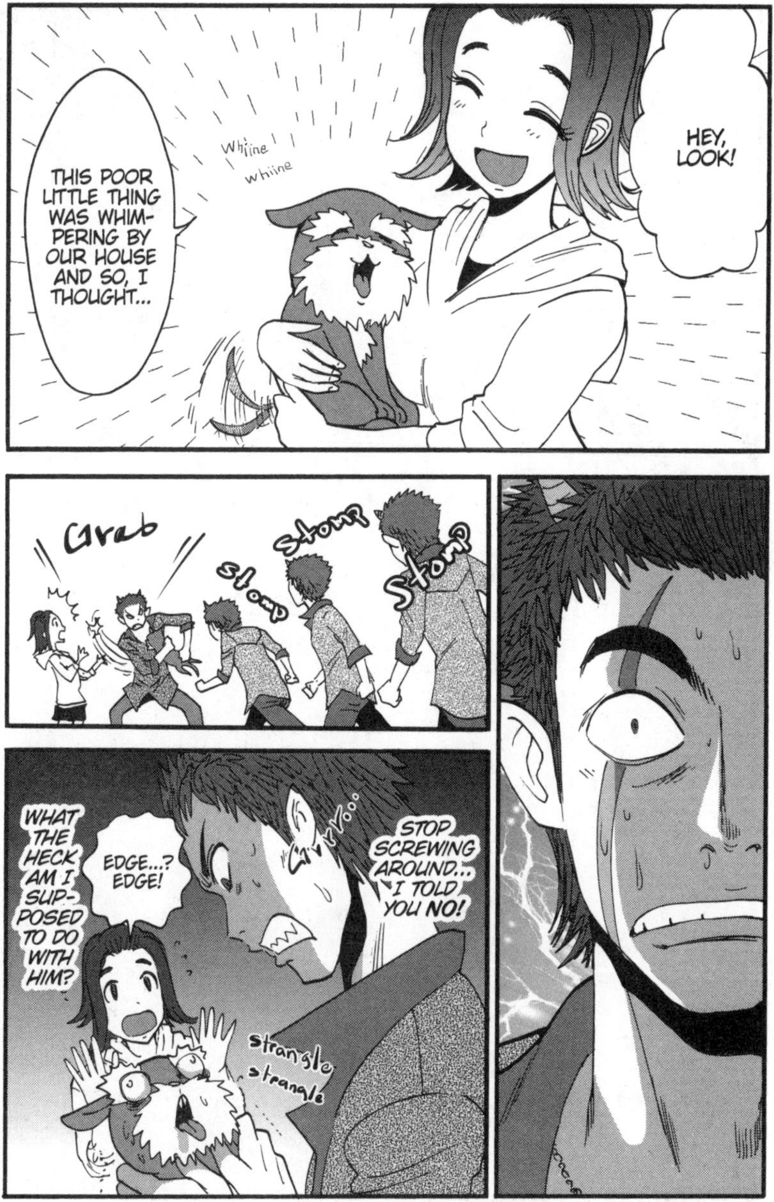
HEY, LOOK!
Whiine whiine
THIS POOR LITTLE THING WAS WHIMPERING BY OUR HOUSE AND SO, I THOUGHT...
Stomp
Stomp
stomp
Grab
STOP SCREWING AROUND... I TOLD YOU NO!
EDGE...? EDGE!
WHAT THE HECK AM I SUPPOSED TO DO WITH HIM?
strangle strangle

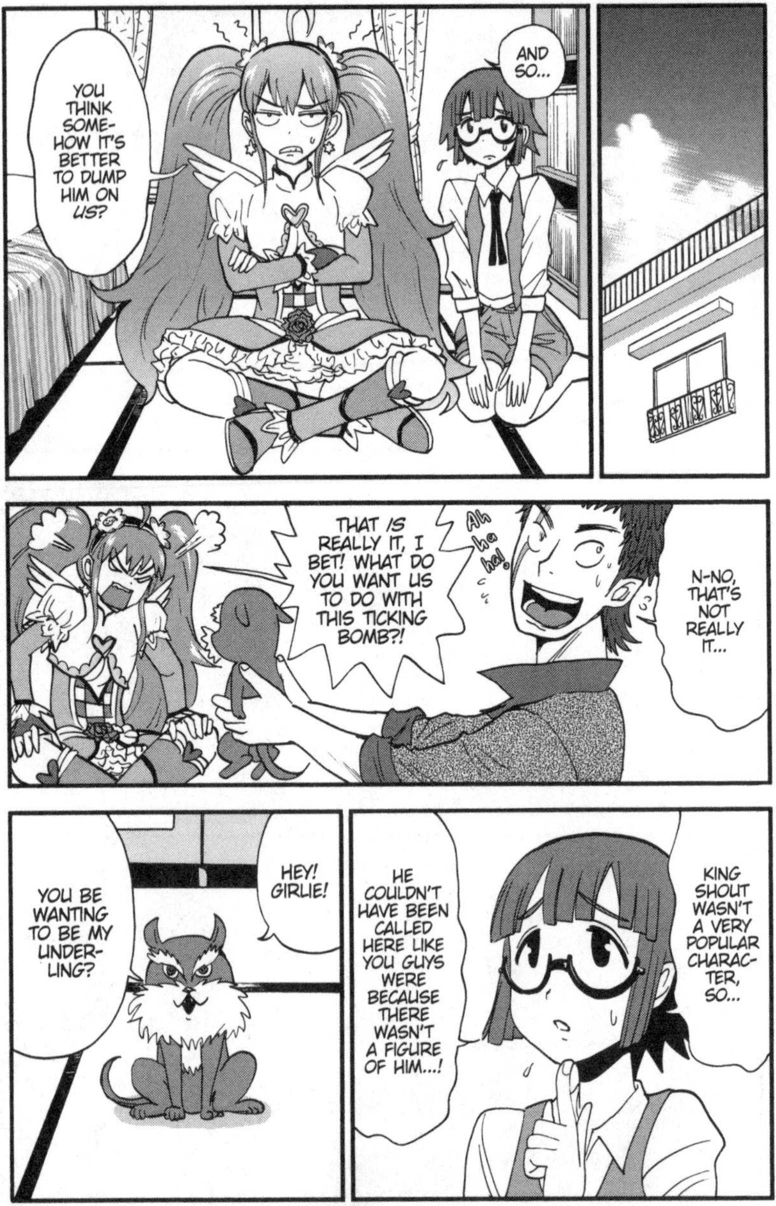
AND SO...
YOU THINK SOMEHOW IT'S BETTER TO DUMP HIM ON US?
N-NO, THAT'S NOT REALLY IT...
Ah ha ha!
THAT IS REALLY IT, I BET! WHAT DO YOU WANT US TO DO WITH THIS TICKING BOMB?!
KING SHOUT WASN'T A VERY POPULAR CHARACTER, SO...
HE COULDN'T HAVE BEEN CALLED HERE LIKE YOU GUYS WERE BECAUSE THERE WASN'T A FIGURE OF HIM...!
HEY! GIRLIE!
YOU BE WANTING TO BE MY UNDERLING?

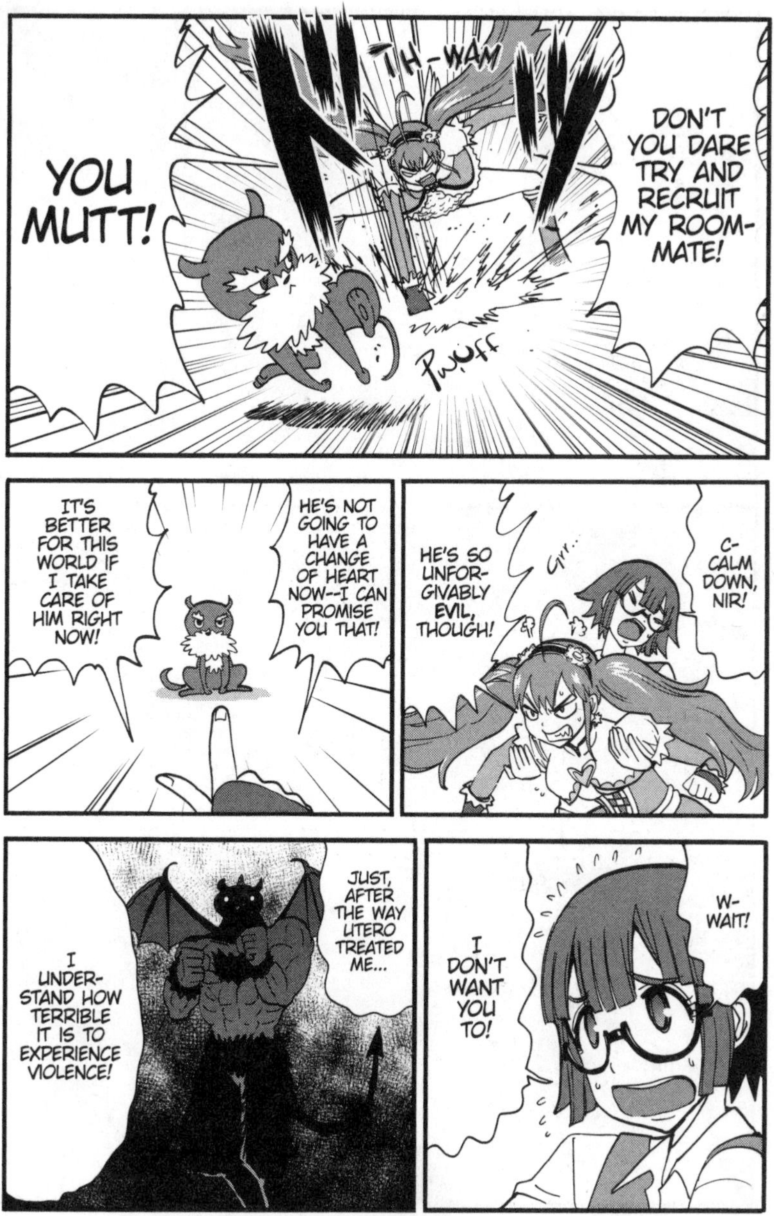
TH-WAM
DON'T YOU DARE TRY AND RECRUIT MY ROOM-MATE!
YOU MUTT!
PWUFF
C-CALM DOWN, NIR!
Grr...
HE'S SO UNFORGIVABLY EVIL, THOUGH!
HE'S NOT GOING TO HAVE A CHANGE OF HEART NOW--I CAN PROMISE YOU THAT!
IT'S BETTER FOR THIS WORLD IF I TAKE CARE OF HIM RIGHT NOW!
W-WAIT!
I DON'T WANT YOU TO!
JUST, AFTER THE WAY UTERO TREATED ME...
I UNDERSTAND HOW TERRIBLE IT IS TO EXPERIENCE VIOLENCE!

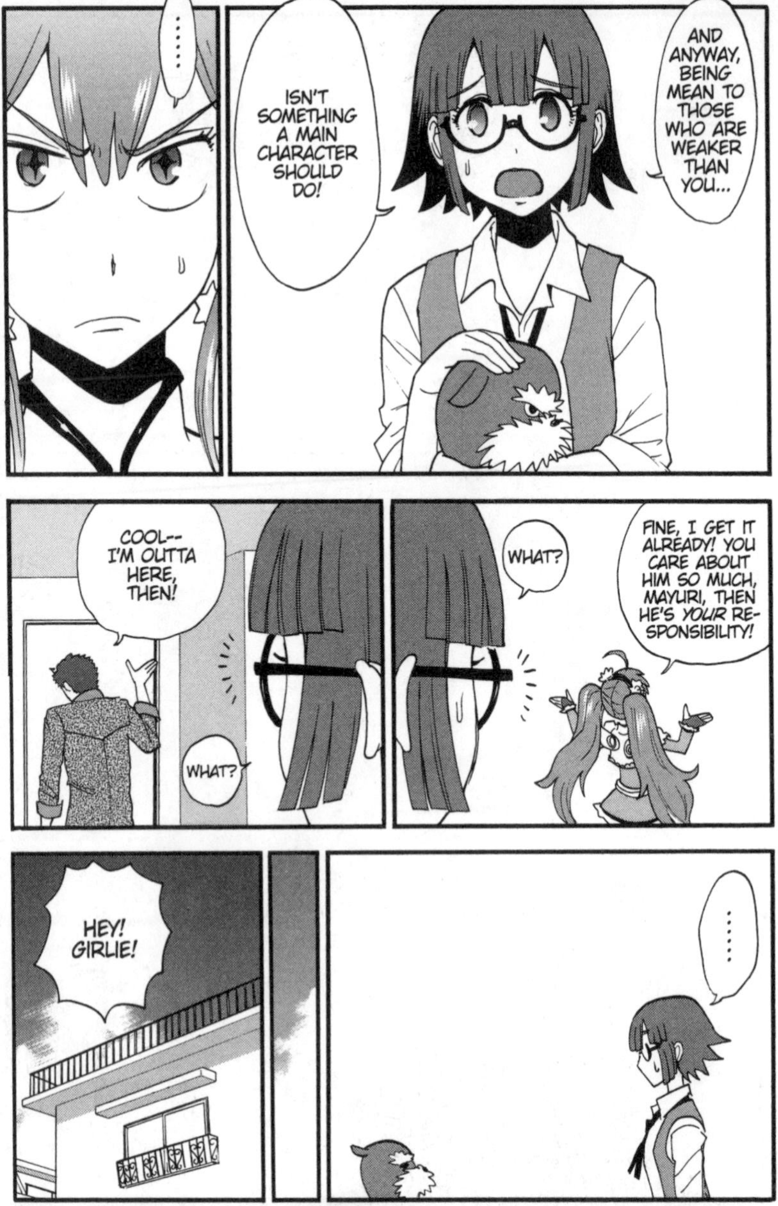
AND ANYWAY, BEING MEAN TO THOSE WHO ARE WEAKER THAN YOU...
ISN'T SOMETHING A MAIN CHARACTER SHOULD DO!
......
FINE, I GET IT ALREADY! YOU CARE ABOUT HIM SO MUCH, MAYURI, THEN HE'S *YOUR* RE-SPONSIBILITY!
WHAT?
COOL-- I'M OUTTA HERE, THEN!
WHAT?
......
HEY! GIRLIE!

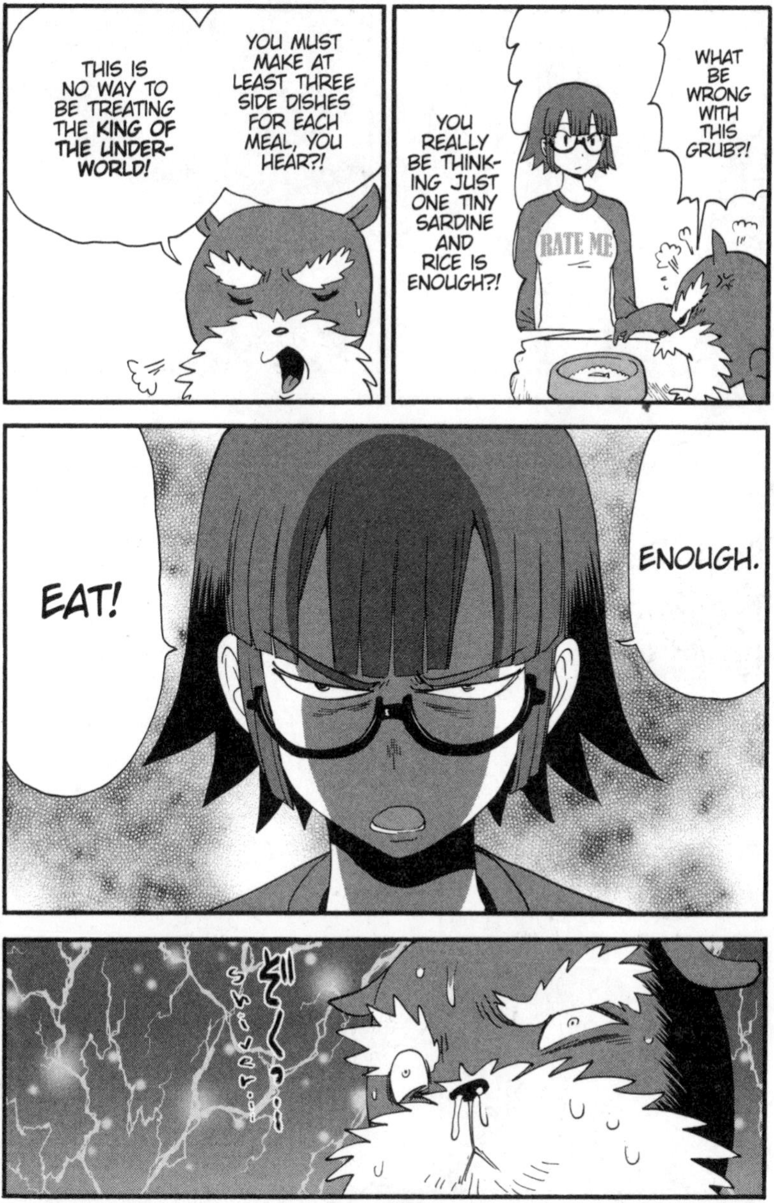
WHAT BE WRONG WITH THIS GRUB?!
YOU REALLY BE THINKING JUST ONE TINY SARDINE AND RICE IS ENOUGH?!
RATE ME
YOU MUST MAKE AT LEAST THREE SIDE DISHES FOR EACH MEAL, YOU HEAR?!
THIS IS NO WAY TO BE TREATING THE **KING OF THE UNDERWORLD!**
ENOUGH.
EAT!
ぞくぅ
shiver...

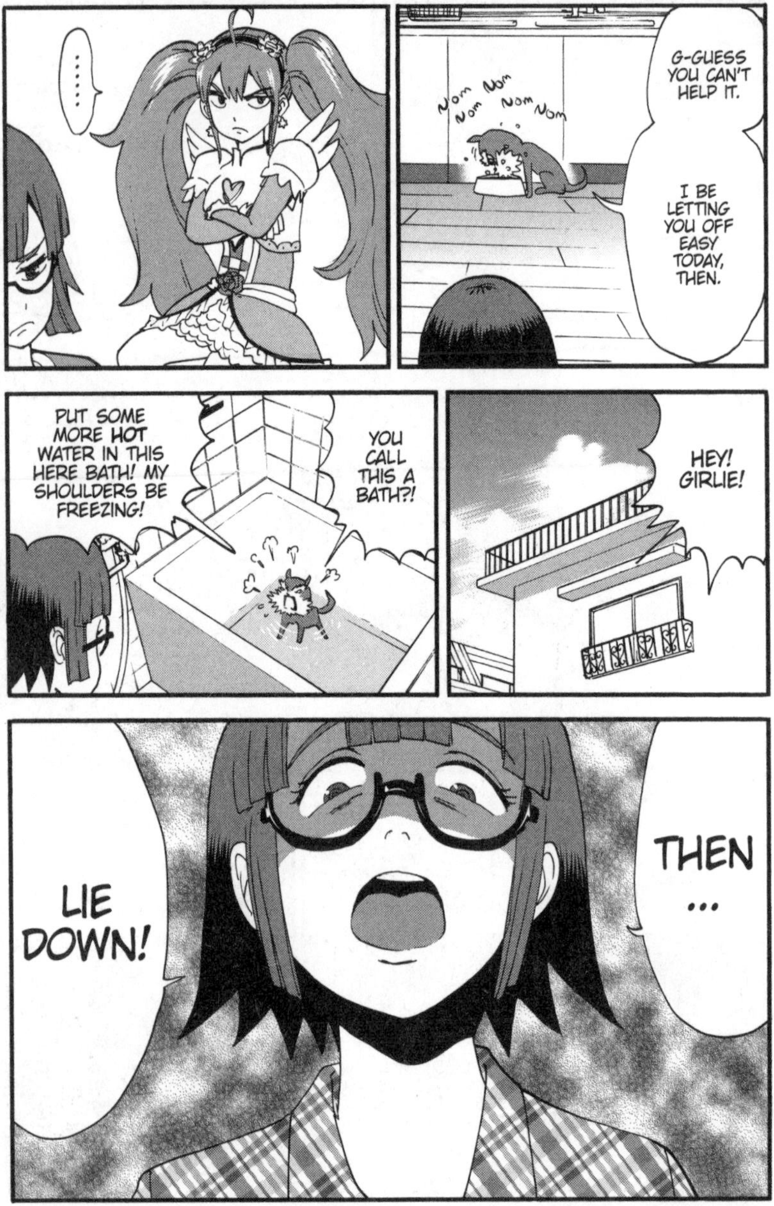
G-GUESS YOU CAN'T HELP IT.
Nom Nom Nom Nom Nom
I BE LETTING YOU OFF EASY TODAY, THEN.
......
HEY! GIRLIE!
YOU CALL THIS A BATH?!
PUT SOME MORE HOT WATER IN THIS HERE BATH! MY SHOULDERS BE FREEZING!
THEN ...
LIE DOWN!

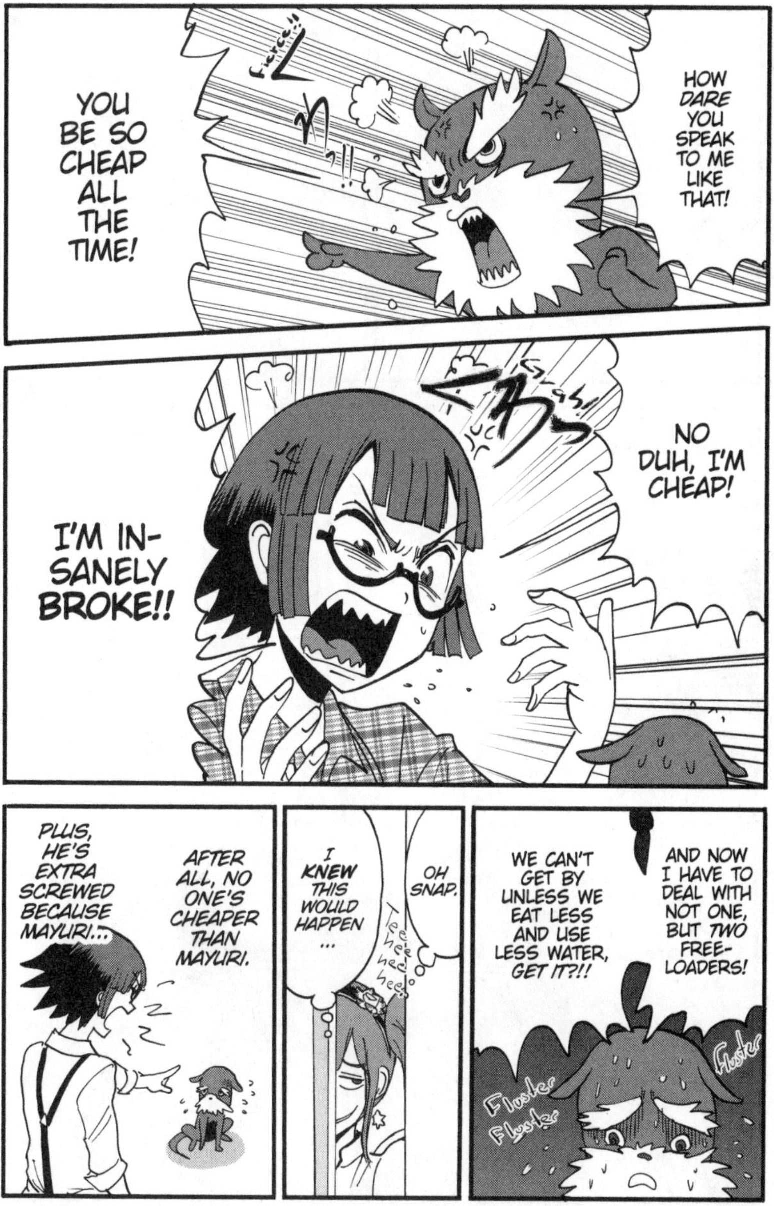
HOW DARE YOU SPEAK TO ME LIKE THAT!
Fierce!!
YOU BE SO CHEAP ALL THE TIME!
NO DUH, I'M CHEAP!
I'M IN-SANELY BROKE!!
AND NOW I HAVE TO DEAL WITH NOT ONE, BUT TWO FREE-LOADERS!
WE CAN'T GET BY UNLESS WE EAT LESS AND USE LESS WATER, GET IT?!!
Fluster
Fluster Fluster
OH SNAP.
I KNEW THIS WOULD HAPPEN...
Tee hee hee hee
AFTER ALL, NO ONE'S CHEAPER THAN MAYURI.
PLUS, HE'S EXTRA SCREWED BECAUSE MAYURI...

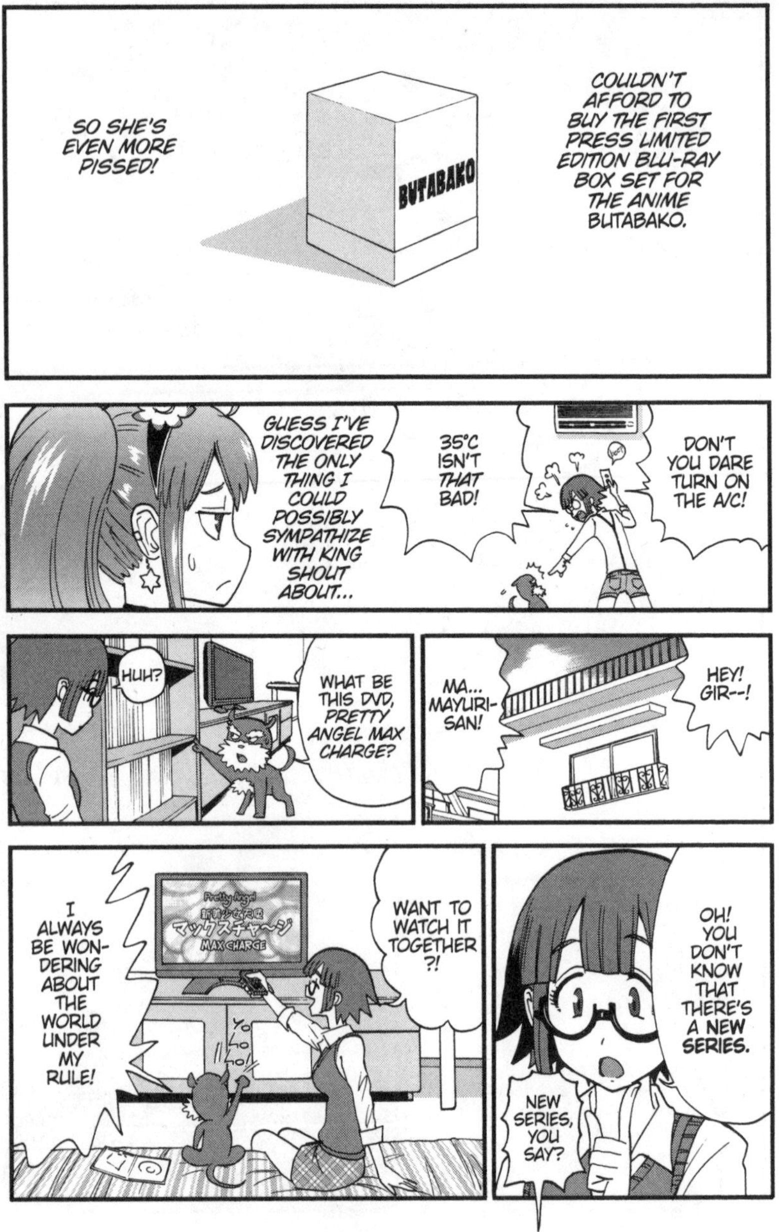

COULDN'T AFFORD TO BUY THE FIRST PRESS LIMITED EDITION BLU-RAY BOX SET FOR THE ANIME BUTABAKO.
BUTABAKO
SO SHE'S EVEN MORE PISSED!
DON'T YOU DARE TURN ON THE A/C!
35°C ISN'T THAT BAD!
GUESS I'VE DISCOVERED THE ONLY THING I COULD POSSIBLY SYMPATHIZE WITH KING SHOUT ABOUT...
HEY! GIR--!
MA... MAYURI-SAN!
WHAT BE THIS DVD, PRETTY ANGEL MAX CHARGE?
HUH?
OH! YOU DON'T KNOW THAT THERE'S A NEW SERIES.
NEW SERIES, YOU SAY?
WANT TO WATCH IT TOGETHER?!
Pretty Angel
マックスチャ〜ジ
MAX CHARGE
I ALWAYS BE WON-DERING ABOUT THE WORLD UNDER MY RULE!

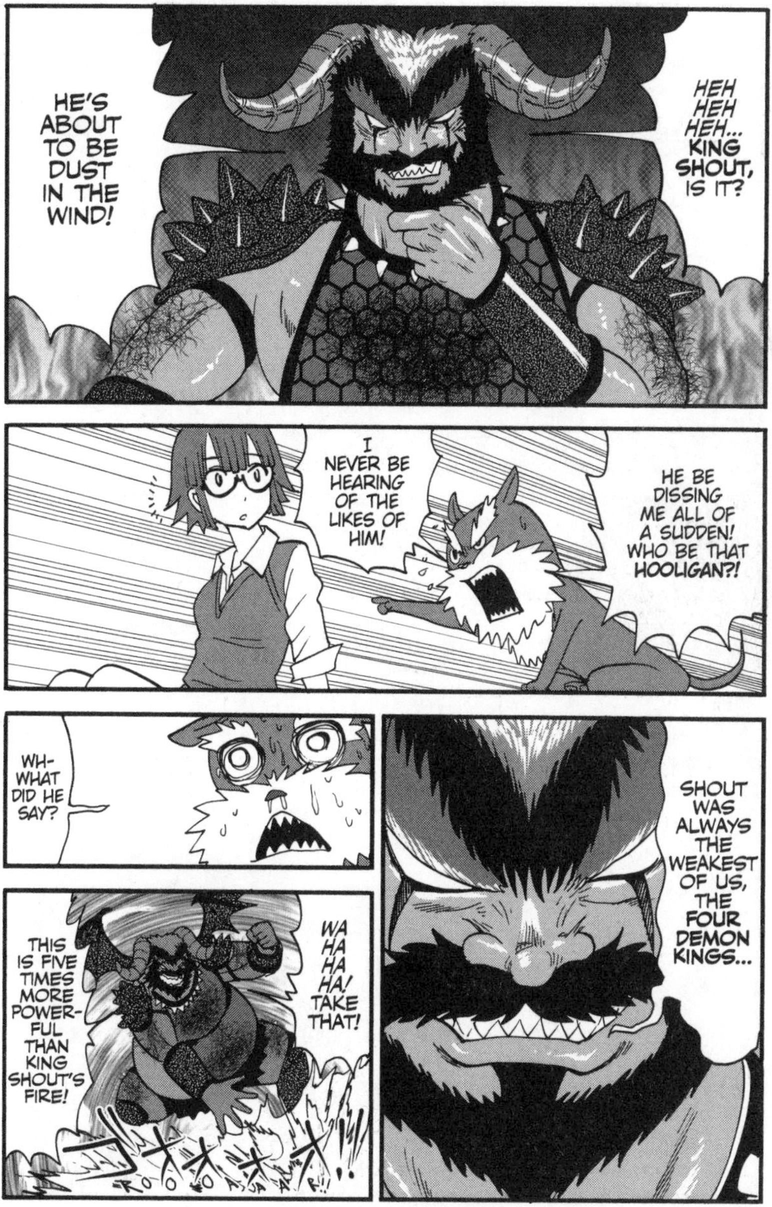
HEH HEH HEH... KING SHOUT, IS IT?
HE'S ABOUT TO BE DUST IN THE WIND!
HE BE DISSING ME ALL OF A SUDDEN! WHO BE THAT HOOLIGAN?!
I NEVER BE HEARING OF THE LIKES OF HIM!
SHOUT WAS ALWAYS THE WEAKEST OF US, THE FOUR DEMON KINGS...
WH- WHAT DID HE SAY?
WA HA HA HA! TAKE THAT!
THIS IS FIVE TIMES MORE POWERFUL THAN KING SHOUT'S FIRE!
ROOOAAAR!!

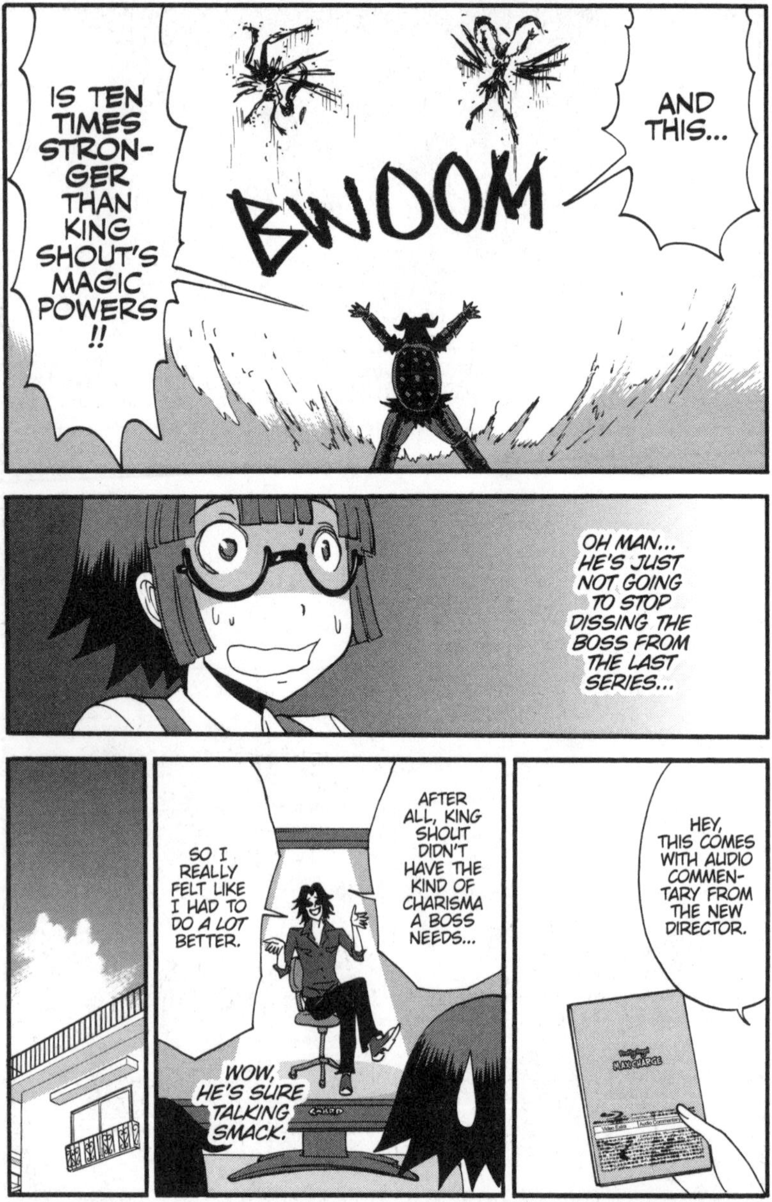
AND THIS...
BWOOM
IS TEN TIMES STRONGER THAN KING SHOUT'S MAGIC POWERS!!
OH MAN... HE'S JUST NOT GOING TO STOP DISSING THE BOSS FROM THE LAST SERIES...
HEY, THIS COMES WITH AUDIO COMMENTARY FROM THE NEW DIRECTOR.
AFTER ALL, KING SHOUT DIDN'T HAVE THE KIND OF CHARISMA A BOSS NEEDS...
SO I REALLY FELT LIKE I HAD TO DO A LOT BETTER.
WOW, HE'S SURE TALKING SMACK.

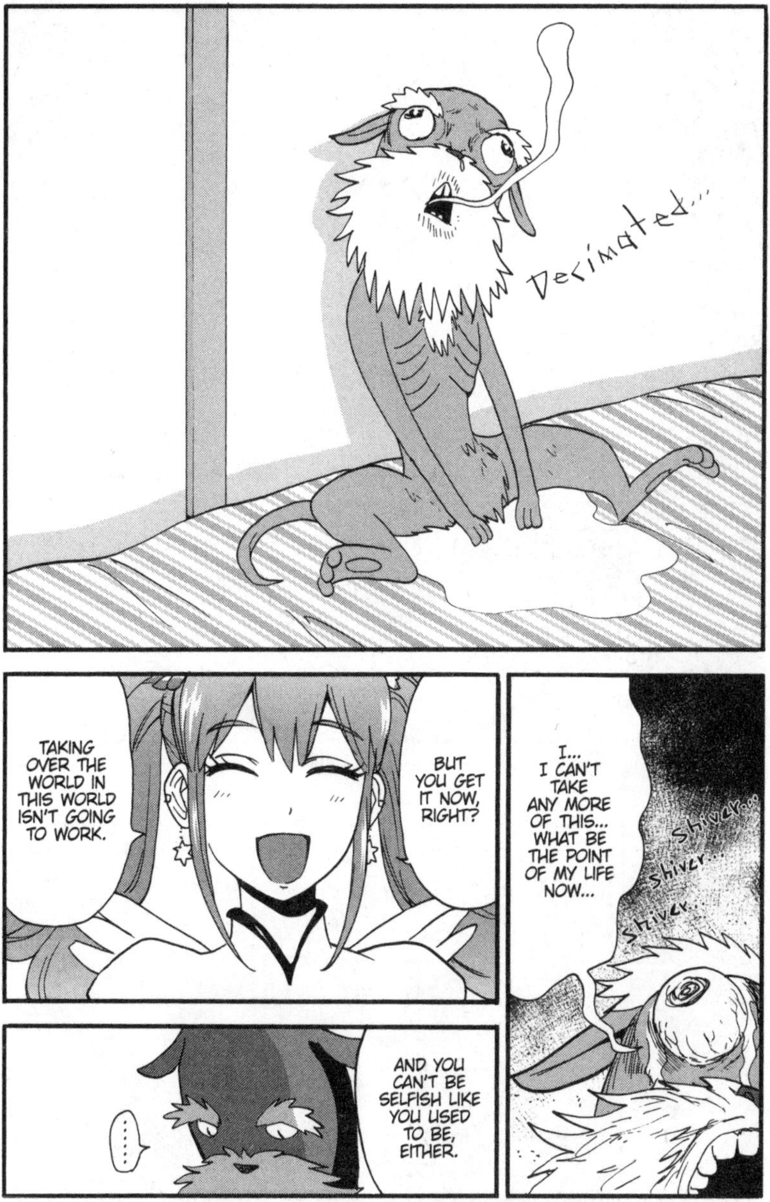
Decimated....
I... I CAN'T TAKE ANY MORE OF THIS... WHAT BE THE POINT OF MY LIFE NOW...
Shiver...
Shiver...
Shiver...
BUT YOU GET IT NOW, RIGHT?
TAKING OVER THE WORLD IN THIS WORLD ISN'T GOING TO WORK.
AND YOU CAN'T BE SELFISH LIKE YOU USED TO BE, EITHER.
......

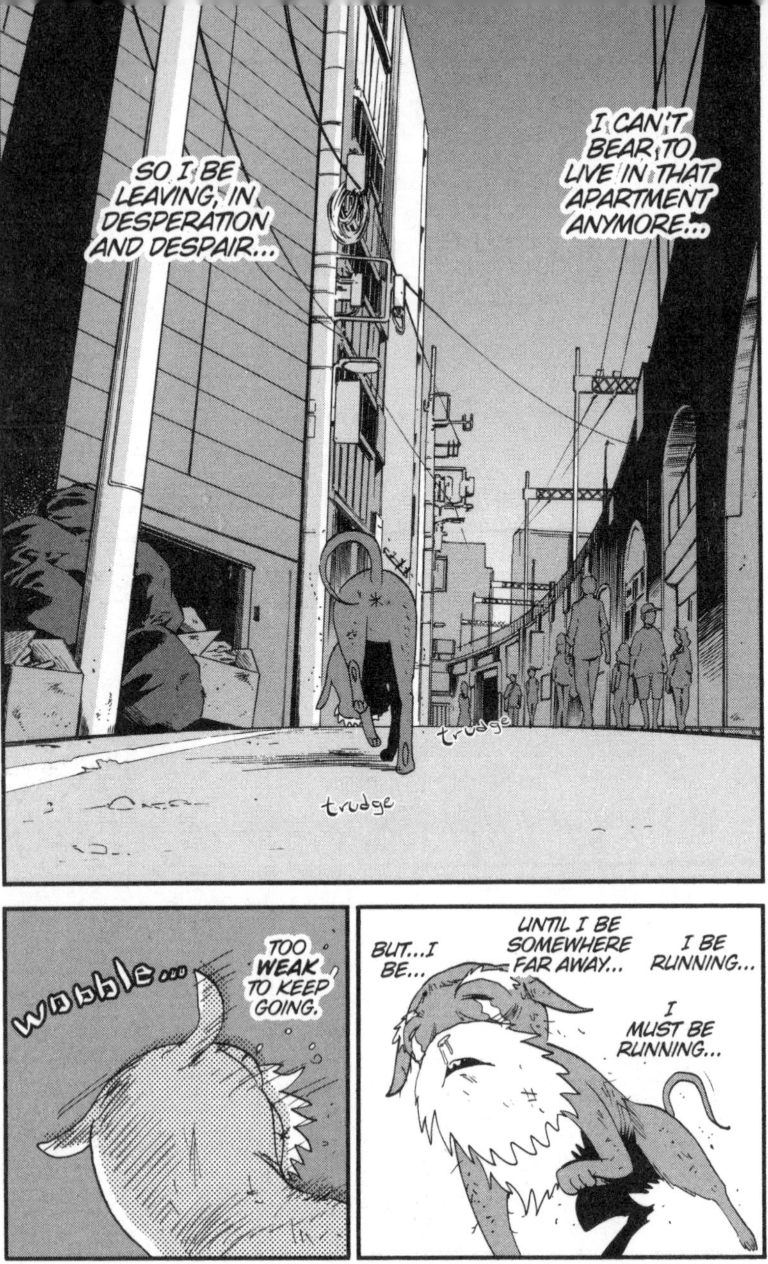
I CAN'T BEAR TO LIVE IN THAT APARTMENT ANYMORE...
SO I BE LEAVING, IN DESPERATION AND DESPAIR...
trudge
trudge
I BE RUNNING...
UNTIL I BE SOMEWHERE FAR AWAY...
I MUST BE RUNNING...
BUT...I BE...
TOO **WEAK** TO KEEP GOING.
wobble...

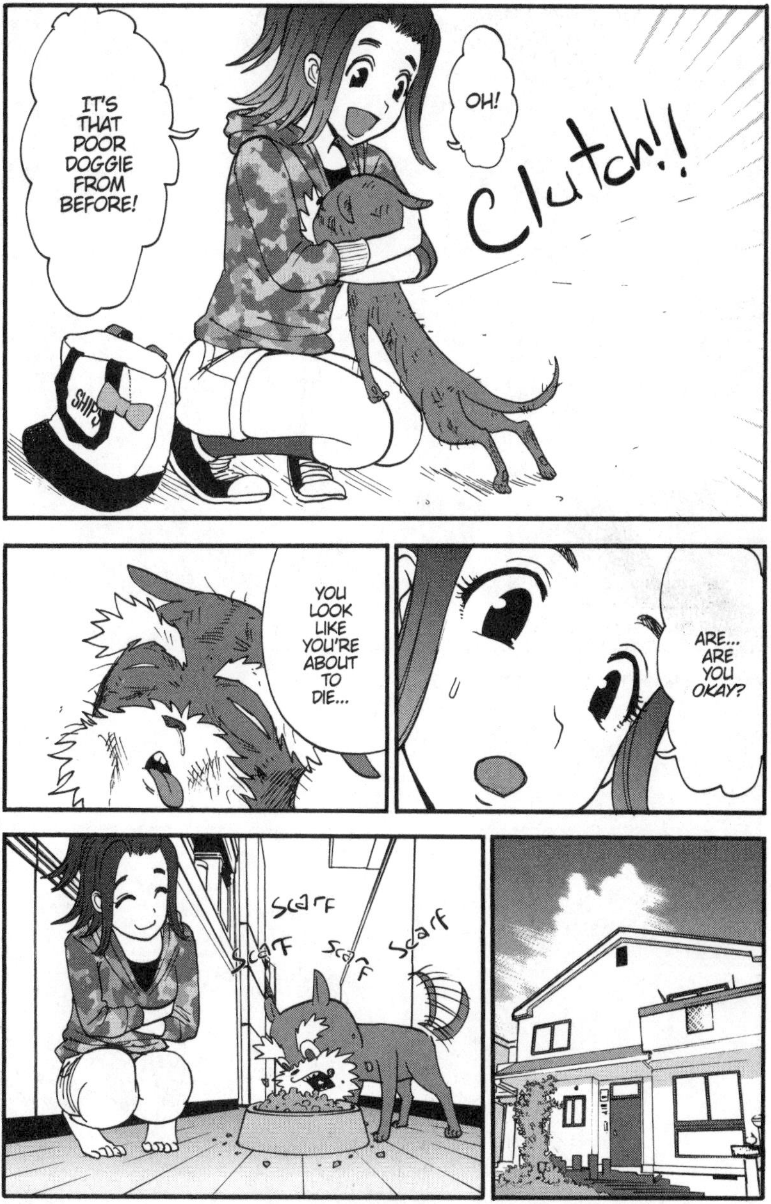
OH!
Clutch!!
IT'S THAT POOR DOGGIE FROM BEFORE!
ARE... ARE YOU OKAY?
YOU LOOK LIKE YOU'RE ABOUT TO DIE...
Scarf
Scarf
Scarf
Scarf

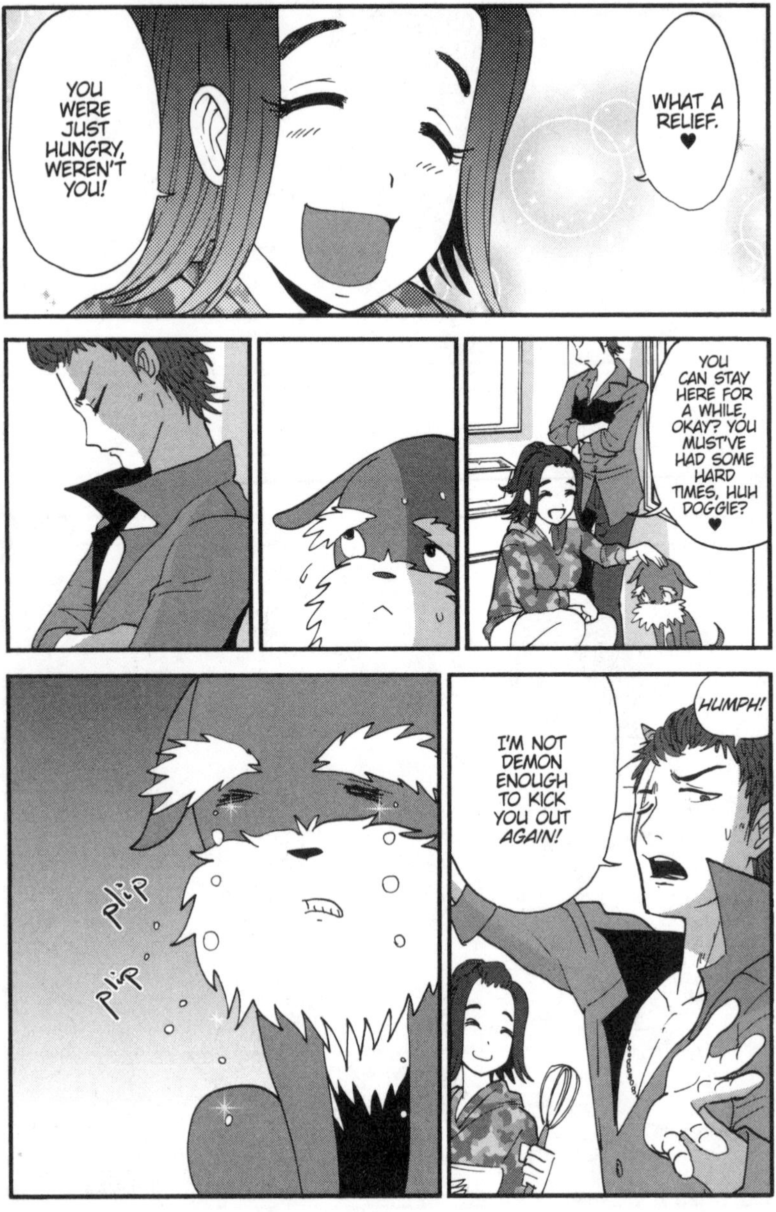
WHAT A RELIEF. ♥
YOU WERE JUST HUNGRY, WEREN'T YOU!
YOU CAN STAY HERE FOR A WHILE, OKAY? YOU MUST'VE HAD SOME HARD TIMES, HUH DOGGIE? ♥
HUMPH!
I'M NOT DEMON ENOUGH TO KICK YOU OUT AGAIN!
plip
plip

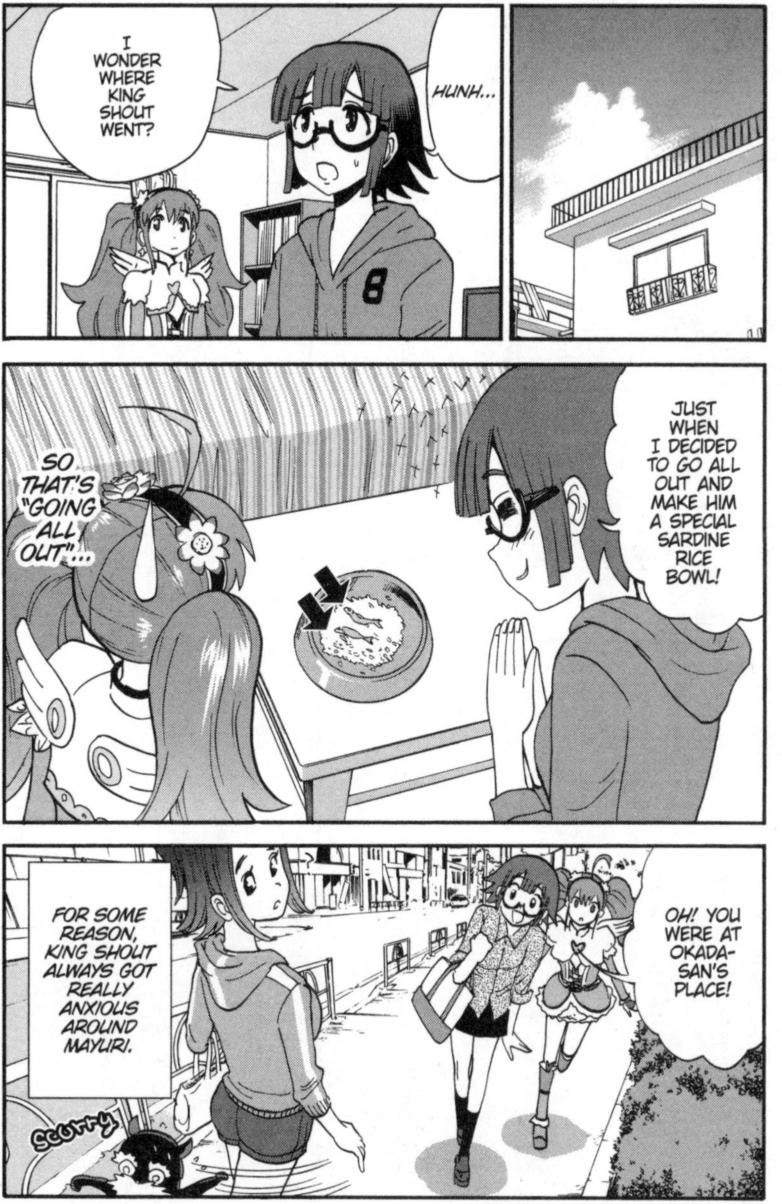
HUNH...
I WONDER WHERE KING SHOUT WENT?
JUST WHEN I DECIDED TO GO ALL OUT AND MAKE HIM A SPECIAL SARDINE RICE BOWL!
SO THAT'S "GOING ALL OUT"...
OH! YOU WERE AT OKADA-SAN'S PLACE!
FOR SOME REASON, KING SHOUT ALWAYS GOT REALLY ANXIOUS AROUND MAYURI.
SCURRY

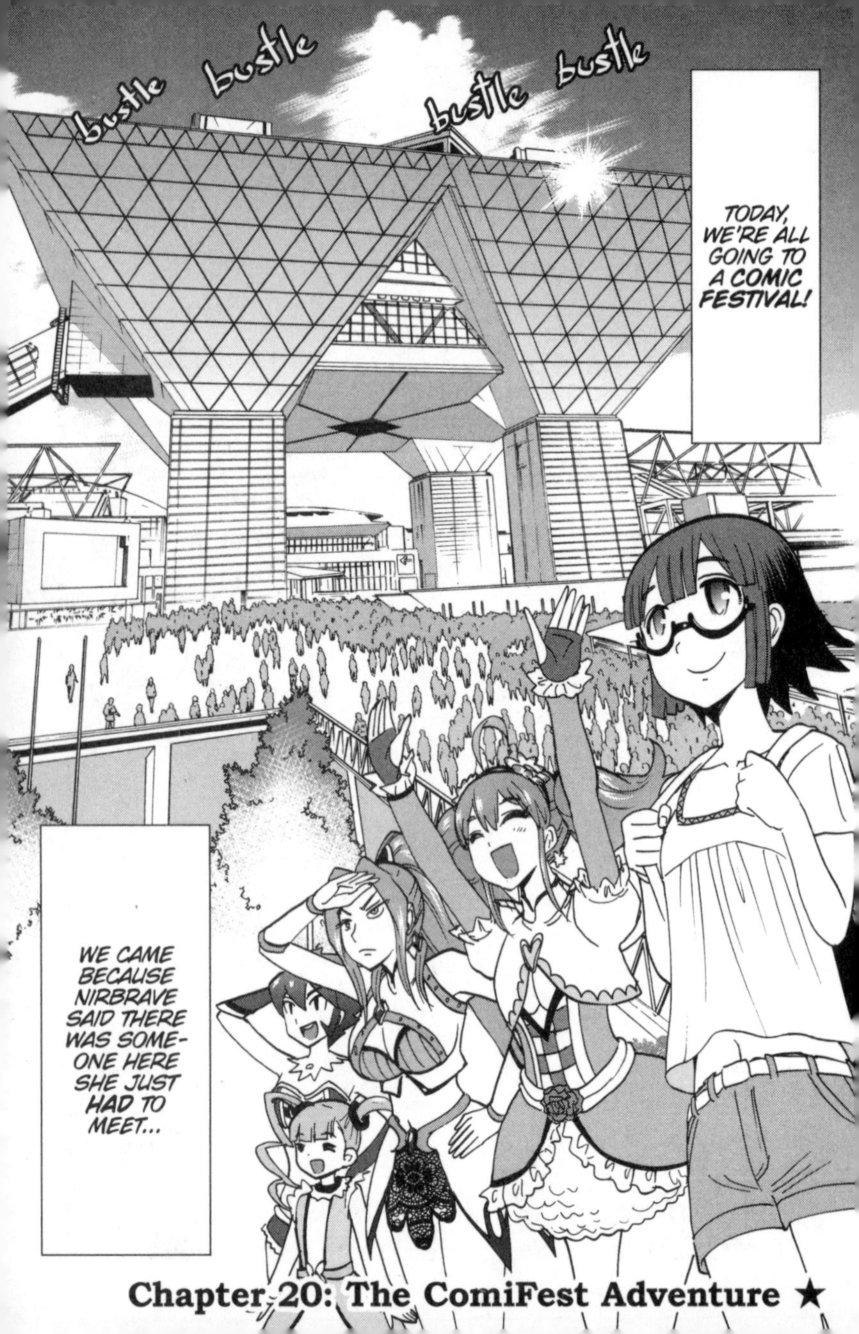

TODAY, WE'RE ALL GOING TO A COMIC FESTIVAL!
bustle bustle
bustle bustle
WE CAME BECAUSE NIRBRAVE SAID THERE WAS SOME-ONE HERE SHE JUST HAD TO MEET...
Chapter 20: The ComiFest Adventure ★

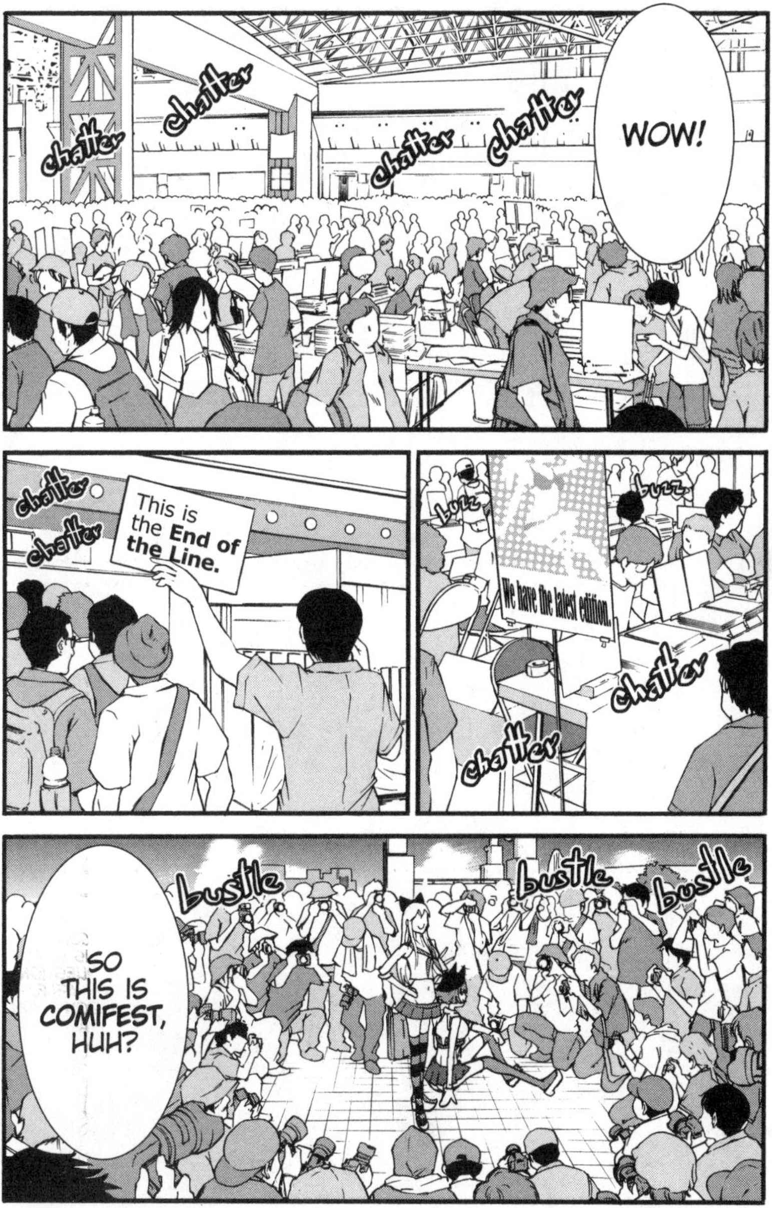
WOW!
chatter
chatter
chatter
chatter
buzz
buzz
We have the latest edition.
chatter
chatter
chatter
chatter
This is the **End of the Line.**
bustle
bustle
bustle
SO THIS IS COMIFEST, HUH?

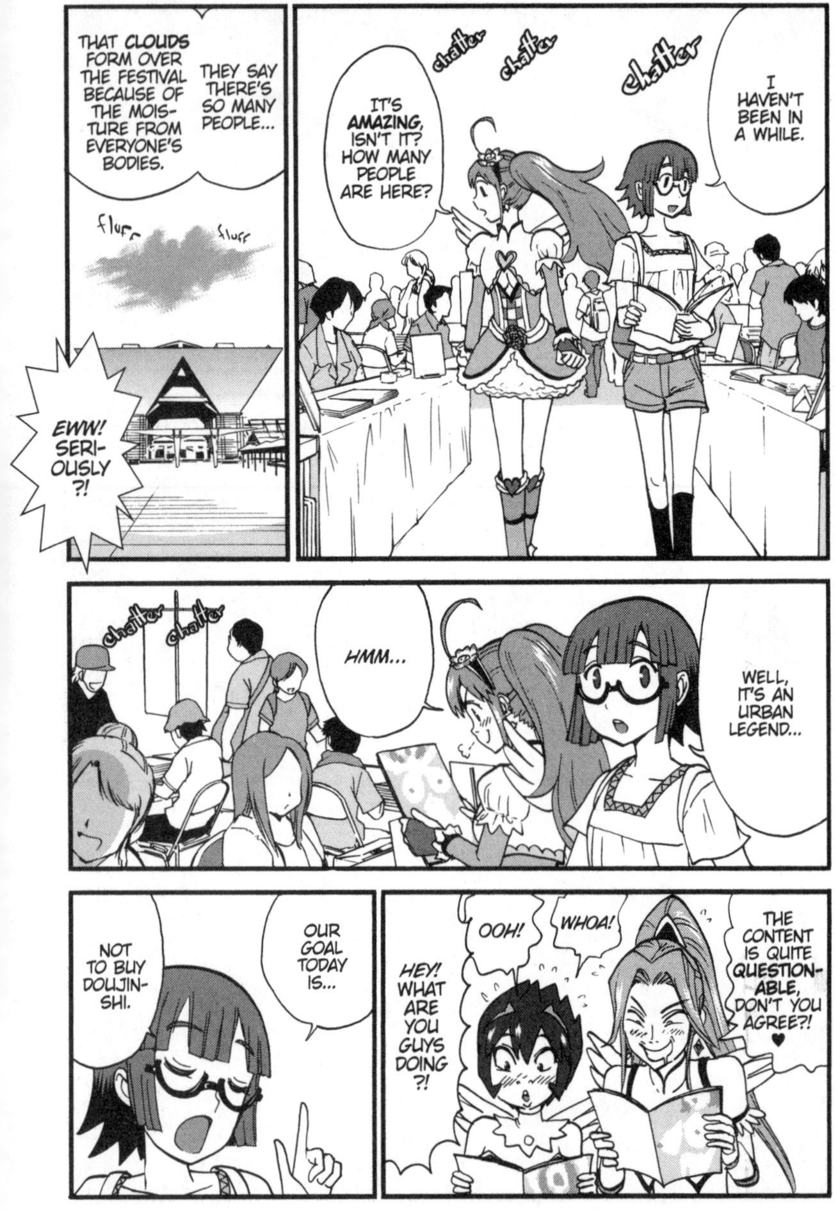
I HAVEN'T BEEN IN A WHILE.
chatter
chatter
chatter
IT'S **AMAZING**, ISN'T IT? HOW MANY PEOPLE ARE HERE?
THEY SAY THERE'S SO MANY PEOPLE...
THAT **CLOUDS** FORM OVER THE FESTIVAL BECAUSE OF THE MOISTURE FROM EVERYONE'S BODIES.
fluff
fluff
EWW! SERIOUSLY?!
WELL, IT'S AN URBAN LEGEND...
HMM...
chatter
chatter
THE CONTENT IS QUITE **QUESTIONABLE**, DON'T YOU AGREE?! ♥
WHOA!
OOH!
HEY! WHAT ARE YOU GUYS DOING?!
OUR GOAL TODAY IS...
NOT TO BUY DOUJINSHI.

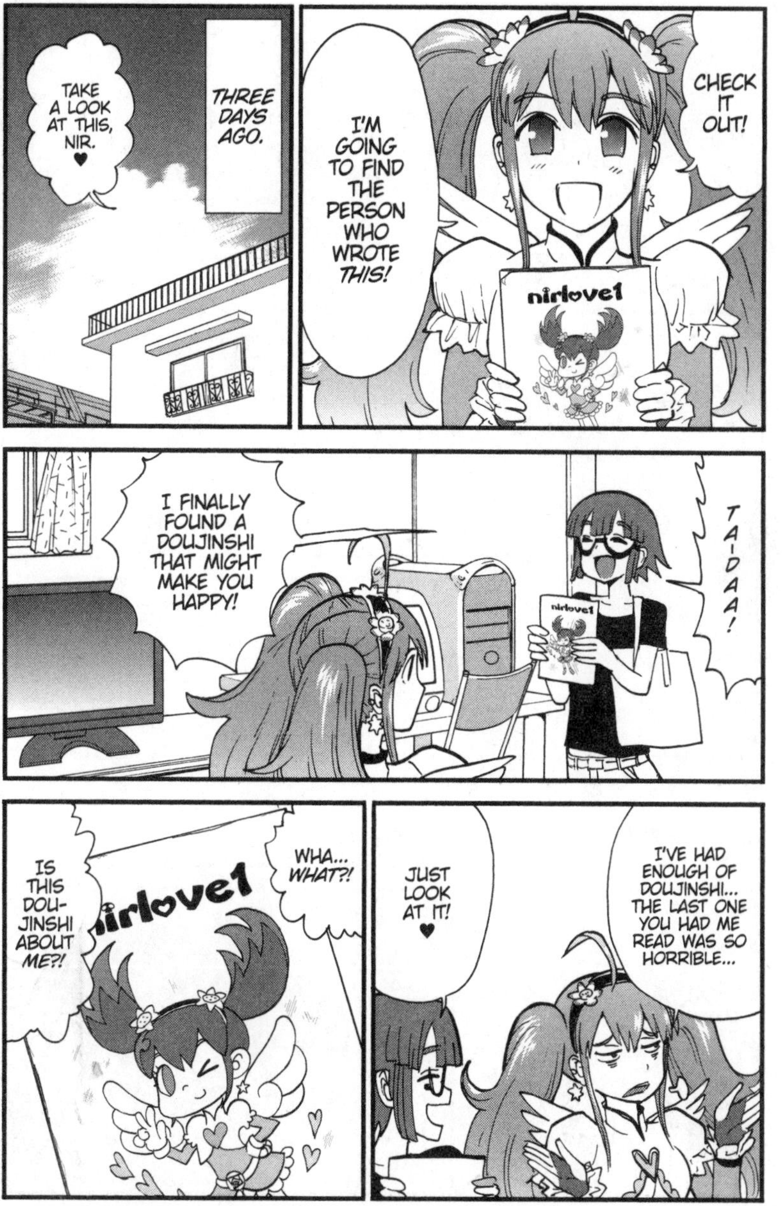
CHECK IT OUT!
I'M GOING TO FIND THE PERSON WHO WROTE *THIS!*
nirlove1
THREE DAYS AGO.
TAKE A LOOK AT THIS, NIR. ♥
TA-DAA!
I FINALLY FOUND A DOUJINSHI THAT MIGHT MAKE YOU HAPPY!
nirlove1
I'VE HAD ENOUGH OF DOUJINSHI... THE LAST ONE YOU HAD ME READ WAS SO HORRIBLE...
JUST LOOK AT IT! ♥
WHA... *WHAT?!*
IS THIS DOUJINSHI ABOUT *ME?!*
nirlove1

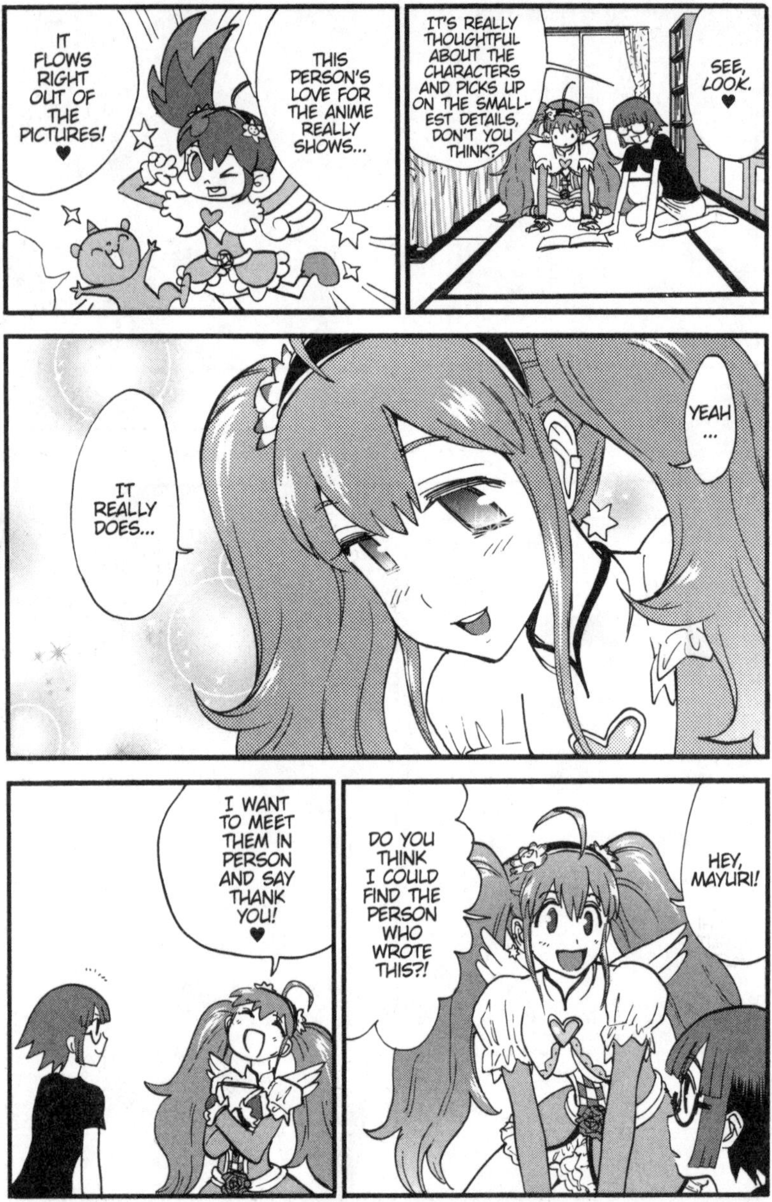
SEE, LOOK. ♥
IT'S REALLY THOUGHTFUL ABOUT THE CHARACTERS AND PICKS UP ON THE SMALL-EST DETAILS, DON'T YOU THINK?
THIS PERSON'S LOVE FOR THE ANIME REALLY SHOWS...
IT FLOWS RIGHT OUT OF THE PICTURES! ♥
YEAH...
IT REALLY DOES...
HEY, MAYURI!
DO YOU THINK I COULD FIND THE PERSON WHO WROTE THIS?!
I WANT TO MEET THEM IN PERSON AND SAY THANK YOU! ♥

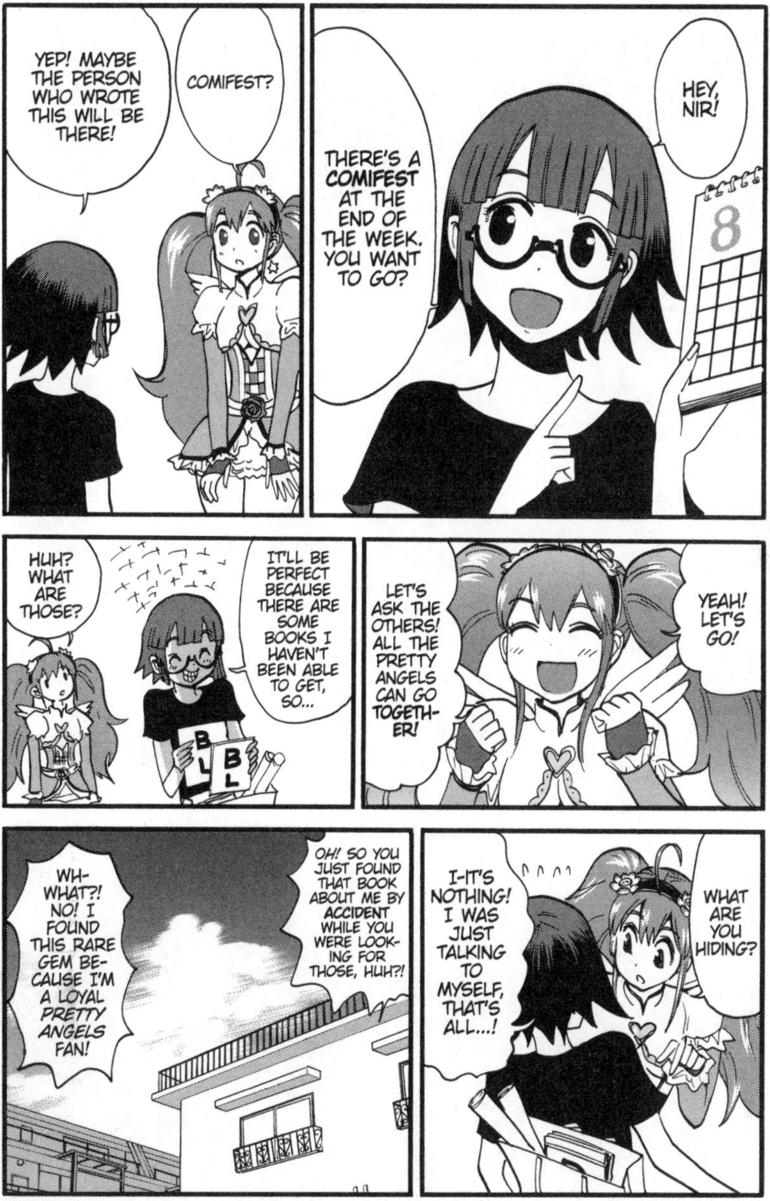
HEY, NIR!
THERE'S A **COMIFEST** AT THE END OF THE WEEK. YOU WANT TO GO?
COMIFEST?
YEP! MAYBE THE PERSON WHO WROTE THIS WILL BE THERE!
YEAH! LET'S GO!
LET'S ASK THE OTHERS! ALL THE PRETTY ANGELS CAN GO **TOGETH-ER!**
IT'LL BE PERFECT BECAUSE THERE ARE SOME BOOKS I HAVEN'T BEEN ABLE TO GET, SO...
HUH? WHAT ARE THOSE?
BL
BL
WHAT ARE YOU HIDING?
I-IT'S NOTHING! I WAS JUST TALKING TO MYSELF, THAT'S ALL...!
OH! SO YOU JUST FOUND THAT BOOK ABOUT ME BY ***ACCIDENT*** *WHILE YOU WERE LOOK-ING FOR THOSE, HUH?!*
WH-WHAT?! NO! I FOUND THIS RARE GEM BE-CAUSE I'M A LOYAL *PRETTY ANGELS* FAN!

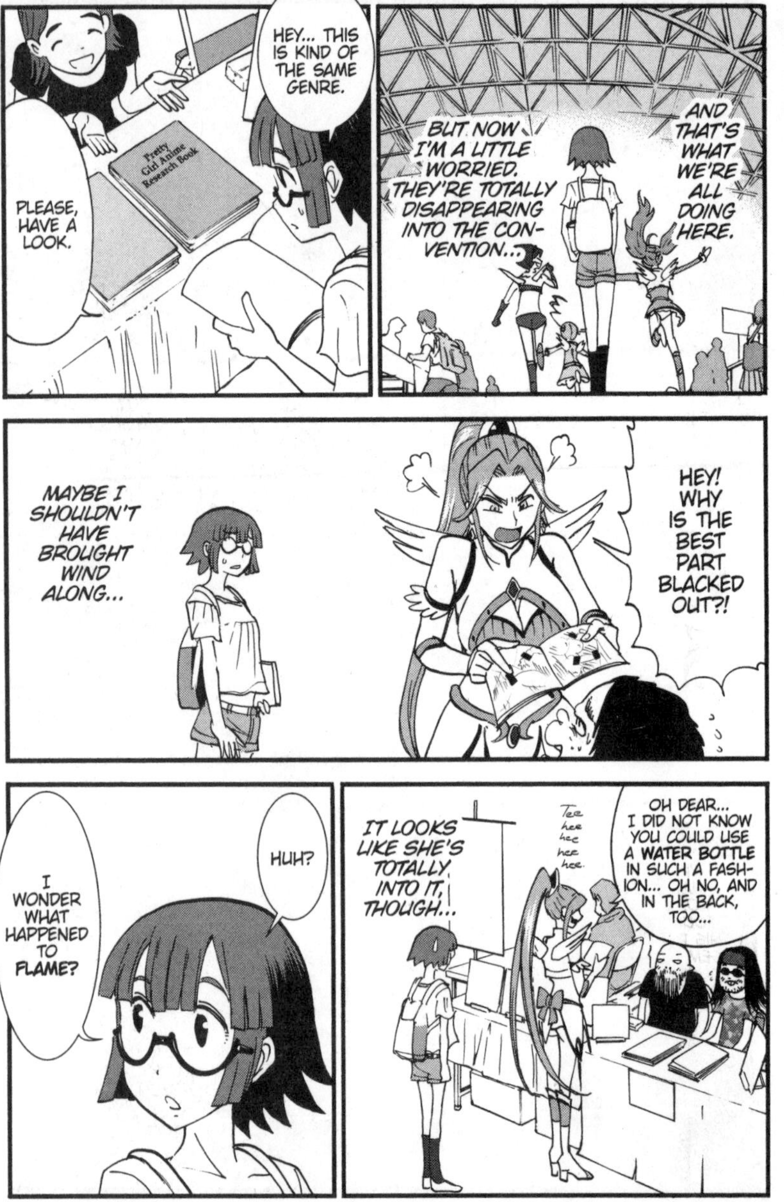
AND THAT'S WHAT WE'RE ALL DOING HERE.
BUT NOW I'M A LITTLE WORRIED. THEY'RE TOTALLY DISAPPEARING INTO THE CON-VENTION...
HEY... THIS IS KIND OF THE SAME GENRE.
Pretty Girl Anime Research Book
PLEASE, HAVE A LOOK.
HEY! WHY IS THE BEST PART BLACKED OUT?!
MAYBE I SHOULDN'T HAVE BROUGHT WIND ALONG...
OH DEAR... I DID NOT KNOW YOU COULD USE A WATER BOTTLE IN SUCH A FASH-ION... OH NO, AND IN THE BACK, TOO...
Tee hee hee hee hee.
IT LOOKS LIKE SHE'S TOTALLY INTO IT, THOUGH...
HUH?
I WONDER WHAT HAPPENED TO FLAME?

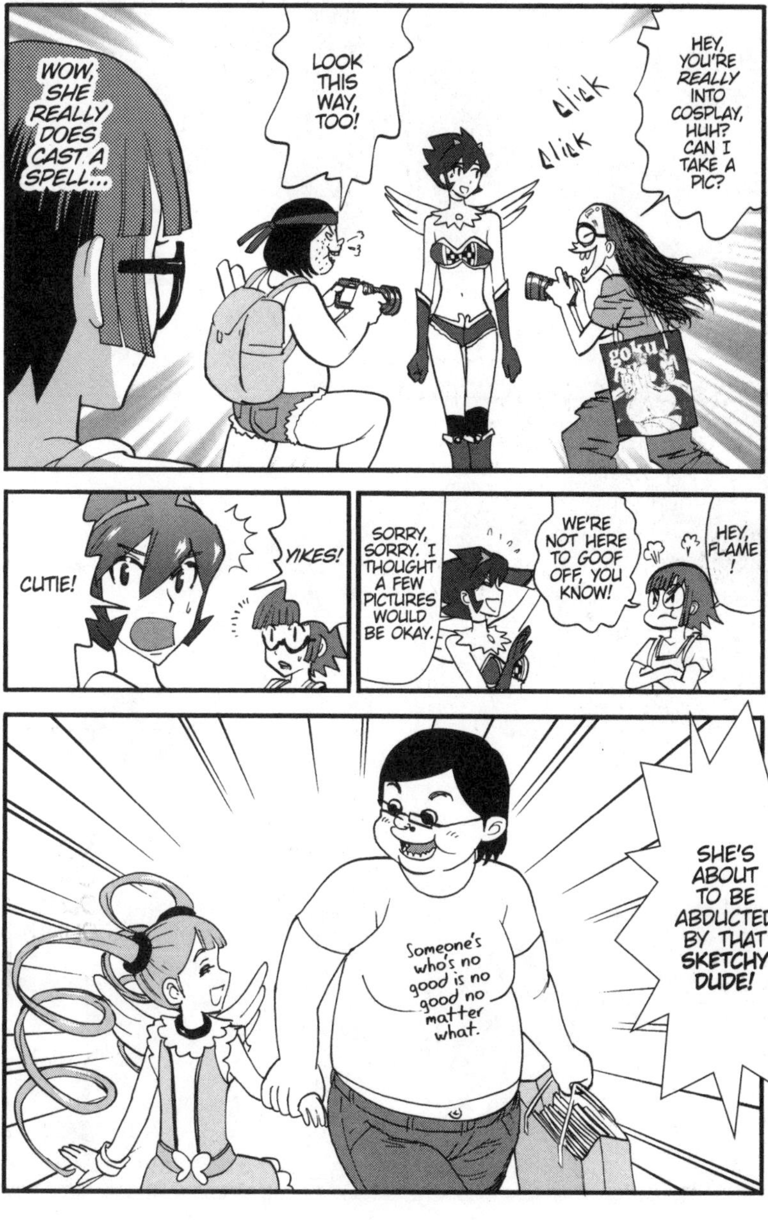
HEY, YOU'RE *REALLY* INTO COSPLAY, HUH? CAN I TAKE A PIC?
click
click
LOOK THIS WAY, TOO!
goku
WOW, SHE REALLY DOES CAST A SPELL...
HEY, FLAME!
WE'RE NOT HERE TO GOOF OFF, YOU KNOW!
SORRY, SORRY. I THOUGHT A FEW PICTURES WOULD BE OKAY.
YIKES!
CUTIE!
SHE'S ABOUT TO BE ABDUCTED BY THAT **SKETCHY DUDE!**
Someone's who's no good is no good no matter what.

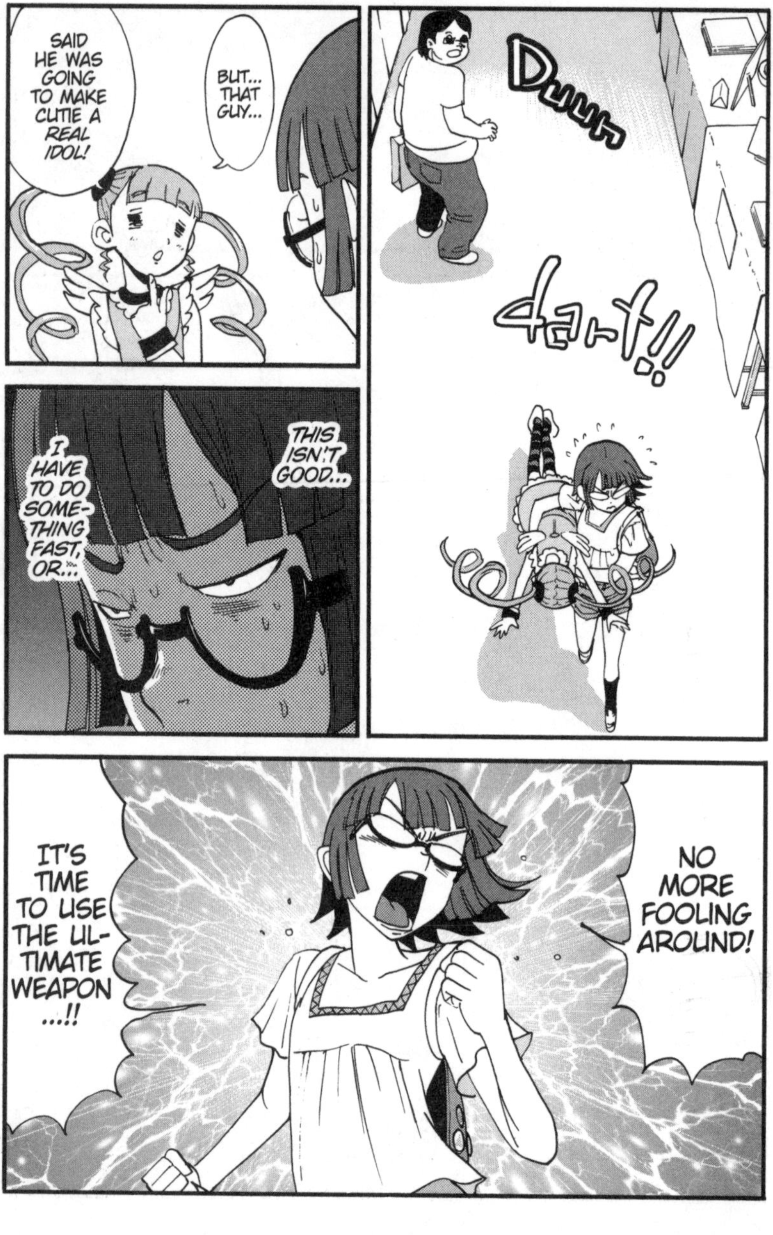
Duuun
dart!!
BUT... THAT GUY...
SAID HE WAS GOING TO MAKE CUTIE A REAL IDOL!
THIS ISN'T GOOD...
I HAVE TO DO SOME-THING FAST, OR...
NO MORE FOOLING AROUND!
IT'S TIME TO USE THE ULTIMATE WEAPON ...!!

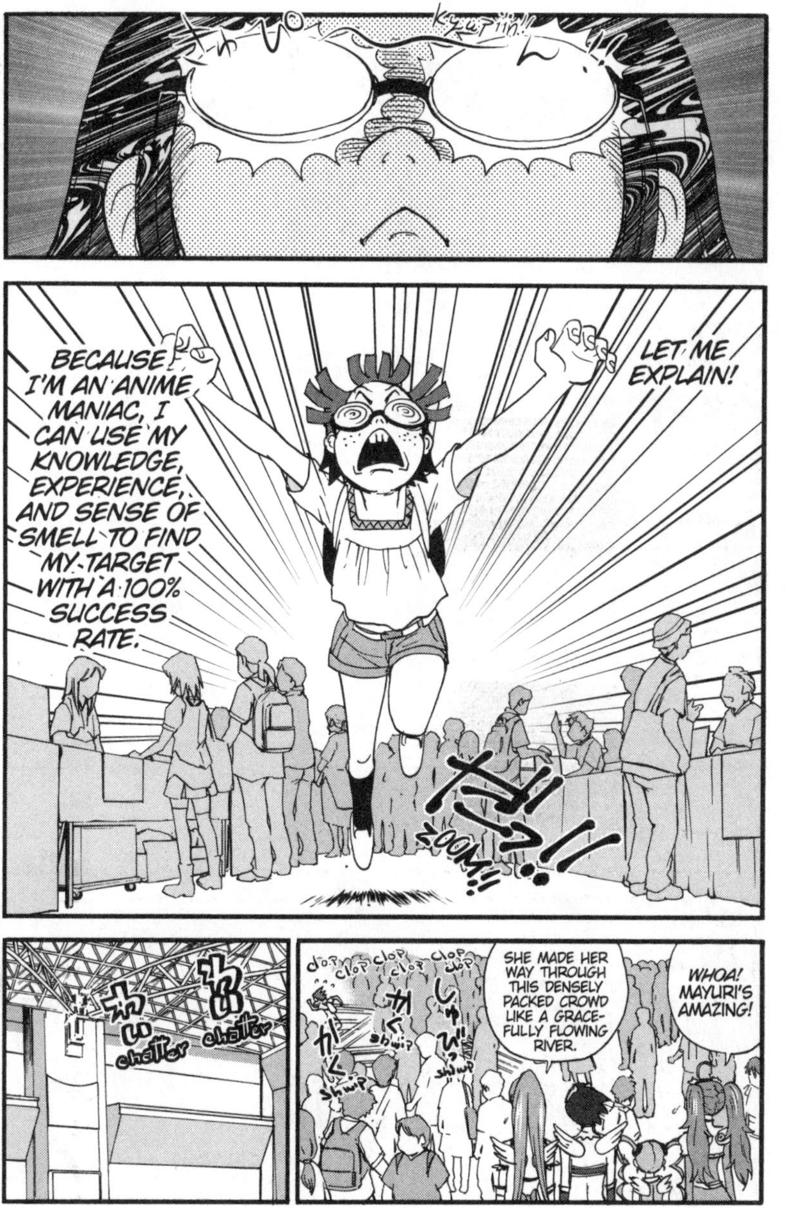
Kyupiin!!
LET ME EXPLAIN!
BECAUSE I'M AN ANIME MANIAC, I CAN USE MY KNOWLEDGE, EXPERIENCE, AND SENSE OF SMELL TO FIND MY TARGET WITH A 100% SUCCESS RATE.
ZOOM!!
WHOA! MAYURI'S AMAZING!
SHE MADE HER WAY THROUGH THIS DENSELY PACKED CROWD LIKE A GRACEFULLY FLOWING RIVER.
clop clop clop clop clop clop
shwip
shwip
shwip
chatter
chatter

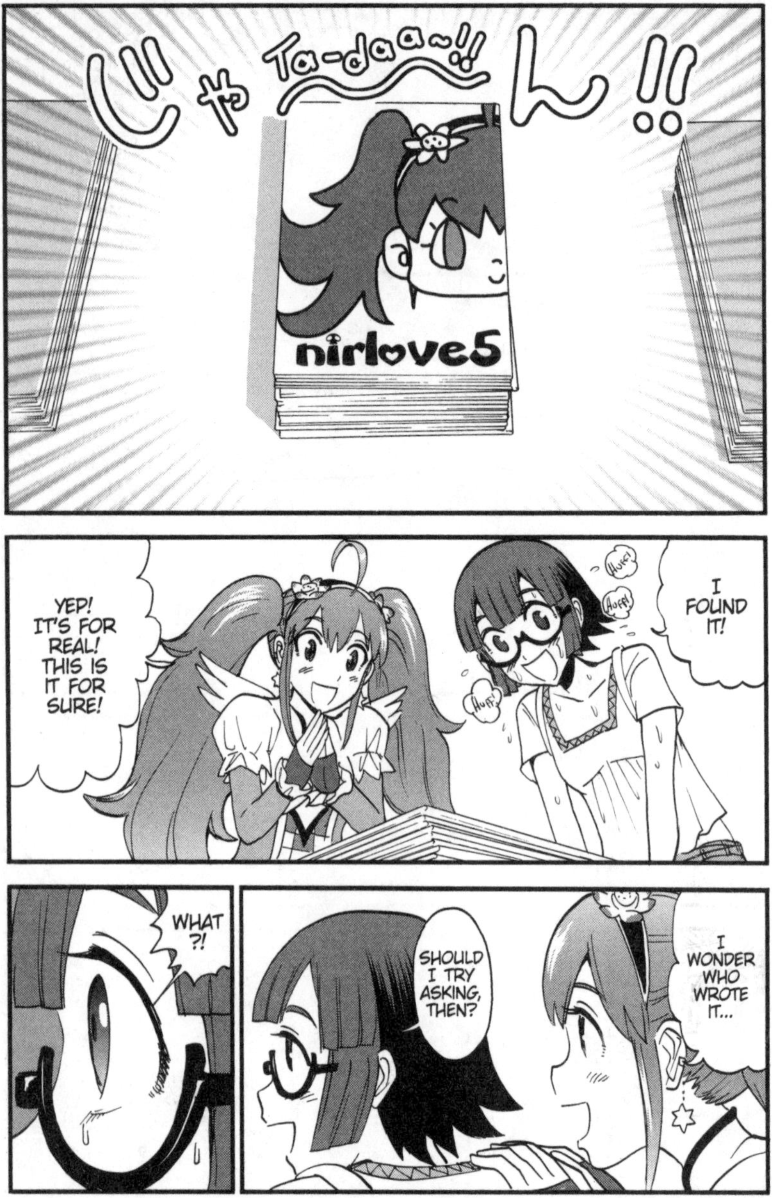
じゃ〜ん!!
Ta-daa~!!
nirlove5
I FOUND IT!
Huff!
Huff!
Huff!
YEP! IT'S FOR REAL! THIS IS IT FOR SURE!
I WONDER WHO WROTE IT...
SHOULD I TRY ASKING, THEN?
WHAT ?!

WAF! GIOOOOOOOOAM!!
WAF!

OH... HA HA! I'M SO HAPPY... I-I HAVE TO THANK HIM...

UH... LIMM... I THINK IT MIGHT BE HIM-- MAYBE?

ARE YOU...THE AUTHOR OF THIS BOOK?

UH, LIMM, EX- CUSE ME!

GLARE

nirlove1

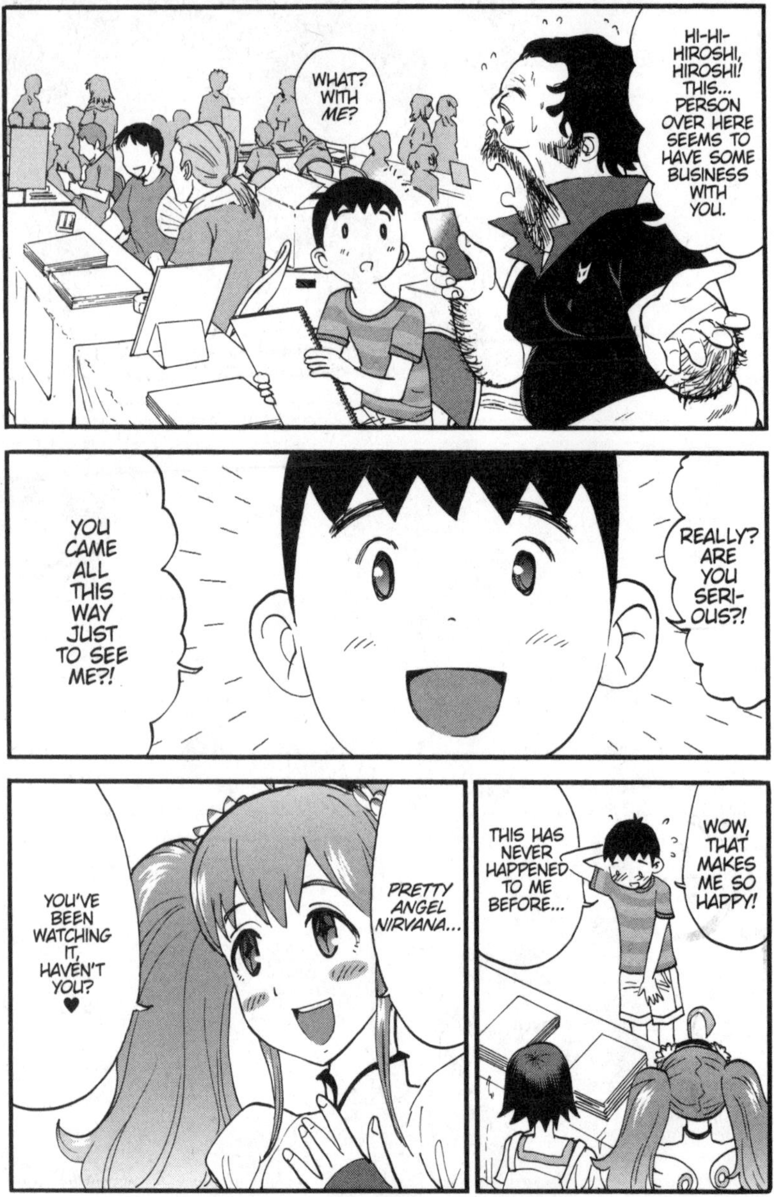
HI-HI-HIROSHI, HIROSHI! THIS... PERSON OVER HERE SEEMS TO HAVE SOME BUSINESS WITH YOU.
WHAT? WITH ME?
REALLY? ARE YOU SERI-OUS?!
YOU CAME ALL THIS WAY JUST TO SEE ME?!
WOW, THAT MAKES ME SO HAPPY!
THIS HAS NEVER HAPPENED TO ME BEFORE...
PRETTY ANGEL NIRVANA...
YOU'VE BEEN WATCHING IT, HAVEN'T YOU? ♥

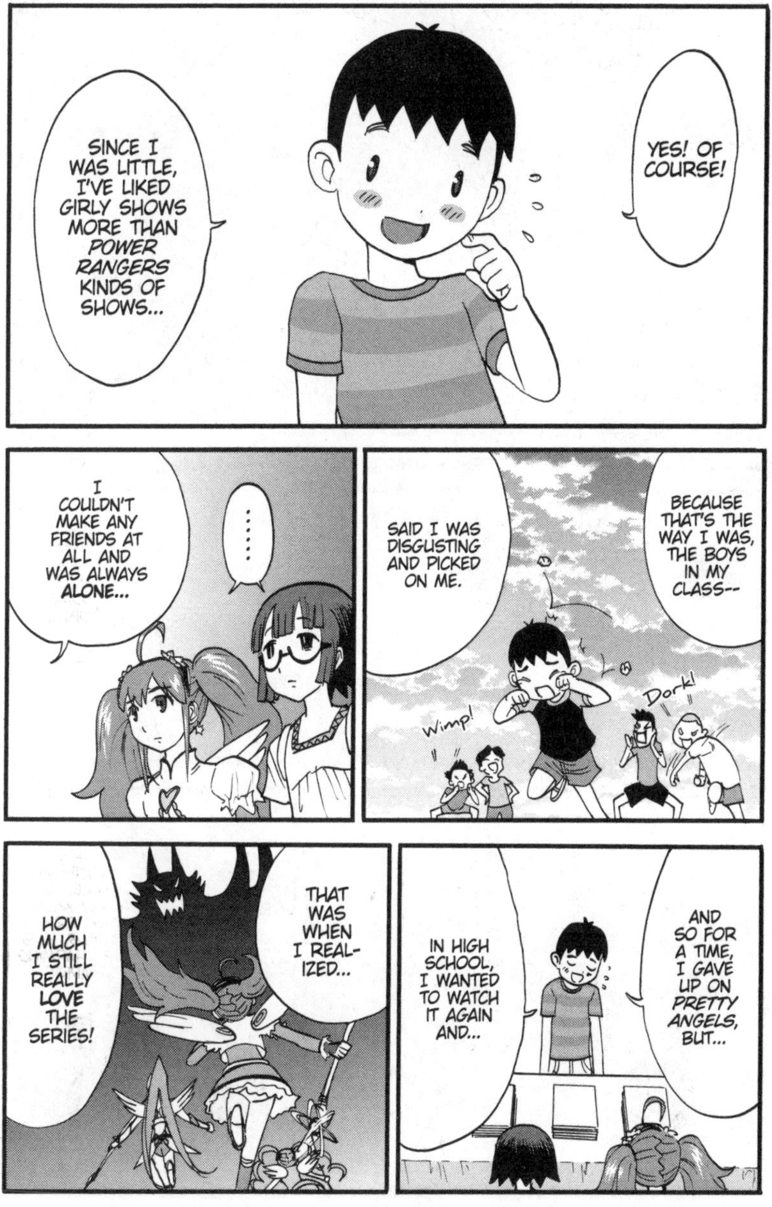
YES! OF COURSE!
SINCE I WAS LITTLE, I'VE LIKED GIRLY SHOWS MORE THAN *POWER RANGERS* KINDS OF SHOWS...
BECAUSE THAT'S THE WAY I WAS, THE BOYS IN MY CLASS--
SAID I WAS DISGUSTING AND PICKED ON ME.
Dork!
Wimp!
......
I COULDN'T MAKE ANY FRIENDS AT ALL AND WAS ALWAYS ALONE...
AND SO FOR A TIME, I GAVE UP ON *PRETTY ANGELS*, BUT...
IN HIGH SCHOOL, I WANTED TO WATCH IT AGAIN AND...
THAT WAS WHEN I REALIZED...
HOW MUCH I STILL REALLY **LOVE** THE SERIES!

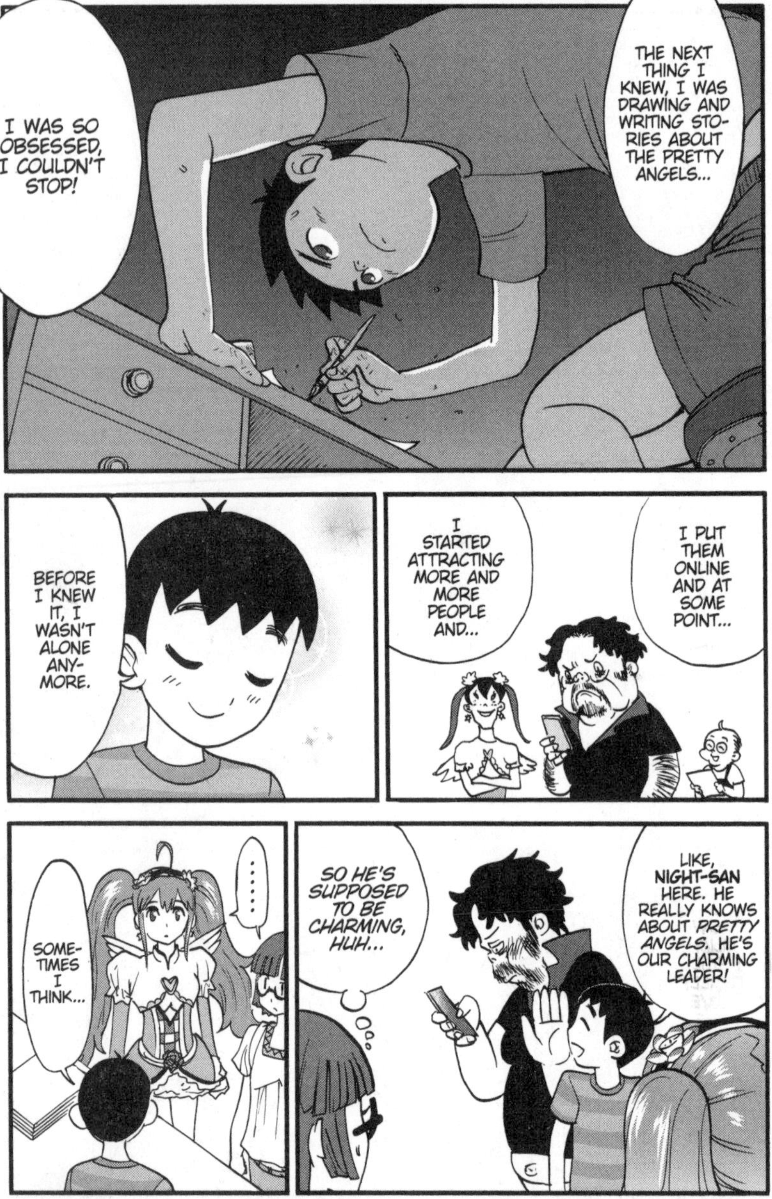
THE NEXT THING I KNEW, I WAS DRAWING AND WRITING STORIES ABOUT THE PRETTY ANGELS...
I WAS SO OBSESSED, I COULDN'T STOP!
I PUT THEM ONLINE AND AT SOME POINT...
I STARTED ATTRACTING MORE AND MORE PEOPLE AND...
BEFORE I KNEW IT, I WASN'T ALONE ANYMORE.
LIKE, **NIGHT-SAN** HERE. HE REALLY KNOWS ABOUT *PRETTY ANGELS*. HE'S OUR CHARMING LEADER!
SO HE'S SUPPOSED TO BE CHARMING, HUH...
......
SOMETIMES I THINK...

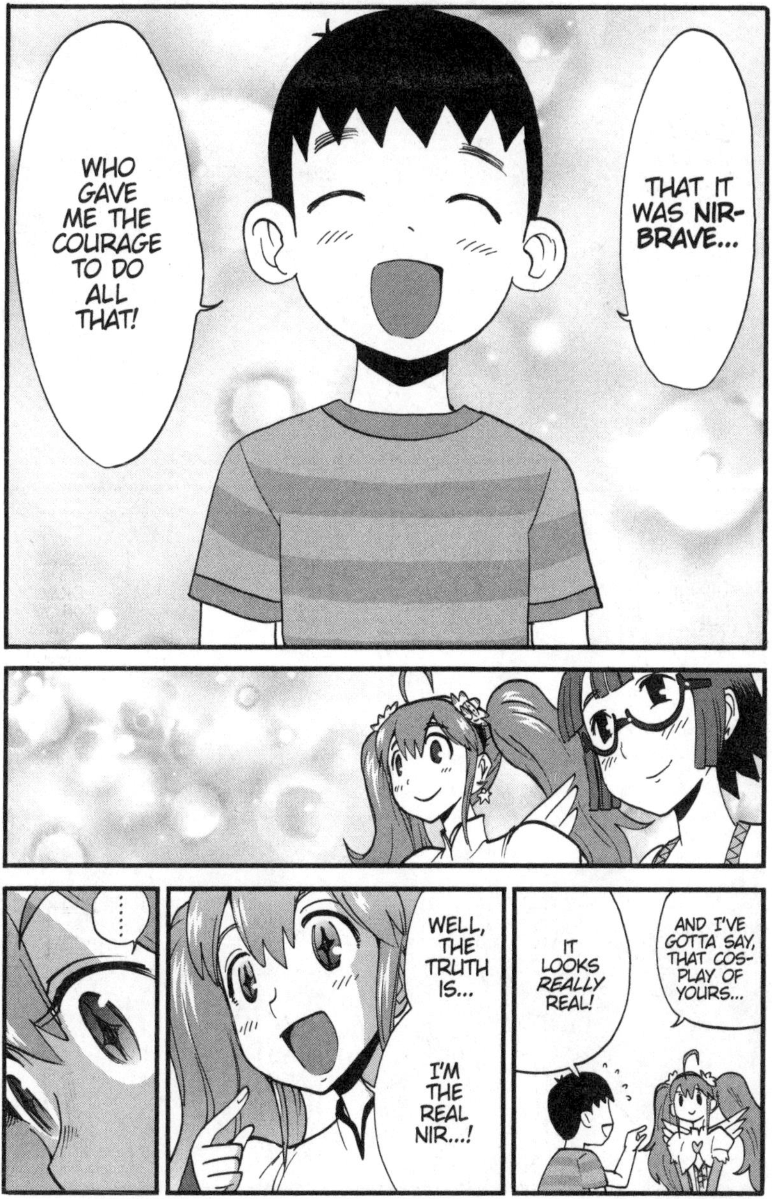
THAT IT WAS NIR-BRAVE...
WHO GAVE ME THE COURAGE TO DO ALL THAT!
AND I'VE GOTTA SAY, THAT COS-PLAY OF YOURS...
IT LOOKS *REALLY* REAL!
WELL, THE TRUTH IS...
I'M THE REAL NIR...!
......

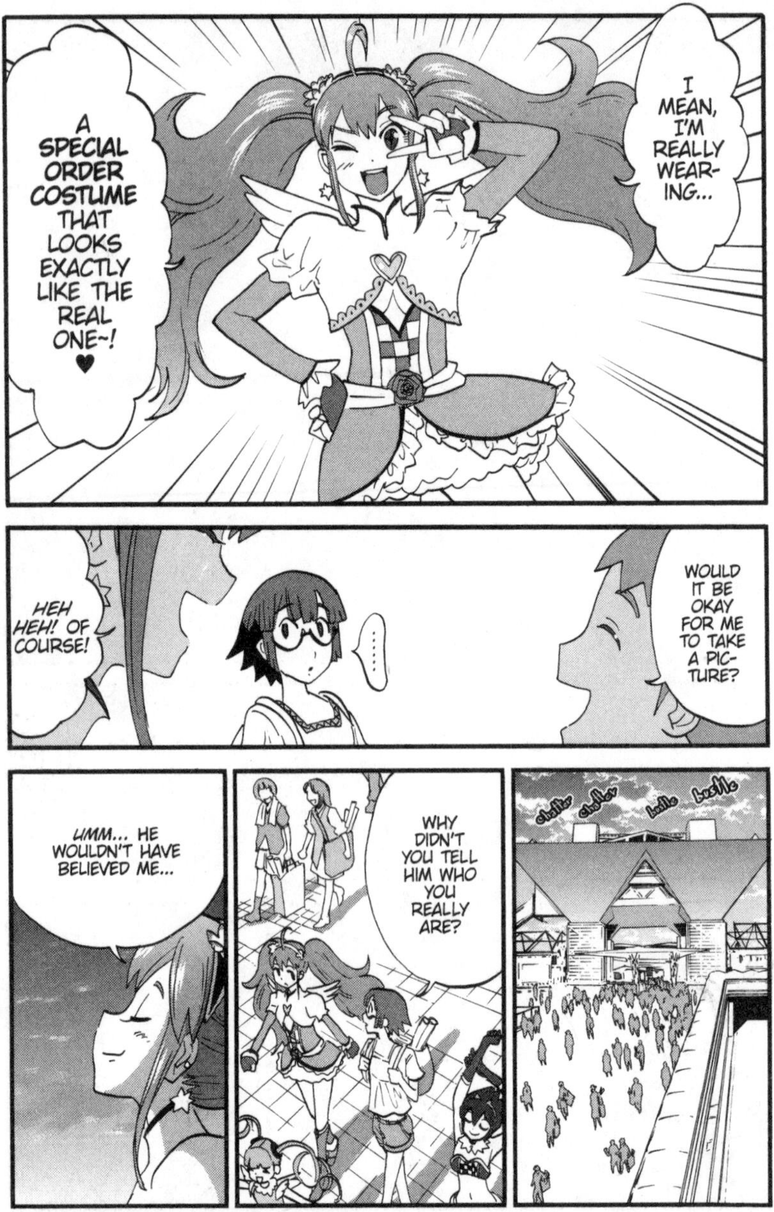
I MEAN, I'M REALLY WEAR-ING...
A SPECIAL ORDER COSTUME THAT LOOKS EXACTLY LIKE THE REAL ONE~! ♥
WOULD IT BE OKAY FOR ME TO TAKE A PIC-TURE?
......
HEH HEH! OF COURSE!
chatter chatter bustle bustle
WHY DIDN'T YOU TELL HIM WHO YOU REALLY ARE?
UMM... HE WOULDN'T HAVE BELIEVED ME...

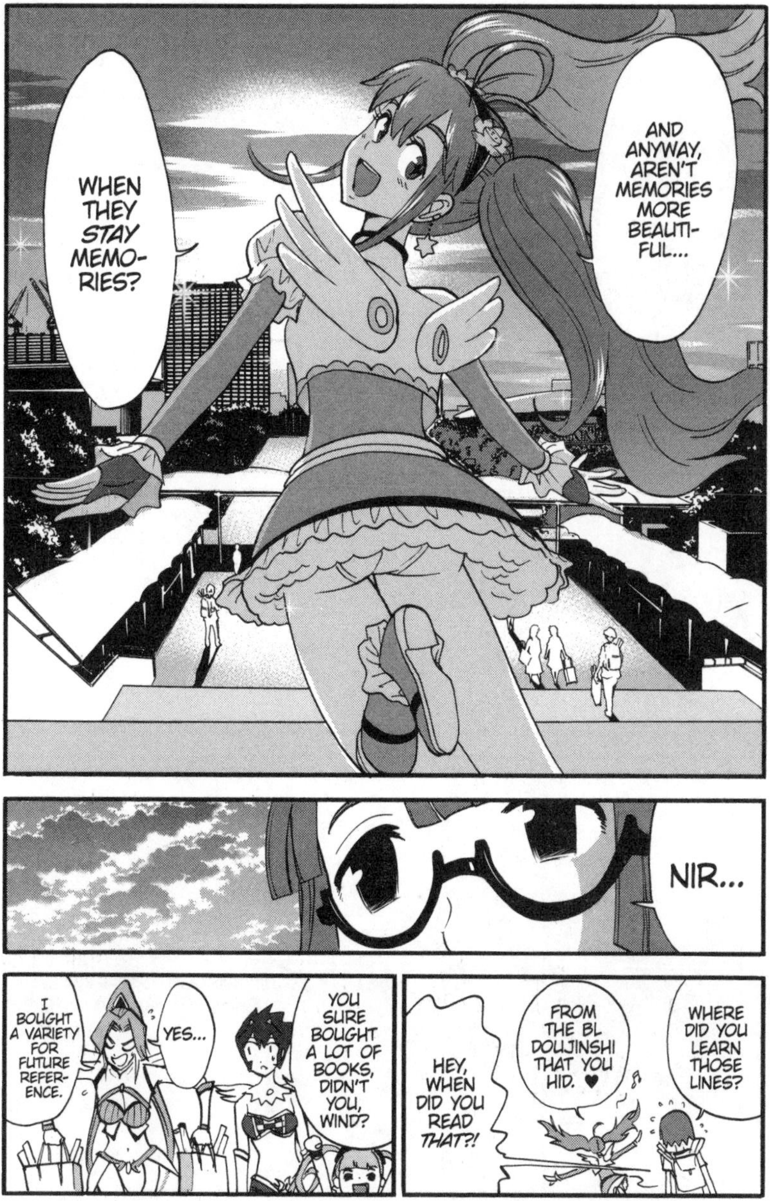
AND ANYWAY, AREN'T MEMORIES MORE BEAUTIFUL...
WHEN THEY *STAY* MEMORIES?
NIR...
WHERE DID YOU LEARN THOSE LINES?
FROM THE BL DOUJINSHI THAT YOU HID. ♥
HEY, WHEN DID YOU READ *THAT*?!
YOU SURE BOUGHT A LOT OF BOOKS, DIDN'T YOU, WIND?
YES...
I BOUGHT A VARIETY FOR FUTURE REFERENCE.

Unmagical Girl (2) - The End

Utero

He's the Beast of Shadows who was, at one time, NirBrave's mascot. Despite his cute appearance, his personality is horrible. According to his backstory, he has a warped sense of love for NirBrave and tries to destroy anyone who might interfere with their relationship--no matter what it takes. The back of his tail is his erogenous zone.

King Shout

He's the supreme ruler of the evil organization Death Metal. Because there was no figure to take his place in this world, he plugged his soul into a stray dog who was about to die. He's pretty much lost all his magical powers but his attitude is still so overbearing that no one wants to have anything to do with him. His favorite dog food is the half-raw kind.

Afterword

Author: Ryouichi Yokoyama

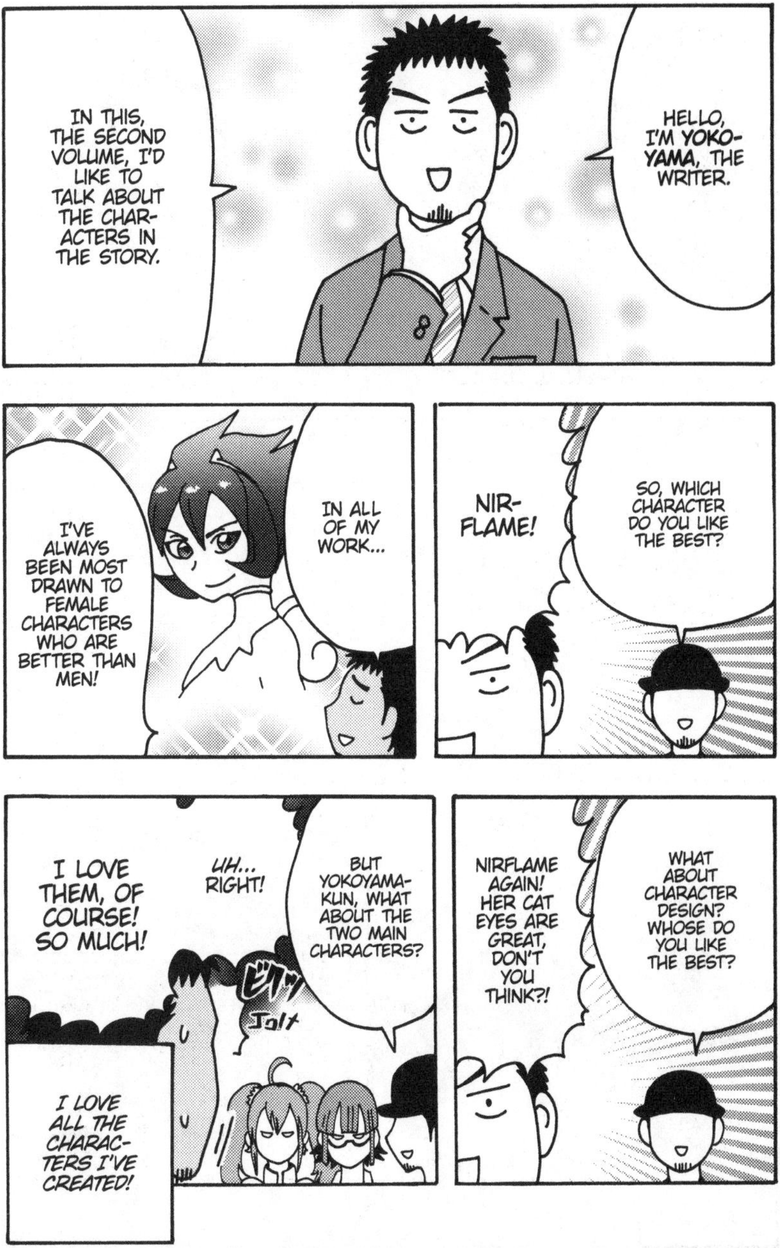
HELLO, I'M YOKOYAMA, THE WRITER.
IN THIS, THE SECOND VOLUME, I'D LIKE TO TALK ABOUT THE CHARACTERS IN THE STORY.
SO, WHICH CHARACTER DO YOU LIKE THE BEST?
NIR-FLAME!
IN ALL OF MY WORK...
I'VE ALWAYS BEEN MOST DRAWN TO FEMALE CHARACTERS WHO ARE BETTER THAN MEN!
WHAT ABOUT CHARACTER DESIGN? WHOSE DO YOU LIKE THE BEST?
NIRFLAME AGAIN! HER CAT EYES ARE GREAT, DON'T YOU THINK?!
BUT YOKOYAMA-KUN, WHAT ABOUT THE TWO MAIN CHARACTERS?
ビクッ
Jolt
UH... RIGHT!
I LOVE THEM, OF COURSE! SO MUCH!
I LOVE ALL THE CHARACTERS I'VE CREATED!

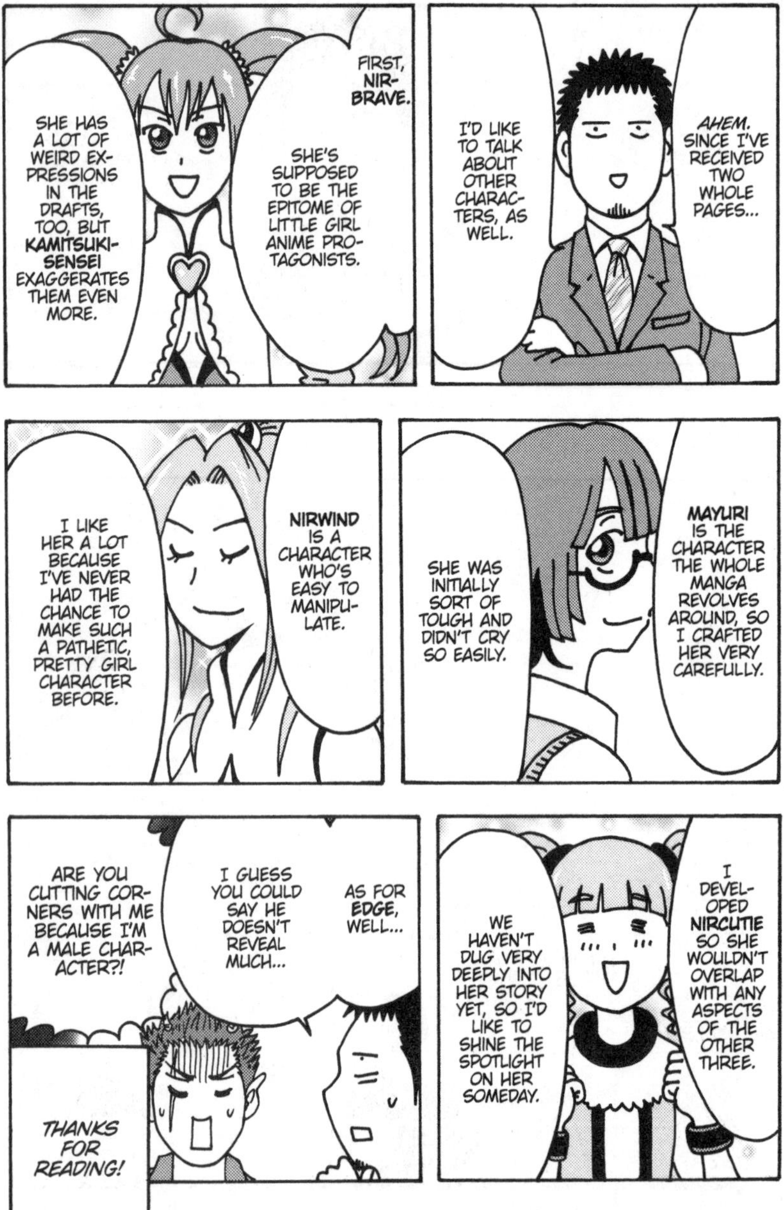
AHEM. SINCE I'VE RECEIVED TWO WHOLE PAGES...
I'D LIKE TO TALK ABOUT OTHER CHARAC-TERS, AS WELL.
FIRST, NIR-BRAVE.
SHE'S SUPPOSED TO BE THE EPITOME OF LITTLE GIRL ANIME PRO-TAGONISTS.
SHE HAS A LOT OF WEIRD EX-PRESSIONS IN THE DRAFTS, TOO, BUT KAMITSUKI-SENSEI EXAGGERATES THEM EVEN MORE.
MAYURI IS THE CHARACTER THE WHOLE MANGA REVOLVES AROUND, SO I CRAFTED HER VERY CAREFULLY.
SHE WAS INITIALLY SORT OF TOUGH AND DIDN'T CRY SO EASILY.
NIRWIND IS A CHARACTER WHO'S EASY TO MANIPU-LATE.
I LIKE HER A LOT BECAUSE I'VE NEVER HAD THE CHANCE TO MAKE SUCH A PATHETIC, PRETTY GIRL CHARACTER BEFORE.
I DEVEL-OPED NIRCUTIE SO SHE WOULDN'T OVERLAP WITH ANY ASPECTS OF THE OTHER THREE.
WE HAVEN'T DUG VERY DEEPLY INTO HER STORY YET, SO I'D LIKE TO SHINE THE SPOTLIGHT ON HER SOMEDAY.
AS FOR EDGE, WELL...
I GUESS YOU COULD SAY HE DOESN'T REVEAL MUCH...
ARE YOU CUTTING COR-NERS WITH ME BECAUSE I'M A MALE CHAR-ACTER?!
THANKS FOR READING!

Our Battle is Just Beginning!
A Manga Based on a True Story

By Kamitsuki Manmaru

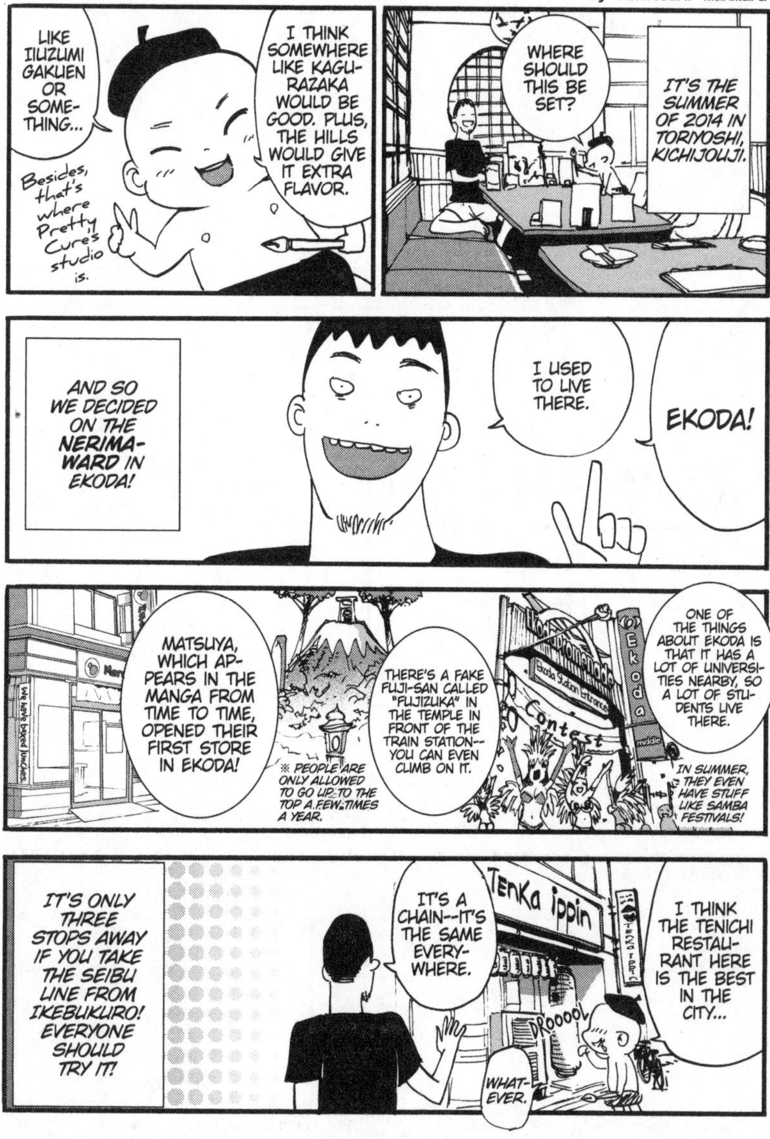
IT'S THE SUMMER OF 2014 IN TORIYOSHI, KICHIJOUJI.
WHERE SHOULD THIS BE SET?
I THINK SOMEWHERE LIKE KAGURAZAKA WOULD BE GOOD. PLUS, THE HILLS WOULD GIVE IT EXTRA FLAVOR.
LIKE IIUZUMI GAKUEN OR SOMETHING...
Besides, that's where Pretty Cure's studio is.
EKODA!
I USED TO LIVE THERE.
AND SO WE DECIDED ON THE NERIMA-WARD IN EKODA!
ONE OF THE THINGS ABOUT EKODA IS THAT IT HAS A LOT OF UNIVERSITIES NEARBY, SO A LOT OF STUDENTS LIVE THERE.
IN SUMMER, THEY EVEN HAVE STUFF LIKE SAMBA FESTIVALS!
Ekoda Promenade
Ekoda Station Entrance
Ekoda
Contest
THERE'S A FAKE FUJI-SAN CALLED "FUJIZUKA" IN THE TEMPLE IN FRONT OF THE TRAIN STATION--YOU CAN EVEN CLIMB ON IT.
※ PEOPLE ARE ONLY ALLOWED TO GO UP TO THE TOP A FEW TIMES A YEAR.
MATSUYA, WHICH APPEARS IN THE MANGA FROM TIME TO TIME, OPENED THEIR FIRST STORE IN EKODA!
We have boxed lunches
I THINK THE TENICHI RESTAURANT HERE IS THE BEST IN THE CITY...
TENKa ippin
DROOOOL
IT'S A CHAIN--IT'S THE SAME EVERYWHERE.
WHATEVER.
IT'S ONLY THREE STOPS AWAY IF YOU TAKE THE SEIBU LINE FROM IKEBUKURO! EVERYONE SHOULD TRY IT!

Secret Production Stories of UNG

Illustrations & text: Ryouichi Yokoyama

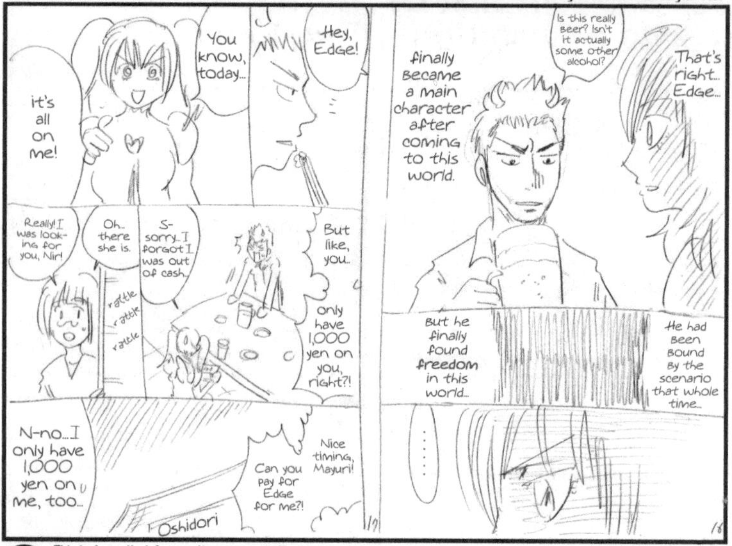
That's right... Edge...
Is this really Beer? Isn't it actually some other alcohol?
finally Became a main character after coming to this world.
He had Been Bound By the scenario that whole time...
But he finally found freedom in this world...
......
Hey, Edge!
You know, today...
it's all on me!
But like, you... only have 1,000 yen on you, right?!
S-sorry... I forgot I was out of cash.
rattle rattle rattle
Oh... there she is.
Really! I was looking for you, Nir!
Nice timing, Mayuri!
Can you pay for Edge for me?!
N-no... I only have 1,000 yen on me, too...
Oshidori

11 This izakaya that frequently appears in the manga is a nostalgic place where I used to get dead drunk. It's cheap and good.

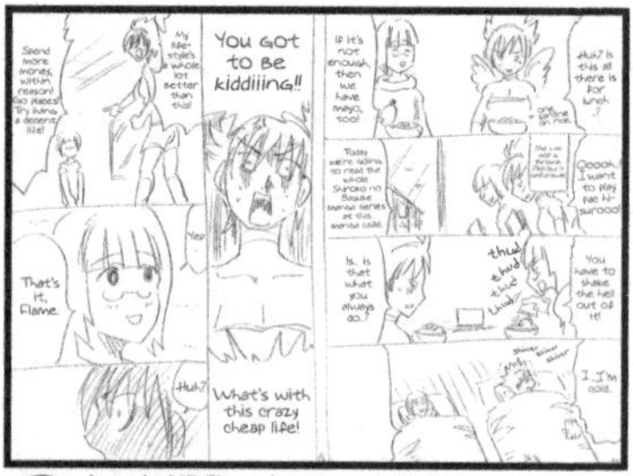
You got to Be kiddiiing!!
That's it, Flame.
What's with this crazy cheap life!

13 I wanted NirFlame to appear early on, you know. It was Manmaru-san's idea to have her live at the curry restaurant.

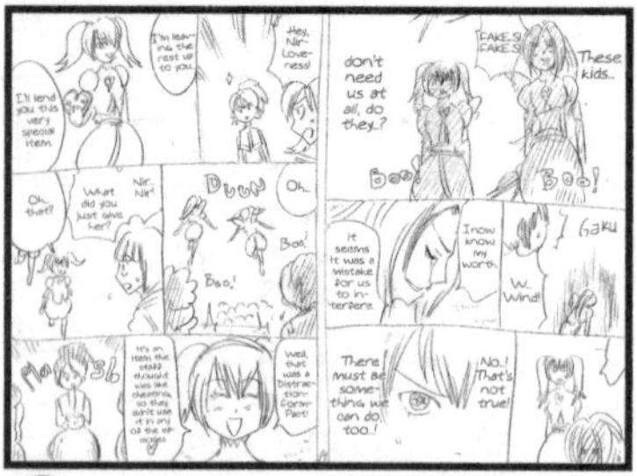
These kids...
don't need us at all, do they...?

12 I wanted to write something about the sorrows of an older generation. Little kids are merciless.

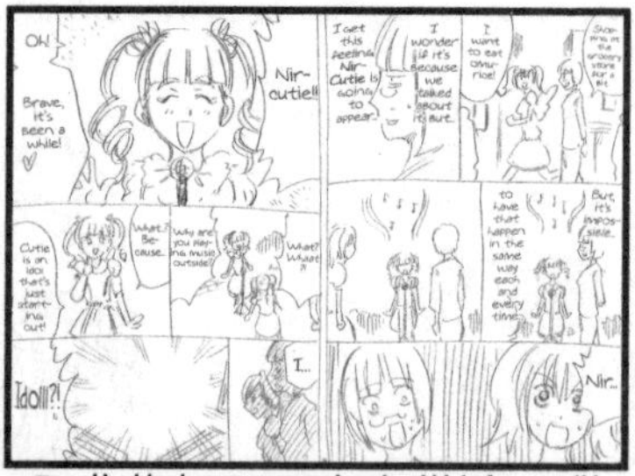
Nir-cutie!!
Idol!?

15 I had to do some research on local idols for something else, so I ended up watching some live. It was perfect timing and I think I made it work out well.

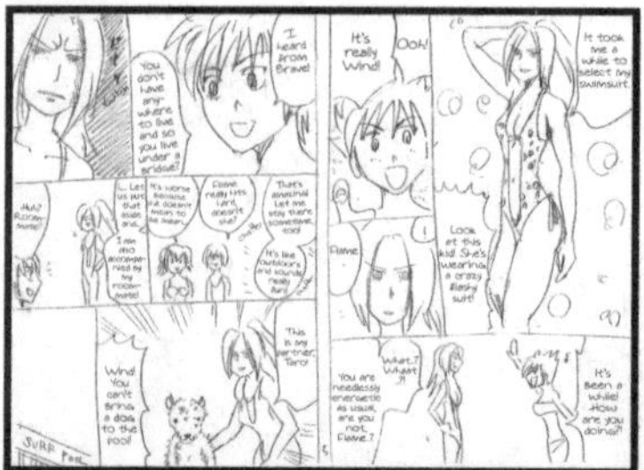
It's really Wind!
I heard from Brave!

14 Manmaru-san said he wanted an episode with swimsuits...! And he's been saying that a lot since the beginning, so I fulfilled his request. Wind's swimsuit is...

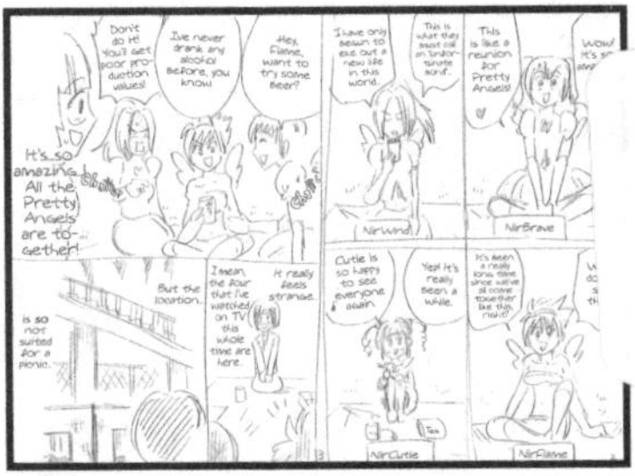
This is like a reunion for Pretty Angels!
This is what they must call an unfortunate sonf.
I have only begun to eke out a new life in this world.
NirBrave
NirWind
It's been a really long time since we've all come together like this, right?
Yep! It's really been a while.
Cutie is so happy to see everyone again.
NirFlame
NirCutie
Hey, Flame, want to try some beer?
I've never drank any alcohol before, you know
Don't do it! You'll get poor production values!
It's so amazing! All the Pretty Angels are together!
It really feels strange.
I mean, the four that I've watched on TV this whole time are here.
But the location
is so not suited for a picnic.

16 **This was a serious episode, so it was really hard for me. You know, because I'm a gag**

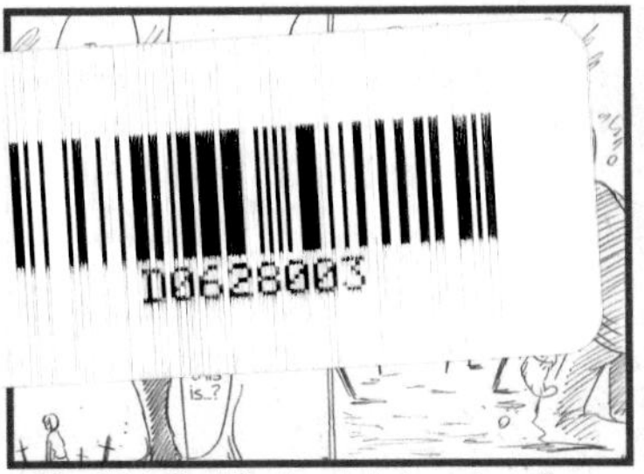
this is..?

17 **This is Utero! The character just came to me like that, so I was really excited while writing that part. I love scummy characters.**

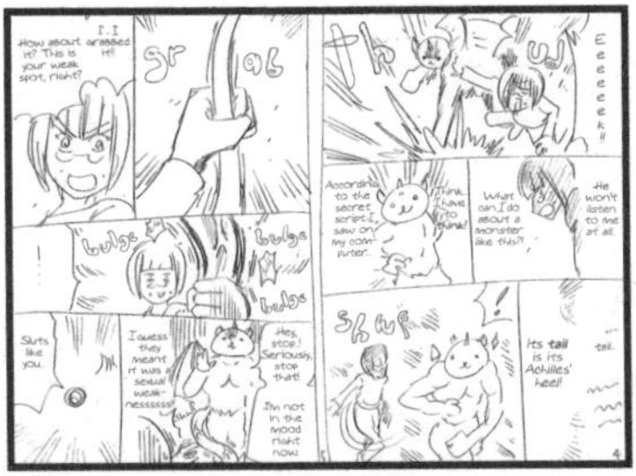
Eeeeeeek!!
He won't listen to me at all.
What can I do about a monster like this?!
Think. I have to think!
According to the secret script I saw on my computer...
tail.
Its tail is its Achilles' heel!
!
I...I grabbed it!!
How about it? This is your weak spot, right?
grab
bulge
!
bulge
bulge
Hey, stop! Seriously, stop that!
I'm not in the mood right now!
I guess they meant it was a sexual weak-nesssss!
Sluts like you.

18 **If you look at just this part, it looks like a battle manga, doesn't it? By the way, I use a lot of musical references for the Pretty Angels and the evil organiza-**

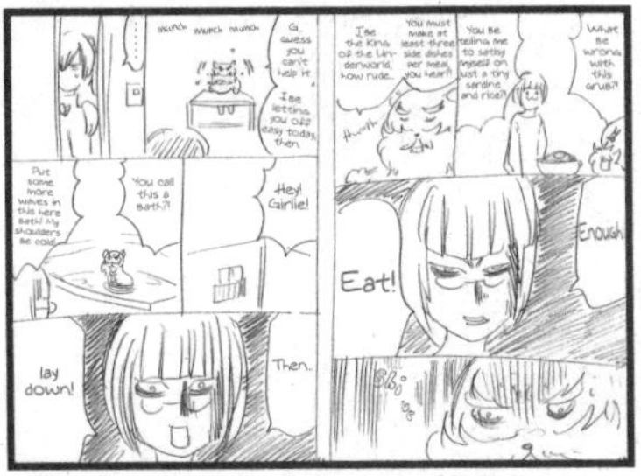
What be wrong with this grub?!
You be telling me to satisfy myself on just a tiny sardine and rice?!
You must make at least three side dishes per meal, you hear?!
I be the King of the Underworld, how rude.
Humph
Enough
Eat!
G... guess you can't help it.
I be letting you off easy today, then
munch munch munch
......
Hey! Girlie!
You call this a bath?!
Put some more waves in this here bath! My shoulders be cold!
Then...
lay down!

19 **The evil leader has finally appeared! By the way, I like rock but I don't listen to death metal.**

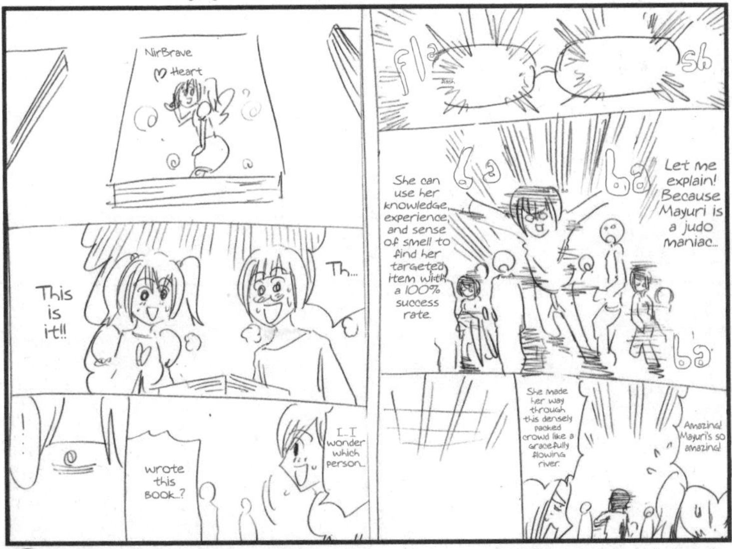
fla
sh
Let me explain! Because Mayuri is a judo maniac...
ba
ba
She can use her knowledge, experience, and sense of smell to find her targeted item with a 100% success rate.
ba
Amazing! Mayuri's so amazing!
She made her way through this densely packed crowd like a gracefully flowing river.
NirBrave
Heart
Th...
This is it!!
I...I wonder which person...
wrote this BOOK...?
!...

20 **Manmaru-san knows more about Comike than I do, so he gave me a lot of pointers. I'd like to appear there someday...**

※ This is from right before the manga was published.